The Contemporary Hollywood Film Industry

Edited by Paul McDonald and Janet Wasko

Blackwell
Publishing

© 2008 by Blackwell Publishing Ltd
except for editorial material and organization © 2008 by Paul McDonald and Janet Wasko

BLACKWELL PUBLISHING
350 Main Street, Malden, MA 02148-5020, USA
9600 Garsington Road, Oxford OX4 2DQ, UK
550 Swanston Street, Carlton, Victoria 3053, Australia

The right of Paul McDonald and Janet Wasko to be identified as the Authors of the Editorial Material
in this Work has been asserted in accordance with the UK Copyright, Designs, and Patents Act 1988.

First published 2008 by Blackwell Publishing Ltd

3   2011

Library of Congress Cataloging-in-Publication Data

The contemporary Hollywood film industry / edited by Paul McDonald and Janet Wasko.
    p. cm.
  Includes bibliographical references and index.
    ISBN 978-1-4051-3387-6 (hardcover : alk. paper) – ISBN 978-1-4051-3388-3
(pbk. : alk. paper) 1. Motion picture industry–California–Los Angeles. I. McDonald,
Paul, 1963– II. Wasko, Janet.
  PN1993.5.U65C64 2008
  384′.80979494–dc22

                                                                    2007014550

A catalogue record for this title is available from the British Library.

Set in 10.5/13pt Minion
by Graphicraft Limited, Hong Kong
Printed and bound in Singapore
by Fabulous Printers Pte Ltd

The publisher's policy is to use permanent paper from mills that operate a sustainable forestry policy,
and which has been manufactured from pulp processed using acid-free and elementary chlorine-free
practices. Furthermore, the publisher ensures that the text paper and cover board used have met
acceptable environmental accreditation standards.

For further information on
Blackwell Publishing, visit our website:
www.blackwellpublishing.com

CONTENTS

List of Figures   viii
List of Tables   xii
Acknowledgments   xiii
Notes on Contributors   xiv

Introduction: The New Contours of the Hollywood Film Industry   1
Paul McDonald and Janet Wasko

PART I   THE STRUCTURE OF THE INDUSTRY   **11**

1   The Studio System and Conglomerate Hollywood   13
    Tom Schatz

2   Financing and Production: Creating the Hollywood Film
    Commodity   43
    Janet Wasko

3   Distribution and Marketing in Contemporary Hollywood   63
    Philip Drake

4   Theatrical Exhibition: Accelerated Cinema   83
    Charles Acland

5   Ancillary Markets – Television: From Challenge to Safe Haven   106
    Eileen R. Meehan

6   Ancillary Markets – Video and DVD: Hollywood Retools   120
    Frederick Wasser

7   Ancillary Markets – Video Games: Promises and Challenges
    of an Emerging Industry   132
    Randy Nichols

8   Ancillary Markets – Recorded Music: Charting the Rise and
    Fall of the Soundtrack Album   143
    Jeff Smith

PART II   INDUSTRY DYNAMICS   **153**

9   Labor: The Effects of Media Concentration on the Film and
    Television Workforce   155
    Susan Christopherson

10 The Star System: The Production of Hollywood Stardom in
    the Post-Studio Era   167
    Paul McDonald

11 Hollywood and the State: The American Film Industry
    Cartel in the Age of Globalization   182
    Manjunath Pendakur

12 Hollywood and Intellectual Property   195
    Ronald V. Bettig

PART III   INTERNATIONAL TERRITORIES   **207**

13 Hollywood and the World: Export or Die   209
    John Trumpbour

14 Britain: Hollywood, UK   220
    Paul McDonald

15 France: A Story of Love and Hate – French and American
    Cinema in the French Audiovisual Markets   232
    Joel Augros

16 Germany: Hollywood and the Germans – A Very Special
    Relationship   240
    Peter Krämer

17 Italy: The Rise and Fall of the Italian Market   251
    Krishna P. Jayakar and David Waterman

18   Latin America: How Mexico and Argentina Cope and
     Cooperate with the Behemoth of the North   264
     Tamara L. Falicov

19   East Asia: For Better or Worse   277
     John A. Lent

20   India: Hollywood's Domination, Extinction, and
     Re-animation (with thanks to *Jurassic Park*)   285
     Nitin Govil

21   Australia and New Zealand: Expats in Hollywood and
     Hollywood South   295
     David Newman

Index   307

LIST OF FIGURES

1.1 *Cleopatra* (1963), an expensive failure for Fox. Produced by Walter Wanger; distributed by 20th Century Fox; directed by Joseph L. Mankiewicz   17

1.2 Monster hit, *Jaws* (1975). Produced by David Brown and Richard D. Zanuck; distributed by Universal; directed by Steven Spielberg   20

1.3 *Batman* (1989), using "the whole machine of the company." Produced by Peter Guber and Jon Peter; distributed by Warner Bros; directed by Tim Burton   28

1.4 *Good Night, and Good Luck* (2005), made through Soderbergh and Clooney's Section Eight production company. Produced by Grant Heslov; distributed by Warner Independent Pictures; directed by George Clooney   34

2.1 From conception to development to production   43

2.2 *The Long Kiss Goodnight* (1996), product of a $4 million script. Produced by Stephanie Austin, Shane Black and Renny Harlin; distributed by New Line; directed by Renny Harlin   47

2.3 *E.T. The Extra-terrestrial* (1982), developed by Columbia but a hit for Universal. Produced by Kathleen Kennedy and Steven Spielberg; distributed by Universal; directed by Steven Spielberg   54

2.4 Disney's corporate headquarters in Burbank, California   57

3.1 Platform releasing helped *My Big Fat Greek Wedding* (1982) to take over $241 million at the North American box office. Produced by Gary Goetzman, Tom Hanks, and Rita Wilson; distributed by IFC Films; directed by Joel Zwick   68

3.2 *Top Gun* (1986), high-concept filmmaking *par excellence*. Produced by Jerry Bruckheimer and Don Simpson; distributed by Paramount; directed by Tony Scott   69

3.3 Distribution of advertising costs in 2005   72

3.4   *Spider-Man* (2002), reaping the revenues across all exhibition windows. Produced by Ian Bryce and Laura Ziskin; distributed by Columbia; directed by Sam Raimi   78

3.5   *Forrest Gump* (1994), a "successful failure." Produced by Wendy Finerman, Steve Starkey, and Steve Tisch; distributed by Paramount; directed by Robert Zemeckis   79

4.1   "Future of Entertainment" cover, *Newsweek* (2005). Whither exhibition?   84

4.2   Façade of the AMC Del Amo 18 megaplex in Torrance, California   87

4.3   Multiplex advertisement featuring both conventional and d-cinema auditoriums, Carmike 16, Wilmington, North Carolina, October 2006   99

5.1   Viacom's *Rugrats* franchise, here honored on the Hollywood Walk of Fame, June 28, 2001   113

5.2   Rupert Murdoch   114

6.1   Boldly going – when Paramount released *Star Trek II: The Wrath of Khan* (1982) on videocassette priced at $40, it became the first "sell-through" release from a Hollywood studio. Produced by Robert Sallin; distributed by Paramount; directed by Nicholas Meyer   124

7.1   US video game software sales and film box-office receipts ($ billion)   132

7.2   Grossing over $131 million at the North American box office, *Lara Croft: Tomb Raider* (2001) proved commercial success can be found with the transfer of game properties to the big screen. Produced by Lawrence Gordon, Lloyd Levin and Colin Wilson; distributed by Paramount; directed by Simon West   134

7.3   *Final Fantasy: The Spirits Within* (2001), from game to film. Produced by Jun Aida, Chris Lee, and Hironobu Sakaguchi; distributed by Columbia; directed by Hironobu Sakaguchi and Moto Sakakibara   139

8.1   "Stayin' Alive" – Tony Manero (John Travolta) struts to the sound of the Bees Gees in the opening of *Saturday Night Fever* (1977). Produced by Robert Stigwood; distributed by Paramount; directed by John Badham   147

8.2   Film and music cross-promotion – the "Maniac" sequence from *Flashdance* (1983). Produced by Jerry Bruckheimer and Don Simpson; distributed by Paramount; directed by Adrian Lyne   148

8.3   *Wedding Crashers* (2005) partying to the sound of the Isley Brothers' "Shout." Produced by Peter Abrams, Robert L. Levy, and Andrew Panay; distributed by New Line; directed by David Dobkin   151

9.1   Militant mouse – mock fighting during a demonstration by the National Association of Broadcast Employees and Technicians and Communications Workers of America outside the gates of Disney's headquarters at Burbank, California, November 6, 1998   158

9.2   Actor Charlton Heston joins the picket outside Paramount Studios
       during the strike by SAG members in August 1980   163
10.1   CAA packaging – Harold Ramis and Bill Murray together in
       Ghostbusters (1984). Produced by Ivan Reitman; distributed by
       Columbia; directed by Ivan Reitman   171
10.2   A $20 million performance – Jim Carrey in *Cable Guy* (1996).
       Produced by Judd Apatow, Andrew Licht, and Jeffrey A. Mueller;
       distributed by Columbia; directed by Ben Stiller   177
11.1   Jack Valenti with President Bill Clinton, addressing television
       executives at the White House, February 29, 1996   184
11.2   Donations of TV/music/movie industries to Democratic and
       Republication politicians   191
11.3   Lobby spending by majors and MPAA, 1997–2000   192
12.1   Former record producer and Republican politican Sonny Bono
       (pictured in February 1996 with the then President of the MPAA
       Jack Valenti and House Speaker Newt Gingrich) campaigned for
       revisions to legislation which led to the passing in 1998 of the
       controversial Copyright Term Extension Act   202
13.1   *Tomorrow Never Dies* (1997), $186 million at the international
       box office. Produced by Barbara Broccoli and Michael G. Wilson;
       distributed by MGM; directed by Roger Spottiswoode   214
13.2   *Alexander* (2004), a production with international credentials.
       Produced by Moritz Borman, Hans De Weers, Jon Kilik, Thomas
       Schühly, and Iain Smith; distributed by Warner Bros.; directed by
       Oliver Stone   216
14.1   Hollywood and Britain reach a harmonious understanding – Julia
       Roberts and Hugh Grant together at the end of *Notting Hill* (1999).
       Produced by Duncan Kenworthy; distributed by Universal;
       directed by Roger Michell   223
14.2   Sohowood – the De Lane Lea post-production house in
       Dean Street, London   227
14.3   The Farmiloe Building, London, masquerades as Gotham City
       police station in *Batman Begins* (2005). Produced by Larry Franco,
       Charles Roven, and Emma Thomas; distributed by Warner Bros;
       directed by Christopher Nolan   227
16.1   Bourne in Berlin – Matt Damon in the lobby of the Westin Grand
       Hotel, Berlin, from *The Bourne Supremacy* (2004). Produced by
       Patrick Crowley, Frank Marshall, and Paul L. Sandberg; distributed
       by Universal; directed by Paul Greengrass   246
16.2   President Thomas J. Whitmore (Bill Pullman) takes the battle to
       the aliens in *Independence Day* (1996). Produced by Dean Devlin;
       distributed by 20th Century Fox; directed by Roland Emmerich   247
17.1   Number of films produced (national productions and international
       co-productions) in Italy, 1945–2004   253

17.2   Box-office admissions (millions) in Italy, 1945–2004   253
17.3   Market share (%) for Italian and US films in Italy, 1950–2004   254
17.4   Primary movie spending as a percentage of GDP in the
       United States and Italy, 1948–2002   256
17.5   Comparison of Italian share of US plus Italian primary movie
       spending vs. market share of Italian films in the home market (%),
       1950–2002   257
18.1   *Amores Perros* (2000) built the reputation of Mexican director
       Alejandro González Iñárritu amongst international audiences.
       Produced by Alejandro González Iñárritu; distributed by Lions
       Gate; directed by Alejandro González Iñárritu   267
18.2   *Y tu mamá también* (2001) became one of the most widely
       distributed foreign-language films from Latin America when
       released in the US. Produced by Alfonso Cuarón and Jorge
       Vergara; distributed by IFC Films; directed by Alfonso Cuarón   268
18.3   The *Titanic* set constructed at Rosarito, Baja California Norte,
       Mexico. From *Building the Ship* (2005), distributed by 20th
       Century Fox Home Entertainment   271
19.1   With a North American box office gross of over $11 million
       Shi mian mai fu (*House of Flying Daggers*) (2004) has contributed
       to raising awareness of East Asian films amongst American
       audiences. Produced by William Kong and Zhang Yimou;
       distributed by Sony Pictures Classics; directed by Zhang Yimou 283
20.1   The India sequence in *Close Encounters of the Third Kind* (1977).
       Produced by Julia Phillips and Michael Phillips; distributed by
       Columbia; directed by Steven Spielberg   288
20.2   When released in India, *Jurassic Park* (1993) became the first
       Hollywood film dubbed into Hindi for a decade. Produced by
       Kathleen Kennedy and Gerald R Molen; distributed by Universal;
       directed by Steven Spielberg   290
20.3   *Deewangee* (2002), borrows from the plot of Paramount's *Primal
       Fear* (1996). Produced by Nitin Manmohan; distributed by Spark;
       directed by Anees Bazmee   291
21.1   Center–periphery model for Hollywood/non-Hollywood industries   297
21.2   Baz Luhrmann directing Nicole Kidman during filming for *Moulin
       Rouge* (2001), which was shot at the Fox studios in Sydney, New
       South Wales   299
21.3   Russell Crowe working with director Peter Weir on the set of
       Master and Commander: The Far Side of the World (2004), a
       co-production between 20th Century Fox, Miramax, and Universal 300
21.4   Peter Jackson and actor Naomi Watts while filming *King Kong*
       (2005)   302

LIST OF TABLES

1.1	US film production and distribution, 1984–1990	24
1.2	Major studio merger and acquisition deals, 1989–2005	26
1.3	Major studio worldwide revenues, 1948–2003	36
2.1	Selected Hollywood production deals or pacts	49
3.1	Average production (negative) and marketing (p&a) costs of a major Hollywood motion picture	63
3.2	Top weekend openings, costs and gross box office 2002–2005 (ranked by opening weekend)	68
3.3	Counting the revenues of the *Spider-Man* franchise	77
4.1	Ten highest box-office revenue countries, 2004	91
4.2	Fifteen countries with the highest number of screens, 2004	92
4.3	Top ten chains in Canada and the US, January 1, 2005	93
4.4	Top ten chains in Canada and the US, October 19, 1995	93
7.1	US video game software sales and film box office receipts ($ million)	135
7.2	Successful video games based on movies, 2001–2005	138
8.1	Bestselling soundtrack albums of all time (total units sold in US)	150
10.1	Leading agencies and star clients, 2006	169
10.2	Who represents whom? Leading Hollywood agents, managers, publicists, attorneys and selected film star clients, 2006	179
13.1	World box office Top 20, 1998 ($ million)	215
13.2	World box office Top 20, 2005 ($ million)	216
14.1	Number of films shown in the UK, 1993–2003	221
14.2	Split of UK box office revenues, US and other distributors, 1991–2000	221
15.1	Films on the main five French television broadcasters by nationality	236
17.1	Primary movie media penetration and usage indicators in the United States and Italy, 2001–2002	258
18.1	Number of Mexican films produced, 1997–2004	266
18.2	Number of Argentine films released, 1997–2004	272

ACKNOWLEDGMENTS

The editors would like to express sincere gratitude to Jayne Fargnoli and Ken Provencher at Blackwell Publishing for their tremendous enthusiasm and support for this collection.

Denzell Richards helpfully assisted in finding sources for certain images, and Mary Erickson provided invaluable editorial assistance.

Paul McDonald would like to thank Tamar, Chloe, and Jessica for sharing in his fascination with all things Hollywood. Janet Wasko thanks Carlos and a multitude of cats for their patience and comfort during the creation of this volume. Thanks to the Ronald Grant Archive for permission to use images which appear in chapter 21.

NOTES ON CONTRIBUTORS

Charles Acland is Professor and Concordia University Research Chair in Communication Studies at Concordia University, Montreal. He is author of *Youth, Murder, Spectacle: The Cultural Politics of "Youth in Crisis"* and *Screen Traffic: Movies, Multiplexes, and Global Culture*, which won the 2004 Robinson Book Prize for best book in communication studies by a Canadian scholar, and he is editor of *Residual Media*.

Joel Augros teaches film at the University of Paris and is the author of *Economie du cinéma américain* (Edilig, 1985) and *El dinero de Hollywood* (Ediciones Paidos Iberica, 2000).

Ronald V. Bettig is an associate professor of communications at the Pennsylvania State University in the College of Communications. He teaches political economy and critical/cultural studies. He has written several works on copyright and culture, including *Copyrighting Culture: The Political Economy of Intellectual Property* (Westview, 1996). He is co-author of *Big Media, Big Money: Cultural Texts and Political Economics* (Rowman & Littlefield, 2003).

Susan Christopherson is the J. Thomas Clark Professor in the Department of City and Regional Planning at Cornell University. Her work focuses on employment and location trends in media industries. In the mid-1980s she conducted a path-breaking study of the motion picture industry in Los Angeles. She collaborated in a study in the mid-1990s which resulted in the award-winning book, *Under the Stars*. She has published studies on the New Media industry in New York and on New York City's role in film, television, and commercial production. She has studied media globalization and trade policy for the United Nations Conference on Trade and Development and has published studies comparing media industry work in the US with that in Sweden and Germany.

Philip Drake is a lecturer in film and media at the University of Stirling, Scotland, and a member of the Stirling Media Research Institute. He has published articles on Hollywood cinema, screen performance, celebrity, and intellectual property rights. He is currently writing a book on Hollywood cinema, and co-editing a forthcoming edition of the journal *Cultural Politics* on the politics of celebrity.

Tamara L. Falicov teaches Latin American cinema and the political economy of film and television industries at the University of Kansas. Her research area is the film industries of Latin America, with a focus on Argentina and Cuba. She is the author of *The Cinematic Tango: Contemporary Argentine Film* (Wallflower Press, 2006).

Nitin Govil teaches film and media studies at the University of California, San Diego, where he is Assistant Professor in the Department of Communication. He is the co-author of *Global Hollywood* (BFI Publishing, 2001) and *Global Hollywood 2* (BFI Publishing, 2005) and is currently co-authoring a book-length study of the Indian film industry. He has also published on digital media outsourcing, Hollywood's copyright unilateralism, media technologies, critical theories of space/place, and crisis and informality in the globalization of "Bollywood."

Krishna P. Jayakar is an associate professor in the College of Communications at the Pennsylvania State University, and teaches telecommunications management and media economics. His research interests include telecommunications policy, intellectual property rights, and film industry economics. Jayakar's research has been published in journals such as *Telecommunications Policy*, the *Journal of Media Economics*, and *The Information Society*. Recently, he received the 2004 Deans' Award for Excellence in Integrated Scholarship. In 2006–7 he served as the head of the Media Management and Economics Division of the Association for Education in Journalism and Mass Communications.

Peter Krämer teaches film studies at the University of East Anglia. He has published essays on American film and media history, and on the relationship between Hollywood and Europe, in *Screen*, *The Velvet Light Trap*, *Theatre History Studies*, the *Historical Journal of Film, Radio and Television*, *History Today*, *Film Studies*, *Scope*, and numerous edited collections. He is the author of *The New Hollywood: From Bonnie and Clyde to Star Wars* (Wallflower Press, 2006), and the co-editor of *Screen Acting* (Routledge, 1999) and *The Silent Cinema Reader* (Routledge, 2004). He has also co-written a book for children entitled *American Film: An A–Z Guide* (Franklin Watts, 2003).

John A. Lent is a professor of international and comparative mass communication with an emphasis on Asian studies at the School of Communication and Theatre, Temple University. He is the author of numerous publications, including *The Asian Film Industry* (University of Texas Press, 1990) and *Animation in Asia and the Pacific*

(John Libbey & Co., 2000); and co-editor (with Gerald Sussman) of *Global Productions: Labor in the Making of the "Information Society"* (Hampton Press, 1998).

Paul McDonald is Professor of Film and Television Studies at the University of Portsmouth. He is the author of *The Star System: Hollywood's Production of Popular Identities* (Wallflower, 2000) and *Video and DVD Industries* (BFI, 2007), and is also joint editor of the International Screen Industries series from the British Film Institute.

Eileen R. Meehan is Professor at Southern Illinois University. She is the author of *Why TV Is Not Our Fault* (Rowman & Littlefield, 2006), co-editor of *Sex and Money* (University of Minnesota Press, 2002) and *Dazzled by Disney?* (Leicester University Press, 2001), as well as authoring numerous articles on the political economy of the media.

David Newman is a Ph.D. candidate in the School of Communication at Simon Fraser University focusing on the political economy of the international film industry and on comparative film policy. Originally from New Zealand, David has lived in Asia and North America since 1987.

Randy Nichols is an assistant professor at Niagara University. His work focuses on video games as cultural commodities and on the impact of new technologies on communication. He has previously published articles on the SimCity franchise and is a reviewer for the Center for Cyberculture Studies. He is currently completing a book, *The Videogames Industry*, due in 2008, for the British Film Institute's International Screen Industries series.

Manjunath Pendakur is Dean of the Dorothy Schmidt College of Arts and Letters at Florida Atlantic University. His research interests are in the political economy of communication, ethnography, cultural studies, and Third World cinema. He has done fieldwork in the US, Canada, Africa, and India. His publications include *Canadian Dreams and American Control: The Political Economy of the Canadian Film Industry* (Wayne State University Press, 1990), *Citizenship and Participation in the Information Age* (edited with Roma Harris) (Garamond Press, 2002), and *Indian Popular Cinema: Industry, Ideology, and Consciousness* (Hampton Press, 2003).

Tom Schatz is Professor of Film at the University of Texas and Executive Director of the UT Film Institute, an innovative program that trains students in independent feature film production. He has written four books on American film, including *Hollywood Genres, The Genius of the System: Hollywood Filmmaking in the Studio Era*, and *Boom and Bust: American Cinema in the 1940s*, and is editor of a four-volume collection on Hollywood from Routledge. His writing on film has appeared in *The New York Times, The Los Angeles Times, Premiere, The Nation, Film Comment, Film Quarterly*, and *Cineaste*.

Jeff Smith is Professor of Film Studies at the University of Wisconsin-Madison. He is the author of *The Sounds of Commerce: Marketing Popular Film Music.*

John Trumpbour is Research Director for the Labor and Worklife Program at Harvard Law School. He is the author of *Selling Hollywood to the World: U.S. and European Struggles for Mastery of the Global Film Industry, 1920–1950* (Cambridge University Press, 2002), which won the Allan Nevins Prize for Literary Excellence in History from the Society of American Historians. He teaches film studies at the Harvard Trade Union Program and has been a guest lecturer on the film industry at Harvard Law School.

Janet Wasko is the Knight Chair for Communication Research at the University of Oregon. She is the author of *How Hollywood Works* (Sage, 2003), *Understanding Disney: The Manufacture of Fantasy* (Polity Press/Blackwell, 2001), and *Hollywood in the Information Age: Beyond the Silver Screen* (Polity Press, 1994) and editor of *A Companion to Television* (Blackwell, 2005) and *Dazzled by Disney? The Global Disney Audience Project* (Leicester University Press/Continuum, 2001), as well as other volumes on the political economy of communication and democratic media.

Frederick Wasser's book *Veni, Vidi, Video: The Hollywood Empire and the VCR* (University of Texas Press, 2001) won the 2003 Marshall McLuhan award. Before becoming a professor, he worked for many years in Hollywood post-production on shows ranging from *Columbo* to *Nightmare on Elm Street Part IV.* Wasser has published articles in *FLOW, Critical Studies in Mass Communication,* the *Journal of Communication, Cinema Journal* and others, and is currently teaching in the Department of Television and Radio at Brooklyn College-CUNY.

David Waterman is Professor in the Department of Telecommunications at Indiana University, Bloomington. His primary area of research is the economics of media industries, and the economics of information more generally. He is co-author (with Andrew A. Weiss) of *Vertical Integration in Cable Television* (MIT Press, 1997), and author of *Hollywood's Road to Riches* (Harvard University Press, 2005), an economic study of the theatrical motion picture industry. He is currently a principal editor of the journal *Information Economics & Policy.*

INTRODUCTION:
THE NEW CONTOURS OF THE HOLLYWOOD FILM INDUSTRY

PAUL McDONALD AND JANET WASKO

When the Hollywood studio Universal released *The Mummy* (Karl Freund, US) in 1932 the film was the latest in the cycle of horror features which the studio made during the decade. Nearly seven decades later, the studio dug over old ground to release *The Mummy* (Stephen Sommers, 1999, US), closely followed by the sequel, *The Mummy Returns* (Stephen Sommers, 2001, US).

At the time the 1932 version was released, Universal stood alongside Columbia and United Artists as one of the "Little Three" studios in Hollywood. Unlike the "Big Five" major studios – Fox, Loews/MGM, Paramount, Radio-Keith-Orpheum (RKO), and Warner Bros. – who dominated the industry through their vertical integration of production, distribution, and exhibition operations, the Little Three formed a weaker secondary tier of studios whose business was confined to producing and distributing films.

By the time the new version of *The Mummy* appeared, the shape of Universal had radically changed, as had the whole of the Hollywood film industry. In the early 1950s the recorded music label Decca became the major shareholder in the studio. Towards the end of the decade the talent agency Music Corporation of America (MCA) bought the Universal studio lot as a facility for its television production division, Revue, and three years later acquired the whole company. After MCA was sold in 1990 to the Japanese electronics manufacturer Matsushita, it was the aim of the new owner to create a hardware-software synergy of consumer electronics and entertainment content. As the studio failed to meet the performance expectations of Matsushita, Universal's film, music, and television operations were sold off in 1995 and consequently *The Mummy* (1999) was made and released through a studio owned by the Canadian drinks and beverages company Seagram. In 1999 *The Mummy* made a sizeable contribution to the $2,931 million revenues which Seagram earned from the film, video, and television operations of the Universal Studios Group. However the spirit and wine business, followed by the Universal Music Group, were the highest-earning segments for Seagram in that year (Seagram, 1999: 60). Subsequently, after Universal was acquired by Vivendi in 2000 as part of the French company's strategy to expand its operations in media and communications, *The Mummy Returns* became the product of a company which historically was more familiar with supplying water.

Universal made the 1932 version of *The Mummy* for less than $200,000. Production of the 1999 version operated on an altogether different economic scale: *The Mummy* (1999) cost in the region of $80 million, while the sequel was even more expensive at $98 million. Principal photography on the new version of *The Mummy* was undertaken during 1998 and the follow-up made two years later. For those years, the Motion Picture Association of America (MPAA), the trade association which represents the major Hollywood studios, calculated the average cost of a film made by its members stood at $52.7 million and $54.8 million respectively (MPAA, 2003: 19). By any reasoning these new takes on *The Mummy* myth were big-budget commitments.

Considering the costs of making the two films, maximizing the audience was a necessity. Although retaining a foothold in the horror credentials of the original 1932 version, Universal's new *Mummy* films explicitly combined elements of action and adventure into the tale. During the 1990s, mixing action and adventure with some light horror had proved marketable to a broad audience, giving Universal its largest hits of the decade with *Jurassic Park* (Steven Spielberg, 1993, US) and *The Lost World: Jurassic Park* (Steven Spielberg, 1993, US). With their tales of derring-do set in a not-too-distant past, the new *Mummy* films also harked back to the Indiana Jones trilogy (Steven Spielberg, 1981, 1984, and 1989, US) with which Paramount had scored such success in the previous decade. By bringing *The Mummy* back from the grave, Universal not only revived its franchise but also reinvented it. Through a hybrid mixing of generic credentials, the reincarnated *Mummy* appealed to a range of audience constituencies, crucially the all-important teenager, young adult, and family audiences, which from the 1970s had become the core market for Hollywood popular film. The appeal and accessibility of the films to this broad constituency of moviegoers was clearly acknowledged by the MPAA, who rated both films PG-13.

When released in the US and Canada at the start of May 1999, *The Mummy* opened on 3,209 screens (two years later in May 2001 the sequel exceeded that scale of release when opening on 3,401 screens) and in the space of two to three months Universal had rolled out the film across international territories. Both films were therefore constructed to make appeals to a broad-based audience, with Universal organizing distribution to make international events of the films. As part of the studio's promotional campaigns, Universal produced a website (www.themummy.com), a now standard tool of film marketing, thereby using new media to carry the films into the old media context of theatrical film exhibition.

At the box office *The Mummy* grossed $155 million in North America and $258 million internationally, while *The Mummy Returns* took $202 million at the North American box office and $227.4 million overseas (D'Alessandro, 2000, 2002). With these takings both films were ranked in fourth place for their respective years in terms of the highest-grossing films at the worldwide box office. At a national level, the films also proved to be hits in international territories. For example, in Germany, Italy, and Spain, at the end of 1999 *The Mummy* was placed amongst the top five highest-grossing films for that year (Dawtrey et al., 2000).

Ticket sales, however, were only part of the story. By the late 1990s the home video market had not only matured but was in the process of being re-energized following the introduction of the new format of Digital Video Disc (DVD), providing a new, rich wave of revenues for Hollywood feature films. For example, five months after its theatrical opening, in October 2001 *The Mummy Returns* was released on VHS and DVD, returning over $50 million in video rentals and $141 million in video sales in North America alone, helping Universal to a 16.8 percent share and third place amongst the studio distributors in the domestic video market that year (*Video Business*, 2001a, 2001b, 2001c). VHS and DVD extended the film's commercial life-cycle and it subsequently also played on pay-television services before receiving its network premiere during February 2004 on ABC (BiB, 2004: p. F-1008).

In keeping with strategies used by all the major studios to exploit the commercial value of their event movies, Universal ensured the new *Mummy* movies were not just films but generators of multiple media products. Universal produced *The Mummy: The Animated Series* for television, which ran for two seasons on Warner Bros.' Kids' WB network. The studio also installed *Revenge of the Mummy: The Ride* attractions at the Orlando and Hollywood sites of its Universal Studios theme park chain. Decca, by now a subsidiary of the Universal Music Group, issued original soundtrack albums to coincide with the releases of the films. Video games for the PlayStation console followed, spawning their own spin-off with *The Scorpion King: Rise of the Akkadian*. Other merchandise appeared in the form of books, posters, action figures, and plastic model kits. For example, Universal Studios Consumer Products Group agreed to a licensing deal with Toy Island to produce a line of action figures to accompany the release of *The Mummy*, while JAKKS Pacific made action figures, play-sets and accessories for the sequel.

To create cross-promotional opportunities, deals with various tie-in partners were agreed. Universal scheduled September 28, 1999, as the street date for the VHS and DVD release of *The Mummy*, timing this to coincide with the increased retail traffic seen during the build-up to Halloween. A week before the video went on sale, Craig Kornblau, president of Universal Studios Home Video, remarked, "Our goal is to own Halloween" (quoted in Arnold, 1999). Cross-promotion deals were signed with Hershey Foods and Polaroid. These cross-promotional deals supplemented Universal's own marketing campaign for the video release while also enabling tie-in partners to feed off the buzz created by the film to promote their own products. With purchases of the video Hershey offered free candy, while rebates on cameras could be claimed from Polaroid. Kornblau reasoned these deals for "[m]ore candy is sold at this time of year than at any other time, and, with the exception of Christmas, more pictures are taken as well. . . . These are natural partnerships." Universal further capitalized on the sense of event created by the video release by also putting out a new direct-to-video animated feature, *Alvin and the Chipmunks Meet Frankenstein*

(Kathi Castillo, 1999, US). Furthermore, releasing the new version of *The Mummy* on video also provided Universal with an opportunity to mine the studio's own library: eight of Universal's horror titles were re-released on VHS and DVD as the Classic Monsters collection, including the original *The Mummy* alongside *Dracula* (Tod Browning, 1931, US), *Frankenstein* (James Whale, 1931, US), *The Wolf Man* (George Waggner, 1941, US), and *Creature from the Black Lagoon* (Jack Arnold, 1954, US). "We have a corporatewide initiative to maximize our horror catalogue," Kornblau commented, adding, "Universal wouldn't exist if it wasn't for horror."

When Universal made the 1932 production it had drawn on the array of in-house service departments based at the studio's Universal City facility. These departments not only worked on *The Mummy* but supported the continuous schedule of films made on the studio lot. With the new *Mummy* films, however, production was organized as separate, self-contained projects. Instead of a set infrastructure of facilities, both productions drew on services from a range of external independent firms while hiring creative and technical personnel through the film industry's freelance labor market. Producer Sean Daniel made the movies through his Alphaville Films outfit, while production services were supplied by the Monaco-based company KanZaman s.a.m., a specialist in providing such services for feature films shot in southern Europe and North Africa. After filming part of the first movie at Shepperton Studios in south-east England, for the second film production returned to Britain for shooting at Pinewood Studios. An array of other companies in the US and UK also contributed to lighting, equipment supply, and post-production. For example, on both films one of the leading names in special effects, Industrial Light and Magic, contributed to creating the visual spectacle of the film. Aside from the UK, further location work was completed in parts of Egypt, Jordan, and Morocco.

Conglomeration, diversification, transnationalization of ownership, multiplication of distribution outlets, escalating production budgets, event movie production, exploitation of ancillary markets, the freelance market for creative and craft labor, and the global dispersal of production: these are just some of the trends which have shaped the contemporary Hollywood film industry. Universal's changing identity and the reinvention of *The Mummy* are symptomatic of those changes. When the 1932 version of *The Mummy* appeared, understanding the business of Hollywood film seemed relatively straightforward. Some of the studios were forging links with radio and the recorded music industries while also experimenting with television, but Hollywood still represented a tightly concentrated cluster of corporations whose main purpose was to make, sell, and show films. Today nearly all the same companies still remain at the center of the Hollywood film industry, but there the resemblances largely end. From the 1960s onwards waves of conglomeration saw ownership of Hollywood change as the film studios became assets folded into far larger corporate structures. Where at one stage conglomeration resulted in the studios becoming part of corporations with wide and diverse portfolios of operations, from the 1980s onwards the Hollywood studios came under the ownership of parent companies more squarely focused on media and communications.

Television not only opened up new markets and exhibition outlets for Hollywood films but also redefined the work of the studios as the major companies diversified into program production and distribution. Divisions between film and broadcasting became blurred, and the emergence from the early 1970s of pay-cable further encouraged the involvement of Hollywood in television. By the end of the 1970s video had also become a viable outlet for films, and at the start of the 1980s the studios were establishing co-ventures or subsidiaries to distribute titles for video rental and sales. As budgets for major Hollywood productions increased at rates which exceeded inflation, so television sales and video releasing provided valuable and increasingly essential new revenue streams. Television had already seen the consumption of Hollywood film migrating from theaters and into the home, but video further encouraged consumers to regard the living-room as the primary space for film viewing. Hollywood films therefore circulated in a market operating through multiple revenue streams and spread across various consumption contexts.

To deal with this range of commercial outlets, the media and communication conglomerates who own the Hollywood film companies now organize numerous divisional and subsidiary operations to make and distribute films through the various media channels. For example, in 2006 Time Warner, parent company of Warner Bros., had operations and holdings organized under seven groupings: Time Inc., Warner Bros. Entertainment, New Line Cinema Corporation, Turner Broadcasting System, Home Box Office, AOL, and Time Warner Cable. Warner Bros. Entertainment in turn contained nine divisions: Warner Bros. Pictures, Warner Bros. Pictures International, Warner Bros. Independent Pictures, Warner Bros. Television Group, Warner Bros. Home Entertainment Group, Warner Bros. Consumer Products, Warner Bros. International Theaters, Warner Bros. Studio Facilities, and DC Comics (Time Warner, 2006: 42–3). It has become a commonplace and a convenience to apply the label "studios" as a way of describing the major Hollywood companies, but holding as it does connotations of a physical production plant used for making films, this label is potentially a misnomer for companies whose divisional structures are now so stretched across many and diverse functions.

As they appear through various commercial outlets, Hollywood films materialize in a plurality of forms. A Hollywood film is now no longer just a movie but also an item of television programming or a digital optical disc. It may also become the source for an original soundtrack album or video game, while its characters or logo may be licensed for use in connection with merchandise and tie-in products, for example toys, apparel, or foodstuffs. All this would suggest that the Hollywood film is now a scattered and fragmented product, taking so many forms that the movie itself disappears. Once a film becomes a slot in the television schedules, a DVD, a game, a book, a ride, or an action figure, it is difficult to simply say what a phenomenon like *The Mummy* actually is. However there is a very definite foundation to the Hollywood film business. Films may enter the market in many forms, but at its core Hollywood remains a business which is not really based on the production of things so much as the control of the rights to use those things. Behind the labyrinthine complexities of conglomeration or the multiple layers of the audio-visual marketplace, the Hollywood film industry fundamentally remains in the business of exploiting intellectual property rights. Hollywood film is a copyright industry, and in this respect the contemporary state of the industry follows exactly the same logic which has determined the conduct of the film business for over a century: the Hollywood corporations are in the business of controlling the legal rights to sell, present, or reproduce films in order to generate profits.

As a result of the history which saw the American film industry consolidate its main production activities in and around Los Angeles, "Hollywood" has been familiarly used to not only name a place but also an industry. Because of these roots "Hollywood" has often been used as shorthand for the American film industry. Box office reporting on behalf of the Hollywood corporations tends to draw a division between the "domestic" market, meaning the US and Canada, and then "international" or "overseas" territories. However by its very own operations, Hollywood's links to any specific national context have become strained. In order to enter overseas markets, in the early decades of the twentieth century American film companies internationalized their distribution operations. Today, international distribution subsidiaries of the major Hollywood companies can be found scattered around the world. In some cases, such as Warner Bros. or National Amusements (majority owner of Viacom, the parent company of Paramount), a "studio" may also own multiplex and megaplex theaters in overseas territories. Because of the escalating costs of making and marketing films, the international box office or video sales now form not only lucrative but necessary markets for Hollywood films. As Hollywood films frequently feature in many territories around the world as the most commercially successful films at the box office, so they have a leading role in forming and defining international audiences for popular film. Consumption of Hollywood film also provides audiences with a set of familiar aesthetic and technological reference points, so that for many moviegoers around the world the visual and aural style of the popular Hollywood feature defines their imagination and understanding of what they accept or expect a film to be. Those aesthetic and technological conventions may in turn become the standards which practitioners in national film industries seek to emulate in the hope of capturing the same popular audience. Indeed, "national" film production may very often involve producers from international territories in forming partnerships with the Hollywood companies through co-production or co-financing arrangements. Furthermore, as the Hollywood companies use international territories for studio facilities and locations, or farm out post-production work to overseas service providers and draw on the international talent pool of creative and craft labor, then Hollywood film production is no longer rooted in clearly defined local or national contexts.

All this points towards the disembedding or deterritorialization of the Hollywood film industry. Indeed, the studio premises of the "Hollywood" film industry have long since decamped outside the immediate confines of Hollywood to other parts of LA. At a different level, since the drive to open up and colonize international markets during the years of World War I onwards, the American film industry has been broadening the geographic extensity of its operations. Today the major

Hollywood corporations may still be managed out of LA, while in turn reporting to parent companies with headquarters in New York or Tokyo, but the Hollywood film industry is firmly established as a globally dispersed business.

To understand Hollywood today it is necessary to look at the major studios or corporations but to also see these as parts of larger media and communications empires. As those corporations are not exclusively involved with the business of movies, the film industry is deeply and complexly involved with relations to other sectors of the audio-visual economy. Films still show in theaters, but their presentation and consumption also take place in many other spaces, particularly the home. Watching movies on DVD in the living-room brings the Hollywood film industry into the most private of spaces at the micro-local level. Yet at the same time the Hollywood film business is stretched and scattered across the globe. "Hollywood" may no longer be in Hollywood, but at least it is in or close to LA; yet it is also in Buenos Aires, Paris, Warsaw, Sydney, Mumbai, and Shanghai. The chapters which follow are therefore seeking to grasp the shape of the contemporary Hollywood film industry by confronting the challenges of thinking across a new set of corporate, technological, spatial, and cultural contours.

How To Use This Book

This collection examines the contemporary organization of the Hollywood film industry. Individual chapters discuss the structure and various dynamics of the industry, while providing diverse perspectives and opinions on the state of the industry. Chapters have been collected together in three parts.

Part I: The Structure of the Industry

This part addresses the structural organization of film production, distribution, and exhibition in Hollywood, and explores the relationships which exist between film and other media industries by the circulation of Hollywood films through various secondary or ancillary outlets.

In chapter 1, **Tom Schatz** presents a historical overview of the evolution of the conglomerate Hollywood system, outlining the current role of the studios as well as independent film practices. He finds that "the movie studios, along with the con- glomerates' 'indie film' divisions, television and cable networks, and myriad other holdings, have become players in a game they no longer control."

In chapter 2, **Janet Wasko** discusses Hollywood financing and production, detailing the various components that currently come together to produce a typical Hollywood film commodity, as well as presenting a few controversial issues that emerge from this process. **Philip Drake** (chapter 3) then examines the nature of film and the cinema experience as products and reviews current trends in film marketing and distribution by the major studios in the domestic North American market. Drake examines the claim that Hollywood is a risky industry by exploring how box-office "profits" are calculated.

The prominent characteristics of contemporary film exhibition are presented by **Charles Acland** in chapter 4. He focuses on four developments in the US context: (1) changing ideas about moviegoing audiences, (2) the concentration of screens in terms of geography and ownership, (3) the release strategies and their impact upon the life-cycle of film, and (4) the coming conversion to digital cinema.

This section also considers inter-media relations through the commercial dispersal of film properties in secondary and ancillary markets. **Eileen Meehan** discusses the relationship between the television and film industries, briefly sketching the film industry's initial interests in television, and focusing on the six firms that deregulation has allowed to dominate film and the ways that those firms embody film's five ancillary markets in television. Meanwhile, in chapter 6, **Frederick Wasser** outlines the home video revolution, describing how home video in its successive forms – first the VCR and now the DVD – contributes more revenue to Hollywood than any other market. Wasser looks at the activities of several groups involved in these markets: manufacturers, audiences, and media industries. **Randy Nichols** discusses another growing market in chapter 7, detailing ties between the video game and film industries. In comparing the two industries, he concludes that the film industry currently wields more power, yet the video game industry is emerging as a formidable challenger. The section concludes with **Jeff Smith**'s discussion of three periods of interaction between Hollywood and the recorded music industry in chapter 8. He discusses recorded music as promotion and cross-promotion, as ancillary revenues for Hollywood companies, and as a means of spreading the risk of Hollywood films.

Part II: Industry Dynamics

This part looks at various dynamics at work in the industry, including labor relations, the systematic promotion of stardom, relations between the film industry and the state, and the control of intellectual property rights.

In chapter 9, **Susan Christopherson** discusses the effects of media concentration on the film and television workforce, examining the labor politics that have emerged in response to the challenges produced by conglomeration and at how the powerful media unions are responding to changing employment conditions. In chapter 10, **Paul McDonald** then examines the Hollywood star system in the post-studio era, and the independent firms (agents, personal managers, publicists, and entertainment lawyers) that undertake the tasks necessary for cultivating, directing, and sustaining the images of leading performers.

Hollywood's relationship with the state is examined in chapter 11, as **Manjunath Pendakur** looks at the MPAA and its role in seeking collaboration and support from the US and other governments. The chapter sketches these relationships in the context of the current phase of globalization and examines the close relationship between the MPAA and the US government. Another important dynamic for Hollywood is explored in chapter 12, as **Ronald Bettig** describes the essential role of intellectual property in the form of copyrights, trademarks, and patents as these shape the structure and performance of the industry.

Part III: International Territories

The final section of the collection explores the involvement of the American film industry in overseas territories through chapters dealing with the major west European nations and other regional markets. **John Trumpbour**'s chapter introduces us to Hollywood and the world, and considers various accounts of how and why Hollywood came to dominate global cinema.

The major west European markets are considered by **Paul McDonald** (UK), **Joel Augros** (France), **Peter Krämer** (Germany), and **Krishna P. Jayakar** and **David Waterman** (Italy). Hollywood's activities in other regions are outlined in chapters by **Tamara L. Falicov** (Latin America), **John A. Lent** (East Asia), **Nitin Govil** (India), and **David Newman** (Australia and New Zealand). Each author discusses the historical and current status of these relationships, while revealing the contradictory impulses which often characterize these relationships as national cinema industries both actively resist but also collaborate with Hollywood.

Note: All dollar amounts given in the text are in US dollars unless otherwise stated.

REFERENCES

Arnold, Thomas K. (1999) "Video Marketers Ready to Scare Up Halloween Sales," *Los Angeles Times*, sect. C, 21 Sept., p. 1.

BiB (2004) *BiB Television Programming Source Books 2005: Films A–M, Indexes*. Philadelphia, PA: North American Publishing Co.

D'Alessandro, A. (2000) "The Top 125 Worldwide," *Variety*, January 24, p. 22.

D'Alessandro, A. (2002) "The Top 125 Worldwide," *Variety*, January 14, p. 23.

Dawtrey, A., M. Williams, L. Foreman, D. Rooney, and J. Hopewell (2000) "Euro B.O. Sings the Blahs," *Variety*, January 3, pp. 9, 22, 24.

MPAA (2003) *US Entertainment Industry: 2002 MPA Market Statistics*. Los Angeles: Motion Picture Association of America.

Seagram (1999) *1999 Annual Report*. Montreal: Seagram.

Time Warner (2006) *Time Warner: 2006 Profile*. New York: Time Warner.

Video Business (2001a) "Year-End Report: Market Share," online at <http://www.videobusiness.com/articles/images/vb/20011231/01_mktshare_big.gif> (accessed December 30, 2006).

Video Business (2001b) "Year-End Report: Rental Data Top-Renters Overall," online at <http://www.videobusiness.com/info/CA627024.html> (accessed December 30, 2006).

Video Business (2001c) "Year-End Report: Sales Data Top-Selling Overall," online at <http://www.videobusiness.com/info/CA627028.html> (accessed December 30, 2006).

PART I

THE STRUCTURE OF THE INDUSTRY

CHAPTER 1

THE STUDIO SYSTEM AND CONGLOMERATE HOLLYWOOD

TOM SCHATZ

Introduction

In August 1995 Neal Gabler, an astute Hollywood observer, wrote an op-ed piece for *The New York Times* entitled "Revenge of the Studio System" in response to recent events that, in his view, signaled an industry-wide transformation (Gabler 1995). The previous year had seen the Seagram buyout of MCA-Universal, Time Warner's purchase of the massive Turner Broadcasting System, and the launch of Dream-Works, the first new movie studio since the classical era. Then on August 1 came the bombshell that provoked Gabler's editorial. Disney announced the acquisition of ABC and its parent conglomerate, Capital Cities, in a $19 billion deal – the second-largest merger in US history, which created the world's largest media company. Disney CEO Michael Eisner also disclosed a quarter-billion-dollar deal with Mike Ovitz of Hollywood's top talent agency, Creative Artists, to leave CAA and run the Disney empire.

For Gabler, the Disney deals confirmed "a fundamental shift in the balance of power in Hollywood – really the third revolution in the relationship between industry forces." Revolution I occurred nearly a century before with the formation of the Hollywood studios and the creation of a "system" that enabled them to control the movie industry from the 1920s through the 1940s. Revolution II came with the postwar rise of television and the dismantling of the studio system by the courts, which allowed a new breed of talent brokers, "most notably Lew Wasserman of the Music Corporation of America [MCA]," to usurp control of the film industry. In the early 1960s, MCA dissolved its talent agency and purchased Universal Pictures, creating a precursor of sorts to the modern media conglomerate. MCA-Universal spearheaded an industry-wide recovery in the 1970s and 1980s, spurred by the deft integration of its film and television divisions and by a new breed of blockbuster films. Leading stars and independent filmmakers still enjoyed unprecedented power and freedom, and so the studios had to share their power with top talent and their agents – most notably the powerhouse agencies like William Morris and Ovitz's CAA, which not only represented talent, but actively "packaged" many of Hollywood's biggest films.

By the 1990s, however, the combined forces of media deregulation, globalization, and new digital technologies were tipping the balance of power back to the studios, thus auguring Revolution III. Disney and the other studios "may have finally found the holy grail," wrote Gabler. "By combining movies, broadcast television, video, foreign video, foreign television, merchandizing, theme parks, soundtrack albums, books and heaven knows what else, Mr. Eisner has devised a new form of vertical integration that takes virtually all of the risk out of movie software." This meant huge paydays for top talent in the short term, but the long-term prognosis for both filmmaking talent and films themselves was bleak. "When risk is vanquished, when even awful movies can be profitable, the stars lose their leverage," opined Gabler, and he closed with a bold assessment of Ovitz's jump to Disney: "The agencies and their clients are no longer the 800-pound gorillas. The studios are back in power. Why else would the greatest agent of them all defect to the enemy?"

In the years that followed, it became obvious that Gabler got it only half-right. There had been a significant power shift in Hollywood, and the Powers That Be were indeed devising new modes of vertical (and horizontal) integration to minimize risk and maximize profits. But the power scarcely resided with the studios of old. The new rulers of Hollywood – and of the global entertainment industry at large – were not the studios but their parent companies, the media giants like Viacom (owner of Paramount Pictures), Sony (Columbia), Time Warner (Warner Bros.), and News Corporation (20th Century Fox), which controlled not only the movie industry but the US television industry as well. Disney, the one studio that had not merged with or been swallowed by a media giant, had in fact become one. "Disney isn't as much a company as it is a nation-state," said Ovitz of his new employer, in an apt analogy that applied to all of the new global media powers (Bart, 1996).

This tectonic shift in the structure and economics of Hollywood actually began a decade earlier when News Corporation bought 20th Century Fox and launched the Fox Broadcasting network. That created a paradigm for the global media giants to come, as the burgeoning New Hollywood steadily morphed into Conglomerate Hollywood, and as the studios' role in the industry drastically changed. The studios were vital to their parent companies' media empires, of course, since Hollywood-produced blockbusters have been the driving force in the global entertainment industry. But the movie studios, along with the conglomerates' "indie film" divisions, television and cable networks, and myriad other holdings, have become players in a game they no longer control.

The Rise and Fall of the Classical Hollywood Studio System

To understand and assess the state of the studio system in contemporary Hollywood, we need to trace its earlier development, along with the complex evolution of the studios themselves and their singular product, the feature-length motion picture. During the classical era, from the 1920s through the 1940s, the "studio system" referred both to a factory-based mode of film production and also, crucially, to the vertical integration of production, distribution, and exhibition. The studio system co-alesced in the 1910s and early 1920s via expansion, merger, and acquisition, and by the 1930s the film industry had evolved into what economists term a "mature oligopoly" – that is, an industry effectively controlled by a cartel of companies (Balio, 1976/1985; Bordwell, Staiger, and Thompson, 1986; Gomery, 1986; Finler, 1988; Schatz, 1988).

Control of the movie industry was exercised by the so-called Big Eight studios, whose filmmaking factories in Hollywood fed their nationwide distribution opera-tions. The most powerful of these firms were the fully integrated Big Five studios – MGM, Warner Bros., 20th Century Fox, Paramount, and RKO – which not only produced and distributed films but operated their own theater chains as well. Meanwhile, the Little Three "major minor" studios – Universal, Columbia, and United Artists (UA) – produced and distributed top feature films but did not own their own theaters. Universal and Columbia were full-fledged movie factories but produced fewer A-class features because they lacked the financial leverage and film-making resources of the Big Five. UA was an anomaly among the studios in that it simply provided financing and distribution to top independent producers like Sam Goldwyn and David Selznick. The 1930s also saw the emergence of several "poverty row" B-movie mills like Monogram and Republic, which were incidental to the studio system since they did not produce A-class features and did not dis-tribute their own films.

The studio system flourished during the Depression and World War II, two national crises that induced the government to sanction (or at least tolerate) the studios' monopolistic control of the film industry. This enabled the studios to maintain their factory operations as well as a "contract system" that kept filmmaking talent at all levels, from top stars to stagehands, directly tied to the company. Studio manage-ment was a classic top-down affair, with the primary power emanating from the home office in New York, which controlled distribution and exhibition (i.e., sales), and passing on to the studio on the West Coast, whose top executives supervised the overall operation of the plant while a corps of supervisors (eventually dubbed "producers") oversaw the production of individual films. The mainstay of the studio system was the A-class feature film, invariably a formulaic "star vehicle" with solid production values and a virtually guaranteed market. The studios also turned out occasional big-budget "prestige pictures" as well as a steady supply of low-cost B-movie fare that comprised up to half their output in the 1930s, which totaled roughly 50 pictures per week and was sold in entire "blocks" to the nation's exhibitors. But it was A-class star-genre films that drove the entire studios system as it reached full maturity during the 1930s and Hollywood entered its legendary Golden Age. Moreover, these star-genre cycles were the basis for each studio's dis-tinctive "house style," which was fundamentally geared to its internal resources, its stables of contract talent, and its overall market strategy.

The 1940s proved to be a watershed era for Hollywood, with an unprecedented boom due to war-related social and economic conditions early in the decade, followed by a drastic industry decline and an abrupt end to the studios' long-standing hegemony. The war boom peaked in 1946, the studios' best year ever in terms of revenues and profits, but by 1947–8 the industry was in a veritable free-fall due to a succession of devastating blows. Foremost among these was the Supreme Court's 1948 Paramount decree, an antitrust ruling that resulted from persistent legal challenges by independent exhibitors, which forced the Big Five studios to sell their theater chains and prohibited the collusive trade practices that were crucial to the studios' control of the motion-picture marketplace. Another was the rapid growth of television, which was propelled by sustained economic prosperity and wholesale changes in postwar American lifestyles – most notably suburban migration and the so-called baby boom. In the span of a decade, "watching TV" replaced "going to the movies" as America's dominant form of habituated, mass-mediated narrative entertainment.

The studios responded – and ultimately survived – by fundamentally changing the way they made movies and did business, thus establishing a modus operandi that still prevails today. Adopting and modifying the UA model, the studios concentrated on financing and distribution rather than production. Lacking the financial resources and contract talent to mass-produce movies for a declining market they no longer controlled, the studios now relied on independent producers to supply "packaged" projects that the studios would "green light" for production, putting up some portion of the budget in exchange for the distribution rights, and often leasing out their production facilities as well. This meant ceding creative control to independent producers and freelance directors, and also to top stars whose "marquee value" gave them tremendous leverage and frequently a share of the profits. This also gave considerable power to the leading talent agencies like William Morris and MCA, with the latter becoming particularly adept at setting up independent companies for its clients. The studios still generated their own films, but they produced fewer, "bigger" pictures – biblical epics and wide-screen Westerns during the 1950s, for instance – which made more sense economically and laid the groundwork for the blockbuster mentality that now prevails.

The Television Era and the New American Cinema

By the mid-1950s all of the studios had weathered the postwar storm except RKO, which was bought by Howard Hughes in 1948 and subsequently mismanaged and dismantled. RKO was essentially defunct by 1957, when the lot itself was purchased by Desilu, the independent television production powerhouse owned by Desi Arnaz and Lucille Ball (of *I Love Lucy* fame), two former RKO contract players. The rise of Desilu had considerable impact on the Hollywood studio system, in that it pioneered "telefilm" series production based on the West Coast, providing a model of sorts for the studios' profitable pursuit of TV series production. The surviving major studios – MGM, Paramount, Warner Bros., and 20th Century Fox – actively resisted telefilm production until 1954–5, when both Columbia (via its Screen Gems subsidiary) and Disney (via its hugely successful *Disneyland* [ABC, 1954–61, US] series) had hit series on prime-time network television. RKO also began selling its old films to TV syndication companies in 1955, providing further impetus for the majors' reconciliation with the upstart industry. In 1955–6 the major studios finally acquiesced, as they began reissuing older films for syndication and, even more importantly, moved headlong into telefilm series production. By 1960 the center of television production in the US had shifted from New York to Hollywood and the studios were turning out far more hours of TV series programming than feature films, having reactivated their B-movie operations to feed TV's voracious appetite for programming. In 1960 the networks also started running Hollywood movies during prime time, which added enormous value to the studios' "libraries" of theatrically released films (Schatz, 1990; Anderson, 1994; Hilmes, 1999).

Despite their growing rapport with the TV industry, the studios struggled during the 1960s due mainly to the continued erosion of the mainstream audience and the over-production of big-budget epics and musicals (in an effort to retain that audience), resulting in a decade-long run of spectacular hits and misses. 20th Century Fox, for instance, careened from financial desperation with *Cleopatra* (Joseph Mankiewicz, 1963, US) to monumental success with *The Sound of Music* (Robert Wise, 1965, US), then saw costly failures like *Doctor Dolittle* (Richard Fleischer, 1967, US), *Star!* (Robert Wise, 1968, US), *Hello, Dolly!* (Gene Kelly, 1969, US), and *Tora! Tora! Tora!* (Richard Fleischer, Kinji Fukasaku, 1970, US) generate net losses of over $100 million in 1969–70, driving the company to the brink of bankruptcy (Finler, 1988: 100). The 1960s also saw an unprecedented surge in film imports and international co-productions, a trend that had been growing throughout the post-war era, and one which threatened the studios' control of the marketplace as well as their narrative and stylistic traditions. These imports ranged from high-cost prestige pictures and art films to low-budget exploitation films, many of them co-financed, co-produced, or simply released by one of the studios. UA was by far the most aggressive and successful in pursuing such deals, which included prestige films like *Tom*

FIGURE 1.1   *Cleopatra* (1963), an expensive failure for Fox. Produced by Walter Wanger; distributed by 20th Century Fox; directed by Joseph L. Mankiewicz

Jones (Tony Richardson, 1963, UK), the Beatles-starring *A Hard Day's Night* (Richard Lester, 1964, UK) and *Help!* (Lester, 1965, UK), the enormously success-ful James Bond cycle, and the Sergio Leone-directed "Spaghetti Westerns" starring Clint Eastwood (Balio, 1987).

During the late 1960s Hollywood began generating an art cinema of its own, spurred by the wave of imports, the demise of the Production Code in 1966–7, and the com-ing of age of the postwar "baby boom" generation – not only as a distinctive (and distinctly counter-cultural) moviegoing market, but a new generation of filmmak-ing talent and studio executives as well. Propelled by the success of *Bonnie and Clyde* (Arthur Penn, 1967, US) and *The Graduate* (Mike Nichols, 1967, US), and aptly termed the New American Cinema by critics and historians, the late 1960s and early 1970s saw the rapid emergence of a director-driven, youth-oriented, art-cinema move-ment that defied the conventions of classical Hollywood narrative, subverted its genre traditions, and openly challenged that studio-controlled mode of production. All of the studios supported the movement, mainly due to the reliability of the youth market, with Paramount, Columbia, and Warner Bros. taking the most aggressive tack. Paramount's releases included *Rosemary's Baby* (Roman Polanski, 1968, US), *Love Story* (Arthur Hiller, 1970, US), and *The Godfather* (Francis Ford Coppola, 1972, US). Columbia's included *Easy Rider* (Dennis Hopper, 1969, US), *Five Easy Pieces* (Bob Rafelson, 1970, US), and *The Last Picture Show* (Peter Bogdanovich, 1971, US). Warner Bros., under the leadership of John Calley, was the most significant contributor to the New American Cinema, producing *Bonnie and Clyde* and *Bullitt* (Peter Yates, 1968, US), *The Wild Bunch* (Sam Peckinpah, 1969, US), *Woodstock* (Michael Wadleigh, 1970, US), *A Clockwork Orange* (Stanley Kubrick, 1971, UK), *Dirty Harry* (Don Seigel, 1971, US), *McCabe and Mrs. Miller* (Robert Altman, 1971, US), *Klute* (Alan Pakula, 1971, US), *Deliverance* (John Boorman, 1972, US), *Mean Streets* (Martin Scorsese, 1973, US), *Badlands* (Terrence Malick, 1973, US), and *The Exorcist* (William Friedkin, 1973, US). This Hollywood new wave proved to be a decidedly mixed blessing for the studios, however, since these films enjoyed the allegiance of the youth market and the adulation of critics but rarely enjoyed cross-over success with mainstream moviegoers and tended to be unsuitable for network television.

While the New American Cinema was geared to a new generation of film-makers and moviegoers, the industry at large underwent significant changes due to a new breed of studio owner. In the course of the 1960s, five of the seven Hollywood studios – Universal, Paramount, Warner Bros., UA, and MGM – changed owner-ship in a merger-and-acquisition wave unlike any since the formation of the studio system a half-century earlier. Spurred mainly by the studios' depressed stock value, this wave was quite distinctive in that all of these were straight buyouts (acquisi-tions, not mergers), and four of the five purchasing companies had no experience of – and little interest in – media entertainment. The only studio acquisition involving a media-savvy buyer was the first of the five buyouts: the 1962 purchase of Universal Pictures and parent company Decca Records by MCA, Hollywood's top talent agency and also its leading television program supplier through its

Revue division. When it bought Universal, MCA dissolved its talent agency (at the insistence of the Justice Department) to concentrate on film and television production, distribution, and syndication. MCA-Universal weathered the industry's 1960s downturn thanks to its successful integration of film and television production, which included the launch of the made-for-TV movie format in a historic pact with NBC, and its continued dominance in telefilm series production (Thompson, 1960; Bruck, 2003).

While the MCA–Universal union was a model of "synergy" – i.e., the coordination of its various media divisions – the other 1960s buyouts involved studio acquisitions by large non-media conglomerates: Paramount by Gulf + Western in 1966; UA by Transamerica in 1967; Warner Bros. by Seven Arts in 1967 and then by Kinney Corporation in 1969; and MGM by Las Vegas mega-developer Kirk Kerkorian in 1969. The Paramount, UA, and Warner Bros. deals involved diversified, deep-pocketed parent companies that enabled the studios to continue operations despite the industry-wide recession. Kerkorian, however, was a financier and real-estate tycoon interested in MGM for its brand name and its library, and with no inclination to underwrite its failing movie production-distribution operation. Kerkorian installed former CBS president James Aubrey as studio head, who began dismantling the studio in the early 1970s. In 1973, the year that Kerkorian opened his MGM Grand Hotel and Casino in Las Vegas (then the largest hotel in the world), Aubrey sold MGM's distribution operation to UA and cut production to only a half-dozen films per year (Bart, 1990a).

The Rise of the New Hollywood

Kerkorian's demolition of the once mighty MGM indicated a widespread loss of confidence in the movie industry at the time, as the combined effects of youth-marketed art cinema and a glut of big-budget flops led to a severe industry recession from 1969 to 1971, with 20th Century Fox, UA, Warner Bros., and MGM all suffering record losses. Feature film production was increasingly perceived as a "loss leader" for the studios, which were valued primarily for their movie libraries and TV divisions. But the historically cyclical movie business soon began an upturn, as films like *Love Story*, *The French Connection* (William Friedkin, 1971, US), *The Godfather*, and *The Exorcist* scored with mainstream moviegoers as well as the youth market. Again MCA-Universal was a major force, vaulting to the top of the movie industry with a string of hits including *American Graffiti* (George Lucas, 1973, US), *The Sting* (George Roy Hill, 1973, US), *Earthquake* (Mark Robson, 1974, US), and *Jaws* (Steven Spielberg, 1975, US). *Jaws* proved to be a genuine industry watershed, marking the birth of the New Hollywood in several crucial ways. Besides putting Steven Spielberg on the industry map (it was his second feature), *Jaws* provided a prototype for the modern blockbuster: a high-cost, high-speed, high-concept entertainment machine propelled by a nationwide "saturation" release campaign, with bookings in a then record 400-plus theaters supported by an

FIGURE 1.2   Monster hit, *Jaws* (1975). Produced by David Brown and Richard D. Zanuck; distributed by Universal; directed by Steven Spielberg

unprecedented network TV ad campaign. *Jaws* was the breakthrough "summer blockbuster," and the first film to gross over $200 million at the box office and to return over $100 million in rental receipts to its distributor – still the measure of a blockbuster hit. The film enjoyed further success via theatrical rerelease and multiple sequels, as well as an aggressive licensing and merchandising campaign that spawned video games, theme-park rides, and myriad other tie-ins (Schatz, 1993).

Jaws sparked a widespread industry recovery that was fueled primarily by a new breed of blockbuster. Domestic grosses totaled $2 billion for the first time in 1975 and rose 40 percent over the next three years, driven by huge hits like *Rocky* (John G. Avildson, 1976, US), *Star Wars* (Lucas, 1977, US), *Close Encounters of the Third Kind* (Spielberg, 1977, US), *Saturday Night Fever* (John Badham, 1977, US), *Grease* (Randal Kleiser, 1978, US), and *Superman* (Richard Donner, 1978, US). The most significant of these films was *Star Wars*, the ultimate New Hollywood commodity – a hip-ironic, genre-blending, male action movie whose characters are essentially plot functions, and whose plot was strategically "open" to reiteration, licensing, and serialization. *Star Wars* surpassed *Jaws* as Hollywood's top all-time box-office hit and quickly evolved into the model New Hollywood "franchise" – i.e., the blockbuster-spawning entertainment machine that exploited and expanded the original hit in an ever-widening range of entertainment products. This was a painful lesson for 20th Century Fox, which granted writer-director George Lucas the sequel rights to *Star Wars* in lieu of his final paycheck. As a result Fox collected only the distribution fees on the subsequent series installments (in 1980, 1983, 1999, 2003, and 2005), while Lucas parlayed his ownership of Hollywood's first billion-dollar franchise into a vast media empire of his own (Pollock, 1999).

The industry recovery accelerated in the early 1980s, fueled by mega-hits like *The Empire Strikes Back* (Irvin Kershner, 1980, US), *Raiders of the Lost Ark* (Steven Spielberg,

1981, US), and *E.T. The Extra-Terrestrial* (Spielberg, 1982, US), as well as the rapid emergence of the home-video and cable industries. Remarkably enough in retrospect, the studios actually resisted the introduction of the videocassette recorder (VCR) into the US market, with Universal and Disney filing a copyright infringement suit against Sony after the 1975 launch of its Betamax VCR in the US. Sony eventually prevailed in a 1984 Supreme Court ruling, but by then it was clear to all parties, especially the studio-distributors, that home-video revenues were a vital revenue source (Wasser, 2001). Meanwhile, Home Box Office (HBO), which in 1975 became the nation's first pay-cable "movie channel," established itself as yet another viable "delivery system" for Hollywood movies, and it was successfully replicated by various other services like Showtime, Cinemax, and The Movie Channel as well (Prince, 2002).

As Hollywood's economic recovery continued throughout the 1980s, the stakes rose at a staggering rate. The average negative cost for studio releases (the amount spent on actual film production) climbed from $9.4 million in 1980 to $26.7 million in 1990 – roughly six time the rate of inflation – while the cost of marketing (prints and advertising, or "P&A") rose from $4.3 million to $11.6 million. The number of movie screens increased by over 50 percent, from 14,000 to 22,000, as the studios became more adept at saturation release campaigns. The studios' domestic theatrical revenues increased from $2.75 billion in 1980 to $5 billion in 1989, while their ancillary markets simply exploded. The principal growth areas throughout the 1980s were in home video and pay-cable, with the overseas markets (both theatrical and video) taking off late in the decade. By 1989 home video, an income source that was virtually nil a decade earlier, was generating more revenue for the studio-distributors than theaters – a trend that would accelerate in the coming years, along with the explosive growth of the overseas market (MPAA, 1990; MPA, 2005). But because these secondary markets were driven by blockbuster hits whose value was established via a saturation marketing campaigns in the US, the Hollywood studio-distributors continued to focus heavily on the domestic theatrical market.

The stakes were rising in terms of talent compensation as well. Top filmmaking talent was rarely if ever tied contractually to a particular studio, except through the studio's ownership of a specific franchise. The alliance of top stars with particular franchises tipped the balance of power in 1980s Hollywood toward top male stars (and their agents), as evidenced by Sylvester Stallone's record payday of $15 million in 1983 for *Rocky IV*, and Paramount's Beverly Hills Cop series starring Eddie Murphy, which was co-produced with (and controlled by) Murphy's production company (Bart, 1990b: 1; Cohn, 1990: 3; Landro, 1990: A1). Equally important were top producer-directors like Lucas and Spielberg who, through Lucasfilm and Amblin Entertainment, respectively, were the chief architects of what *Variety*'s A. D. Murphy termed "the modern era of super-blockbuster films." With the 1989 release of their third Indiana Jones collaboration, Lucas and Spielberg were responsible for eight of the ten biggest box-office hits in movie history, all of which surpassed $100 million in domestic rentals (Murphy, 1989: 26; *Variety*, 1992: 86).

The Changing Industry Structure in the 1980s

In terms of the structure and conduct of the studios, the most significant development in the 1980s was the concerted move toward "synergy" or "tight diversification" – a key aspect of the film industry for the next two decades (Mickelthwait,
1989: p. 5). This was a function of the studios' efforts to become more efficient
multi-faceted media corporations, focusing on their filmed entertainment divisions
while taking full advantage of new delivery systems and revenue streams. The quest
for synergy was spurred by multiple factors, notably the dramatic growth of home
video and cable, the Reagan-era policies of deregulation and free-market economics,
and the obvious impulse to enhance (and exploit) the value of their blockbuster
hits. In some cases, the move to tight diversification involved radical downsizing,
as with Warner Communications and Gulf + Western, which shed their non-media
assets to focus on media and entertainment – with G+W changing its name to
Paramount Communications in 1989 to underscore this new focus. Other cases
involved radical expansion via acquisition, most notably Coca-Cola's purchase of
Columbia Pictures in 1982, and the buyout of 20th Century Fox in 1984–5 by Rupert
Murdoch's News Corporation.

While the Coke–Columbia alliance failed to click, News Corporation–Fox proved
to be one of the most important mergers in industry history. The deal was orchestrated by Barry Diller, who began his career at ABC before moving to Paramount
in the 1970s, and then left Paramount for Fox in 1983 after the death of G+W boss
Charles Bludhorn (as did Michael Eisner, Diller's protégé at ABC and Paramount,
who left for Disney in 1984). Diller convinced Murdoch to invest in and ultimately
to buy Fox, thus giving the studio a deep-pocketed parent company with global
media holdings ranging from newspapers and magazines to satellite and cable. He
then created a fourth US broadcast network, Fox Television, which launched in 1986
and soon was competing successfully with ABC, CBS, and NBC (Block, 1990). The
success of the News Corporation–Fox alliance underscored the logic of synergy when
properly employed, as well as the impact of cable and the rapidly eroding power
of the Big Three TV networks – an erosion so severe, in fact, that all three changed
hands in 1985–6, due to their declining market value and audience share, and to
the general uncertainty in the industry (Auletta, 1992).

News Corporation–Fox also highlights the importance of the Reagan administration's free-market economic policies and media deregulation campaign, which
led to the steady relaxation of both ownership restrictions and antitrust activities
by the Federal Communication Commission (FCC) and the Justice Department.
Several studios began buying theaters, which had been prohibited since the 1948
Paramount decree. But given the current industry structure and the proliferation
of delivery systems, the Old Hollywood model of vertical integration – i.e., production–distribution–exhibition within the film sector – no longer made sense. Far
more effective was the News Corporation–Fox strategy of multiple "pipelines" to
consumers (satellite, cable, broadcast, as well as print) delivering content created
and owned by the parent company's media divisions. Another key regulatory con-

cern was the FCC's Financing and Syndication ("Fin-Syn") Rules, passed in 1970, which prohibited the networks from owning and syndicating their own programs, as well as the cross-ownership of film studios and TV networks. These rules ensured the studios' production and ownership of TV programming, a crucial revenue source that was threatened by FCC chairman Mark Fowler's media deregulation campaign. Despite Fowler's stated intent to roll back Fin-Syn, the effort was stymied throughout the 1980s thanks to heavy lobbying by Motion Picture Association of America (MPAA) president Jack Valenti, the highest-paid lobbyist in the US, as well as Lew Wasserman's gentle pressuring of his former client and close friend, Ronald Reagan (Holt, 2001–2).

Disney also exploited new technologies and delivery systems, creating synergies that were altogether unique among the studios, and that finally enabled the perpetual "mini-major" to ascend to major studio status. Mired during the early 1980s at the very bottom of the studio heap in terms of output and market share, Disney began a dramatic surge after a fierce internal power struggle that brought in Michael Eisner, Frank Wells, and Jeffrey Katzenberg to run the company in 1984 (Taylor, 1987). The three executives concentrated on several key areas: live-action theatrical films produced for mature audiences under the new Touchstone banner, created in 1983; an innovative syndication operation geared to home video, where it planned to reissue Disney's classic films; a pay-cable operation, The Disney Channel, also launched in 1983, that focused on family fare; and an aggressive return to network television series production. Disney's fortunes quickly improved thanks to Touchstone hits like *Splash* (Ron Howard, 1984, US) and *Down and Out in Beverly Hills* (Paul Mazursky, 1986, US), along with hit network TV series and, perhaps most importantly, the successful repackaging of Disney's animated classics for both home video and theatrical reissue. By 1988 Disney enjoyed the industry's leading market share, and had revamped the animation division under Katzenberg, which was preparing *The Little Mermaid* (Ron Clements, John Musker) for release in 1989 – the same year that Disney launched a chain of retail stores to further exploit its revitalized brand (Stewart, 2005).

While Disney flourished in the 1980s due to its successful diversification and its response to changing industry conditions, two other struggling studios, MGM and UA, fell even further due to their inability to adapt. The studios merged in 1981 to create MGM/UA, a union precipitated by the spectacular failure of UA's *Heaven's Gate* (Michael Cimino, 1980, US) – a $40 million write-off that induced UA owner Transamerica to sell the studio. Meanwhile, Kirk Kerkorian was planning to expand MGM's operations, which he had severely cut a decade earlier, and he decided to acquire UA to enhance the effort. The results were uneven at best, however, so the mercurial Kerkorian went to Ted Turner, who was sorely in need of content for his sprawling cable TV empire. In 1985 the Turner Broadcasting System (TBS) acquired MGM/UA, which Turner promptly dismantled, selling everything except for the massive library (which included some 3,650 film titles) – thus crippling MGM/UA as a viable film studio while giving TBS the world's largest film and television library (Balio, 1987; Bart, 1990a).

As these two traditional studio powers were all but obliterated during the
1980s, new studios rapidly emerged. The most important were Orion and TriStar,
two upstart "mini-majors" that grew increasingly powerful and important in the
course of the decade. Orion was an independent production company created in
1978 by several former UA executives, including Arthur Krim, who left over
differences with owner Transamerica. The company enjoyed early success with
mid-range auteur vehicles and comedy hits, most notably Woody Allen's films. TriStar
was an explicit product of media synergy, formed in 1983 as an alliance between
CBS-TV, Columbia Pictures (then owned by Coca-Cola), and HBO (owned by Time,
Inc.). By 1985 both CBS and HBO had pulled out. TriStar was effectively a subsidiary of Coca-Cola, operating separately from Columbia Pictures and releasing
about the same number of films as Orion (Wyatt, 2000). The mid-1980s also saw
the rapid emergence of a new breed of smaller companies, due to the combined
effects of the booming theatrical market and the explosive growth of the home-
video industry with its new class of "direct-to-video" features. A few companies
like Carolco, Vestron, Cannon, DEG (DeLaurentiis Entertainment Group), and New
Line enjoyed success both as independent producer-distributors and also in partnership with the major studios, which relied heavily on "negative pickups" – i.e.,
independent productions that the studios opted to finance and distribute – to fill
out their release slates.

The surviving major studios along with mini-majors Disney, TriStar, and Orion
all released 15 to 20 films per year during the 1980s, split fairly evenly between
in-house productions and negative pickups. Meanwhile the new breed of smaller
producer-distributors like Vestron and New Line evolved into a veritable sub-
industry, radically increasing Hollywood's overall output of feature films (see
table 1.1). As the figures in table 1.1 indicate, the majors were distributing about
one-third of all theatrical releases by the late 1980s, and actually producing less than

TABLE 1.1   US film production and distribution, 1984–1990

	1984	1985	1986	1987	1988	1989	1990
Majors' in-house productions	81	70	67	72	75	73	90
Majors' indie pickups	57	36	54	75	66	76	61
TOTAL MAJORS	138	106	121	147	141	149	151
US indie releases	132	150	197	172	166	112	102
Direct-to-video releases	36	36	115	142	165	103	51
No US distribution	62	64	96	111	129	120	134
Total: no US theatrical release	98	100	211	253	294	223	185
Subtotal: US indie prodns	287	287	463	500	526	411	348
TOTAL US PRODUCTIONS	368	357	530	572	601	484	438
% with no theatrical release	27%	28%	40%	44%	49%	46%	42%

Source: Variety, 1991: 12.

20 percent of the total feature film output. Nonetheless, the majors and mini-majors took in the lion's share of the film revenues from both the theatrical and home-video markets, with the latter proving to be as hit-driven as the nation's drivers – as the corporate moniker of the leading US video rental chain, Blockbuster, well indicated (Wasser, 1990).

Another significant challenge to studio hegemony involved top filmmaking talent and the leading agencies, most notably William Morris, CAA, and ICM, which formed a veritable cartel during the 1980s and exercised far more authority over Hollywood filmmaking than any studio. Besides representing most of the talent required to produce top features, these agencies were adept at packaging major studio productions, with the agency and its clients exercising enormous creative control and siphoning off a sizable portion of the revenues through "participation" deals. The sheer size of William Morris was awesome, with over 500 agents and literally thousands of clients, but CAA under Mike Ovitz was arguably the more powerful industry force. At least one top studio executive, Universal's Frank Price, lost his job for relying too heavily on Ovitz, but even after Price was replaced by Tom Pollock, Universal could scarcely cut its ties to Ovitz and CAA. The agency's client list of some 150 directors, 150 actors, and 300 writers included the cream of Hollywood's talent crop, and Ovitz personally handled Steven Spielberg, Martin Scorsese, Spike Lee, and Oliver Stone, all of whom had multi-picture deals with Universal (Cieply, 1989; Davis, 1989; Prince, 2000).

Ovitz's power reached a peak of sorts in 1990, when *Premiere* magazine put him atop its Hollywood "power list" – ahead of MCA-Universal's Lew Wasserman, Warner's Steve Ross, Disney's Michael Eisner, and Paramount's Barry Diller (numbers two through five, respectively) (*Premiere*, 1990). Ovitz's film-related deals were crucial to that ranking, of course, but even more important was the fact that Ovitz now brokered not only talent and package deals but actual media mergers. In 1989, Sony hired Ovitz as a consultant on its buyout of Columbia-TriStar; then in 1990 Sony's chief Japanese manufacturing rival, Matsushita Electrical, hired Ovitz to identify a studio acquisition target and to personally broker the deal. Ovitz decided on MCA-Universal, and he personally handled the negotiations between the Japanese hardware giant and the Hollywood studio (Griffin and Masters, 1996; Bruck, 2003).

The 1990s and Beyond: The Studio System in Conglomerate Hollywood

Ovitz's role in the Sony–Columbia and Matsushita–MCA deals underscored the power of Hollywood's top agents and talent agencies, but the mergers themselves were far more significant. In fact these two acquisitions, along with the 1989 merger of the US media titans Time Inc. and Warner Communications, marked a watershed in Hollywood's history, as the logic of synergy and tight diversification met the larger forces of globalization, digitization, and US media deregulation. In a five-year span from 1990 to 1995, the New Hollywood rapidly transformed into Conglomerate

TABLE 1.2   Major studio merger and acquisition deals, 1989–2005

1984–5: News Corporation buys privately owned 20th Century Fox for an estimated
        $750 million.
1989: Time Inc. acquires Warner Communications for $9.1 billion.
1989: Sony acquires Columbia-TriStar for $4.8 billion.
1990: Matsushita buys MCA/Universal for $6.6 billion.
1990: Pathé acquires MGM/UA for $1.43 billion.
1993: Disney buys Miramax for $80 million.
1994: Viacom buys Paramount for $9.5 billion.
1994: Viacom buys Blockbuster for $8.4 billion.
1994: Spielberg, Katzenberg, and Geffen announce the creation of DreamWorks SKG.
1995: Seagram buys MCA (80% stake) from Matsushita for $5.7 billion, and renames it
        Universal Studios.
1995: Disney buys Capital Cities/ABC for $18.3 billion.
1995: Time Warner buys Turner Broadcasting System (TBS) for $9.1 billion. Deal
        includes New Line and Castle Rock, which TBS purchased in 1993.
1999: Viacom buys CBS for $35.6 billion.
2000: Vivendi buys Seagram for $34 billion, creating Vivendi Universal.
2000: AOL merges with Time Warner in a stock deal with an estimated value of
        $160 billion to $183 billion. Company name reverts to Time Warner in 2003, with
        AOL as a subsidiary.
2003: GE buys Vivendi Universal (80% stake) in a deal valued at $14 billion, creates NBC
        Universal.
2005: Viacom (Paramount) buys DreamWorks for $1.6 billion.

Dates indicate announcement of deal, not the final approval(s) or effective dates (which generally
    occurred up to a full year later).
The announced dollar amount of each deal varies widely according to many factors – notably
    current stock value and assumption of debt.
An excellent source for researching and charting media mergers is the *Columbia Journalism Review*'s
    "Who Owns What" site, online at <http://www.cjr.org/tools/owners/>.

Hollywood, as a new breed of media giants took command of the US film and
television industries and became the dominant powers in the rapidly expanding
global entertainment industry (see table 1.2).

The Time–Warner merger primarily involved print and filmed entertainment
interests, recalling the News Corporation–Fox union of 1984–5. Sony–Columbia
and Matsushita–MCA, meanwhile, created "hardware-software" alliances prompted
by technological innovation and a booming home-video market on the verge of
global expansion. The two Japanese tech-manufacturing giants had battled for
control of the VCR and home-video market a decade earlier, and now both were
looking for Hollywood-based "content providers" as they geared up for high-
definition (HD) digital television and the next-generation home-video technology,
the digital video disc (DVD). The new studio owners also brought two more

foreign-based, multi-national players into the Hollywood mix. With the 1990 acquisition of MGM/UA by the Italian conglomerate Pathé Communications, in fact, four of the eight original Hollywood studios were foreign-owned. (Australian Rupert Murdoch became an American citizen in 1985 to accommodate US media regulations when News. Corp acquired Fox, or the total would have been five.)

The merger-and-acquisition wave initiated in 1989–90 continued with Viacom's purchase of Paramount Pictures and Blockbuster Entertainment in 1994, the launch of cable networks by Warner Bros. ("The WB") and Paramount ("UPN") in 1995, and literally dozens of other media mergers. And the wave crested in 1994–5 with the deals mentioned at the outset: the launch of DreamWorks SKG by three consummate Hollywood players, Steven Spielberg, Jeff Katzenberg, and David Geffen; Seagram's acquisition of MCA-Universal from Matsushita; Time Warner's purchase of TBS; and Disney's buyout of Cap Cities/ABC. These coincided with the FCC's final phase-out of Fin-Syn in 1995 and Congress's passage of the Tele-communications Act of 1996, which culminated the media deregulation campaign begun during the Reagan era. With these two decisive strokes, the government not only sanctioned but encouraged cross-ownership of film, television, cable, music, publishing, and other media and entertainment interests – thus propelling the rise of a cadre of media giants that would integrate several once distinct media industries (movies, television, cable, music, publishing, et al.) into a worldwide entertainment industry with the film studios at the epicenter, and with "filmed entertainment" as its key commodity.

The decade ended with Viacom's 1999 purchase of its former parent company, CBS, which was spun off when the FCC's Fin-Syn rules first took effect in the 1970s. That merger was soon to be overshadowed by two other studio-driven deals spurred by the explosive growth of the internet, the World Wide Web, and the new-media economy. In early 2000 AOL and Time Warner announced their $180 billion merger, by far the biggest in US history and some 20 times the value of the 1989 Time–Warner merger. Months later the French water, wastewater, and energy giant Vivendi, which had been moving aggressively into telecommunications and media, announced its purchase of Universal from Seagram. By the time the AOL–Time Warner and Vivendi–Universal deals were finalized, however, the digital economy was collapsing and both mergers were effectively doomed. In 2003 AOL-Time Warner reverted to Time Warner, with AOL a mere subsidiary, and a year later Vivendi sold most of its stake in Universal to General Electric, owner of NBC, which promptly created "NBC Universal."

At that point all four of the US broadcast TV networks were directly aligned with a Hollywood studio, and all were owned and controlled by global media con-glomerates. Indeed, Conglomerate Hollywood had attained oligopoly status by the early 2000s, with six companies – News Corporation, Sony, Time Warner, Viacom, Disney, and General Electric – taking in over 85 percent of the movie revenues and supplying over 80 percent of the primetime TV programming in the US, by far the world's richest media market (Epstein, 2005a). The term "Big Six" was commonly used in the industry trade press to reference either the conglomerates or their

FIGURE 1.3 *Batman* (1989), using "the whole machine of the company." Produced
by Peter Guber and Jon Peter; distributed by Universal; directed by Tim Burton

studios, which were increasingly adept at coordinating their respective operations
and objectives. Key to this effort, of course, was the Hollywood blockbuster, which
was re-engineered to accommodate the changing – and steadily expanding – media
landscape. That process began at the very outset of the conglomerate era with the
"blockbuster summer" of 1989, when hit sequels to the Indiana Jones, Lethal
Weapon, Back to the Future, and Ghostbusters franchises were eclipsed by *Batman*
(Tim Burton), the biggest box-office hit in a record year when the domestic box
office surpassed $5 billion for the first time ever. Released just as the Time Warner
merger took effect, *Batman* created a new paradigm for Hollywood blockbusters.
In studio head Terry Semel's words: "The first picture that blew us out [after the
merger] was *Batman*. . . . It was the first time we utilized the whole machine of the
company. The marketing, the tie-ins, the merchandising, the international"
(Brown, 1996). Despite the huge success in 1990 of more modest films like *Pretty
Woman* (Garry Marshall, US), *Home Alone* (Chris Columbus, US), and *Ghost*
(Jerry Zucker, US), the studios inexorably turned their attention away from
mid-range star-genre projects in favor of event films and "tentpole" pictures – i.e.,
mega-hits that could carry a studio's entire production slate and drive the parent
company's far-flung entertainment operations as well.

This strategy view was bolstered enormously by the foreign market surge during the 1990s, as media conglomeration and globalization proved to be mutually
reinforcing phenomena, with Hollywood-produced blockbusters as a principal
catalyst. In fact the studios' overseas markets attained much the same status in
the 1990s that the home-video market had a decade earlier – i.e., a hit-driven
"secondary" or "ancillary" market that produced more revenue than the primary

(and once sacrosanct) domestic theatrical market (Balio, 1998). A scan of the studios' worldwide box-office revenues well indicates the soaring economic stakes of the conglomerate era as the foreign markets took off. As of October 2006, 47 of the top 50 all-time worldwide box-office hits had been released after 1990 (all but *E.T.* and the first two Star Wars films), and 90 of the top 100. The majority of these were franchise films, with the Star Wars, Lord of the Rings, and Harry Potter series accounting for 10 of the top 20 all-time global hits. Moreover, the vast majority of these top hits, including 33 of the top 35, earned far more overseas than in the US (Box Office Mojo, 2006).

The "Indie Film" Movement

While studio-produced blockbusters are the prime movers in the global movie marketplace, the domestic US market since the early 1990s has become increasingly split between these major studio releases on the one hand and low-budget "indie" films on the other. Indeed, one of the more significant and paradoxical aspects of the conglomerate era has been the emergence of an independent film movement, which also caught on in 1989–90, just as conglomeration was heating up, but was not a studio-induced phenomenon. In 1989 independent art-film distributor Miramax enjoyed a run of hit releases including *sex, lies and videotape* (Steven Soderbergh, US), *My Left Foot* (Jim Sheridan, Ireland/UK), and *Cinema Paradiso* (*Nuovo Cinema Paradiso*, Giuseppe Tornatore, Italy/France), that established the company as an indie powerhouse and enabled it to move aggressively into active production. Then in 1990 New Line Cinema, a well-established producer-distributor that specialized in low-end genre films, notably horror and teen pictures, enjoyed a major breakthrough with *Teenage Mutant Ninja Turtles* (Steve Barron, US/ Hong Kong), which grossed over $100 million in the US to become the most successful independent film in box-office history. These and other hits made Miramax and New Line prime acquisition targets, and soon the two independent powers were swept up in the conglomerate wave. In 1993 Disney bought Miramax Films for $60 million and in early 1994 Turner Broadcasting acquired New Line Cinema along with its "specialty" art-cinema division, Fine Line Films, and indie producer Castle Rock Entertainment in a billion-dollar deal (Wyatt, 1998: 84). The value of those acquisitions was underscored in 1994 with the release of Miramax's *Pulp Fiction* (Quentin Tarantino, US), New Line's *The Mask* (Chuck Russell, US) and *Dumb & Dumber* (Peter Farrelly, US), and Castle Rock's *The Shawshank Redemption* (Frank Darabont, US).

The acquisition of successful independents like Miramax and New Line was one of two key strategies deployed by Conglomerate Hollywood to commandeer the indie movement. The other was to launch indie divisions of their own – i.e., quasi-autonomous production-distribution operations that specialized in low-budget, "indie style," target-marketed films. The first of these conglomerate-owned indies was Sony Pictures Classics, created in 1992 (and essentially a repackaged version of the recently folded Orion Classics), followed by Fox Searchlight in 1995, Paramount Classics in 1998, Universal's Focus Features in 2002, and Warner Independent in 2003. While these companies came to dominate the high end of the indie film market – i.e., films with stars and other name talent, and with budgets over $10 million – another (sub)species of indie filmmaker emerged that handled lower-cost (even micro-budget) films in the "genre" and "specialty" categories – horror, action, or ethnic films, for instance. This market has been dominated by genuinely independent producers, who were responsible for their own financing, although these companies invariably relied on the studios for distribution – including newly created subdivisions like Sony Screen Gems and Miramax's Dimension Pictures that were created to handle genre and specialty films.

The most visible and commercially successful films in this category have been low-budget horror hits that have spawned minor franchises – films like *Saw* (James Wan, 2004, US) and *Hostel* (Eli Roth, 2005, US). The former was co-produced by Evolution Entertainment and Twisted Pictures, and its worldwide release (in the-atrical and all other media) was handled by Lionsgate (formerly Lions Gate), the powerful Vancouver-based indie producer-distributor that has remained stead-fastly independent but often collaborates with Conglomerate Hollywood, as it did on *Hostel*. Lionsgate handled the domestic (North American) theatrical release of that film, while Sony Screen Gems handled foreign theatrical and Sony Home Entertainment handled the DVD release – a major revenue generator for this kind of product. Cable television also has become involved in the indie movement, par-ticularly in the lower-budget genre and specialty realm. Key here was the mid-1990s launch of the two pay-cable outfits, the Independent Film Channel (IFC) and the Sundance Channel – with the brand association of the latter further underscoring the growing importance of the Sundance Film Festival to the indie movement (Schamus, 1998; Biskind, 2004). The most prominent example of this trend has been *My Big Fat Greek Wedding* (Joel Zwick, 2002, US/Canada), which was pro-duced by Gold Circle Films, co-financed by HBO, and distributed by IFC Films. Another is the Spanish-language production *Y tu mamá también* (Alfonso Cuarón, 2001, Mexico), which was produced by Alianza Films, released in North America (US and Canada) by 20th Century Fox, released in Mexico by IFC Films, and dis-tributed on home video by MGM Home Entertainment.

As these trends indicate, the indie film movement by the early 2000s had devel-oped into a highly complex industry phenomenon, due to the proliferation of new players, many of which gained instant status and leverage thanks to breakthrough hits, as well as the conglomerates' multiple indie-film divisions. Moreover, the con-glomerates' studio operations grew steadily more complex as the expanding indie market led to an increase in their indie subsidiaries, most of which were effectively distinct from the parent company's major studio. Time Warner, for instance, brought New Line, Fine Line, and Castle Rock into the fold in 1995, all of which operated separately from Warner Bros. Pictures. In the early 2000s Time Warner added Warner Independent, HBO Films, and Picturehouse which also enjoyed complete autonomy from their major-studio counterpart.

Thus by the early 2000s Hollywood was generating three fairly distinct classes of feature film via three different types of producer. The dominant products were big-budget blockbusters and high-cost star vehicles handled by the six major studio pro-ducer-distributors, with an occasional high-end film coming from another division like Time Warner's New Line, Sony's TriStar, and Disney's Touchstone Pictures. Budgets on the major studios' pictures averaged $100 million, with roughly one-third of that total spent on marketing (prints and advertising) due to their massive release campaigns. The second class of Hollywood features included art films, specialty films, and other niche-market fare handled by the conglomerates' indie subsidiaries, with the parent company providing the capacity to "go wide" in the event of a break-out hit like Focus Features' *Eternal Sunshine of a Spotless Mind* (Michel Gondry, 2004, US) or Searchlight's *Sideways* (Alexander Payne, 2004, US). Budgets on these indie-subsidiary films averaged $40 million per release in the early 2000s, with $10 million–$15 million spent on marketing (MPA, 2006: 12). The third class of film included genre and specialty films handled by independent producer-distributors with release campaigns of only a few dozen (or possibly a few hundred) screens in select urban markets. Films in this category comprised over half of the 500 or so features released in the US per annum in the early 2000s, and usually cost less than $10 million – frequently less than $5 million – with minuscule marketing budgets that increase if and when a particular film performs.

In terms of revenues and market share, the difference between the conglomerate-owned film companies and the true independents is stark indeed. Taken together, the MPAA-member companies – i.e., the conglomerates' major studios and indie subsidiaries – comprise roughly one-third to one-half of all theatrical releases, but they generally account for 75 to 85 percent of all box-office revenues. In 2005, for instance, the conglomerate's film divisions released 190 of the 535 feature films released theatrically in the US, and those 190 films took in 85.7 percent of the total domestic box office. When the major studios' tentpole releases are factored into the equa-tion, the imbalance is even more pronounced – and the studios' blockbuster-driven "economies of scale" are even more evident. In 2005, the top five major studio releases alone earned more domestically ($1.4 billion) than *all of the 345 independent releases combined* ($1.2 billion) (MPA, 2006: 12).

Reconciling the "Two Hollywoods"

Some major fault lines have developed in Hollywood during the conglomerate era, most notably the rift between the conglomerate-owned companies and the true inde-pendents, as well as the rift between the blockbuster-driven mentality of the major studios and the indie-film ethos of all the other Hollywood producer-distributors. Some filmmakers and industry observers have argued that, as the conglomerates and major studios invade the indie realm, both the production process and the prod-ucts themselves lose their indie edge. As James Schamus, the veteran independent producer and long-time partner of indie auteur Ang Lee, put it: "more and more, as the studios finance and distribute 'independent' films, independent producers find themselves rather dependent employees. This is because the 'independent' cinema has quickly become a victim of its own success, a success that has made the independent film game look more and more like a microcosm of the studio business" (Schamus, 1998). And industry observers have noted the emergence of an "indie blockbuster" strategy with films like Miramax's *The English Patient* (Anthony Minghella, 1996, US), *Good Will Hunting* (Gus Van Sant, 1997, US), and *Shakespeare in Love* (John Madden, 1998, US/UK) (Perren, 2003, 2004).

Despite the conglomerates' systematic efforts to annex the indie film movement, the split between the blockbuster-driven major studios and their "Indiewood" counterparts remains a key characteristic of the conglomerate era. Indeed, the rift has led to the perception of "two Hollywoods" that carries both aesthetic and economic ramifications (*New York Times Magazine*, 1997). An astute assessment of this rift from an independent filmmaker's viewpoint appeared in a *Variety* guest column by writer-director Alexander Payne, published just weeks before the release of *Sideways*, by Fox Searchlight, which, on the heels of *Citizen Ruth* (1996, US), *Election* (1999, US), and *About Schmidt* (2002, US), confirmed Payne's stature as Hollywood's leading indie auteur (Payne, 2004). As a "Hollywood director," wrote Payne, "I resent the cleft between what we consider studio movies and independent movies." He then mounted a stinging critique of studio movies, which he deemed "not films but glorified cartoons" that "exploit banality and violence," formula fare designed for world-wide consumption "as readily and predictably as McDonald's hamburgers," commodities designed "to maximize profits . . . at the tremendous, tragic expense of our culture."

Despite the studios' "imprisonment by corporate edicts and market forces" that impel them "to feed the increasingly mercurial 'tentpole' beast," however, Payne was encouraged by "a strong trend of cinema – big and commercial as well as small and personal – aspiring to be human, intelligent, respectful of the audience and director-driven." This latter point was both the "central issue" and defining characteristic of the indie film movement for Payne: "Cinema is independent only to the degree that it reflects the voice of one person, the director (in conjunction with his or her hand-picked creative team)." Payne saw this imperative at work on several fronts: the persistent efforts of established auteurs like Scorsese and Steven Soderbergh to make films on their own terms; the emergence of new talent like Sophia Coppola and Michael Moore; the US release that the indie subsidiaries provided to foreign auteurs like Pedro Almodóvar and Zhang Yimou; the widening conglomerate trend toward indie subsidiaries like Searchlight and Focus; and the studios' willingness to entrust blockbuster franchises to "strong and thoughtful directors." Taken together, mused Payne, these may be signs of a Hollywood renaissance. "I want and expect studios to finance personal, risky and political cinema – as they did in the much-vaunted 1970s."

There is no going back to the 1970s, of course, when Hollywood came as close to being a "director's cinema" as it is ever likely to do. But it is important to note that Conglomerate Hollywood, whatever its overriding commitment to high-yield blockbusters, is also heavily invested in the indie movement itself and also, crucially, in the active cross-fertilization of the two Hollywoods. What Payne terms "the cleft between studio movies and independent movies" might also be seen as a symbiosis of sorts, a dynamic tension that has become integral to the "studio system" in its current configuration. One might argue, in fact, that the two Hollywoods could not exist without one another in structural and economic terms, and that Conglomerate Hollywood provides a remarkable range of creative opportunities for filmmakers (like Payne) with the talent, clout, inclination, and audacity to pursue them. While many successful directors clearly operate on one side of the studio/indie divide or the other, others manage to migrate constantly between them, working on blockbusters and art films, niche-market and specialty films, even cable and television projects.

In some cases top directors have crossed this divide while working with the same studio, often through corporate alliances or their association with a specific franchise. Spielberg's Amblin Entertainment has been closely allied with Universal Pictures for over two decades, and has produced a remarkable range of pictures including the back-to-back 1993 hits, *Jurassic Park* and *Schindler's List*, exemplars of the studio/indie split. The Amblin–Universal alliance has survived the launch and eventual Viacom buyout of DreamWorks as well, with Spielberg and Universal remaining veritable partners in the billion-dollar Jurassic Park franchise. Likewise Clint Eastwood's Malpaso Productions and Warner Bros., a relationship that dates back to the 1970s and has produced literally dozens of important films, ranging from Dirty Harry franchise films to Eastwood-directed conglomerate-era hits like *Unforgiven* (1992, US), *Mystic River* (2003, US), and *Million Dollar Baby* (2004, US), that have solidified Eastwood's stature as an indie auteur.

Steven Soderbergh, whose *sex, lies and videotape* catalyzed the indie movement, has had perhaps the most varied and complex career of any conglomerate-era auteur. After spending the 1990s in the indie trenches doing low-budget art films, Soderbergh enjoyed a breakout hit with *Erin Brockovich* (2000, US) for Columbia TriStar. Since then he has been prolific and eclectic in his filmmaking, successfully working "the system" at all levels. He did *Traffic* (2000, Germany/US) for USA Films (shortly before its transformation into Universal's indie division, Focus Features), an effective blend of edgy art film and political thriller that featured top stars and a budget of roughly $50 million. Soderbergh then did an unabashedly "commercial" project for Warner Bros., *Ocean's Eleven* (2001, US/Australia), a franchise-spawning entertainment machine with an all-star cast and a budget approaching $100 million. He followed that with *Full Frontal* (2002, US), a $2 million experiment in collaborative digital cinema. Soderbergh also has moonlighted as an executive producer, using his considerable clout to facilitate indie projects like *Far From Heaven* (Todd Haynes, 2002, France/US), *Good Night, and Good Luck* (George Clooney, 2005, US), *Syriana* (Stephen Gaghan, 2005, US), and *A Scanner Darkly* (Richard Linklater, 2006, US).

Several Soderbergh films have starred George Clooney and Julia Roberts, who have been equally adventurous in their project selection, and who also have played

FIGURE 1.4   *Good Night, and Good Luck* (2005), made through Soderbergh and
Clooney's Section Eight production company. Produced by Grant Heslov; distributed by
Warner Independent Pictures; directed by George Clooney

the system and helped nurture the indie movement. In fact the indie surge has relied
heavily on the mobility of top stars who are willing to work on indie projects for
far less than their studio rates. Clooney's career is especially telling in terms of
his relationships with both Soderbergh and Warner Bros. In 1997 Clooney segued
from a hit Warner Bros. TV series, *ER*, to the lead in *Batman and Robin* (Joel
Schumacher, 1997, US/UK), and then rose to top stardom in three subsequent Warner
releases: *Three Kings* (David O. Russell, 1999, US/Australia), *The Perfect Storm*
(Wolfgang Peterson, 2000, US/Germany), and *Ocean's Eleven*. The latter marked the
debut of Soderbergh–Clooney's independent production company, Section Eight
Ltd., which partnered with Warner Bros. for the big-budget "Oceans" films, and
on several other indie-scale projects as well – including *Syriana* for Warner Bros.
and *Good Night, and Good Luck* for Warner Independent, both of which featured
Clooney in key supporting roles and simply could not have been made without his
"marquee value," as well as his and Soderbergh's clout at Time Warner.

   Soderbergh's handling the "Oceans" films also indicates a trend by the major
studios to hire indie auteurs to direct high-stakes blockbuster series. Here again Warner
Bros. provides an illuminating case. Warner actually started this trend with Tim
Burton on the first two Batman films, but then replaced him with a more "commercial" director, Joel Schumacher, on the third and fourth installments (in 1995
and 1997). Warner also launched its high-stakes Harry Potter series with mainstream
filmmaker Chris Columbus, who had directed *Home Alone* and *Mrs. Doubtfire* (1993,
US). By then the tide was turning, however, due in part to two other Time Warner
franchises. While the Columbus-directed Potter films in 2001 and 2002 were huge

hits, the concurrent Lord of the Rings films from New Line enjoyed far more critical prestige and demographic reach, thanks to the talent and stature of indie auteur Peter Jackson. Warner Bros. also released but did not actively produce the Matrix trilogy (1999, 2003, 2003), which was handled by two then obscure indie filmmakers, the Wachowski brothers, Andy and Larry. At that point Warner Bros. reversed its field, replacing Columbus with indie auteurs on subsequent Potter installments – Alfonso Cuarón on the third and Mike Newell on the fourth – and then relaunched the Batman franchise under director Christopher Nolan, whose films included the indie hits *Memento* (2000, US) and *Insomnia* (2002, US), as well as its Superman franchise under Bryan Singer, whose earlier films included the indie hit *The Usual Suspects* (1995, US/Germany), as well as the X-Men series for Fox.

Batman Begins (2005, US) and *Superman Returns* (2006, Australia/US) were successful by any measure, and especially in terms of the parent company's all-important bottom line. Despite production costs in excess of $150 million, both returned over $350 million in their worldwide theatrical release, with literally hundreds of millions yet to come in home-video, pay-cable, et al. (Box Office Mojo, 2006). Both Warner Bros. franchises were firmly re-established with sequels immediately in the works – and with Nolan and Singer aboard, reinforcing the trend of attaching indie auteurs to high-stakes franchises, and underscoring the vital importance of directorially "re-authoring" an established narrative formula via distinctive, stylized treatment, to enhance its prospects for a successful revival.

New Millennium – New Equilibrium

Warner Bros.' franchise revivals also were significant in terms of production financing. The Batman and Superman films initiated a five-year, 25-film deal between Warner Bros. and Legendary Pictures, a co-financing and co-production pact that gave Warner a $500 million infusion and gave Legendary access to the studio's inactive properties (Foreman, 2005). The deal set off a predictable round of snickers about wolves, sheep, and Hollywood accounting, but Legendary's investors included savvy and cautious financial institutions, and the deal was one of several during 2005–6 in the $300–$500 million range between studios and other highly reputable institutions, all of them geared to the production of blockbuster-scale films (Galloway, 2006; Kelly, 2006). Besides bringing welcome new funding into the studio coffers, this massive infusion of studio production financing signaled two other key aspects of Conglomerate Hollywood's development. First of all, large investors were satisfied enough with the conglomerates' fiscal "transparency" and responsibility to tolerate the byzantine nature of motion picture accounting and the studios' reputation for financial chicanery. Second, the worldwide movie marketplace was now so lucrative that it was difficult for Hollywood-produced blockbusters *not* to make money. Warner's star-driven, effects-laden spectacles geared for global release, such as *The Last Samurai* (Edward Zwick, 2003, US) and *Troy* (Wolfgang Petersen, 2004, US/Malta/UK), may cost roughly $200 million to produce and release, but even mediocre films like these routinely returned $500 million within a year of their initial release, with cable and DVD now assuring the studio-distributor a much longer "shelf-life" than was the case even a decade earlier. Major hits and franchise installments are in another category altogether, with billion-dollar returns becoming routine when all revenue sources (including merchandising and licensing) are taken into account.

Not only were studio-produced blockbusters almost assured of turning a profit by the early 2000s; so too were the studios themselves – or rather their parent companies, thanks to their increasingly well-integrated media entertainment divisions. The film studios in 2004–5 publicly bemoaned box-office slumps and a slowdown in DVD sales, but their laments scarcely hold up if one considers their parent conglomerates' full range of production, distribution, and delivery operations. By then the Big Six conglomerates owned all of the major film studios and broadcast networks, along with over 60 cable networks, and had attained a level of synergy across their movie, television, and home entertainment sectors that resulted in unprecedented revenues and profits. In the words of Edward Jay Epstein, among the most thorough and insightful industry analysts of recent years, the "relentless marriages" between the film studios and television networks has been the defining feature and ultimate outcome of media deregulation and conglomeration, and "the union between Hollywood and TV has paid off handsomely" (Epstein, 2005d).

The payoff, in fact, has been simply astounding. According to the MPAA's international division, the Motion Picture Association (MPA), industry revenues have increased nearly fourfold (in inflation-adjusted dollars) since the mid-1980s, when the conglomerate era began to coalesce. Consider the worldwide studio receipts contained in a "strictly confidential" MPA report to its members – i.e., the Big Six conglomerates' filmed entertainment divisions – which clearly indicates how the sustained economic surge of the past quarter-century has relied on all facets of these diversified media giants (Epstein, 2005a: 20) (see table 1.3).

Equally impressive are the conglomerates' net revenues – i.e., profits – which may be driven by movie hits but are actually realized in the television and home

TABLE 1.3   Major studio worldwide revenues, 1948–2003

Year	Theatrical	Video/DVD	Pay-TV	Free TV	TOTAL
1948	6.90	0	0	0	6.90
1980	4.40	0.20	0.38	3.26	8.20
1985	2.96	2.34	1.04	5.59	11.9
1990	4.90	5.87	1.62	7.41	19.80
1995	5.57	10.60	2.34	7.92	26.43
2000	5.87	11.67	3.12	10.75	31.40
2003	7.48	18.90	3.36	11.40	41.10

* Inflation-adjusted to 2003 (in $ billion).
Source: *2003 MPA All Media Revenue Report*, cited in Epstein, 2005a: 20.

entertainment sectors. By the early 2000s, despite the rise in box-office receipts, the studios' worldwide theatrical motion-picture market had become a "loss leader," due mainly to the massive marketing costs involved in launching global blockbuster films. But once those costs are absorbed and the movies' market value is established, particularly in an age when most moviegoing is done at home in front of a television screen, the "ancillary" TV and home-video markets generate enormous profits. In 2004, for instance, the MPA reported that the Big Six grossed $7.4 billion in worldwide box-office receipts, but marketing costs of $9.6 billion resulted in net losses of $2.2 billion in the worldwide theatrical sector. Meanwhile the conglomerates' collective television revenues were $17.7 billion and their home-video/DVD revenues totaled $20.9 billion, which yielded net profits of $16 billion and $14 billion, respectively, thanks to the low sales and marketing costs associated with these sectors (MPA Consolidated Television Sales Report, cited in Epstein, 2005c).

Thus Conglomerate Hollywood reached a new equilibrium in the early 2000s, whereby a balance and integration of its overall media operations generated record revenues and profits while enabling the Big Six media giants to enjoy collective dominion over an ever-expanding entertainment marketplace. This is not to say that all six companies are configured in quite the same way, nor that their conduct and performance in the global media marketplace are altogether consistent from one company to the next. What *is* consistent from one company to the next is the combination of three film-related areas of production and distribution: the major studio with its emphasis on blockbusters and big-budget star vehicles; the indie sub-divisions geared to low-cost specialty and niche-market films; and the television division, focused as ever on high-volume TV series output.

In terms of production, the exemplary Hollywood conglomerate in recent years has been News Corporation, a model of tight diversification whose filmed entertainment divisions performed at optimal levels. According to a May 2006 *Fortune* profile, Fox and Warner Bros. are "the biggest and best-run of the six major Hollywood studios," with Fox's recent performance particularly impressive. Fox Filmed Entertainment was News Corporation's biggest and most profitable division in 2005, with a $4.5 billion investment in production, marketing, and distribution yielding an operating profit of $1.2 billion. The movie division enjoyed success in all sectors, ranging from blockbuster hits like *Star Wars: Episode III – Revenge of the Sith* (George Lucas, 2005, US) and *Fantastic Four* (Tim Story, 2005, US) from the 20th Century Fox studio to indie hits like *Sideways* and *Napoleon Dynamite* (Jared Hess, 2004, US) from indie subsidiary Fox Searchlight. Fox Television was the leading supplier of primetime TV shows, with franchise series like *24* scoring both in the ratings and in DVD sales (*Economist*, 2006; Gunther, 2006).

Equally important to the conglomerates' success has been their combined control not only of film and television distribution but also, crucially, media "delivery" via television and cable networks, ownership of cable systems, and so forth. The one media giant noticeably out of step in this area has been Sony Pictures Entertainment, owner of Columbia TriStar, which failed to keep pace with the rest of the Big Six due largely to its lack of substantial broadcast or cable network holdings. This dearth of "pipelines" to media consumers helps explain why

Sony teamed with cable giant Comcast in the $4.5 billion purchase of MGM/UA in 2005, a deal that dramatically expanded Sony's massive film and TV series library while giving it a valuable cable ally. Even more importantly, this crucial scarcity explains why Sony would take the enormous risk of developing its own high-definition DVD format, the so-called Blu-ray Disc system. If it succeeds, this strategy definitely would offset Sony's pipeline deficiencies, giving it a stake in the entire home entertainment industry when the "next-generation" high-def DVD technology supplants the current system. The odds against success are considerable, however, considering the competing HD-DVD system being developed by arch-rival Toshiba that augurs a "format war" similar to the one Sony waged – and lost – against Matsushita on the VCR front three decades earlier. A format war also will prove costly to all of the Big Six as content suppliers, thus precluding the kind of rapid diffusion enjoyed by the original DVD format and the windfall profits that accompanied that historic rollout (Belson, 2005, 2006).

Although a format war over next-generation DVD technology may prove troublesome to Conglomerate Hollywood, it is not likely to upset the new equilibrium enjoyed by the media giants. A far greater threat to that equilibrium – and to the conglomerates' hegemony over the global entertainment industry at large – involves the internet and broadband delivery of media content. While media "convergence" has been a buzzword for decades, the full-scale merging of "old" media like film and television and the new digital media has been waylaid by relatively slow deployment of high-speed internet delivery of media and graphics to consumers, and particularly to the home. With high-speed internet service becoming ubiquitous, the entertainment landscape is being rapidly transformed and the established media powers are making way for – and cutting deals with – internet powers like Yahoo and Google, telecom giants like AT&T and Verizon, cable companies like Comcast, and a host of smaller online outfits like MySpace and YouTube. The key issue for Conglomerate Hollywood is not whether to pursue new media delivery, but how – and how aggressively – to do so, despite the fact that the current system is currently working so well. Time Warner is in a particularly favorable position due to its AOL division, of course, although several of the other media giants are moving aggressively into the new-media arena. In July 2005, for example, Rupert Murdoch announced News Corporation's acquisition of three internet companies (for a total of $1.4 billion), including the phenomenally successful online social-networking site, MySpace (Siklos, 2005; *Economist*, 2006).

Other media giants have been less aggressive or have taken another tack altogether, as with Sony's Blu-ray gambit. Perhaps the most radical approach involved Viacom, whose principal owner Sumner Redstone announced in 2005 that "the age of the conglomerate is over," and that he planned to split the company into two entities, Viacom and CBS Inc., thus reverting to a pre-conglomerate mode. None of the other conglomerates followed suit, predictably enough, and the split, which took effect in early 2006, proved to be ill advised in the short term (Szalai, 2005; Fabrikant, 2006). But it did allow Viacom, now free of the stable but slow-growing television division, to aggressively pursue high-risk, fast-growth, new-media prospects. These included YouTube, a video-sharing website that Viacom went after in a fierce bidding war with Google and Yahoo. Google prevailed, acquiring YouTube in October 2006 for $1.65 billion – the first major media acquisition for the emerging media giant. By then Google's market value had surged to a phenomenal $132 billion, roughly equal to the *combined* market value of the top two Hollywood conglomerates, Time Warner and Disney (*Fortune*, 2006; Sorkin, 2006).

The rise of Google is but one indication that Conglomerate Hollywood faces serious challenges in terms of media distribution and digital delivery, which could lead to yet another revolution of the magnitude of those described by Gabler, since distribution has always been the key to the studios' power within the film and television industries. This may bode well for the studios, if not for their parent companies. As the trinity of post-industrial forces that begat Conglomerate Hollywood – i.e., conglomeration, globalization, and digitization – continue to stoke the fires of change, and as the media giants struggle to maintain their control of the media-entertainment system at large, the creation and quality of media content is likely to become an increasingly important issue. This may force the studios, ironically enough, to concentrate more fully on media production – a focus that has steadily been lost since the classical era.

REFERENCES

Anderson, C. (1994) *Hollywood TV: The Studio System in the Fifties.* Austin: University of Texas Press.

Auletta, K. (1992) *Three Blind Mice: How the TV Networks Lost their Way.* New York: Vintage Books.

Balio, T. (ed.) (1976/1985) *The American Film Industry.* Madison: University of Wisconsin Press.

Balio, T. (1987) *United Artists: The Company that Changed the Film Industry.* Madison: University of Wisconsin Press.

Balio, T. (1998) "'A Major Presence in All of the World's Important Markets': The Globalization of Hollywood in the 1990s," in S. Neale and M. Smith (eds.), *Contemporary Hollywood Cinema.* New York: Routledge.

Bart, P. (1990a) *Fade Out: The Calamitous Final Days of MGM.* New York: Doubleday.

Bart, P. (1990b) "Stars to Studios: Pass the Bucks," *Variety*, September 24, pp. 1, 108.

Bart, P. (1996) "The Art of Non-Communication," *Variety*, December 16–22, pp. 4, 98.

Belson, K. (2005) "Technology: A DVD Standoff in Hollywood," *The New York Times*, July 11, p. C1.

Belson, K. (2006) "In Sony's Stumble, the Ghost of Betamax," *The New York Times*, February 26, sect. 3, p. 1.

Biskind, P. (2004) *Down and Dirty Pictures: Miramax, Sundance, and the Rise of Independent Film.* New York: Simon & Schuster.

Block, A. B. (1990) *Outfoxed: The Inside Story of America's Fourth Network.* New York: St. Martin's Press.

Bordwell, D., J. Staiger, and K. Thomson (1986) *The Classical Hollywood Cinema: Film Style and Mode of Production to 1960.* New York: Columbia University Press.

Box Office Mojo (2006) "All Time Worldwide Box Office Grosses," online at <http://www.boxofficemojo.com/alltime/world/?pagenum=1&p=.htm>.

Brown, C. (1996) "The Years Without Ross," *Premiere*, January, p. 36.

Bruck, C. (2003) *When Hollywood Had a King: The Reign of Lew Wasserman, who Leveraged Talent into Power and Influence.* New York: Random House.

Cieply, M. (1989) "Inside the Agency," *Los Angeles Times/Calendar*, July 2, pp. 5–7, 23, 29, 30.

Cohn, L. (1990) "Stars' Rocketing Salaries Keep Pushing Envelope," *Variety*, September 24, pp. 3, 168.

Davis, L. J. (1989) "Hollywood's Most Secret Agent," *The New York Times Magazine*, July 9, pp. 25–7, 51–3, 74–5.

Economist (2006) "Old Mogul, New Media," January 21, pp. 65–7.

Epstein, E. J. (2005a) *The Big Picture: The New Logic of Money and Power in Hollywood.* New York: Random House.

Epstein, E. J. (2005b) "Hollywood's Death Spiral," *Slate*, July 25, online at <http://www.edwardjayepstein.com/mpa2004.htm> (accessed July 17, 2007).

Epstein, E. J. (2005c) "Hollywood's Profits, Demystified," *Slate*, August 8, online at <http://www.slate.com/id/2124078/> (accessed July 17, 2007).

Epstein, E. J. (2005d) "Rise of the Home-Entertainment Economy," Motion Picture Association, 2005 Worldwide Market Research, online at <http://www.edwardjayepstein.com/mpa2004.htm> (accessed July 17, 2007).

Fabrikant, G. (2006) "A Surprise after the Split: Viacom Struggles as CBS Holds its Own," *The New York Times*, June 22, p. C1.

Finler, J. (1988) *The Hollywood Story.* New York: Crown.

Foreman, L. (2005) "Legendary Warners Deal," *The Hollywood Reporter*, June 22, p. 1.

Fortune (2006) "Fortune 500 2006," online at <http://money.cnn.com/magazines/fortune/fortune500/industries/Entertainment/1.html> (accessed July 17, 2007).

Gabler, N. (1995) "The Revenge of the Studio System," *The New York Times*, August 22, p. A15.

Galloway, S. (2006) "Film Finance," *The Hollywood Reporter*, April 11, online at <http://indiefliks.com/article2.asp> (accessed July 17, 2007).

Gomery, D. (1968) *The Hollywood Studio System.* New York: St. Martin's Press.

Griffin, N., and K. Masters (1996) *Hit and Run: How Jon Peters and Peter Gruber Took Sony for a Ride in Hollywood.* New York: Touchstone.

Gunther, M. (2006) "Fox the Day after Tomorrow," *Fortune*, May 17, online at <http://money.cnn.com/2006/05/15/magazines/fortune/chernin_futureof_fortune_052906/index.htm> (accessed July 17, 2007).

Hilmes, M. (1999) *Hollywood and Broadcasting: From Radio to Cable.* Urbana: University of Illinois Press.

Holt, J. (2001–2) "In Deregulation We Trust: The Synergy of Politics and Industry in Reagan-Era Hollywood," *Film Quarterly*, 55(2), Winter, pp. 22–9.

Kelly, K. (2006) "Creative Financing: Defying the Odds, Hedge Funds Bet Billions on Movies," *The Wall Street Journal*, April 29, online at <online.wsj.com/article_print/SB114627404745739525.html> (accessed July 17, 2007).

Landro, L. (1990) "Paramount's Problems with Eddie Murphy Soul Honey of a Deal," *The Wall Street Journal*, August 13, pp. A1, A6.

Mickelthwait, J. (1989) "A Survey of the Entertainment Industry," *The Economist*, December 23, pp. 3–18.

MPA (2006) "*U.S. Theatrical Market: 2005 Statistics.*" Los Angeles MPA Worldwide Market Research Analysis.

MPAA (1990) *U.S. Economic Review.* Los Angeles: Motion Picture Association of America.

Murphy, A. D. (1989) "Twenty Years of Weekly Film Ticket Sales in U.S. Theaters," *Variety*, March 15–21, p. 26.

New York Times Magazine (1997) "The Two Hollywoods: A Special Issue," November 16.

Payne, A. (2004) "Declaration of Independents," *Variety*, September 7, online at <www.variety.com/index.asp?layout=indies2004> and at <http://www.alexanderpayne.net/articles/misc/misc_04.html> (accessed July 17, 2007).

Perren, A. (2003) "sex, lies and marketing: Miramax and the Development of the 'Quality Indie' Blockbuster," *Film Quarterly*, 54(2), Winter 2001–2, pp. 30–9.

Perren, A. (2004) "A Big Fat Indie Success Story? Press Discourses Surrounding the Making and Marketing of a 'Hollywood' Movie," *Journal of Film and Video*, 56(2), Summer, pp. 18–31.

Premiere (1990) "Hollywood Power List," online at <http://www.premiere.com/feature/2820/the-power-list-history.html> and <http://www.imdb.com/features/15thanniversary/1990> (accessed July 17, 2007).

Prince, S. (2002) *A New Pot of Gold: Hollywood Under the Electronic Rainbow, 1980–1989.* New York: Scribner's.

Pollock, D. (1999) *Skywalking: The Life and Films of George Lucas*, updated edn. New York: Da Capo.

Schamus, J. (1998) "To the Rear of the Back End: The Economics of Independent Cinema," in S. Neale and M. Smith (eds.), *Contemporary Hollywood Cinema.* New York: Routledge.

Schatz, T. (1988, 1996) *The Genius of the System: Hollywood Filmmaking in the Studio Era.* New York: Pantheon; Metropolitan Books.

Schatz, T. (1990) "Desilu, *I Love Lucy*, and the Rise of Network TV," in R. Thompson and G. Burns (eds.), *Making Television: Authorship and the Production Process.* New York: Praeger.

Schatz, T. (1993) "The New Hollywood," in J. Collins, H. Radner, and A. P Collins (eds.), *Film Theory Goes to the Movies.* New York: Routledge.

Siklos, R. (2005) "News Corporation Buys and Internet Company," *The New York Times*, July 19, p. C6.

Sorkin, A. R. (2006) "Dot-Com Boom Echoed in Deal to Buy YouTube," *The New York Times*, October 10, p. A1.

Stewart, J. B. (2005) *Disney War: The Battle for the Magic Kingdom.* New York: Simon & Schuster.

Szalai, G. (2005) "Redstone: Viacom Split Signals End of an Era," *The Hollywood Reporter*, June 15, p. 1.

Taylor, J. (1987) *Storming the Magic Kingdom: Wall Street, the Raiders and the Battle for Disney.* New York: Knopf.

Thompson, E. T. (1960) "There's No Show Business Like MCA's Business," *Fortune*, July, pp. 114–19, 152, 154, 159, 160, 165.

Variety (1991) "U.S. Feature Production and Release History," April 15, p. 12.

Variety (1992) "Top 100 All-Time Film Rental Champs," January 6, p. 86.

Wasser, F. (2001) *Veni, Vidi, Video: The Hollywood Empire and the VCR.* Austin: University of Texas Press.

Wyatt, J. (1998) "The Formation of the 'Major Independent': New Line and Miramax," in S. Neale and M. Smith (eds.), *Contemporary Hollywood Cinema.* New York: Routledge.

Wyatt, J. (2000) "Independents, Packaging, and Inflationary Pressure in 1980s Hollywood," in S. Prince (ed.), *A New Pot of Gold: Hollywood Under the Electronic Rainbow, 1980–1989.* New York: Scribner's, pp. 142–59.

CHAPTER 2

FINANCING AND PRODUCTION: CREATING THE HOLLYWOOD FILM COMMODITY

JANET WASKO

While a good deal of attention is devoted by the press and within cinema studies to the production of Hollywood films, the coverage typically focuses on anecdotal stories about celebrities or analysis of production style. And even though there is more popular coverage of Hollywood's box-office results these days, the complete context of the production and distribution process is often less obvious. This chapter will outline the various components that currently come together to produce a typical Hollywood film commodity, as well as some discussion of controversial issues that emerge from this process.

The production of a Hollywood motion picture – from development to theatrical release – typically takes from one to two years. During this time, raw materials and labor are combined to create a film commodity that is then bought and sold in various markets. Film production has been called a "project enterprise," in that no two films are created in the same way. Nevertheless, the overall process is similar enough to permit a description of the production process for a "typical film."

Contrary to popular belief, Hollywood films do not begin when the camera starts rolling, but involve a somewhat lengthy and complex development and pre-production phase during which an idea is turned into a script and preparations are made for actual production followed by post-production (see figure 2.1).

concept (writer/producer)>>manager/agent>>producer>>

studio executive: development deal>>

studio prez/chair: green light>>

production>>post-production

FIGURE 2.1   From conception to development to production

Acquisition and Development

Film Concepts/Properties

Ideas for Hollywood films come from many sources. Some screenplays are from original ideas or fiction; some are based on actual events or individuals' lives. However, a good number of Hollywood films are adaptations from other sources, such as books, television programs, comic books, and plays, or represent sequels or remakes of other films.

The prevailing wisdom is that around 50 percent of Hollywood films are adaptations. An informal survey of *Variety*'s top 100 films by gross earning for the years 2001 and 2002 and for all time revealed that Hollywood films often draw on previous works for inspiration. Books, biopics, and sequels to previous blockbusters represent primary sources used by the industry, while both comic book and video games represent emerging frontiers. Perhaps more importantly, films based on previous works consistently rate among the highest-grossing films.

These points draw attention to the issue of creativity, a topic that attracts a good deal of attention, both inside and outside of the film industry. Most importantly, there are economic factors that contribute to this ongoing reliance on recycled ideas, already proven stories, and movie remakes and sequels. Repetition of stories and characters may also have cultural significance. Nevertheless, it is relevant at this point to at least question some of the common claims made about the originality and genius of Hollywood fare.

In Hollywood, film material rather quickly becomes known as property, defined by the industry as "an idea, concept, outline, synopsis, treatment, short story, magazine article, novel, screenplay or other literary form that someone has a legal right to develop to the exclusion of others and which may form the basis of a motion picture." An underlying property is "the literary or other work upon which rights to produce and distribute a motion picture are based." (Cones, 1992: 413)

The idea of a property implies some kind of value and ownership, and thus involves copyright law. In fact, copyright is a fundamental base for the film industry as commodities are built and exploited from the rights to specific properties. A copyright can be described simply as a form of protection provided by law to authors of "original works of authorship," including literary, dramatic, musical, artistic, and certain other intellectual works. This protection is available to both published and unpublished works. (For more discussion of intellectual property and Hollywood, see chapter 12 in this volume.) A film idea that develops from another source usually already involves a set of rights. For instance, book contracts usually specify film rights. Thus, even before a screenplay is produced, ownership rights (and usually some kind of payment or royalties) may be involved. That is, unless a source is in the public domain, which means either that the work was not copyrighted or the term of copyright protection has expired. The material therefore is available for anyone to use and not subject to copyright protection. The rights to film ideas are often contested, with infamous lawsuits emanating from squabbles over copyright infringement, plagiarism, etc.

Overall, the Hollywood script market is relatively complex, as there are many ways that a script may emerge. An idea, a concept, or a complete film script may originate with a writer, an agency or manager, a producer or production company, a director, or a studio executive. In each case, a slightly different process is involved.

The players

Before describing the script market, it will be helpful to introduce some of the players involved in the process: writers, agents and managers, lawyers, and producers. In Hollywood, powerful people are often referred to as "players." However, in this discussion, all participants in the process will be referred to as players, with the important distinction that some players are more powerful than others.

Writers. Everyone in Hollywood seems to have a screenplay or an idea for a film. It is not uncommon that directors or producers also are writers. However, only a relatively small number of writers actually make a living from screenwriting and typically writers have little clout in the industry.

In the past, writers typically had studio contracts or deals to develop ideas or options, from which scripts were written. More recently, a major writer works with an agent or manager to sell an idea or script (which sometimes is packaged to include talent) to a producer, who then tries to interest a studio executive in a development deal.

Agents/agencies. Writers, as well as other Hollywood players, often use agents, managers, or lawyers, to represent them in business negotiations and career planning. Generally, an agent or agency serves as an intermediary and represents a client. Agents typically negotiate employment contracts, sell scripts, help find financing, or act as intermediaries between two or more companies that need to work together on a project. The standard commission for agents is 10 percent, thus *Variety*'s name for agencies, 10-percenters. In addition, the agency gets an interest in possible future versions of the product (for example, a television show that is syndicated), in the form of royalties and residuals.

Agencies often are assumed to have tremendous clout and power in Hollywood, especially for their ability to put together film packages. The major talent agencies are closely held and many of their intangible assets are hard to value. But some aspects of the business – such as its ability to take a sizable stake in the profits generated from packaging television shows – can generate substantial revenues.

Agencies also can become involved with product placement deals (or the arrangements made for branded products to be featured in films). Not only are agencies often aware of film projects from their conception, they represent writers who can add a product or company name to a script in the first draft and then sell that placement to corporate clients. In addition, directors represented by the agencies can be encouraged to feature the product prominently in the film.

Management companies. Recently, managers and management companies have been developing as power players in Hollywood. Managers are similar to agencies in that they advise talent and perform other similar functions. Managers receive fees of 15 percent or more, and have been aggressively moving into agencies' territories. More importantly, management companies are allowed to develop and produce film and television projects, a function that gives them a considerable advantage over agencies. In other words, talent managers have been allowed a more extensive role in their clients' careers than talent agents.

Entertainment lawyers. The legal framework for motion picture production and distribution is built from contract, copyright, labor, and competition law. More specifically lawyers may focus on finance, liability, litigation, intellectual property, contracts, copyrights, production and distribution rights, syndication, taxation, and publication within the entertainment industries.

Obviously, a wide range of agreements and contracts is used during the production and distribution of a motion picture. For instance, option agreements are used to acquire rights to a literary property, and often combined with a literary property acquisition agreement. In addition, the ownership rights of a literary property must be researched, as well as film titles. Defamation and privacy issues also are legal considerations during the pre-production process.

Other legal agreements are involved in the financing of a motion picture, although these vary according to the type of financing. As discussed below, bank financing or presale contracts may be involved and thus require complex and important legal contracts.

Entertainment lawyers also are involved in negotiating agreements that deal with talent, resolving disputes, and drawing up contracts – lots of contracts for lots of deals. The contracts involved in the distribution and licensing of films and film-related products may seem never-ending, and all of them involve constant legal expertise.

Producers. A producer typically guides a film through development, pre-production and production, acquires a script, selects talent, secures financing or convinces a studio to fund the film. However, there are many kinds of producers, including executive producer, line producer, associate producer, and co-producer. Sometimes a producer's credit is given to a power player who contributes in some way to getting a project off the ground.

It's possible that a producer may initiate a project, but work under the supervision of one of the major studios, receiving a straight producing fee ($250,000 to $500,000), plus some kind of participation in the net profit. Other producers may be involved with production companies that handle the acquisition, development, and packaging of material for production, and have ongoing relationships with major distributors (more in the next section).

The script market

So an idea or concept for a film or an original screenplay may originate with a writer, producer, or director, who may work with an agent/manager to interest a producer in the property. A producer also may purchase an option (a temporary purchase of rights to a property for a specific period of time for a fee). Others who may become involved in the script market are development executives (who work with a project through development) and trackers (studio people who specifically follow the script market). (See Taylor, 1999, for more background on these players.)

The process of selling the idea or script may include a pitch, that is, when a writer (typically) verbally describes a project or story to a development executive or other potential buyer. Since the end of the 1980s, pitches have been somewhat difficult to arrange and probably only possible for established screenwriters. However, pitches have not disappeared and may become more common in the future, as some of these processes are cyclical.

Many scripts are written in hopes of purchase by a producer or studio and referred to as spec scripts. The process often involves readers or script analysts who prepare script coverage for studio executives, producers, and agents who do not have time to read every script. Coverage includes a short synopsis of the screenplay, a rating of the script (from poor to excellent), plus an overall assessment as to whether to consider, recommend, or pass on the project. Most scripts (one estimate is 99 percent) receive a recommendation of pass. Readers are interns, students, recent graduates, or aspiring screenwriters, who may receive $25–$50 per script.

An agent also can circulate a spec script, trying to build a buzz around the property and create a bidding war. The sale of spec scripts boomed throughout the 1990s, as did the prices paid for them. After Shane Black (*Lethal Weapon*: Richard Donner, 1987, US) sold *The Last Boy Scout* (Tony Scott, 1991, US) for $1.75 million in 1990, the "million-dollar script" became commonplace. Then, only a few years later, Black received $4 million for *The Long Kiss Goodnight* (Renny Harlin, 1996, US).

Despite attempts by the studios to hold script prices down, by the end of the 1990s million-dollar scripts were "almost routine," and even unknowns have succeeded in selling spec scripts. For instance, M. Night Shyamalan, when he was basically a

FIGURE 2.2   *The Long Kiss Goodnight* (1996), product of a $4 million script. Produced by Stephanie Austin, Shane Black and Renny Harlin; distributed by New Line; directed by Renny Harlin

Hollywood newcomer, received $2.25 million for *The Sixth Sense* (1999, US) spec script, with a green light (a go-ahead for production) on its purchase (Taylor, 1999).

Some think that the spec script process is increasingly problematic, as the bidding process boosts the appeal of mediocre scripts that then attract inflated prices. Taylor (1999) notes that nearly all spec scripts must be rewritten before they are produced, but many are especially weak and the selection process is often irrational.

One of the alleged problems is that everyone is looking for the next big hit, the next blockbuster, or the next franchise (a movie that spawns merchandising and sequels). And since no one knows what will actually work, decisions are not based on quality, but the moneymaking potential of the material. In other words, a "bottom-line mentality" prevails. As one producer notes, "I would say 90 percent of the screenplays are purchased based on financial concerns and . . . what it's going to bring the studio. It really starts at the financial end" (Taylor, 1999: 58).

Other problems have to do with the "scare factor" – executives scared of losing their jobs, as well as scripts that are bought because of their potential as star vehicles or potential packages.

Another trend has been the high-concept film – an easily expressed, extremely commercial idea, where the story can be told in a few lines. High-concept films are usually action or melodrama with recognizable stars. (For a thorough discussion of high-concept films, see Wyatt, 1994.)

Production companies

Concepts or script ideas sometimes are initiated in-house or within a major studio. After securing the rights to an idea or the movie rights to an existing literary property, a studio may hire a writer to prepare a script, or at least a first draft, often with the guidance of the studio's development staff. Obviously, these films proceed quite differently from independent or out-of-house films. However, the exact roles played by various producers, studios, and production companies in the evolution of a script and an eventual film are sometimes difficult to assess. As one report has noted, "The often-complex transactions involved in bringing a film to market make analysis of the production industry difficult. Without detailed inside knowledge it can be impossible to determine the actual producer of a film" (Grummitt, 2001: 4). But it also must be noted that most of the scripts developed by the studios, no matter where they originate, never actually get produced. Estimating the number of scripts that do not emerge as finished films is nearly impossible, for the reason noted above.

However, it is possible to determine how many films are released and by whom. Of the 185 films released by members of the Motion Picture Association of America (MPAA) and their subsidiaries in 2000, one estimate is that the studios themselves released 109 films, while their subsidiaries were responsible for 76. One hundred of these films were actually produced or co-produced by the studios, at a cost of approximately $5.5 billion. These films accounted for 75 percent of the North American box office in 2000 (Grummitt, 2001: 5). (Note: the number of films released by MPAA members in 2005 was 190, which was around the same as in 2000.)

TABLE 2.1   Selected Hollywood production deals or pacts

DISNEY
Boxing Cat (Tim Allen)
Jerry Bruckheimer
Garry Marshall
Hyde Park (co-financer)
Mirage
Quentin Tarantino
Craven/Maddalena
Los Hooligans
(Robert Rodriguez)

DREAMWORKS
Aardman
ImageMovers
(Robert Zemeckis)
Eddie Murphy
Zanuck

FOX
Conundrum
Lightstorm
(James Cameron)
New Regency
Scott Free
Spiritdance
(Forest Whitaker)
State Street

NEW LINE
Benderspink
Chick Flicks
Contrafilm
Landscape

PARAMOUNT
Alphaville
Carsey-Werner Lakeshore
Lion Rock (John Woo)

MTV
Nickelodeon Revelations
(Morgan Freeman)

SONY
Spyglass (equity partner)
Revolution

MGM
Hyde Park (co-financer)
Irish DreamTime
(Pierce Brosnan)
Side Street

UNITED ARTISTS
Banyan Tree (Matt Dillon)
Mr. Mudd (John Malkovich)

UNIVERSAL
Imagine
Kennedy/Marshall
Mandalay (co-financer)
Morgan Creek
(distribution only)
Tribeca (Robert De Niro)
Working Title
Focus Features
Priority
River Road

WARNER BROS.
Malpaso (Clint Eastwood)
Section Eight (George
Clooney, Steven Soderbergh)
Village Roadshow
Jerry Weintraub

Source: *Variety*, 2005.

Some players have ongoing arrangements or production contracts (pacts) with the studios for development and output. Many pacts involve production companies, but some individual players also have pacts with a specific studio or company. *Variety* categorizes pacts as follows:

- a first-look deal, which may provide a producer with overhead (and which may be supplemented by additional outside financing);
- an equity partnership, under which a studio and a company's backers share in both the shingle's overhead and profits;
- a distribution deal, under which a company is wholly financed by outside partners and utilizes only the studio's distribution and marketing arms. (Variety, 2001)

Table 2.1 presents a few examples of pacts that were in place during 2005. While some of these companies represent important players in the industry and are able

to command preferential deals, because of their dependence on the majors for distribution, their "independence" is still relative. Daniels, et al. (1998: 213) call them
dependent-independent producers, although others in the industry still refer to them
as independent. It also is revealing to find that the top box office films often involve
these companies with on-going pacts with the major studios.

Although it has been argued that the spec system provides opportunities for new
writers, the market is still quite selective. Taylor (1999) has described it as a "closed
auction," while another producer poses an interesting question:

> Are agencies inhibiting free trade as a result of only giving it to such and such indi-
> vidual? The agencies say, "We're gonna give this spec to you, you, and you to look
> at first, and we are going to decide who we want to give it to." That, to me, is a closed
> market, and they are basically monopolizing their talent and distributing it to certain
> individuals. (quoted in Taylor, 1999: 57)

For instance, 20th Century Fox purchased film rights to Michael Crichton's novel
Prey for close to $5 million in 2002. Fox executives were approached about the rights
several weeks before they received the manuscript and concluded the deal over one
weekend. The book was sent only to Fox – a rare event in Hollywood, where literary rights are typically shopped to the highest bidder and ultimately spread across
several companies (see McNary, 2002).

The most successful writers and producers don't always go through the spec script
process, per se. As illustrated by the Crichton example above, some players with an
established track record have the clout to "short-circuit the standard development
process and have a film approved on the strength of their interest alone" (Daniels,
Leedy, and Sills, 1998).

Again, it is impossible to estimate how many ideas or concepts for films and scripts
based on those ideas do not make it to the development stage. Many elements must
come together for a film to actually become a commodity. One might argue that
some films that actually do make it to the screen should not have been developed
or produced. But it seems clear that some ideas and scripts have a better chance
than others.

Development deals

Development generally refers to the initial stage in the preparation of a film, or in
other words, those activities related to taking an idea or concept and turning it into
a finished screenplay. More specifically, the development stage may include activities
related to organizing a concept, acquiring rights, preparing an outline, synopsis,
and treatment, as well as writing, polishing, and revising script drafts (see Benedetti,
2002; Cones, 1992). Again, film properties develop differently, depending on who
is involved and when. While it may be risky to generalize, a "typical" or "model"
process will be described here.

Development deals are agreements with a studio or production company to
provide funding for a writer, producer, or director to develop a project. Not all

projects receive the same amount of funding and many don't make it through the full series of development steps. Development financing may come from different sources – the major studios draw on corporate funds, while independents may draw on a wider variety of sources, as discussed below. Development deals also may include contingencies that must be met before the movie can move into actual production. The process, which can take as little as eight months or as long as two years, may involve the approval of the writer, script, budget, director, and lead actors.

Often the first step is for the writer to prepare a treatment, which outlines the scenes, major characters, action, and locations in about 20–50 pages. A first draft, second draft, rewrite, and polish usually follow a treatment. At every step, various participants or players offer suggestions in the form of development notes.

If they haven't been arranged already through a package deal, for instance, directors and main stars may be hired at this point. These players may receive front-end payments, which would include their salaries and other perks which are negotiated, and back-end payments, such as profit participation, or some kind of share in the receipts from the film.

Deferred payments involve cast or crew members who receive some or all of their compensation after the film is released in order to reduce production costs. A deferred fee is generally paid from revenues generated from a completed motion picture, and if a movie is not finished, or it does not generate significant revenue, then the deferred payment holder may not be paid for his or her contribution.

Film costs/budgets

During development, a line producer is hired to oversee physical production of the film, which includes preparing the preliminary board and budget. The budget is organized with above-the-line and below-the-line costs, which also is the way that labor is referred to. Above-the-line costs include major creative costs or participants (writer, director, actors, and producer) as well as script and story development costs. Below-the-line items are technical expenses (equipment, film stock, printing, etc.) and "technical" labor.

Generally, motion picture production is labor-intensive, meaning the largest part of the budget is spent on labor. The cost of key talent (especially actors/actresses) is a significant part of the budget for a typical Hollywood film. Above-the-line talent can often represent 50 percent of a production budget, and has been identified as one of the key reasons why the costs of Hollywood films have skyrocketed.

The average cost of producing a Hollywood feature film has increased dramatically over the last few decades. One measure of a film's expense is the negative cost or the amount spent on actual production costs. However, there also are additional costs involving studio overheads and interest expenses. Thus, the actual cost of manufacturing a completed negative may be inflated beyond what was actually spent to produce the film. As reported by the MPAA, in 1975 the average negative cost was around $5 million; by 2007 that amount was around $65 million. (Marketing costs will be discussed in the next chapter.)

Financing

Financing usually is arranged during development and becomes a significant factor in determining whether a film will be made and who will be involved. Again, financing strategies and funding sources are different for major films and independents. A funding source's influence or involvement in the production/distribution of a film also may vary, depending on the clout of the major participants or players.

Funding sources. While financing is a major challenge for most independent filmmakers, it is less problematic for film projects that involve the major studios. The entire cost of development and production typically will be paid by the studio, which will then own the film outright.

It is important to note at this point that the major Hollywood companies do not fund film production solely through profits. At least the potential for extensive resources is available through the studios' well-heeled parent corporations, as well as the ongoing financial relationships with banks and other financial institutions. These sources may provide capital for various activities, including film production. While these financial sources (especially banks) may not become involved in decisions about which films to produce, they are always involved in the financial health and overall management of the company and become more involved and restrictive when a company is doing poorly. (See Wasko, 1982, for more discussion of Hollywood's historical relationship with financial institutions.)

Production loans for individual films also are possible from banks; however, collateral is always required to secure the loan and a distribution agreement with a major studio is often required. Independent filmmakers may find it especially difficult to find bank financing; however, some financial institutions specialize in this type of business. A few large banks have many years of experience in dealing with Hollywood companies (City National, Chase National, Chemical, and Bank of America). Meanwhile, other financial institutions have ventured into the film-financing business, but often find it to be quite challenging, as well as requiring a good deal of specialized expertise.

Independent producers often are forced to rely heavily on presales to other distribution outlets, such as TV networks, pay-cable channels, and home-video companies. In other words, a producer may arrange for production financing from a pay-TV channel, in exchange for the right to run the film first in the pay-TV market. Similar rights in foreign territories also are sources of funding, especially for independent films. The availability of such funding fluctuates, sometimes providing ample funds for film production, at other times drying up completely.

Another source of production funding is investment capital in the form of a limited partnerships, which may be organized for a specific film or group of films. Several general partners (often, the producers) may initiate and control the partnership, with limited partners serving as investors with no control and no financial liabilities beyond the amount they have invested.

Sources of funding for Hollywood films come and go, as financing schemes seem to be as trendy as Hollywood fashion. For instance, around 2005–6, hedge funds were the hot item, with many of the studios, as well as some production companies, arranging funding from such private equity funds. For instance, Miramax founder Harvey Weinstein raised $490 million in hedge funds for the new company The Weinstein Co. Typically, these funds involve a slate of films, rather than an individual picture.

Meanwhile, other sources of funding may include merchandising and product placement arrangements. While not all films may be able to tap these sources, it is not uncommon for Hollywood films to feature numerous products that are not accidental, but purposely placed in exchange for fees that may offset production costs.

Independent filmmakers also may seek grants from various sources. For example, the film *Stand and Deliver*'s (Ramón Menédez, 1988, US) budget of $1.37 million came from the Corporation for Public Broadcasting, American Playhouse, ARCO Corporation, National Science Foundation, and Ford Foundation, in addition to a few product placement deals.

Co-productions. Actually, cooperative production ventures have been prevalent in the past and US film production in Europe has a long history, albeit with numerous ups and downs. Co-productions grew dramatically in the late 1980s as companies were not just picking up films for distribution or simply financing projects, but becoming active in "creative partnerships."

Sometimes complete funding is provided, through a combination of presales and a domestic US distribution agreement. Financing is available from distribution companies, pay-TV (such as HBO) and cable companies (such as Turner and the USA Network). Such financing may be available for independents, especially if the film has overseas potential. However, when such co-production funds are slim, projects associated with the US majors (again) have the advantage.

Completion guarantees. It is possible that a financier or bank may require a completion guarantee to assure that the film is actually finished. A completion bond is a form of insurance that guarantees financing to complete a film in the event that the producer exceeds the budget. If a bond is invoked, the completion guarantor sometimes assumes control over the production, as well as receiving a preferential position over other investors in recouping funds.

Green lights, development hell, turnaround

When all of these various elements are in place (which may take many years), a film project may receive a green light from a studio executive and move into (pre)production. If a script is in development but never receives production funds, it is said to be in development hell. A former screenwriter has estimated that 85 percent of studio-purchased spec scripts end up in development hell (Taylor, 1999). However, even if a film is not produced, the studios are able to recoup development costs from other films' budgets as part of studio overhead charges.

Development itself is a controversial process, especially because of the constant rewriting of scripts. The major studios tend to have different philosophies about development, including the number of projects in development, who becomes involved in the rewriting process, etc. In addition, decisions about which films are given a green light are made based on many factors, not just the quality of the idea or con-

FIGURE 2.3   *E.T. The Extra-terrestrial* (1982), developed by Columbia but a hit for Universal. Produced by Kathleen Kennedy and Steven Spielberg; distributed by Universal; directed by Steven Spielberg

cept. For instance, a film may provide a vehicle for a star or director or it may be a high-powered studio executive's special project. However, favored film projects may also never receive a green light because of management changes.

Even though one studio may abandon a project, it is possible for another one to pick up the project and make it into a successful film. Again, if a studio project is abandoned, the costs are written off the studio's overhead or perhaps charged to a producer's multi-picture deal. A classic example was *E.T. The Extra-Terrestrial* (Steven Spielberg, 1982, US), which was developed and dropped by Columbia Pictures, but picked up by Universal. As they say, the rest is history.

Pre-Production

Pre-production begins when a developed property is approved for production and may take from two to six months, of course with the usual proviso that every film is different. While 400–500 films are released in the US each year by Hollywood companies, obviously many, many film ideas or scripts never reach the production stage. However, if a major film does begin production, it will usually be completed, as too much money has already been invested in the project for it to be abandoned.

Organizing production

After a film is given a green light, various elements are assembled that are necessary to manufacture the film. Locations are scouted and selected, final casting is done, and key production personnel are hired. Each of these areas will be discussed further below.

Meanwhile, the final budget, shooting script, and shooting schedule also are prepared. A line producer or unit production manager handles some of these details and the logistics of the entire company and production process. Although these positions are similar, a line producer often has greater creative involvement.

Decisions are made as well about the equipment needed during production. Often, production companies hire or lease machinery, tools, or gear needed for production as rentals eliminate the need to purchase and maintain equipment.

In addition, an account is established for the film, with all costs, time, and materials charged against a job or charge number. Importantly, producers or studio representatives review charges on a regular basis, watching for costs that may be inappropriately charged to the film. Motion picture accountants explain that this "job-order cost procedure" is similar to the process used in specialty manufacturing or accounting systems used by service businesses (Daniels, Leedy, and Sills, 1998: 183). This process becomes especially important when the revenues and costs for a film are eventually distributed.

Locations

Decisions are often made about locations during development and firmed up during pre-production. Decisions about whether to shoot on a studio lot or another location involve creative judgments, but are also very much influenced by economic factors. A script may call for a specific location; however, recreating the site in a studio or on a back lot may in the end be less costly.

While a good deal of production for Hollywood films takes place at studios and on location in and around Hollywood and the San Fernando Valley, film companies also are often drawn to other locations for economic reasons. For instance, during 2001, around 170 features were shot in New York City, with film and TV companies spending $5 billion on production in the city and that activity generated $500 million in tax revenues for the city. These days, film production is being deliberately lured away from southern California, by film commissions offering various incentives, as well as the attraction of lower labor costs.

Film commissions. Film commissions at the local, state, and national levels attempt to attract productions to their locations. The first commission was formed in the US in the late 1940s. More commissions developed in response to the need for local government liaisons who could coordinate local services such as police, state troopers and highway patrols, road and highway departments, fire departments, park rangers, and all of the other essential municipal and government services for location shooting. The Association of Film Commissioners (AFCI), formed in 1975, represents a worldwide network of more than 300 commissions from 30 countries.

As more production companies began to look for realistic and varied locations, more cities and states began to see the need for production coordination liaison. But most importantly, they were also keenly aware of the economic benefits brought by film and video production companies to their areas. Indeed, a multiplier effect has been experienced as the local economy can benefit by as much as three times the amount that a production company actually spends on location.

The services provided by film commissions have expanded in response to the growth of on-location filming. Film commissions provide a number of services for film producers, from scouting locations within their area to troubleshooting with local officials and helping cut through paperwork and bureaucratic red tape. Some provide economic incentives, such as tax rebates and hotel discounts for location scouts. Others offer a variety of other free services like research for screenwriters or liaison work with local government agencies.

Film commissions have been set up by cities, counties, states, provinces, or federal governments, and are generally operated and funded by various agencies of government, such as the governor's office, the mayor's office, the county board of supervisors, chambers of commerce, convention and visitors' bureaus, travel commissions, and business and economic development departments. Their primary responsibility is to attract film and video production to their areas so that the companies will hire local crews and talent, rent local equipment, use hotel rooms, rental cars, catering services, and other goods and services supplied on location. While attracting business to their area, they also attract visitors. Film scenes at a particular location are "soft-sell" vehicles that also promote that location as a desirable site for future tourism and industry.

Various incentives are offered to attract film production to locations. For example, the state of Louisiana launched a major production-incentives program featuring film production tax credits in 2002. Under the new legislation, qualifying productions could earn tax credits of up to 15 percent of the total production expenditures in the state. In addition, a financing fund was organized to attract producers to the state.

Fragmentation and runaway production

Because of the proliferation of film production in many locations, some attention has been given to the issue of whether the US motion picture industry is still centralized in Southern California. Some scholars argue that the film industry is characterized by flexible specialization, with activities fragmented at different locations. From their base in urban planning, Michael Storper and others argue that the film industry has been restructured from the integrated, mass-production studio system of the 1930s and 1940s (a Fordist model) to a disintegrated and flexible system based on independent and specialized production (a post-Fordist model). Thus, the film industry provides an example of flexible specialization's viability for other industrial sectors to emulate (Storper and Christopherson, 1987).

While these interpretations describe some important changes in the US film industry of the late twentieth century, the analysis is severely handicapped by the emphasis on production and the neglect of the key roles played by distribution, exhibition, and financing. Aksoy and Robins have provided an excellent critique of the flexible specialization thesis:

For them [Storper and Christopherson] the major transformation in the American film industry is centered around the reorganization of production, and, more particularly, around the changing relationship between technical and social divisions of labor in production. It is as if the Hollywood industrial story begins and ends with the production of films. (Aksoy and Robins, 1992)

The flexible specialization argument also overlooks the considerable concentration of post-production in California. Even with growing post-production activities in Florida, Vancouver, and Toronto, an argument can be made that Hollywood is still a focal point for production planning, post-production, and distribution. A Hollywood insider explains it this way:

There is still some truth to the notion of Hollywood as a place located in Southern California. The district of Hollywood is still more or less the geographic center of a cluster of production facilities, soundstages, office buildings, and studio ranches, stretching from Culver City, Venice, and Santa Monica in the south, to Glendale, Burbank, North Hollywood, and even the Simi Valley in the north. The dozen or so companies that control more than half of the world's entertainment have headquarters in Los Angeles, within a thirty-mile radius of Hollywood. The executives, agents, producers, actors, and directors are there. The meetings to decide what movies will be made are held there. At some point, every major figure in world entertainment has to come to Hollywood, if only to accept an Academy Award. (Vogler, 1997)

Nevertheless, shooting on location is common for various reasons. In some discussions of this issue, economic runaway has been defined as "U.S. -developed

FIGURE 2.4   Disney's corporate headquarters in Burbank, California. Photo by Associated Press

feature films, movies for television, TV shows or series, which are filmed in another country for economic reasons" (DGA, 1999). A Screen Actors Guild (SAG)/Directors Guild of America (DGA) study of runaway production in 1999 reported that the total economic impact as a result of US economic runaway film and television production was $10.3 billion in 1998, up more than fivefold since the beginning of the decade (Monitor, 1999).

The report noted that Canada had captured the vast majority of economic runaways, with 81 percent of the total. Although US domestic feature film production grew 8.2 percent annually from 1990 to 1998, US features produced in Canada grew 17.4 percent annually during the same time period. In addition to the substantial impact on DGA and SAG members (directors, unit production managers, assistant directors, principal and supporting actors, stunt and background performers), the guild's study noted that the greatest impact in terms of lost employment opportunities was felt by below-the-line workers.

Further, the total employment impact of US runaway production on entertainment industry workers rose 241 percent from 1990 to 1998, with the number of full-time equivalent positions lost rising from 6,900 in 1990 to 23,500 in 1998 – a cumulative total of 125,100 positions. Meanwhile, a Department of Commerce study released in 2001 mirrored the DGA/SAG findings, concluding that film and TV work continues to leave the US at an accelerating rate (US Dept. of Commerce, 2001).

Some small anti-runaway advances have emerged in recent years, such as streamlined local permitting and California's $45 million, three-year incentive program, which reimburses filmmakers for permits, public equipment, and safety costs.

Labor markets/labor organizations

While actors and directors receive much of the attention and publicity, the Hollywood workforce includes a wide range of laborers, from carpenters and office workers to artists and lab technicians. According to MPAA data, 591,800 people were employed in the US motion picture industry in 2001.

Hollywood workers sell their labor to employers in a labor market that is both similar to and different from other industries. Generally, the motion picture production is labor-intensive and the industry is highly unionized. Hollywood unions and guilds negotiate basic agreements, which specify minimum salaries (or scale), working conditions, residuals, benefits, etc. However, individual workers also negotiate their own contracts, sometimes with the assistance of an agent or manager, as explained above. (More discussion of labor can be found in chapter 9 in this volume.)

Principal Photography/Production

Principal photography is usually the most costly part of manufacturing a film and typically takes 6–12 weeks. Again, there are always exceptions.

While the structure of production is relatively flexible, it is similar to that of the construction industry. In other words, film productions are organized as short-term combinations of directors, actors, and crews, plus various subcontractors who come together to construct a motion picture.

A good deal of attention has been given to this part of the production process, which may be seen as the most glamorous and/or creative part of the manufacture of the film commodity. While some economic issues may emerge during principal photography, only a few will be mentioned briefly here. Obviously, there is always the issue of adhering to the budget, and the problems that may lead to over-budget productions. Creative decisions inevitably will be influenced by the availability of funds.

In addition, the clout or power of various players has enormous influence on decision-making on the set, as the influence or involvement of producers, investors, or studio representatives (collectively called "The Suits") may add a chilling effect to the creative process.

Post-Production

Although editing usually begins during principal photography, it continues after shooting concludes, as other elements of the film are added: scoring, mixing, dialog, music, sound effects, and special effects. Post-production may take 4–8 months. As noted above, some of these activities may take place in other locations; however, post-production is still mostly centralized in Hollywood.

Hollywood services industry

An infrastructure for film production and post-production has developed in the Los Angeles area, which includes a wide range of motion picture-related businesses. Many companies are involved in servicing the motion picture industry, including those that deal with film stock, laboratories, camera equipment, sound recording and equipment, properties, costumes, set design and construction, lighting equipment, etc. There is even an association for the businesses that manufacture, supply, and produce entertainment equipment, called the Entertainment Services and Technology Association.

Though some of these services may be offered in other locations, Los Angeles is still a centralized location for most of these activities. For instance, Los Angeles is home to roughly 400 sound stages with more than 4.4 million square feet of space.

Special effects (f/x)

The area of special effects has grown dramatically over the last decades, as new computer and digital technologies continue to produce a wide range of filmic magic. Because of the significance of this area, a bit more detail might be of interest. Obviously, these possibilities have implications for the type of films that are made and an influence on production costs as well.

The aim of special effects has been to create things that don't actually exist. Some of the techniques used by the earliest filmmakers, such as double exposures and miniaturized models, are still employed. *King Kong* (Merian C. Cooper and Ernest B. Schoedsack, 1933, US) represented a landmark in special effects and incorporated many of the same techniques used by today's special effects teams: models, matte paintings for foreground and backgrounds, rear projections, miniature or enlarged props and miniaturized sets, combined with live action.

However, the use of computers, robotics, and digital technologies over the last 20 years has added to the sophistication of the effects process, and also enhanced the filmmaker's ability to create nearly anything imaginable on film. There is a wide variety of optical or special effects, which are constantly changing, as every film has its own set of unique requirements which inspire effects masters to create new techniques.

Creating a Film Commodity

It is fairly uncontroversial to state that decisions made about which scripts are sold, how they are developed, and which ones are green-lighted and actually produced are guided by a bottom-line or box-office mentality, at least for major Hollywood films. Obviously, such decisions also affect the creativity of the players involved. For instance, as a script goes through the development process, it's often changed and reworked to the point that some writers don't even recognize their original work. As Kawin explains:

> A script may pass through the hands of many writers before it is ready to be produced, and even the revised final is likely to be modified by the director and the actors while the picture is being shot. The editor, too, may affect the "script" by deleting a line or a speech that turned out not to play well, and the decisions that follow previews may entirely change the outcome of a story. (Kawin, 1992: 310)

Important decisions about what is shot (or not shot) during principal photography and the final cut also are made by those in positions of power. While the last stage of the editing process involves a director's cut, the final version of the picture is almost always in the hands of the distributor or the financier of the film, unless a director has a good deal of clout. For instance, as another industry insider reports: "I have seen bad test screenings, where the director of the film has final cut and the head of the studio wants the director to change the movie, fix the ending" (Levy, 2000). Generally, creativity is tempered by clout and power, and decisions are made within the parameters of the box office.

However, even with the prevailing financial mentality, those with power or clout often don't know any better than anyone else what will be popular with an audience. As screenwriter William Goldman wrote in *Adventures in the Screen Trade*, "nobody knows anything in the movie business because no one can predict popular taste" (Goldman, 1989: 39). Goldman explains further: "nobody really knows which films will be big. There are no sure-fire commercial ideas anymore. And there are no unbreakable rules." While these remarks echo the claims of riskiness which Hollywood frequently repeats, the industry also tries to eliminate this uncertainty in various ways – by focusing on blockbusters featuring well-known stars and/or by basing films on already recognizable stories and characters.

While success in Hollywood may be unpredictable, explanations abound. For instance, some claim that the movies that get made reflect the executive mentality; but the movies that are successful reflect the audience (Squire, 1992: 95). This explanation, however, underestimates the amount of effort and expense that is devoted to convincing audiences to see or buy a film or the products associated with the film. Marketing and promotion begin during production, continue during shooting, and become especially significant upon a film's release.

As noted previously, the production of Hollywood films attracts a good deal of attention from the press, academics and the public. It also attracts a good deal of capital. The total investment in producing or acquiring films for release in the US in 2000 was $7.75 billion (not including advertising or marketing expenses) (Grummitt, 2001: 5). Thus, it becomes especially important to understand the factors that contribute to the creation of a Hollywood film commodity.

NOTE

This chapter has been adapted from Janet Wasko (2003) *How Hollywood Works.* London: Sage.

REFERENCES

Aksoy, A., and K. Robins (1992) "Hollywood for the 21st Century: Global Competition for Critical Mass in Image Markets," *Cambridge Journal of Economics* 16(1), pp. 1–22.

Benedetti, R. (2002) *From Concept to Screen*. Boston: Allyn & Bacon.

Cones, J. W. (1992) *Film Finance and Distribution: A Dictionary of Terms*. Los Angeles: Silman-James Press.

Daniels, B., D. Leedy, and S. D. Sills (1998) *Movie Money: Understanding Hollywood's (Creative) Accounting Practices*. Los Angeles: Silman-James Press.

DGA (1999) "DGA/SAG Commissioned Study Shows Total Economic Impact of U.S. Economic Runaway Production Reached $10.3 Billion in 1998 (June 25, 1999)," online at <http://www.dga.org/news/pr_expand.php3?143> (accessed July 18, 2007).

Goldman, W. (1989) *Adventures in the Screen Trade: A Personal View of Hollywood and Screenwriting*. New York: Warner Books.

Grummitt, K.-P. (2001) *Hollywood: America's Film Industry*. Leicester: Dodona Research.

Kawin, B. F. (1992) *How Movies Work*. Berkeley, CA: University of California Press.

Levy, F. (2000) *Hollywood 101: The Film Industry.* Los Angeles: Renaissance Books.

McNary, D. (2002) "Crichton Nabs a Foxy $5 Mil," *Variety,* July 25, p. 1.

Monitor (1999) *US Runaway Film and Television Production Study Report.* Santa Monica, CA: Monitor Company.

Squire, J. E. (ed.) (1992) *The Movie Business Book,* 2nd edn. New York: Simon and Schuster.

Storper, M. and S. Christopherson (1987) "Flexible Specialization and Regional Industrial Agglomerations: The Case of the U.S. Motion Picture Industry," *Annals of the Association of American Geographers,* 77(1), pp. 104–17.

Taylor, T. (1999) *The Big Deal: Hollywood's Million-Dollar Spec Script Market.* New York: William Morrow & Co.

US Dept. of Commerce (2001) *The Migration of U.S. Film and Television Production: Impact of "Runaways" on Workers and Small Business in the U.S. Film Industry.* Washington, DC.

Variety (2001) "Facts on Pacts 2001," online at<http://www.variety.com/index.asp?layout=chart_pass&charttype=chart_pact2001&dept=Film> (accessed July 18, 2007).

Variety (2005) "Facts on Pacts (2005) (Spring)," online at <http://www.variety.com/index.asp?layout=chart_pass&charttype=chart_factspacts2005spring&dept=Film#ev_top> (accessed September 1, 2006).

Vogler, C. (1997) "The Writer's Journey," in C. De Abreu (ed.), *Opening the Doors to Hollywood.* New York: Three Rivers Press.

Wasko, J. (1982) *Movies and Money: Financing the American Film Industry.* Norwood, NJ: Ablex Publishing.

Wyatt, J. (1994) *High Concept: Movies and Marketing in Hollywood.* Austin: University of Texas Press.

CHAPTER 3

DISTRIBUTION AND MARKETING IN CONTEMPORARY HOLLYWOOD

PHILIP DRAKE

Distribution and marketing are amongst the least widely understood aspects of the contemporary Hollywood film industry yet, in comparison to film production, these sectors are the focus of activity for many of its workers. Marketing costs, usually referred to by the industry as "print and advertising" (or "P&A"), now account for around one-third of the total cost of a major studio-released feature film, equal to around half of the "negative cost" (the cost of production). According to the Motion Picture Association of America (MPAA), the average marketing cost of a studio film in 2005 was $36.19 million, which, once added to an average production cost of $60 million, took the average total cost of a major released film to nearly $100 million (MPAA, 2006). This has led commentators in trade magazines such as *Variety*, *The Hollywood Reporter*, and *Screen International* to question the sustainability of blockbuster economics in the industry. The long-term trend in costs has clearly been upwards although, as table 3.1 below shows, total costs have leveled out in recent years and may even have started to fall in real (inflation-adjusted) terms.

TABLE 3.1   Average production (negative) and marketing (p&a) costs of a major Hollywood motion picture*

	Negative cost $m	P&A cost $m
2005	60.0	36.19
2004	62.4	34.35
2003	63.8	39.05
2002	58.8	30.62
2001	47.7	31.01
2000	54.8	27.30
1995	36.4	17.74

* Figures not adjusted for inflation.
Source: MPAA, 2003, 2005, 2006.

Over the last two decades the Hollywood film industry has seen a number of important developments, including the consolidation of video and the rise of DVD as the largest studio revenue earners, which now eclipse the theatrical box office. Box-office takings currently account for less than a quarter of total revenues and have become increasingly "front-loaded," earning the majority of receipts in the opening two weeks of exhibition, meaning that films need to make an almost instant impact in order to avoid being dropped from screens by exhibitors. According to market analysts Merrill Lynch, by the early 2000s as much as 50 percent of theatrical box office was generated in the first week of release, compared to only around 20 percent in 1990 (cited in Marich, 2004: p. x). A consequence of front-loading has been a reduction in time allowed in the exhibition window for theatrical release, and the further embedding of movie marketing into Hollywood's mode of production. For medium- to high-budget films the "opening weekend" – usually defined as the three-day period, Friday to Sunday – is seen as an indicator not only of predicted theatrical revenue but also of the value of the film in overseas markets and a partial determinant of its sell-through price in distribution windows such as television and home video – what is known in the industry as its "marquee value." Theatrical box-office figures are seen as a measure of how the film can be valued and exploited as a licensable property over its life-cycle, and across different formats. Box-office data therefore matters not simply in terms of immediate financial receipts but, more importantly, by operating as a signal of value in other media markets.

Before we consider each of the different aspects of film marketing and distribution it is worth examining the nature of film and the cinema experience as products. The peculiarities of Hollywood films as cultural goods are: (a) the ticket price of cinema admission is not variable across individual films but set at the same level for all films; (b) films are product-differentiated in more complex ways than other categories of product; (c) film revenues are streamed across a lengthy time period; (d) consumption of the product does not exhaust it; for it is not "used up" by watching or depleted for other viewers, so there is an element of non-rivalry in consumption; and (e) admission might buy the social experience of cinemagoing rather than to see a particular film. Cinemagoing can therefore be considered a risky activity for consumers in that they are buying a product based only upon the promise of a pleasurable experience, and risky for film financers in that they cannot guarantee demand for a particular film and cannot alter ticket price to balance supply and demand for each film. The satisfaction gained by consumption can only be judged afterwards, feeding into positive and negative word-of-mouth recommendations by audiences. A consequence of this, as Arthur De Vany (2004) has demonstrated, is that box-office receipts are notoriously difficult to predict. Marketing is therefore a key means for the industry to establish product recognition and differentiation, and attempt to reduce these risks by highlighting the marketable elements prior to a film's release. This is important because often only a week is given by exhibitors to evaluate whether a film will attract a wide audience.

Such factors mean that Hollywood is often characterized as a risky industry. Major films require a massive financial investment without any guarantee of recouping their cost at the box office. Indeed when faced with criticism (as, for instance, during the 1993 GATT negotiations) the MPAA emphasizes risk in defense of Hollywood's economic dominance in overseas markets. It argues that only the major Hollywood studios are willing to take the major risks that lead to global success, and should not be penalized for risk-taking by trade tariffs or quotas. According to such industry rhetoric only a few films become profitable in their theatrical release, and blockbuster smashes are needed to offset box-office failures. Leaving aside the circularity of such an argument (for critiques see Wasko, 2003; Miller et al., 2005), we should note that the definition of success requires further scrutiny. Hollywood has always had a vested interest in being seen as a risky business, yet has evolved elaborate mechanisms over the last 30 years to ensure financial survival. Later in this chapter we will examine the claim that most studio films lose money by exploring how box-office "profits" are calculated. What is true is that the market for Hollywood films operates under what economists call "asymmetric information" – incomplete information between producers and consumers – and this leads to difficulties in reliably predicting success or otherwise, hence surprise box-office "hits" and "flops." Marketing, especially saturation marketing targeted at the opening weekend, can be seen as one industrial response to this issue.

The rest of this chapter aims to offer an overview of film marketing and distribution by the major studios in the domestic North American market. There are currently six major studios, taking into account the acquisition in 2005 of MGM/United Artists by Sony Pictures, and of DreamWorks SKG by Paramount Pictures in early 2006. The dominant big multi-media conglomerate studios are Warner Bros./New Line, 20th Century Fox, Universal Pictures, Walt Disney/Miramax/Touchstone, Sony Pictures/Columbia and Paramount Pictures. These "Big Six" all distribute their films and the films of others, mainly through their eponymous domestic distribution divisions which include Warner Bros. Pictures, 20th Century Fox Pictures, Universal Pictures, Buena Vista (part of Disney), Sony Pictures, and Paramount Motion Picture Group (which includes Paramount Pictures and DreamWorks SKG). The "domestic" market includes both the United States and Canada, which in theatrical distribution is conceived of as a single territory and equal to approximately half of global box-office revenue. Some aspects of overseas distribution, which accounts for around half of revenues, are considered later in this volume in the chapters exploring Hollywood's presence in international territories. Hollywood is a transnational industry and the majors have significant distribution interests in international markets, an example of this being United International Pictures (UIP), a joint venture between Paramount and Universal Pictures, which distributes films in numerous overseas territories. The majors also form alliances with local distributors, such as Metrodome in the UK, or star-owned companies such as Mel Gibson's Icon Pictures.

Broadly, the rest of this chapter will be divided into three sections: first, it will explain the basic processes involved in motion picture marketing and their place in the contemporary Hollywood mode of production; second, it will examine distribution agreements and the calculation of profits, and finally it considers the implications of Hollywood's dominance in these areas.

Motion Picture Marketing and Distribution in Hollywood: An Overview

Marketing is of great importance to Hollywood, and necessary to the process of building consumer awareness about studio products. Marketing is not simply reactive, responding to consumer demand, but also attempts to both anticipate and create demand. The film industry has long recognized the importance of marketing its products, as exemplified by the elaborately designed and much-loved posters used in the earliest years of the twentieth century. Traditionally Hollywood studios managed their marketing through in-house publicity departments by carefully controlling the publicity generated around their stable of stars and limiting advertising spend to trailers, newspapers, and radio. As film consumption was a regular activity for many audiences, the studios were able to rely upon information gathered by frequent cinemagoing and exposure to trailers and posters, together with the mass appeal of stars or popularity of particular genres. In the decades of the classical Hollywood studio system between approximately 1920 and 1960, the studios also became associated with particular genres – most famously MGM musicals and Warner Bros. gangster pictures – which gave them brand identity.

After the 1948 Paramount decree the major film studios gradually became less associated with a particular roster of stars or identifiable genres, and the well-documented decline in theatrical audiences meant that marketing departments needed to create greater awareness for their products against a backdrop of the rise in popularity of television and reduced control over cinema exhibition chains (Bordwell, Staiger, and Thompson, 1985). Due to anti-trust restrictions, films had to be sold in blocks of five titles, and so the major studios resorted to a greater reliance on individual stars, marketing, and wider release patterns to draw audiences. They soon discovered that their market power lay in financing deals, controlling access to distribution networks (including television) and the exploitation of film rights, rather than maintaining costly and under-utilized studio production facilities (Wasko, 2003). As the international and television markets became increasingly important so the value of their film archives began to rise, and this strategy began to make sound business sense. In economic terms the marginal cost of distributing a film is low compared to the fixed costs of its production. As attendances fell and ticket prices went up, the small cost of additional prints made a reduction in production, wide release strategies and large marketing campaigns all effective ways of maximizing revenues. These changes were a rational response to shifts in the structure of the industry, encouraging the proliferation of blockbuster-driven release and marketing strategies pioneered by the hugely successful *Jaws* (Steven Spielberg, 1975, US) and *Star Wars* (George Lucas, 1977, US), amongst others (see Earnest, 1985; Wyatt, 1994).

Since the 1970s marketing has thus been a central part of Hollywood's business. As a result of the challenge to cinema presented by television, the 1960s shift in audience demographics towards a youth market, and a competing range of leisure activities, the film industry had to work hard at attracting an increasingly fragmented audience (Vogel, 2001). In response Hollywood started to utilize network television for its advertising, a move that significantly raised costs but allowed a far greater advertising reach than other media. These factors also brought changes in film distribution, with a national saturation release replacing the road-shows that once toured films across the US slowly building audiences. "Platform releasing," running a film in a few key cities before gradually widening the release to provincial areas, is still used for films which primarily recruit audiences through word of mouth, or art-house films with a limited P&A spend; however, most major Hollywood films are now simultaneously released in many cities. Previously so-called "wide" domestic release patterns of 500 film theaters in the mid-1970s were regularly extended to over 2,000 screens by the 1980s (a "saturation" release) and over 3,000 screens ("super-saturation") by the turn of the twenty-first century. With multiple screens showing the same film in many multiplex cinemas, major films can now be domestically released on over 4,000 screens – opening on so-called "playdates" – capitalizing on nationwide marketing campaigns and providing an additional marketing push for spin-off ancillary products such as video games and toys. For example, in November 2001 the film *Harry Potter and the Sorcerer's Stone* (Chris Columbus, 2001, US) was released in 3,672 locations in the US but on over 8,000 screens, grossing over $90 million in its opening three-day weekend (Fellman, 2006: 366).

Robert Friedman, a former Chief Operating Officer at Paramount studios and President of Advertising and Publicity at Warner Bros., suggests that the competition for audience awareness invariably now requires a blanket push in terms of both release strategy and marketing spend to avoid being forced out of the cinemas by other films (Friedman, 2006: 284). However, films that are platform-released do occasionally perform spectacularly well at the box office. *My Big Fat Greek Wedding* (Joel Zwick, 2002, US), for instance, cost only around $5 million to make but grossed $241.4 million with a marketing spend of around $30 million (Marich, 2004: 57). *The Passion of the Christ* (Mel Gibson, 2004, US) generated record-breaking box office of $370 million for an independently produced and distributed film costing only $30 million, largely due to publicity and word of mouth generated through churches and their congregations. Table 3.2 shows recent top-opening, three-day-weekend grosses, clearly dominated by major studios.

High Concept and Beyond

According to Justin Wyatt in his 1994 book *High Concept: Movies and Marketing in Hollywood*, there are strong links between marketing and contemporary Hollywood filmmaking, and these can be encapsulated by the term "high concept." High concept refers to a mode of filmmaking where the core narrative premise can

TABLE 3.2   Top weekend openings, costs, and gross box office 2002–2005 (ranked by opening weekend)*

	Estimated negative cost $m	Distributor	Release date	Opening weekend box office $m	Gross box office $m
Spider-Man 2	200	Sony	6/4/04	115.8	373.4
Spider-Man	139	Sony	5/3/02	114.8	403.7
Star Wars: Episode III – Revenge of the Sith	113	Fox	5/19/05	108.4	380.3
Shrek 2	75	DreamWorks	5/19/04	108.0	436.7
Harry Potter and the Goblet of Fire	150	Warner Bros.	11/18/05	102.7	289.2
Harry Potter and the Prisoner of Azkaban	130	Warner Bros.	6/4/04	93.7	249.4
The Matrix Reloaded	150	Warner Bros.	5/15/03	91.8	281.5
Harry Potter and the Chamber of Secrets	100	Warner Bros.	11/11/02	88.3	253.0
The Day After Tomorrow	125	Fox	5/28/04	85.8	186.7
Bruce Almighty	81	Universal	5/23/03	85.7	242.6

* Figures not adjusted for inflation.
Source: MPAA, 2003, 2004, 2005, 2006.

FIGURE 3.1   Platform releasing helped *My Big Fat Greek Wedding* (1982) to take over $241 million at the North American box office. Produced by Gary Goetzman, Tom Hanks, and Rita Wilson; distributed by IFC Films; directed by Joel Zwick

FIGURE 3.2   *Top Gun* (1986), high-concept filmmaking *par excellence*. Produced by
Jerry Bruckheimer and Don Simpson; distributed by Paramount; directed by Tony Scott

be easily summarized and communicated, with an assembly of elements that foreground narrative transparency and didacticism. For example *Under Siege* (Andrew
Davis, 1992, US) could be described as *"Die Hard* on a boat." From the early 1980s
producing partners Don Simpson and Jerry Bruckheimer became exemplary expo-
nents of the high-concept philosophy with their films *Flashdance* (Adrian Lyne, 1983,
US), *Beverly Hills Cop* (Martin Brest, 1984, US) and *Top Gun* (Tony Scott, 1986, US).

Analyzing industrial changes in Hollywood during the 1980s, Wyatt suggested
that film marketing began to directly feed into production and aesthetic decision-
making. Thus a particular project might be described in terms of its "elements"
and "properties" – the hooks upon which a marketing campaign might be based,
such as stars or spectacular special effects. Wyatt, in appropriately high-concept fashion, summarizes the strategy as "the look, the hook, and the book": the linking of
market branding and film style, the use of elements to hook audiences, and the
maximizing of synergies in ancillary markets through licensing of movie tie-in products such as novels and merchandising. Film style therefore became an important
component of high-concept movie-making, as the "total look" of the film provided
a way of differentiating between films in the marketplace. Perhaps the most famous
example of integrated marketing is Steven Spielberg's blockbuster *Jurassic Park* (1993,
US), where the theme park shown in the film was branded in the same manner as the
film itself, and the merchandising depicted in the film was available for film audiences
to purchase (Balides, 2000). Such films can be described as "commercial intertexts"
(Meehan, 1991), integrating aesthetics with marketing opportunities, and conforming
film form to the economic imperatives of Hollywood as a profit-making industry.

Movie Marketing Practices

The importance of marketing, in terms of success of a film, is like air to all of us. It
is a crucial resource that you must be breathing from the beginning. The minute you

start the process of deciding to make a film and you're communicating that vision
to anyone, you're in the process of selling. If you don't understand that, you're not
in show business. You're just not.
– Peter Guber producer and former chairman and CEO of Sony Pictures (Guber, 2001)

Lucas spent US$115 million to produce *The Phantom Menace*, Fox spent about
US$50 million to make anyone who lived in the US know "Star Wars" was back. Fox
also lined up deals for further merchandising and publicity. Toy-maker Hasbro paid
a quarter of a billion dollars for toy rights; Pepsi agreed to spend US$2 billion to pro-
mote *The Phantom Menace* – and two future sequels – along with its soft drinks. *Star
Wars: Episode 1 – The Phantom Menace* opened to a record US$28.5 million-worth
of tickets on its first day, setting a new record. The twentieth century's final blockbuster was born. (Gomery, 2003: 72)

Marketing a film involves conceptualizing it as a brand. Often this brand may already
have existing consumer recognition, as in the *Spider-Man* and *Batman* franchises
or film sequels, which assume a familiarity based on the earlier films. For other
films the function of marketing is to establish the film as a recognizable brand with
strong audience appeal. Film marketing can be broadly divided into the following
activities: (1) product marketing, advertising, and promotion; (2) market research;
(3) publicity; and (4) ancillaries and merchandising. We will now briefly examine
the first three of these in turn. The final category is dealt with in the later section
on distribution and in more detail elsewhere in this volume in chapters 7 and 8,
on video games and recorded music.

Product marketing, advertising, and promotion

Even before a large-scale project enters production, planning will have started on
its marketing campaign. Indeed marketing may play a role in deciding whether a
film is even put into production in the first place (see the market research section
below). Friedman argues that marketing a film is "like a race, in that each discip-
line may start at different times, but all finish together, at the target, opening weekend" (2006: 284). For major studio releases, marketing and advertising strategies
are formulated during pre-production and constantly revised throughout. The
casting of the principal actors and other significant elements will determine
marketing strategy. For instance the marketing campaign might focus upon a
major star such as Julia Roberts or Brad Pitt, or a highly recognized narrative, such
as the film adaptations of the massively successful *Harry Potter* books, or it might
showcase spectacular action sequences or special effects, as in the *Matrix* trilogy.
Brand recognition of studios is weak in Hollywood but, possibly uniquely amongst
the contemporary studios, Disney and Pixar have been able to achieve recognition through their distinctive style of computer-generated animation, displayed
in the family-oriented hits *Toy Story* (John Lasseter, 1995, US), *Finding Nemo*
(Andrew Stanton and Lee Unkrich, 2003, US), or *Cars* (John Lasseter and Joe Ranft,
2006, US).

The starting point in developing a marketing campaign for a particular film is the formulation of a marketing strategy. This will involve reviewing the screenplay and production schedule in order to put in place arrangements for the creation of promotional materials, such as the shooting of a "making of" documentary, interviews with the principal actors and creative personnel, and publicity photographs from the set. Taglines are reproduced on posters, summarizing the basic concept of the film, for instance "In space no one can hear you scream" used for *Alien* (Ridley Scott, 1979, UK). The most important and costly element of a campaign is the creation of advertising trailers and subsequent buying of media space or "spots." This usually involves the employment of specialist outside boutique agencies. The aim of the trailer is to condense the film's highlights and showcase its elements, creating a narrative image of the film in the minds of audiences. The boutique agencies will produce a variety of trailers for cinema, television, and internet advertising from either the dailies or the rough cut of the film, if available. Usually different materials will be produced for different markets. Advertising appealing to a particular demographic, for instance, may run in niche media outlets, or different trailers may be produced for overseas territories. These will usually include a 90-second "teaser" trailer, often screened by cinemas many months before release, as well as a full two-minute trailer used for theatrical and television distribution. Trailers can cost upwards of $250,000, and between 20,000 and 30,000 prints are distributed to cinemas in the domestic market. Similarly key art for the graphics of the marketing material – the design that forms the center of all promotional material produced for the film and its print campaign – can cost around $200,000 (Marich, 2004: 10). Print advertisements usually include a striking image from the film or of its stars, and later may carry a favorable quote from a review by a critic as a form of product endorsement. Work will also be conducted upon a film website, often at a pre-production stage of the film, as this is now an important and cost-effective means of film marketing. Creating a launch website allows a potential audience to follow the production process, which can be especially beneficial if the film is a recognizable franchise such as the *Spider-Man* or *Star Wars* series, which already have significant and active fan bases. Film websites often also host exclusive promotional material such as downloads of behind-the-scenes footage, interviews, previews, games, posters, and other free promotional material that can be circulated amongst fans and spread "buzz" about the film.

The largest part of the promotional budget is the media spend – the amount of money paid to purchase media spots. The huge rise in spending on advertising in the last 20 years can be mainly attributed to rises in the cost of reaching a wide audience on network television, now costing up to $600,000 for a 30-second commercial during peak audience viewing times, such as the Thursday evening comedy slot on NBC (Marich, 2004: p. x). The cost of television advertising is measured in levels of gross rating points (GRPs), the level of audience per dollar reached. In a recent study on the effectiveness of film marketing spending it has been argued that the increased cost of television advertising reflects the decreased reach of the media networks due to audience fragmentation (Gilbert-Rolfe,

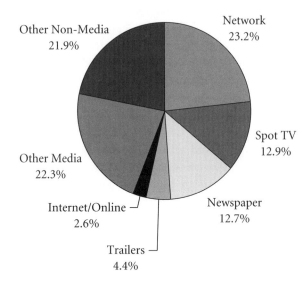

FIGURE 3.3   Distribution of advertising costs in 2005
Source: MPAA, 2005.

Merchant, and Moroian, 2003: 5). In 2003 Nielsen Media Research estimated the Hollywood film studios were the fifth largest spenders on advertising in the United States, paying a total of $3,472 million, of which over $2,500 million was on television, with the next largest spend, a surprisingly high figure of $546 million, on local newspaper advertising. According to Robert Marich (2004) an industry rule of thumb is that the creative costs of marketing are usually about five percent of the total media spend, hence an average $100 million major film will have a marketing budget of around $30 million, of which approximately $1.5 million will be spent on creating marketing materials and the rest spent on advertising spots. James Gilbert-Rolfe et al. (2003: 30) estimate that approximately 85–90 percent of the marketing costs are committed or spent prior to the opening weekend as a way of securing product recognition with audiences. The allocation of spending by the major studios on different media spots can be seen in figure 3.3.

The relative decline in box-office revenues compared to those from DVD and television also means that marketing strategies now conceive of films as potential franchises producing revenues over longer-term life-cycles. This leads to a willingness to invest larger amounts in marketing as a way of brand-building. The theatrical release for a film therefore also functions as an important advertisement for the film in other windows such as DVD and television sales, justifying a high media spend.

Market research

Market research assesses the opportunities and potential success of the marketing strategy for a particular film, and includes previewing, market analysis, and tracking surveys. It will often "test" marketing material, for instance by asking a sample audience to respond to a particular advertising campaign idea or measuring their recall of a trailer. Marich (2004: 26) divides market research into the following practices: (1) concept testing, which evaluates reactions to a film idea and is fairly rare; (2) positioning studies, which analyze a script for marketing opportunities; (3) focus groups, which probe viewers' opinions about a film in small groups prior to release; (4) test screenings, which involve the previewing of films prior to theatrical release; (5) tracking studies, which gauge (often by telephone polling) an audience's awareness of a film on a weekly basis prior to and during theatrical release; (6) advertising testing, which measures responses to marketing materials such as trailers and television advertisements; and finally (7) exit surveys, that measure audience reactions after seeing the film in the cinema. Market research also tends to divide audiences into what is known as "quads" – a quadrant dividing audiences into male/female and aged under or over 25.

Like advertising, the studios usually outsource market research to specialist firms. There are three main market research companies serving the Hollywood studios: the National Research Group (NRG, founded in 1978 by Joe Farrell and part of VNU who also own Nielsen Media Research), MarketCast (part of Reed Elsevier) and Online Testing Exchange (OTX). It is not unusual for a studio to spend over $1 million on market research for a single film, a relatively small investment when $30 million may be spent on advertising and another $60 million on production. Test screenings have garnered the most media attention of the above methods, not least due to well-publicized disputes that sometimes occur when a film tests "badly" and where the creative talent is requested to change the film. For example, the endings of both *Fatal Attraction* (Adrian Lyne, 1987, US) and *The Interpreter* (Sydney Pollack, 2005, US) were changed due to negative feedback from testing. A more recent problem, compounded by the internet, has been the leaking of preview results. If exhibitors hear of poor results they are less likely to book the film for as many screens, meaning it has less chance of being successful. Notoriously the *Ain't it Cool News* website run by Harry Knowles acquired a reputation for breaking news about upcoming Hollywood films in advance of their release. The site came to public attention in 1997 when it posted negative reviews from preview screenings of *Batman and Robin* (Joel Schumacher, 1997, US), claiming to have obtained test screening data from industry insiders. The film performed badly at the box office, leading to speculation about whether the leaked reviews had damaged ticket sales. By contrast *The Blair Witch Project* (Daniel Myrick and Eduardo Sánchez, 1999, US) is often cited as an example of a film that generated huge box-office revenues without any major marketing spend, relying instead on positive word of mouth and an ingenious internet campaign (which included leaking trailers to *Ain't it Cool News*). Its domestic box office of $140.5 million was very impressive against a much-publicized budget of $35,000, although the marketing spend to achieve this probably did eventually run into many hundreds of thousands of dollars.

Publicity

Whilst promotion is the paid-for marketing coverage bought by the studios to keep the product in the mind of the customer, publicity refers to media coverage for which no payment is made. Reviews, interviews, and suchlike do not usually involve a direct payment to the media, and are therefore less directly controlled by the studio and, arguably perhaps, more trusted by audiences. Not that such publicity is entirely independent of Hollywood, however. Studios have long used publicity departments to manage and regulate media coverage of their products, and their ability to control access to stars gives them a degree of editorial control and gatekeeping power (able, for instance, to refuse interviews with unsympathetic journalists). One famous early example of studio manipulation was the much-mythologized publicity stunt that took place in 1910 around the apparent "death" of the star Florence Lawrence. It is claimed that Carl Laemmle, who had lured the star from Biograph to the Independent Motion Picture Corporation (IMP), started a rumor about her death in a car accident. After gaining worldwide media attention he placed an advertisement in *Moving Picture World* announcing "We nail a lie," denouncing the story and including a photo of Lawrence with information about her new film.

Whilst such faked stories announcing the death of stars are rare, Hollywood has always worked closely with the media in order to manage and court publicity. This is unsurprising, as the studios know that carefully placed "exclusives" with film stars are an extremely valuable and cost-effective means of bringing audiences into the cinema. For newspapers, magazines, and television shows such "exclusives" are a reliable means of increasing their own audiences, hence publicity is often of mutual benefit assuming negative coverage can be avoided. Television chat shows, interviews, premiere appearances, and the like are all ways in which star profiles can be leveraged in support of film marketing, and often amount to world tours in support of a particular film. One staple of film publicity is the press junket. This is a very cost-effective way of garnering media coverage and involves the principals (usually the stars and director) being interviewed by a large – often international – assembly of journalists over two to three days in a location such as a prestigious hotel. Junkets tend to involve a series of heavily regulated interviews, where ground rules are stipulated and questions about the film on release are encouraged.

Most major films also have a unit publicist, an on-site publicity manager who is available during the making of the film. Material such as behind-the-scenes footage, interviews with cast and crew, filming of special effects construction, stills of set design, storyboards, and so on are all compiled during the making of the film, as these are not only used for electronic press kits but also for supplementary material for website and DVD promotion. According to Friedman a half-hour behind-the-scenes show can cost from $75,000 to $350,000 (2006: 286). Traditionally the publicity department arranged for still photography of the film production. Whilst this is still a key activity, their role has dramatically widened to become a form of media manager. It is not uncommon for television film review shows, such as the BBC's long-running *Film* series in the UK (which started in 1972), to report from the set of a film whilst in production, helping to create "buzz" about a film and reaching a large television audience at negligible cost.

Other important components of film publicity include film reviews and awards. Film journalists are invited to special previews of the film, and if their reviews are positive, quotes will often feature in subsequent advertising. It is unclear whether negative reviews are able to seriously damage a film's commercial prospects, but it seems likely that this may depend upon the kind of film. For example critics are often seen as more influential over the success of arthouse films than they are for blockbusters, whose audiences are thought to take less notice of reviews. Nonetheless Hollywood publicists build close relationships with film journalists and use the lure of access to creative talent and lavish film premieres as a way of wooing critics. Finally, awards given to talent at ceremonies – most significantly the annual Academy Awards, but also the Golden Globe Awards and the Cannes film festival – are all prized by the studios as they both bring artistic credibility and prestige to the studio and also usually translate into substantially increased revenues in all windows (Wasko, 2003: 209–10).

Distribution and Ancillaries

> The bulk of our business is distribution. Probably three quarters of our employees are involved in generating revenues. Out of the other quarter, most are involved in counting revenues, and then we have about twelve people who are involved in actually making movies. The bulk of our business is financing, distribution and accounting. We have a huge staff that does nothing but license our pictures in all markets around the world.
> – Strauss Zelnick, former President and Chief Operating Officer of 20th Century Fox (Zelnick, 1996: 21)

> Having a blockbuster film allows you to charge more for almost everything else you do that year, because of the way movies are packaged in with other business deals and other films. So the hits are really the locomotives that drag the rest of the train down the tracks. (Gerbrandt, 2001)

As we have seen, during the last 30 years the major Hollywood studios have sought to maintain indirect control over film distribution networks and adopted a saturation release strategy as the most effective way of establishing brand recognition, minimizing their risk and maximizing their revenues. Asu Aksoy and Kevin Robins (1992) have described distribution and finance as the "critical hubs" of Hollywood, so important are they to the industry. Virtually all films that are widely distributed are distributed through the major studios. Although about three-quarters of US productions are "independent" in the sense that they are not financed by the majors, these films also need to be distributed by the major studios if they are to gain access to marketing and distribution techniques such as a saturation release and high-budget media advertising. Independent producers often view a distribution deal with a major studio as a prerequisite to obtaining financing for production, and many independent production companies obtain such agreements by doing pre-production development for the majors, who often then have "first-look" options on new projects. Furthermore acquisitions are frequently made of films that are completed and produced outside of the studio and then distributed by the majors. These are termed "negative pick-ups" and comprise a substantial part of studio output, often outnumbering the studio's own production slates and offering an attractive risk-sharing alternative to in-house productions.

The studios' distribution divisions are highly profitable in their own right. The charges levied by Hollywood distributors, including upon their own films, are nearly always far more lucrative for the studios than the direct profits returned from the pictures themselves, although they are extremely coy about revealing exact figures. To understand why this should be the case we first need to explore the process of film distribution. A simplified description is as follows: producers make a deal with a distribution company (usually a division of a major) to book their film in cinemas. This will usually involve a run of two to six weeks with a sliding scale of payments made to both the distributor and exhibitor (the theater) and a minimum guaranteed to the former ("the floor"). The exhibitors deduct the "nut" from the weekly "gross" (box-office receipts) to pay towards the cinema's weekly overheads, although they primarily rely upon massive mark-ups on soft drinks and confectionery for their revenues. The distributors of the film collect the "rental" receipts (box office minus the nut and minus the sliding percentage for the exhibitor) and collect a distribution fee charged for releasing the film. Major distributors then receive a substantial percentage of the gross, usually starting at around 60–70 percent in the first week and falling to 30–40 percent later, when the arrangement tips back in favor of the exhibitor. The distributor also deducts marketing costs and overheads such as interest charges. Finally, fees for any gross participants (personnel whose contracts give them a percentage of the gross box-office revenues) are deducted, and the remaining revenue is returned to the producer. These are termed "net profits," and from these the producer can theoretically pay net profit participants. However, as we shall see, in theatrical release films rarely declare any "back-end" net profits due to the many "off-the-top" deductions listed. This does not mean, of course, that the Hollywood studios receive no profit, only that the revenues made from the theatrical release are primarily channeled back to the studio in the form of distribution charges, an accounting sleight of hand.

In addition to the theatrical release, the major Hollywood studios – as the above quotes by the industry insiders suggest – generate substantial additional revenues through ancillary markets. According to a recent study, domestic theatrical box office grosses now represent less than 15 percent of the total revenues, with the remaining 85 percent from these so-called "ancillary" markets (Gilbert-Rolfe, Merchant, and Moroian, 2003: 65). The word ancillary is thus somewhat misleading, as ancillaries can include the international theatrical market, DVD and video, pay television and network syndication, and further windows for films and related spin-off products. As table 3.3 shows, in the case of the hugely successful *Spider-Man*

TABLE 3.3   Counting the revenues of the *Spider-Man* franchise ($m)

		Spider-Man	*Spider-Man 2*
Production budget		139	200
P&A budget			
	US	50	57
	estimated worldwide	100	110
Box-office gross			
	US	403.7	373.5
	worldwide	821.7	783.5
US TV rights			
	Fox, TBS/TNT	60	
	Fox, FX		50
Related tie-ins			
toy sales licensing revenue split with Marvel		109	
marketing deal with Burger King			40
US DVD revenue			
	to July 2004	338.8	
	to end 2004		162
US VHS revenue			
	to July 2004	89.2	
	to end 2004		11

Source: Nash, 2005, 2006.

franchise, the success in theatrical markets led to a "tent-pole" effect, supporting revenues from other windows, including merchandising and television rights. Put simply, the success of the films in theaters directly fed their success in other markets. The significance of DVD as an important source of income is evident in the table, and revenue from windows such as DVD sell-through and television rights continue to accrue well into the future, returning profits to the studio and gross participants of the film.

This strategy of releasing a film over time across different media windows is known as "windowing." Traditionally it follows a predetermined sequence – the theatrical release is followed by licensing to pay cable and satellite distributors, home video/DVD, and television networks. The timing of these windows is important, and marketing strategy will be closely linked to the timings of the various releases. Recent trends, however, have closed the time difference between windows, in part an effect of industry attempts to combat illicit internet downloading of films. Industry commentators have speculated about whether in the near future the major studios will adopt similar models for film distribution over the internet, with the introduction of new payment mechanisms (Silver and Alpert, 2003; Taylor, 2006). Recent innovations in the internet distribution of music, such as the commercial

FIGURE 3.4 *Spider-Man* (2002), reaping the revenues across all exhibition windows. Produced by Ian Bryce and Laura Ziskin; distributed by Columbia; directed by Sam Raimi

success of Apple's iTunes music store, and the widespread take-up of broadband internet access in the US, suggest that similar mechanisms for the downloading of films by payment transaction will become increasingly important as sources of revenue for the Hollywood studios in the near future.

Distribution and Creative Accounting

> I'm not interested in box-office and I never have been. I'm interested in profitability.
> – Sherry Lansing, former Paramount Chairman and CEO (cited in Epstein, 2005: 125)

To understand why most films do not make any net profit, yet Hollywood thrives, we need to consider Hollywood's so called "creative accounting" in more detail (Daniels, Leedy, and Sills, 1998). As we have seen, net profits give little indication of the overall profitability of a film. The accounting amortization and profit-participation procedures adopted during the last two decades mean that the studios have an incentive to reinvest (and add these charges) so revenues can continually be offset against ongoing costs, thus avoiding tax and pay-outs to net participants. In an astute analysis of financial accounting in the film and television industries, Harold Vogel has shown, by comparing the balance sheet of *Who Framed Roger Rabbit?* (Robert Zemeckis, 1988, US) with that for *Commando* (Mark L. Lester, 1985, US), that a higher-grossing film may in fact make a "net loss" while a film which sold far few tickets may record a profit (2001: 132). Despite grossing over $200 million in worldwide theatrical revenue, television rights, and home video, the former film declared a net loss of nearly $20 million after distribution fees, marketing costs, production costs, interest on capital, and gross participations and deferments were taken into account. The second film, despite grossing only $65 million, actually made a $2.7 million profit, due to its much lower participation and deferments costs and a lower interest on capital due to its smaller budget. As revenues are top-sliced so early in the accounting process, then "failures" are not uncommon. However due to lucrative "first dollar gross" deductions by distributors, these failures can be extremely profitable for the distribution divisions of the major studios.

A more recent example of a "successful failure" is *Forrest Gump* (Robert Zemeckis, 1994, US), which despite grossing $382 million domestically declared a reported net "loss" of $62 million (Pfeiffer, Capettini, and Whittenburg, 1997: 320). The calculations for this "loss" were as follows. From $191 million in gross receipts (after the exhibitor deductions of 50 percent of revenues) the distributor Paramount charged a distribution "cost" (that included P&A) of $67.2 million, plus a further distribution fee of 32 percent of receipts (another $61.1 million) and interest overheads on the distribution cost of 10 percent (another $6.7 million). Gross participants (principally star Tom Hanks and director Robert Zemeckis) received 16 percent of gross revenues at $30.6 million, and the studio deducted an overhead of 15 percent or $14.6 million as well as an additional interest charge for financing the film of $6 million. This left a loss of $62 million once the production (negative) costs of $66.8 million had been deducted. The film therefore declared a net loss despite returning substantial revenues to the studio through distribution ($128.3 million) and finance ($21.3 million). This brings to mind Arnold Schwarzenegger's speech at the 1998 Academy Awards, where he joked that so extraordinary was the box-office success of *Titanic* (James Cameron, 1997, US), the highest-grossing film of all time, that even the Hollywood film industry could not believably argue that it had made a loss.

The relationship between distributors and exhibitors in terms of box-office revenue also gives studios a far larger share of box office in the early weeks of release

FIGURE 3.5 *Forrest Gump* (1994), a "successful failure." Produced by Wendy Finerman, Steve Starkey, and Steve Tisch; distributed by Paramount; directed by Robert Zemeckis

and therefore incentivizes a high marketing spend and wide saturation release. Furthermore, the power of high-profile creative talent creates an upward push on costs, as the gross participants, high distribution costs, and overheads strip out revenues and prevent films from ever moving into net profits, despite being profitable ventures overall. As Vogel comments:

> The existence of profitable studio enterprises in the face of apparent losses for the "average" picture can be reconciled only when it is realized that the heart of a studio's business is distribution and financing and that, therefore, the brunt of marketing and production-cost risk is often deflected and/or transferred to (sometimes tax-sheltered) outside investors and producers. (2001: 97)

Understanding Hollywood's profitability requires a close scrutiny of its arcane accounting procedures and costs, such as this practice of amortizing costs against receipts over time. If gross receipts are misleading, "net profits" are even more so, merely reflecting what remains of gross receipts after deductions of the distribution fees, expenses, taxes, overheads, interest, negative costs, deferments, all gross participations, and a number of other charges have been deducted. In the *Art Buchwald vs. Paramount* legal case (1990), the film *Coming to America* (John Landis, 1988, US) grossed $350 million but declared a net deficit, leading to legal action by writer Art Buchwald. During the case the star Eddie Murphy famously referred to net participation as "monkey points," so unlikely were they ever to declare a profit. The actual profitability of major films is thus almost impossible to calculate, as it is necessary to untangle all charges and revenue streams (present and deferred) that flow to studios, stars, distributors, and all other parties, hence the common saying within the industry that net profit is that which is left to be apportioned after everyone has participated in and profited from the grosses.

Conclusions

This chapter has described contemporary Hollywood's marketing and distribution activities. Identifiable trends over the last two decades include an escalation of spending on marketing and the normalization of a saturation release schedule that allows only around six weeks for theatrical release. Marketing positions each film in order to attract an audience in the opening three-day weekend and avoid being forced out by other products, hence the symbolic significance of the opening three-day weekend box-office figures. In terms of revenues the theatrical release has been displaced by other windows as Hollywood's core sector although, as we have seen, its precise financial contribution depends largely upon how we calculate profitability. Cinema exhibition retains an important price-setting and marketing role for these windows and is the most significant determinant of their success. Extensive media coverage of Hollywood means that the opening box-office performance is also often seen as a judgment about popularity and quality, meaning that opening weekend grosses also convey word-of-mouth information to consumers. Thus theatrical box office may in part be exactly that: theater, the "show" of Hollywood's business, a marketing platform for a product that reaps its major profits in other windows such as DVD, pay television, and network syndication over long periods of time.

The preceding discussion has also stressed the need to conceptualize Hollywood as a *rights* industry. The major studios are conglomerates that maintain their economic power primarily through their access to and control over global distribution networks, where these rights are exploited (Miller et al., 2005). As much as Hollywood makes movies, Hollywood is in the business of acquiring, licensing, and regulating media rights. Strategic alliances with international distributors, and their own distribution divisions overseas, enable the major Hollywood studios to sell each film at a different price and maintain arm's-length control over international film markets by regulating the supply and timing of their products. Due to both geographical and technological changes, such as the consumer adoption of DVD and the opening of new markets (for example, China), Hollywood's content libraries have dramatically increased in value in the last two decades. This allows the risk of current productions to be continually offset against the flow of revenues from their back catalogs. As revenues from the international box office often now exceed domestic box office, and revenues from ancillaries often exceed box office itself, control over distribution – whether in cinemas, on television, or on the internet, domestic and international – is and will continue to be of primary importance to the Hollywood film industry for the foreseeable future.

ACKNOWLEDGMENTS

I would like to thank Bruce Nash of *The Numbers* (www.the-numbers.com) and Nash Information Services for providing me with Hollywood industry data.

REFERENCES

Aksoy, A., and K. Robins (1992) "Hollywood for the 21st Century: Global Competition for Critical Mass in Image Markets," *Cambridge Journal of Economics*, 16(1), pp. 1–22.

Balides, C. (2000) "Jurassic Post-Fordism: Tall Tales of Economics in the Theme Park," *Screen*, 41(2), pp. 139–60.

Bordwell, D., J. Staiger, and K. Thompson (1985) *The Classical Hollywood Cinema: Film Style and Mode of Production to 1960*. London: Routledge.

Daniels, B., D. Leedy, and S. Sills (1998) *Movie Money: Understanding Hollywood's (Creative) Accounting Practices*. Los Angeles: Silman-James Press.

De Vany, A. (2004) *Hollywood Economics: How Extreme Uncertainty Shapes the Film Industry*. London: Routledge.

Earnest, O. J. (1985) "*Star Wars*: A Case Study of Motion Picture Marketing," in B. A. Austin (ed.), *Current Research in Film, Audiences, Economics and Law*, vol. 1. Norwood, NJ: Ablex Publishing, pp. 1–18.

Epstein, E. J. (2005) *The Big Picture: Money and Power in Hollywood.* New York: Random House.

Fellman, D. R. (2006) "Theatrical Distribution," in J. E. Squire (ed.), *The Movie Business Book,* 3rd edn. Maidenhead: Open University Press, pp. 362–74.

Friedman, R. G. (2006) "Motion Picture Marketing," in J. E. Squire (ed.), *The Movie Business Book,* 3rd edn. Maidenhead: Open University Press, pp. 282–99.

Gerbrandt, L. (2001) "Interview with PBS," online at <http://www.pbs.org/wgbh/pages/frontline/shows/hollywood/interviews/gerbrandt.html> (accessed July 31, 2006).

Gilbert-Rolfe, J., U. Merchant, and V. Moroian (2003) *Drivers of Marketing Spending in Motion Pictures.* Los Angeles: UCLA Anderson School of Management.

Gomery, D. (2003) "The Hollywood Blockbuster: Industrial Analysis and Practice," in J. Stringer (ed.), *Movie Blockbusters.* London: Routledge, pp. 72–83.

Guber, P. (2001) "Interview with PBS," online at <http://www.pbs.org/wgbh/pages/frontline/shows/hollywood/interviews/guber.html> (accessed July 31, 2006).

Marich, R. (2004) *Marketing to Moviegoers.* London: Focal Press.

Meehan, E. R. (1991) " 'Holy Commodity Fetish, Batman!': The Political Economy of the Commercial Intertext," in R. E. Pearson and W. Uricchio (eds.), *The Many Lives of Batman: Critical Approaches to a Superhero and his Media.* London: Routledge, pp. 47–65.

Miller, T., N. Govil, J. McMurria, R. Maxwell, and T. Wang (2005) *Global Hollywood 2.* London: British Film Institute.

MPAA (2003) *US Entertainment Industry: 2002 MPA Market Statistics.* Los Angeles: Motion Picture Association of America.

MPAA (2004) *US Entertainment Industry: 2003 MPA Market Statistics.* Los Angeles: Motion Picture Association of America.

MPAA (2005) *US Entertainment Industry: 2004 MPA Market Statistics.* Los Angeles: Motion Picture Association of America.

MPAA (2006) *US Entertainment Industry: 2005 MPA Market Statistics.* Los Angeles: Motion Picture Association of America.

Nash, B. (2005) "Research," email from *The Numbers*/Nash Information Services to the author, December 7, 2005.

Nash, B. (2006) "Research," email from *The Numbers*/Nash Information Services to the author, January 9, 2006.

Pfeiffer, G., R. Capettini, and G. Whittenburg (1997) "*Forrest Gump* – Accountant: A Study of Accounting in the Motion Picture Industry," *Journal of Accounting Education,* 14(3), pp. 319–44.

Silver, J., and F. Alpert (2003) "Digital Dawn: A Revolution in Movie Distribution?" *Business Horizons* September–October, pp. 57–64.

Taylor, P. (2006) "Coming Soon: Films on File," *Financial Times,* May 31, p. 12.

Vogel, H. L. (2001) *Entertainment Industry Economics.* Boston, MA: Cambridge University Press.

Wasko, J. (2003) *How Hollywood Works.* London: Sage.

Wyatt, J. (1994) *High Concept: Movies and Marketing in Hollywood.* Austin: University of Texas Press.

Zelnick, S. (1996) "Twentieth Century Fox," in R. Ohmann (ed.), *Making and Selling Culture.* Hanover, NH: Wesleyan University Press, pp. 18–33.

CHAPTER 4

THEATRICAL EXHIBITION: ACCELERATED CINEMA

CHARLES ACLAND

Individualism rules the world of entertainment. The contemporary environment of mobile, hand-held, and personalized technological trinkets is a most astounding manifestation of this dominant common sense. New leisure commodities boast of their contribution to an über-individualism, the extremes of which suggest an omniscient role for every lowly creature toting a cellphone, an MP3 player, or a PlayStation Portable (PSP). *Newsweek* (2005) mirrored this direction when they adorned the cover of their "Future of Entertainment" issue with a track-suited model holding a cellphone, TV remote, iPod, PSP, laptop computer, and electronic day-minder in each of her six hands. This goddess figure, arms extended in a radiating pose, sits cross-legged and appears to be levitating, perhaps ironically referencing Hinduism. A sky-blue backdrop creates an impression of meditative serenity. The gravity-defining human form becomes command central for desires that exceed the grasp of a mere two hands. The image of technological abundance, and the selection it implies, is ultimately one of universal control located at the site of the single person.

With the imagined centrality of the consuming and controlling individual, it is no wonder communal and shared entertainment seems out of step. Live theater, music, and sport thrive, but so too does the sale of private box-seats and exclusive corporate engagements for top performers. "Free" broadcast television is finally succumbing to video-on-demand, personal video recorders, and à la carte cable channel selection. Privately subscribed satellite radio, wherein companies market their services as access to a bottomless collection of records, challenges the public-ness of radio broadcast. Most visibly, and germane to this chapter, moviegoing has been battered for years, often with popular and industry critics alike becoming Cassandras to herald the imminent burial of this beloved practice. Films on videotape and DVD can be owned in multitudes and collected to reflect individual tastes, home theaters can be tailored to personal preferences, and living-room showtimes can be infinitely variable. With such individually mastered and orchestrated viewing conditions, how could there still be a place for the trudging, weather- and transport-dependent, journey to the movie theater, giving oneself over to the pre-

FIGURE 4.1   "Future of Entertainment" cover, *Newsweek* (2005). Whither exhibition? Photo by C. J. Burton. Copyright 2005 Newsweek, Inc. All rights reserved. Reprinted with permission

determined schedule and surrendering to the unpredictability of public contact? And during flu season, no less!

With this in mind, public screens are changing, responding to different opportunities and occasions for moving image culture. Some may still weep about the fractured hegemony of celluloid, but motion pictures have been divided among broadcast and video technologies for ages. The fact that moviegoing competes for a place among an ever-widening array of viewing situations is nothing new or surprising. Nonetheless, the current ubiquity of moving images is impressive. They appear as added features for cellphones, PSPs offer feature films uniquely compatible with their hand-held screen, and the MP3 market expects to do for television what it did for music. CinemaNow and Movielink are currently the top download providers for movies. Demonstrating the importance of telephony for film circulation, Movielink is part of the AOL empire and grew from the Moviefone ticketing service (*Screen Digest*, 2005b). Apple iTunes and Amazon.com have also added movie downloads to their services (Avery, 2006). Expanding moving image circulation takes unusual turns that challenge our presumptions about exhibition. *Variety* cheekily claimed that, with 37 percent of Hollywood's DVD sales, Wal-Mart should be understood as the "largest distrib outlet in the film biz" (Learmonth, 2005: 1). Even McDonald's tested DVD rental kiosks in 100 Denver area restaurants (Amdur, 2004), and Starbucks has struck a deal with Lions Gate to promote and sell DVDs of select films (Gray and Kelly, 2006). These expanded windows of distribution and exhibition alter the ordinary landscape of moving image culture, along with the structure of the entertainment business, which confronts intermediality at the level of industry, technology, and consumption. Films generate revenue outside of cinemas, theatrical runs can benefit other exhibition windows, and exhibitors are in a multimedia business beyond feature film presentation. Most importantly, these factors alter our notions of film spectatorship and the meaning of movie-going's cultural and economic vitality.

This chapter will describe some of the prominent characteristics of contemporary film exhibition, showing how the very structure of industry and cultural practice is bending to economic and technological change. Focusing on the US context, four developments will be addressed: (1) changing ideas about moviegoing audiences; (2) the concentration of screens in terms of geography and ownership; (3) release strategies and their impact upon the life-cycle of film; and (4) the coming conversion to digital cinema.

The current US film industry was profoundly altered by the return to the exhibition business by major studios Universal, Columbia, Warner Bros, and Paramount, beginning in 1986. As a result, such corporate entities became increasingly interested in the entire lifespan of a film as it moves from format to format. This ownership shake-up prompted a sector-wide reassessment of the particular nature of the service offered by movie theaters, with many settling on the need to upscale the cinemas themselves and to reshape the moviegoing experience to be distinctive and desirable enough for people to leave the comfort of the living-room couch and proximity to the refrigerator. The result was the multiplex building and refurbishing of the 1990s. This so-called megaplex boom introduced as industry standard cup-holders, state-of-the-art sound systems, and larger lobby space where one might find restaurants, bars, party rooms, and video arcades. Most significantly, this industry makeover increased the number of screens at a given site, as well as in total. This was initially meant to lead to a wider slate of film titles, though this never really came to pass. Instead, the megaplex era reduced the number of theaters, as locations with two to four screens closed in favor of double-digit screen venues.

Consequently, we have seen the expansion of start-times, with the same film appearing on several screens, a feature that appeals to individualized convenience. Multiple start-times funnel cinematic taste such that opening-night crowds can be shuffled from one sold-out performance to another screening half an hour or so later.

Megaplexes cater to other forms of individualized experience. The wider variety of concessions, from the highbrow bulk fancy candies to the plebeian nachos and melted cheese, flatters different palates. The larger, high-backed seats and steeper grade of the rows suggest semi-isolation from other audience members as one sinks into an approximated intimacy with the screen. The most pronounced version of this private-in-public cinematic experience has been the pricey VIP screens at some chains, with sofa-like seating in small auditoriums. These modifications sought to bring exhibition into line with an expanding range of audiovisual entertainment, doing so by marking the irreproducible qualities of megaplex spectatorship and by making moviegoing consistent with the streams of individualistic, convenience-driven models of cultural consumption. This upscaling of cinemagoing is further evidenced by the steady increase in ticket price, and it routinely gets credit for audience increases or spikes in box-office revenue. The logic, however, appeared fatally flawed once waves of theater chains had to file for bankruptcy protection in the early 2000s, largely due to the over-extension of cinema building and refurbishing.

Film exhibition and distribution is, ultimately, charged with the task of propelling texts and viewers through the world. As theatrical exhibition moves people to a specially designed location for communal viewing, its circulation of film is to add up to the movement of revenue and profit. Importantly, movement is central. Broadly speaking, culture is not a static museum of precious artifacts, pinned behind glass or suspended in formaldehyde. Taking cues from Raymond Williams (1977), it consists in the ordinary, "whole," patterns of practice. Williams's work challenges us to capture and accommodate the range of dynamism cultural practice represents. Culture circulates and travels, carrying ideas, stories, and things across time and through space. This restlessness has been investigated by Walter Benjamin (1936) in the cult and exhibition value of art forms, Harold Innis (1951) in time- and space-bias media, and Greg Urban (2001) in the replication and dissemination functions of culture. Their differing approaches and conclusions still settle upon the consequences of the ways culture moves and to what broad effect.

And, no different from other cultural commodities, motion pictures have a life-cycle through which their cultural and economic impact rises and falls. This life-cycle encompasses the range of media forms through which a cultural text travels, something that has been elaborated with respect to popular music by Will Straw (1990) and Keir Keightley (2004). For many distributors, the later stages of a film commodity are more lucrative than theatrical release. This is definitely the case for the major studios, who saw about a quarter of their 1996 feature film revenue (24.5 percent) coming from theatrical rentals, with 28.7 percent from DVD sales, 23.8 percent from video sales for rental, and 23.1 percent from other sources, including television and pay-per-view sales, for a total of $11.3 billion. In 2004 this had become 47.9 percent DVD sales, 23.1 percent theatrical, 12 percent video rental,

FIGURE 4.2   Façade of the AMC Del Amo 18 megaplex in Torrance, California.
Courtesy of AMC

and 17.1 percent other for a total of $19.1 billion (Belson, 2005: C1). In organizing the relations between media in this life-cycle, exhibition, and its sister sector distribution, bundle the appearance of some films, accelerate the arrival and departure of releases, and leave a greater waiting period for others. Doing so shapes the *current cinema*, that temporally defined set of "new" films, or what we commonly call those "in theaters now" and which are temporarily available nowhere else.

The reconfiguration of film exhibition is not unique to our era. Indeed, there has been mutability in film performance contexts, practices, and technologies throughout the entire course of cinema history. Not giving this fact full consideration has been a lacuna for film and media studies, which has instead tended to assume stability in exhibition. Only recently has a sub-area loosely designated "exhibition studies" emerged to document the historical making and remaking of

cinema's exhibition contexts. Research has drawn from political and economic exam-
inations of the film industry and from cultural theory's attention to the everyday
practices of moving image consumption. In these studies we find the particularity
of public cinematic exhibition and reception forged by strategically drawing connections with some cultural and leisure practices, while turning away from others
(see Hansen, 1991; Gomery, 1992; Waller, 1995; Stokes and Maltby, 1999, 2001, 2004;
Jancovich and Faire, 2003; Grieveson, 2004; Stewart, 2005; and Allen, Maltby, and
Stokes, forthcoming).

With this emphasis on the joint economic and cultural dimensions of theatrical
exhibition, and with a conceptual focus on exhibition's role in the movement of
film culture, I ask the following: What special role does theatrical exhibition play
in the overall life-cycle of films? What will that special place of moviegoing look
like given that the same texts will be versioned for an ever-expanding array of audiovisual attractions? And what of the economic enterprise invested in essentially a
single point in the process, i.e., theatrical exhibition?

The Audience May Not Be Listening

The most pronounced uncertainty for contemporary exhibition has been a slide
in attendance. While overall assessments vary, exhibitors see a long history of
hemorrhaging audiences as habitual moviegoing becomes occasional and irregular,
having been abandoned for several successive generations of television-related
entertainments. The high point in US moviegoing of the mid-1940s is now but a
twinkling and ever-receding memory of a golden era. Recently, US attendance slipped
6.3 percent between 2002 and 2004. Still, between 1993 and 2003 the US witnessed
nearly 19 percent growth in admissions (MPAA, 2005: 7). Western Europe and
the Americas account for a clear majority of world box-office revenue, with the
latter taking 47 percent of total world box office (*Screen Digest*, 2005i: 271).
Consequently, the moviegoing practices of those regions steer the decision-making
of the major film corporations. Moreover, rising ticket prices keep money flowing.
For instance, average US ticket prices increased 16.6 percent from $6.04 in 2003 to
$7.04 in 2004 (*Screen Digest*, 2005i: 273). So, even though attendance may fall, box
office can still climb. This was the case for 2004, in which year domestic US box
office rose to a record high of $9.5 billion (or second highest, in adjusted dollars,
after 2002), even though admissions fell 2.1 percent from 2003 (*Screen Digest*, 2005i:
275).

Aggregate market data about film exhibition grounds corporate decision-making,
and every twitch in audience patterns sends shock waves through stock markets
and studio boardrooms. But it does not stay confined to those air-conditioned
cloisters; it also forms and circulates popular impressions of the practice itself.
The entertainment business has expanded its presence in popular news. Books like
Dade Hayes and Jonathan Bing's (2004a) *Open Wide: How Hollywood Box Office
Became a National Obsession*, which chronicles the industry activity surrounding

the theatrical release of three US films, attempt to keep the public abreast of what is ostensibly industry information. A convenient illustration of these changes is a comparison between two of Peter Biskind's books. The earlier *Easy Riders, Raging Bulls: How the Sex-Drugs-and-Rock 'n' Roll Generation Saved Hollywood* (1998) is a gossipy retelling of the rise of the New Hollywood cinema of the 1960s and 1970s as a story of passionate auteurs. The sequel, *Down and Dirty Pictures: Miramax, Sundance, and the Rise of Independent Film* (2004), is an equally gossipy narrative about American film in the 1980s and 1990s, but it shifts the focus from filmmakers to dealmakers, that is, producers, agents, and distributors. The industry is the story in this later work. In this context, a broad reading public shares the fits and fears of the industry, becoming a figure of parody with the father in *Win a Date with Tad Hamilton!* (Robert Luketic, 2004, US) who, though living in West Virginia, sees himself as a Hollywood insider, quoting box-office expectations and sporting a "Project Greenlight" T-shirt.

While reasons to celebrate or chastise market exploitation and shareholder wealth abound, summer 2005 offered special anxiety for North American film exhibitors and distributors. For 19 weeks in a row, weekend domestic box office was lower than the same weekend of the previous year. This broke the 20-year record of 17 diminished weekend grosses from 1985 (Nielsen EDI, 2005). Successive Monday newspapers presented dim comparisons with the previous year's weekend performance and popular magazines turned to trade reporters for explanations, as *Entertainment Weekly* did when they published a special report from *Variety* stalwart Hayes (2005). Popular media chronicled the ulcerated stomachs and sweaty brows of Hollywood investors through the summer of 2005 as though they were attending to a barometer of national health. Slumping box office and attendance was more than bad economic posture; for some, it marked the global demise of US cultural standing as well as the decrepitude of the cherished cultural institution of moviegoing. During those consecutively diminishing weekends, exhibitors and distributors began to try some novel methods to attract audiences. Theater chain American Multi-Cinemas (AMC) offered a money-back guarantee for *Cinderella Man* (Ron Howard, 2005, US), and major distributor 20th Century Fox enticed groups with a four-for-the-price-of-three deal for *Star Wars Episode III: Revenge of the Sith* (George Lucas, 2005, US) (Kelly, 2005).

In the end, the 2005 box-office disappointment captured in trade and popular publications shows more than diminishing returns and inflated expectations. It presents the importance of the art of empirical portraiture. Moviegoing may consist in fond memories of intimacy, wondrously ornate venues, and surprising emotive experiences. Or it may be made up of stormy mid-screening departures, uninspiring generic surroundings, and boredom. But for members of a class of entrepreneurs, invested in the profit-making possibilities of theatrical exhibition, moviegoing exists as an agglomeration of ticket sales, concessions purchases, and cheap labor. Consequently, eyes fix upon consumer trends evident in statistical representations of moviegoing. Audience monitoring and box-office tabulations are decisive features in the construction of an impression of moviegoing. The key measurements include attendance numbers, grosses, ticket prices, and average box office per screen. Together, these indicators guide an overall sense of market vitality relative to competing films, exhibitors, and distributors. These are the much-debated terms of success for exhibitors and distributors, which in turn become what general movie fans – those ersatz "insiders" – understand as the triumph or defeat of a title or a summer.

Under-appreciated elements in the commercial film business, then, are those companies who compile and circulate this much-coveted information. Entertainment Data Incorporated (EDI) has been the premier box-office data-gathering agency since its establishment in 1976. Its methods relied heavily upon weekly waves of phone calls to individual theaters. Recognizing the rising value of cultural consumption information, AC Nielsen purchased EDI in 1997, and four years later Dutch publishing and data analysis giant VNU acquired AC Nielsen (for detail on VNU, see Miller et al., 2005). Competitor Rentrak appeared on the scene in 2003, growing from a videotape rental tracking firm founded in 1988 into a high-tech box-office monitoring agency, to challenge Nielsen EDI's supremacy. Though Nielsen EDI had developed an elaborate international network of box-office tracking and cross-media analysis through its parent VNU, Rentrak offered a system that accessed exhibitors' cash registers to track box office in real time. Rentrak's method featured speedier results than the weekend phone calls of Nielsen EDI, not to mention circumventing the potential embellishments of self-reported data. The real-time reporting became a quick hit with screen-obsessed studio executives at Fox, who were the first to sign on to watch Rentrak's weekly horse race of winning films. Nielsen EDI began to add similar real-time tracking, ultimately firing 60 percent of its call-center staff in October 2004 (Snyder, 2004b).

Unlike Rentrak, which provides information to corporate subscribers only, some of Nielsen EDI's composite information appears in newspapers and magazines. Consequently, Nielsen EDI's changing methodology was nothing less than a massive shift in the *public* understanding of weekly snapshots of theatrical exhibition. It represented a sea-change in how interested industry participants and popular audiences make economic activity visible and comprehensible. An immediate comparison can be made with the music industry's adoption of SoundScan. There too the networking of music retail cash registers replaced the traditional phone call reporting, and the results were nothing less than dramatic. Overnight, presumably under-represented and marginal genres appeared to be substantial segments of the popular music market (see McCourt and Rothenbuhler, 1997).

The issue here is not one of accuracy, and I don't dispute evidence of an overall decline in 2005 box office. The issue concerns methods of data-gathering and analysis. Quite simply, one cannot compare directly data gathered via two different methods. Throughout the summer of 2005, trade papers were awash with articles bemoaning the decrease in weekend box office compared to 2004. Those publications noted the anomaly of the unusually strong independent films *The Passion of the Christ* (Mel Gibson, 2004) and *Fahrenheit 9/11* (Michael Moore, 2004), which, if taken out of the mix, made 2005 box office not seem off pace (Bart, 2005: 1; Snyder,

2005: 6). Representatives of theatrical organizations went to great pains to restore faith in their sector, pointing to long-term gains rather than short-term dips (Lichtman, 2005). Not once have I seen an article explain that the two years represent two different research methodologies. As such, Nielsen EDI's claims – e.g. a record number of consecutive weeks or weekends of decreasing box office for 2005 when compared to 2004 – are of limited value. Of the two companies, only Rentrak can fully compare the two years, and they have not released their 2005 tallies to the public. In short, industry statistics, and how information businesses gather and circulate data, are powerful determinants of what one sees, records, and assesses of moviegoing practice. They show the discursive construction of the audience, revealing the process by which this ephemeral cultural practice leaves traces. Industry information as tabulated and interpreted by outfits like Nielsen EDI and Rentrak are concrete mechanisms that materialize market changes and abstract notions of success, becoming the basis upon which exhibitors make decisions about their business.

Concentrating Ownership and the Changing Life-Cycle of Films

Whatever changes are in process, we are far from consigning theatrical exhibition to the dust. Table 4.1 shows the top box-office revenue countries for 2004, with a world total of $24 billion. Significantly, these ten countries represent 79.4 percent of that total, with the domestic US market representing half of that. This level of concentration of revenue sources shows the highly competitive nature of just a few markets, and of the US market especially. Relatively small shifts in the US, then, become tremors felt by a sizeable portion of the international industry. Paying

TABLE 4.1   Ten highest box-office revenue countries, 2004

	$ billion	% change from 2003*	% share of total world box office
USA	9.539	0.5	39.7
Japan	1.950	3.8	8.1
France	1.411	15.3	5.9
UK	1.411	3.7	5.9
Germany	1.111	5.0	4.6
Spain	0.860	8.2	3.6
Italy	0.718	10.3	3.0
India	0.707	6.9	2.9
Canada	0.699	−4.1	2.9
South Korea	0.676	7.9	2.8
Total top ten	19.082		
World total	24.000		

* As measured in their respective national currencies.
Source: *Screen Digest*, 2005i: 271.

TABLE 4.2   Fifteen countries with the highest number of screens, 2004

	Screens	% change from 2003	Screens per million people
China	38,496	−8.3	29.2
USA	36,652	2.4	124.8
India	10,500	−4.5	9.5
France	5,302	0.1	88.1
Germany	4,870	0.0	59.0
Spain	4,390	3.2	102.8
Italy	3,762	3.7	65.0
UK	3,475	1.2	57.7
Mexico	3,248	1.6	31.2
Canada	3,190	13.0	99.9
Japan	2,825	5.4	22.1
Brazil	1,988	9.4	9.9
Russia	1,986	9.8	13.4
Australia	1,909	0.1	94.9
South Korea	1,400	23.9	29.1

Source: Screen Digest, 2005i: 270.

attention to the dispersion and volume of cinema screens reveals how selective and specialized moviegoing has become. Table 4.2 presents the 15 countries with the highest number of cinema screens. Comparing screens per million people shows us the variation between the highly screened context of the US, with 124.8/million to the historically "underscreened" country of Brazil with 9.9/million. Most pronounced is the degree of global concentration of movie theaters. These 15 countries account for 85.7 percent of the world total, and about a quarter are in the US.

The geographic concentration of screens has accompanied a dramatic concentration of movie theaters into larger chains. The five chains with the most screens in Canada and the US at the beginning of 2005 were Regal (6,521 screens), AMC (3,548), Cinemark (3,257), Loews (2,176), and Carmike (2,175). Together, these chains held 17,677 screens, or 44.4 percent of the total 39,842 screens in those two countries. Compare this to 1995, where the top five chains (Carmike, UATC, AMC, Cineplex Odeon, and Cinemark USA) together held 9,376 screens, representing 31.7 percent of the 29,613 total screens (MPAA, 2001; Statistics Canada, 1999) (see tables 4.3 and 4.4). At the time of writing, AMC and Loews are in the process of merging, making for an even more concentrated American and Canadian exhibition environment.

Traditionally a highly concentrated sector, Canada experienced even further consolidation when the two largest chains merged. In 2005, Cineplex Galaxy acquired Famous Players from its parent Viacom, with the federal competition bureau requiring the sale of 35 theaters (Blackwell, 2005a). When all transactions are complete, Cineplex will have nearly 1,300 screens and over 60 percent market share in

TABLE 4.3 Top ten chains in Canada and the US, January 1, 2005

	Screens	Sites	New screens in 2004
1. Regal Entertainment Group	6,521	560	213
2. AMC Entertainment	3,548	230	33
3. Cinemark USA	3,257	304	160
4. Loews Cineplex Entertainment	2,176	200	−659
5. Carmike Cinemas	2,175	282	−64
6. National Amusements	1,415	115	15
7. Century Theaters	1,000	78	70
8. Famous Players	794	84	−28
9. Cineplex Galaxy	775	86	608
10. Kerasotes Showplace	572	75	28

Source: Boxoffice, 2005.

TABLE 4.4 Top ten chains in Canada and the US, October 19, 1995

	Screens	Sites	New screens in 1995
1. Carmike Cinemas	2,375	520	433
2. UATC	2,333	417	97
3. AMC	1,730	235	94
4. Cineplex Odeon	1,535	329	−90
5. Cinemark USA	1,403	180	189
6. General Cinema	1,200	200	−40
7. National Amusements	979	112	26
8. Regal Cinemas	961	122	257
9. Sony Theaters	900	155	32
10. Hoyts Cinemas	620	88	59

Source: Boxoffice, 1995.

Canada (Blackwell, 2005b). This accounts for about 40 percent of all screens. Empire became the next largest chain, with 403 screens, after acquiring most of those divested by Cineplex, with about 12.6 percent of screens (Screen Digest, 2005c). Thus, two chains control over half the screens in Canada.

The impact of concentration is substantial. There are economies of scale in arranging concessions deals and negotiating terms for film rental. Beyond this, the distribution of screens and the agglomeration of chains tell of the uneven development of cinematic life. Theaters comprise circuits for the flow of moving images, channeling where and in what circumstances first-run feature films appear. Concentration of ownership tips the weight of the cinematic world toward a handful of economic and cultural powers. That world also tips away from a sizeable majority of countries and communities. In other words, contemporary mainstream exhibition is not disappearing. Faced with a proliferation of non-theatrical sites and situations of film consumption, that more reified temple of the cinephile – the movie theater – is ever more tightly bound up with prestige, exclusivity, and urbanity.

One does not have to be a card-carrying cinephilic snob to hold the big-screen experience as the situational ideal for spectatorship. Yet one has to equally admit that, nevertheless, most films are seen – whether enjoyed or disparaged as second-best situations – in other locations, from the cramped, semi-obstructed video projection in airplanes to individualized hand-held PSPs. As a result, we need to think about the velocity of motion pictures as they move from screen to screen, format to format, and hence from a cultural circuit of relative exclusivity to other more accessible circuits. Commercial theaters remain a space of high visibility for a text that may be encountered later in its multimedia life-cycle, as a video, pay-per-view, DVD, VCD, cable, or broadcast commodity. The speed of the traveling film artifact alters the consistency of the related cultural practice and engagement. The three vectors of exhibition temporality are running time of the film performance, length of theatrical run, and schedule of openings (see Acland, 2003). The last two are evident in releasing strategies. A most time-honored strategy is platform releasing, in which a film opens gradually in select venues and cities. In 2003 and 2004, it remained the case that the majority of films released in the US (53 percent) were non-wide releases of less than 500 prints, some of which would be followed by the slow build of platforming (*Screen Digest*, 2004h: 372). This strategy now tends to be associated with smaller-budget films, without large promotion and distribution budgets, or prestige films that count on building critical praise to draw in audiences. The other main strategy is wide releasing. The upper end of this will see films open on 6,000 screens and in several national markets at once. Wide releasing means that there is a simultaneous national and increasingly international presence for a film. In 2003, the average prints per release was 3,469 for the top 70 films in the US, which represented approximately 9.5 percent of domestic screens (*Screen Digest*, 2004e). The prominence of opening weekend saturation releases accounts for the soaring marketing budgets, in turn making greater box-office revenue essential for a profitable return on production investments and fortifying a hit-driven exhibition economy. It is only in the contemporary context of such saturation releasing that a film can boast that it will open "worldwide," as trailers for *The Da Vinci Code* (Ron Howard, 2006, US) proclaimed.

Having said that, the internationalization of US distribution, much touted since the 1990s, has not wavered from a fairly consistent domestic/foreign split of around 50/50 (Groves, 2004c), with some annual variances. *Variety* reporter Don Groves suggested that attention to international releasing was partly due to the rising clamor for the limited number of domestic screens, writing, "One factor driving the day-and-date global campaigns is that the foreign market isn't gridlocked like the Stateside market" (2004a: 8). Industry analysts attribute international day-and-date openings of films, continued multiplexing, and exploitation of high-profile film franchises for the rise of international box office (McNary, 2005). The simultaneous openings in multiple markets can generate fast grosses, and are a bid against piracy, but it is also adds to marketing costs, which averaged $39 million for 2003 (Groves, 2004b).

A consequence of the growing investment in wide releasing has been that the concentration of box office around opening weekends has intensified. The opening weekends for wide-released films accounted for 24.7 percent in 1999, 29.5 percent in 2001, and 30.3 percent in 2003 of total box office, on average (Nielsen EDI, 2004). Films that drew $15 million and more on their opening weekends saw their box-office revenue drop an average of 38 percent by the second weekend in 2000. Four years later, in 2003, that drop was 49 percent. Industry commentators credited this drop to the growing size of saturation openings, the crowding of release schedules with more films, and a general decline in the quality of the works themselves (Snyder, 2004a: 6). The aging of cultural commodities is to be expected, and through time there is a conventional cheapening of the artifact as its original shine dulls. Over the years, libraries clear their shelves of 16mm prints, and video retail and rental outlets manage their backlog with discount bins and cheaper rentals for older tapes and DVDs. Works can be dressed up with the ornamentation of connoisseurship, which is part of the genius of DVD extras, box sets, and collector's editions. In this way, a gilded frame brightens a fading commodity. And rapid drop-off rates are now part of DVD releasing as well (Mohr, 2005: 1). The point is that widening release strategies set the terms for the speedy aging of a film's theatrical release, calling for related strategies of accommodation.

The reigning centrality of opening weekends thus prompts a reconfiguration of commodity life-cycle. The time between theatrical and DVD releases had shrunk to an average of four months and 16 days in 2004 for the major studios (Mohr, 2005: 1). The life-cycle is undergoing even more significant revision in relation to other media. One possible future is manifest in Steven Soderbergh's deal with 2929 Entertainment for six films that would appear in theaters, on DVD, and on cable simultaneously (Mohr, 2005: 1). The theatrical screen is a limited window for audiences, a rare situation for film viewing especially when compared to the expanding timeframe of other formats. It is, however, a primary revenue source for exhibitors, who consequently try to fill up their services with impressive and fast performers. This varies with the differing place of exhibition in overall corporate structure. Disney has been among the most resolute in its disinterest in owning theaters just as AMC is steadfastly a film exhibitor. In contrast Viacom, majority-owned by exhibitor chain National Amusements, owns the broadcaster CBS, Paramount film studio, and has been active in the acquisition of theaters, as well as videotape and DVD rental through the Blockbuster chain. In other words, these are divergent corporate investments in the life-cycle of film commodities and their relation to other media enterprises.

The mutating film format provides other challenges. A prominent concern arises when the migration from one to another is not sanctioned by the authorized copyright holders. DVDs of surreptitiously recorded theatrical releases and networks of online movie file sharers have grown exponentially. Conceptually speaking, contemporary piracy involves an unsanctioned acceleration of a film's life-cycle. It jump-starts a path of circulation and exchange, one that will eventually be available, but

too soon and without approval from or benefit for the original producers and financial participants. Put differently, piracy is a form of cultural speeding. The Motion
Picture Association of America (MPAA) estimates $3.5 billion in annual losses to
piracy (Triplett, 2005: B1).

The source of pirated copies is a matter of debate. When *Puños Rosas* (*Pink Punch*:
Beto Gómez, 2004, Mexico) appeared in pirate versions before it had hit commercial screens, the Guadalajara Iberoamerican Film Festival received accusations of
being the source (Bensinger, 2004). It remains likely that a good portion of bootleg prints originate from inside the industry (Cohen, 2005b). Former MPAA chief
Jack Valenti's short-lived plan to limit the distribution of voters' DVD copies of
Academy Award nominees was one effort to respond to this fact. Still, many come
from hand-held digital cameras recording films in conventional theaters, evident
from the skewed angles, the grainy image, the muddied audio, and the occasional
sound of audience response. Multiplexes in the US have introduced security guards,
metal detectors, searches of patrons, and auditorium surveillance with night vision
goggles. More cruelly, perhaps, Montreal audiences on the opening weekend of *Harry
Potter and the Goblet of Fire* (Mike Newell, 2005, UK/US) were subjected to a pre-
show anti-piracy skit, performed in mime (Brownstein, 2005).

One action has been to release films in multiple markets faster, in effect fighting speed with speed. This has been one of the stated rationales for international
wide releasing, reasoning that every day a popular film is playing in one location
but not another is an incentive for an underground market to fill that temporal
gap with illegal product. Similarly, some distributors have begun to release films
on different media early in their cultural and economic lives. Distributors accelerate the life-cycle, cutting into the immediate DVD availability of pirated films by
tightening the gap between theatrical and home viewing contexts (Ludemann, 2005).
They develop different release strategies for different countries. For instance,
Warner released *The Sisterhood of the Traveling Pants* (Ken Kwapis, 2005, US) in
China on DVD and in theaters elsewhere (Jones, 2005b).

The estimated cost of losing business to pirated DVDs is borne by exhibitors and
distributors. The actual cost, however, is lost in a fog of alarmist tales told by the
same supposedly injured parties. Rough estimations typically, and erroneously, assume
that consumers of bootleg DVDs are prospective movie patrons who would have
attended the cinema had they not acquired the film in another fashion. And rare
is consideration of the way black market distribution can actually build audiences
for films. Such was the case of *The Football Factory* (Nick Love, 2004, UK), for which
pirated DVDs became a "guerrilla marketing strategy" and helped raise box-office
receipts (Thomas, 2004).

Despite uncertainty about the effects of piracy on exhibitors and distributors,
the MPAA's response has been to transform part of its operations to focus on policing. They actively cooperated with governments and policing agencies to push
for investigations and enforcement abroad. They have been trying to educate the
public on the issue of copyright, with online information and movie trailers on the
topic. The MPAA has also established a tip hotline, but will pursue action only in

those operations with at least 30 copying units. Overall, the tone is decidedly milit-aristic, with Operation Eradicate being launched in December 2004 to attack Asian piracy (Jones, 2005a). MPAA head Dan Glickman, in his best Elliott Ness manner, proclaimed, "`You can click, but you can't hide'" (Cohen, 2005b).

So, as the MPAA rallies domestic and international efforts to combat this leak in revenue, exhibitors are caught between two related threats to their operations. They must contend with the narrowing theatrical window as distributors move films through their multi-media incarnations faster. Theatrical runs become even briefer peaks into the overall life of a film. And the circulation of bootleg copies of the-atrical releases presumably challenges the uniqueness of a first-run feature. The narrowing theatrical window is one effort to combat piracy, which of course leaves exhibitors with an even shorter timeframe for their end of the film's economic prospects.

Digital Projections

One of the most talked-out shifts in exhibition is post-celluloid presentation, and 1999 stands as "year zero" for the possible mass conversion of theaters to this mode of projection and distribution. The number of fully equipped digital screens went from 12 in 1999 to 182 in 2003 (*Variety*, 2005). The next two years saw this num-ber leap to 335 in 2004 and to 407 by July 2005 (*Screen Digest*, 2005g). As can be expected during a time of transition, the terms used are highly imprecise. "Digital cinema" can refer to any form of video projection', "e-cinema" tends to indicate the lower-end systems, of which there are thousands worldwide, and "d-cinema" tends to be reserved for the higher end, meaning 2,000 (2K) or more lines of high-resolution, digital projection systems. Note that in the existing literature "e" and "d" are often inverted. Furthermore, without any standard system in place, "digital cinema" can involve any number of delivery methods, including disk or drive deliv-ery, satellite relay, or fiber optic transmission.

Efforts have been made to coordinate the transition. Seven Hollywood majors – Disney, Fox, MGM, Paramount, Sony Pictures Entertainment, Universal, and Warner Bros. – formed Digital Cinema Initiatives (DCI), charging it with smooth-ing the way for d-cinema, making recommendations for industry-wide technical specifications, conversion financing – a considerable expense that exhibitors do not wish to be burdened with – and security standards. Though DCI questioned whether or not 2K was an acceptable standard, and some argued for 4K as a more suitable goal for the industry, they ultimately did set the minimum resolution at 2K, placing d-cinema above the 1,080 for HDTV and the 480 for North American tele-vision ((Digital Cinema Initiatives, 2005; McBride, 2005).

A major factor is that, regardless of the method used to get moving images and sounds to theaters, digital cinema will dispense with the transportation of film can-isters (Marriott, 1999; *Globe and Mail*, 2002). Some, like John Belton (2003), have questioned d-cinema's claims to revolutionary status, seeing instead a reinforcement of existing practices. While generally accurate, the mode of delivery *is* most un-settling to reigning understandings and operations of theatrical cinematic events. Digital systems, with cheaper delivery of *any* video or televisual text, expand genres emphasized by exhibitors. They accommodate one-time audiovisual performances for specialized audiences, whether video displays for corporate clients, live perform-ances, or sporting events. At the moment, contrary to the promises of eventual cost savings, d-cinema actually costs about $2,000 more per copy than traditional celluloid reels (Fritz, 2005). Despite this, there are advantages. Digital projection systems eliminate the exhibitor's labor of assembling film reels and appending trail-ers for platter projection systems. Currently, film canisters arrive at theaters, at which time an employee assembles them into a single large roll and places it on the hor-izontal platter for the duration of the film's run. Counting on exhibitors to attach trailers is unreliable from the distributors' perspective, with some estimates indi-cating that only 60 percent of trailers shipped make it to the screen (Hayes and Bing, 2004b: 52).

Most industry and scholarly discussions focus on the quality of the projected image and worry about the final "death of cinema" as we move into a post-celluloid era. And yet, so far, there is no indication that celluloid will be eliminated completely. Contrary to many predictions, rare is the feature that does not use celluloid at some point the process, and digital video is not necessarily cheaper as the money saved on film stock is often lost in the longer lighting set-ups required for digital cameras. In 2004, worldwide sales of film stock increased 10 percent for 16mm and 5 percent for 35mm (Cohen, 2005a). Most surprisingly, some argue that d- and e-cinema could help entrench celluloid even further. For years there have been calls, led by director James Cameron, to increase frame rates above the standard 24 frames per second. A major stumbling block in this experimentation is that new film projectors would be needed and the film prints would be heavier and more expensive. D-cinema, however, not only eliminates these super-sized prints, but also does not restrict shoot-ing specifications, which makes alternate film rates feasible (Cohen, 2005a). And as conversion accelerates, freshly developed 3-D systems for digital projection and screens will gain spotlight status, with Cameron to release his first feature fiction film since *Titanic* (1997), currently called *Avatar* (2009), in theaters equipped with this new technology.

By 2005 there were over 12,000 e-cinema screens worldwide (*Screen Digest*, 2004d). In Canada and the US, e-cinema has developed rapidly, and the push has largely come from advertising. Advertising-heavy pre-show packages of slides, trivia, and commercials are attractive to exhibitors, though they hold patrons hostage to ever longer streams of ads. The lengthening programs have led to complaints about start times not being as advertised. Just as audiences sit down to a cluttered advertising environment, advertisers can be irritated as well when they discover their products lost in a glut of commodity appeals.

The most developed e-cinema operation is Regal's Digital Content Network (DCN) whose pre-shows are part of a centrally controlled closed circuit. Regal has signed on other exhibitors, including Georgia Theater Company, to its e-cinema network,

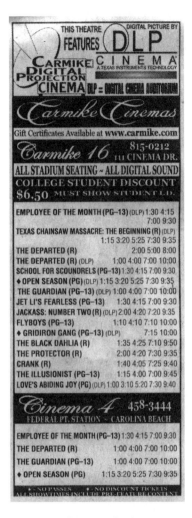

FIGURE 4.3   Multiplex advertisement featuring both conventional and d-cinema auditoriums, Carmike 16, Wilmington, North Carolina, October 2006. Courtesy of Carmike Cinemas

showing "The 2wenty" pre-show program and presenting live concerts, corporate meetings, and DVD launches (*Screen Digest*, 2005g). Following suit, AMC set up National Cinema Network (NCN) and Screenvision converted Loews Cineplex's US screens for digital pre-show advertising (*Screen Digest*, 2005e). The weight of this sector has only been gaining, with a 20 percent increase in advertising revenues in 2004, to reach a total of $374 million. Consider, too, the 41 percent increase in other on-site advertising, such as in-lobby displays, and one sees that exhibitors are banking on these revenue streams as insurance against fluctuations in box office (*Screen Digest*, 2005d). Theaters become inward-turning multimedia billboards.

Representing a monumental transformation in how films reach audiences, a key concern has been to maintain the existing industrial structure, with the same parties (i.e. Hollywood major and mini-major distributors) reaping whatever benefits accrue. Exhibitors do not necessarily have distributors' interests in mind, and have been spurred on to experiment with non-Hollywood filmed programs. The financial and technological roadblocks to d-cinema's development notwithstanding, exhibitors have used less advanced systems to screen events other than feature films, including live sports, wrestling, popular music, operas, ballets, Broadway musicals, and television programs, not to mention the rental of facilities for corporate events (*Screen Digest*, 2003). AMC used their e-cinema system to release the independent feature *Evergreen* (Enid Zentelis, 2005, US) on 114 screens, then considered to be the widest d- or e-cinema release (*Screen Digest*, 2004b). They followed this with a two-week e-cinema run of *The Final Cut* (Omar Naim, 2004, Canada/Germany) from distribution innovator Lions Gate Films (*Screen Digest*, 2004a). Currently, concentration among these cinema advertising companies is afoot, with AMC's NCN merging with Regal's renamed DCN, CineMedia, forming a new company that will serve both chains, and over 30 percent of the domestic market, called National Cinemedia (NCM) (*Screen Digest*, 2005h). With AMC's merger with Loews, the concentration of the theatrical and cinema advertising market rises. Cinemark is in the process of equipping its screens as part of NCM, which will boast 13,400 screens, or a full 36 percent of US screens (*Screen Digest*, 2005g).

Both e- and d-cinema involve a struggle for control of the filmed commodity in the theater. For the high-end d-cinema, a distributor delivers the entire work, on which trailers can already be attached, thus avoiding the uncertainty of leaving this task to exhibitors. DCI initially proposed to deliver work to a single d-cinema projector/server unit. This would effectively limit an exhibitor's ability to move a film from one auditorium to another, which is a primary advantage of multiplexes, i.e., the managers' ability to move films to smaller-sized auditoriums as their audiences dwindle. The National Association of Theatre Owners (NATO) participated in the d-cinema conversion debate, putting forward a resolution for standards of image and sound quality, technical uniformity and competition, security and operational control, and financing and roll-out plans. They too hoped to make d-cinema a singular, uniform, and identifiable experience (*Screen Digest*, 2004g). One of the concessions NATO won was a mechanism by which they could shift films between screens at a given site (*Screen Digest*, 2005a: 110).

While the US and Canada have seen their e-cinema networks expand rapidly due to advertising, other locations have had different experiences. In return for a cut of box-office and advertising revenue, Brazil's Rain Networks has been paying to convert a circuit of 120 digital screens to receive films transmitted over an intranet (Cajueiro, 2004: 11), showing "art" films from Brazil, Europe, and mini-majors including Lions Gate. Unlike the usual method of selling advertising in weekly blocks, Rain has been selling it per screening (*Screen Digest*, 2004c). Other alternative cinema circuits using e-cinema include Sweden's Folkets Hus, India's Mukta Adlabs, and Thailand's Shin-EGV Theaters, all of which use some form of fiber optic cable to deliver film content to disparate screens. While this low-end format does not have the superior image quality of d-cinema, it boasts faster distribution of new works and can compete with the piracy that arises due to the temporal lags in availability between cities and regions (*Screen Digest*, 2004f). Shout Africa introduced e-cinemas as an inexpensive way to reach South Africa's largely underserved non-urban audience, partly with local films (de Jager, 2005). Directed toward the majority black population, Shout Africa made some films available in Zulu and Xhosa (*Screen Digest*, 2005f). CinemaNet (formerly DocuZone) has more than 150 screens dispersed across Europe in which it opens documentary films simultaneously (Whiteman, 2004). The closest comparable initiative in the US is a company called Screening Room Digital Cinemas, which is building a network of e-cinemas with food menus that will access a centrally orchestrated schedule of art and alternative programming (*Screen Digest*, 2005a: 111).

Digital projection and delivery systems, whether d- or e-cinema, are new paths for the circulation of audiovisual material, and through them we are witnessing convergences between exhibition, cable, computer, and satellite technologies. These changes to the very nature of the theatrical exhibition context alter the temporality of the current cinema, as we witness shorter run times, wider or more selective openings, and flexible release calendars. Moreover, with e-cinema, exhibitors are investing in a revenue stream other than box office, namely advertising, and are actively reimagining what they will present and from where their audiovisual programs arrive.

Though I have concentrated upon the larger mainstream chains, it is apparent that other types of film circuits are developing, and here the alternative e-cinema chains of CinemaNet and Shout Africa point to innovations not yet evident in Canada and the US. Furthermore, it is important to acknowledge that this does not come close to exhausting the range of venues and situations. While repertory and second-run cinemas have dwindled in North America, film festivals have expanded and diversified. In Montreal alone there were more than two dozen film festivals in 2005, ranging from Vues d'Afrique to the Image + Nation International Film Festival. The festivals present hundreds of films that will never receive theatrical release in the US and Canada in university auditoriums, specially designated sites, and mainstream multiplexes. To be sure, Montreal is a festival-rich city, and may not be the most typical example of the role film festivals play elsewhere. Nonetheless, it does capture the fact that film exhibition involves both an international common ground of blockbusters *and* a more specialized vision of local and world cinema. The film festival circuit is primarily urban and fragments cinemagoing interests into geographic, genre, and topic categories. In reference to the circuits of American popular music, Philip Ennis (1992) discussed short and long loops for music economies. The former consists of markets, audiences, and artists that together can sustain a degree of recognition and coherence for a local musical scene. These can connect to form a national "loop," with some short-loop performers or songs making it to far-flung showcases. The difference between metropolitan festival cultures and international film traffic exhibits something comparable to Ennis's temporally and spatially defined loops.

With expanded multi-media exhibition windows, theatrical release is but one of the varying tracks for the movement of films. The acceleration of exhibition, as some of those multi-media tracks draw closer together, continues the conversion of the theater into something like a newsstand, whose periodicals are available for anywhere from a single day to a few weeks, as opposed to, say, the long-term holding goals of a library. Similarly, compare the long, multi-year runs of successful Broadway productions (*The Phantom of the Opera* and *The Producers*) to the short runs of experimental theater. With film, the short run of the blockbuster marks rapid economic gleaning and looks ahead to lucrative prospects on DVD, where the smaller "art" or "indie" film has a slower release pace and hence may spend more time in its few theaters, and may now appear nearly simultaneously on DVD. In both the Broadway and film cases, the differing temporality is partly determined by senses of financial and aesthetic risk, though in inverse proportions. The shorter film run signals a reduction of financial and aesthetic risk for a dominant industry logic, while the longer run tends to accommodate the smaller, more offbeat, non-blockbuster fare.

The notion of cultural temporality figures in the work of Pierre Bourdieu. Describing the difference between avant-garde and middlebrow theater, he wrote, "The opposition between the two economies, that is to say, between two relationships to the 'economy', can thus be seen as an opposition between two life-cycles of the cultural production business, two different ways in which firms, producers and products *grow old*" (1986: 104). Importantly, what we might describe as "slow" and "fast" cultures become correlates of cultural and symbolic capital. With film, then, an emerging system of cultural hierarchy is evident, one that articulates technology with location and style. For instance, one can foresee a split between local, alternative, or art features nudging their way into the less advanced advertising-dominated e-cinema format, and the bright colors and high-resolution of d-cinema being reserved for the upper end of transcontinental big-budget productions from major distributors. Many prevailing forces are structuring occasions for cinematic life, including multi-format distribution channels, ownership and geographic concentration, release strategies, piracy, and digital delivery/projection. These forces are prompting a reconstitution of theatrical exhibition, one that depends upon exhibition's place in the corporate investment mix. Still, there is a lived dimension to this as well, that is, a shared and engaged culture that responds to the influence of the economic structuring, but that cannot be reduced to it exactly. And the organization of this commercial culture-in-common depends upon selective access to the various paths and speeds of film traffic.

NOTE

Thanks to Keir Keightley, Paul McDonald, Janet Wasko, and Haidee Wasson for comments on this research, and thanks to Peter Lester for research assistance.

REFERENCES

Acland, C. R. (2003) *Screen Traffic: Movies, Multiplexes, and Global Culture*. Durham: Duke University Press.

Allen, R., R. Maltby, and M. Stokes (eds.) (forthcoming) *Hollywood and the Social Experience of Movie-going*. Exeter: University of Exeter Press.

Amdur, M. (2004) "McDonald's Eyes New Meal Ticket in DVD Biz," *Variety*, May 31–June 6, p. 6.

Avery, S. (2006) "Apple Raises Curtain on Movie Service," *Globe and Mail*, September 13, pp. B1, B12.

Bart, P. (2005) ". . . But Is All That Angst Justified?," *Variety*, June 27–July 10, pp. 1, 4.

Belson, K. (2005) "A DVD Standoff in Hollywood," *New York Times*, July 11, pp. C1, C6.

Belton, J. (2003) "Digital Cinema: A False Revolution," *October*, 100 (Spring), pp. 99–114.

Benjamin, W. (1936; 2002) "The Work of Art in the Age of its Technological Reproducibility," in H. Eiland and M. W. Jennings (eds.), *Walter Benjamin, Selected Writings*, vol. 3: *1935–1938*. Cambridge: Belknap Press of Harvard University Press, pp. 101–33.

Bensinger, K. (2004) "Piracy Blame Put on Fest," *Variety*, June 28–July 11, p. 10.

Biskind, P. (1998) *Easy Riders, Raging Bulls: How the Sex-Drugs-and-Rock 'n' Roll Generation Saved Hollywood*. New York: Simon & Schuster.

Biskind, P. (2004) *Down and Dirty Pictures: Miramax, Sundance, and the Rise of Independent Film*. New York: Simon & Schuster.

Blackwell, R. (2005a) "Cineplex Plans Real Estate Sale to Pay for Blockbuster Takeover," *Globe and Mail*, June 30, p. B7.

Blackwell, R. (2005b) "Cineplex Road to Viacom Ran Through Ottawa," *Globe and Mail*, June 25, p. B3.

Bourdieu, P. (1986; 1993) *The Field of Cultural Production*. New York: Columbia University Press.

Boxoffice (1995) "Giants of Exhibition," December, pp. 30–3.

Boxoffice (2005) "The Fabulous Fifty," January, p. 32.

Brownstein, B. (2005) "Montreal Stealing the Shows: Film Piracy Capital," *The Gazette*, November 18, pp. A1, A4.

Cajueiro, M. (2004) "Arthouse Circuits win Digital Race," *Variety*, August 2–8, pp. 1, 13.

Cohen, D. S. (2005a) "Film Not Ready to Cede to Tape," *Variety*, April 18–24, p. 7.

Cohen, D. S. (2005b) "Pirates Wreak 'Revenge'," *Variety*, May 23–9, p. 5.

De Jager, C. (2005) "South African Villages Get D-Cinema," *Variety*, April 4–10, p. 11.

Digital Cinema Initiatives (2005) *Digital Cinema System Specifications*, July 20, Hollywood: Digital Cinema Initiatives, LLC.

Ennis, P. H. (1992) *The Seventh Stream: The Emergence of Rocknroll in American Popular Music*. Hanover: Wesleyan University Press.

Fritz, B. (2005) "Digital Doldrums Sink In: D-Cinema Still Mired in Tech, Funding Frustrations," *Variety*, April 11–17, p. 5.

Globe and Mail (2002) "Major Studios Agree to Set Digital Standards," April 4, p. R2.

Gomery, D. (1992) *Shared Pleasures: A History of Movie Presentation in the United States*. Madison: University of Wisconsin Press.

Gray, S., and K. Kelly (2006) "A Movie and a Latte? Starbucks Plans Push into Film Business," *Globe and Mail*, January 12, p. B16.

Grieveson, L. (2004) *Policing the Cinema: Movies and Censorship in Early-Twentieth-Century America*. Berkeley: University of California Press.

Groves, D. (2004a) "Summer Takeoffs Stack Up O'seas: Opening-Weekend Pressure Drives Studios to Count on Supersized Foreign Grosses," *Variety*, February 14–20, pp. 8, 59.

Groves, D. (2004b) "Touting Tentpoles = Towering Tabs: Wide Releases Worldwide Prove Pricey for Majors," *Variety*, April 5–11, p. 8.

Groves, D. (2004c) "U.S. Pix Bigger O'seas: Still Room to Grow in Many Markets, Say Distrib Exex," *Variety*, June 21–7, p. 12.

Hansen, M. (1991) *Babel and Babylon: Spectatorship in American Silent Film.* Cambridge, MA: Harvard University Press.

Hayes, D. (2005) "If You Had Rented a DVD You'd Be Home Now," *Entertainment Weekly*, May 13, pp. 13, 14, 16.

Hayes, D., and J. Bing (2004a) *Open Wide: How Hollywood Box Office Became a National Obsession.* New York: Hyperion/Miramax Books.

Hayes, D., and J. Bing (2004b) "Tyranny of the Trailer: Fate of Tentpoles Rests on Coming Attractions," *Variety*, February 23–9, pp. 1, 52, 53.

Innis, H. (1951) *The Bias of Communication.* Toronto: University of Toronto.

Jancovich, M., and L. Faire, with S. Stubbings (2003) *The Place of the Audience: Cultural Geographies of Film Consumption.* London: BFI Publishing.

Jones, A. (2005a) "China's Shoppers Shun Legal Superstore Vidpix," *Variety*, February 21–7, p. 13.

Jones, A. (2005b) "Control Geeks: H'wood Deploys Innovative Initiatives in China," *Variety*, June 27–July 10, p. B6.

Keightley, K. (2004) "Long Play: Adult-Oriented Popular Music and the Temporal Logics of the Post-War Sound Recording Industry in the USA," *Media, Culture & Society*, 26(3), pp. 375–91.

Kelly, K. (2005) "Jittery Theatres Pitch Money-Back Movies," *Globe and Mail*, June 29, p. B11.

Learmonth, M. (2005) "Store Wars!," *Variety*, November 14–20, pp. 1, 62.

Lichtman, H. (2005) "Don't Believe the Hype," *Boxoffice*, September, pp. 26, 28.

Ludemann, R. (2005) "Narrow DVD Windows Choke Chains," *Variety*, June 27–July 10, p. B2.

Marriott, M. (1999) "Digital Projectors Use Flashes of Light to Paint a Movie," *New York Times*, May 27, p. G7.

McBride, S. (2005) "Hollywood Studios Reach Pact on Standards for Going Digital," *Wall Street Journal*, July 27, p. B3.

McCourt, T., and E. Rothenbuhler (1997) "*SoundScan* and the Consolidation of Control in the Popular Music Industry," *Media Culture & Society*, 19(2), pp. 201–18.

McNary, D. (2005) "Think Local, Act Global: O'seas B.O. Cools but Exhibs and H'wood Still Happy," *Variety*, June 27–July 10, pp. B1, B8.

Miller, T., N. Govil, J. McMurria, R. Maxwell, and T. Wang (2005) *Global Hollywood 2.* London: BFI Publishing.

Mohr, I. (2005) "War of the Windows: Pic Biz Frets as B.O. Fades & DVDs Usurp Key Dates," *Variety*, June 27–July 10, pp. 1, 82.

MPAA (2001) "2001 US Economic Review," online at <http://www.mpaa.org/useconomicreview/2001Economic>.

MPAA (2005) *U.S. Entertainment Industry: 2004 MPA Market Statistics*, Los Angeles: Motion Picture Association of America.

Newsweek (2005) "The Future of Entertainment," September 26–October 3, front cover.

Nielsen EDI (2004) "Box Office News," *Variety*, February 16–22, p. 23.

Nielsen EDI (2005) "Box Office News," *Variety*, May 16–22, p. 14.

Screen Digest (2003) "Exhibitors Eye Alternative Revenue Streams," October, p. 291.

Screen Digest (2004a) "AMC and Lions Gate Team for E-Cinema Release," October, p. 311.

Screen Digest (2004b) "AMC Digital Indie Film Uses Low-End Ad Network," September, p. 277.

Screen Digest (2004c) "Brazil's Digital Indie Cinema Network Makes Gains," October, p. 293.

Screen Digest (2004d) "Cinema Advertising Evolves," December, pp. 366–9.

Screen Digest (2004e) "Maximum Print Runs Increasing," November, p. 328.

Screen Digest (2004f) "Thai Companies to Set Up E-Theaters Network," May, p. 153.

Screen Digest (2004g) "U.S. Exhibitors Unite on D-Cinema Terms," December, p. 374.

Screen Digest (2004h) "U.S. Releases Are Getting Wider," December, pp. 370–2.

Screen Digest (2005a) "Digital Cinema Year Six," April, pp. 109–16.

Screen Digest (2005b) "Download-to-Own VoD: Year One," June, p. 168.

Screen Digest (2005c) "Empire Theatres Consolidates on Cineplex Sale," September, p. 280.

Screen Digest (2005d) "Europe Leads Digital Screen Rise," October, p. 291.

Screen Digest (2005e) "Largest Digital Ad Network Launches in U.S.," April, p. 123.

Screen Digest (2005f) "New E-Cinema Network for Rural South Africa," April, p. 118.

Screen Digest (2005g) "U.S. Pre-Show Booming as Digitisation Takes Hold," September, p. 279.

Screen Digest (2005h) "U.S. Screen Ad Market Signs of Concentration," April, p. 123.

Screen Digest (2005i) "World Cinema Markets Reviewed," September, pp. 269–76.

Snyder, G. (2004a) "Big Dippers Haunt H'wood: Second Weekend Drop-Offs Lead to Lower Total Takes," *Variety*, August 9–15, pp. 6, 45.

Snyder, G. (2004b) "H'wood in a Numbers Crunch: Firms Race to Dominate Box Office Tracking Biz," *Variety*, October 11–17, p. 7.

Snyder, G. (2005) "B.O. Bashers and Slipped Discs: Studios A-OK on Bigscreen, but Shifts in DVD Biz Could Have Big H'wood Impact," *Variety*, June 6–12, pp. 6, 46.

Statistics Canada (1999) *Movie Theatres and Drive-ins, 1997–98, Cultural Statistics*. Ottawa: Culture, Tourism, and the Centre for Education Statistics.

Stewart, J. (2005) *Migrating to the Movies: Cinema and Black Urban Modernity*. Berkeley: University of California Press.

Stokes, M., and R. Maltby (eds.) (1999) *Identifying Hollywood's Audiences: Cultural Identity and the Movies*. London: BFI Publishing.

Stokes, M., and R. Maltby (eds.) (2001) *Hollywood Spectatorship: Changing Perceptions of Cinema Audiences*. London: BFI Publishing.

Stokes, M., and R. Maltby (eds.) (2004) *Hollywood Abroad: Audiences and Cultural Exchange*. London: BFI Publishing.

Straw, W. (1990) "Popular Music as Cultural Commodity: The American Recorded Music Industries, 1978–1985," Ph.D. dissertation, McGill University, Montreal.

Thomas, A. (2004) "Pirated DVD Boots Up Buzz for Soccer Hooligan Pic," *Variety*, May 10–16, p. 8.

Triplett, W. (2005) "Politics Ups Role in War on Piracy," *Variety*, June 27–July 10, pp. B1, B9.

Urban, G. (2001) *Metaculture: How Culture Moves through the World*. Minneapolis: University of Minnesota Press.

Variety (2005) "Hot Number," March 21–7, p. 6.

Waller, G. A. (1995) *Main Street Amusements: Movies and Commercial Entertainment in a Southern City, 1896–1930*. Washington: Smithsonian Institution Press.

Whiteman, B. (2004) "Docs to D-cinemas," *Variety*, August 30–September 5, p. 8.

Williams, R. (1977) *Marxism and Literature*. New York, Oxford University Press.

CHAPTER 5

ANCILLARY MARKETS – TELEVISION: FROM CHALLENGE TO SAFE HAVEN

EILEEN R. MEEHAN

An industry-by-industry approach to media research illuminates how each medium operates as a distinct economic endeavor. Such an intensive examination of an individual industry at a particular point in time allows a researcher to explore in depth the relationships, contingencies, and practices through which participants make the end product or service available (Mosco, 1979; Cantor, 1980; Gitlin, 1983; Wasko, 2003). It also allows researchers to see connections by tracing how companies in one industry make their products an integral part of another industry (Wasko, 1994; Kunz, 2006; Meehan, 2006). Combining these approaches illuminates processes by which firms structure themselves, negotiate and construct their business environments, deal with new challenges, and sometimes rearticulate their industries. Looking at separate industries allows us to distinguish film from television. Attention to connections and negotiation reminds us that all industrial relations are dynamic and that particular governmental policies may foster or militate against the integration of film and television. To understand these ideas, this chapter briefly sketches the film industry's initial interests in television, regulatory action barring the studios from ownership of television, and the studios' accommodation to that through the development of ancillary markets in television. The bulk of the chapter looks at the six firms that deregulation has allowed to dominate film and ways that those firms embody film's five ancillary markets in television.

At this writing, film's Big Six are the Disney Corporation, General Electric, National Amusements, News Corporation, Sony, and Time Warner. Each follows the same general pattern in circulating their movies. Each firm releases it films to movie theaters and then repackages them as DVDs and videocassettes in their home entertainment operations. Films are licensed in sequence to pay-per-view operations, premium cable channels, and television networks or basic cable channels. Finally, they are syndicated on networks or cable channels (Balio, n.d.). Theatrical release determines the film's market value for its subsequent repackaging on DVD and video as well as for its licensing to different television-based venues. Today, the television industry may seem like the film industry's best friend, but that was not always the case.

Making Television Safe for Film

Hollywood's interest in the emerging medium of television dates from the 1920s and includes experiments with the developing technology, an alternative model of television as home theater, applications for television frequencies, as well as investments in broadcasting companies that were exploring television (Anderson, 1994; Hilmes, 1990; Wasko, 1994). The evidence suggests that studios clearly wanted to control the development and implementation of television technology. Securing that control required the assistance of the Federal Communication Commission, which regulated television's development by articulating technical standards and operating rules and through the FCC's exclusive right to license the use of television frequencies for experimentation or broadcast.

Historically, companies like General Electric, Westinghouse, and AT&T played significant roles in articulating early regulations and policies for radio. For television in the late 1940s, the broadcast industry's standard bearers were the Radio Corporation of America (RCA), which owned two national radio networks under the NBC label, and the Columbia Broadcasting System, which owned the CBS radio network. FCC decisions tended to favor requests by radio broadcasters, thereby organizing television in terms of radio with programming that was sponsored by advertisers and defined as radio-with-pictures. By 1953, the studios' campaign to define and control television distribution and technology was essentially over just as the Paramount decree, the Supreme Court's decision that the studios should divest their theaters, went into effect. From 1946 to 1953, studios had suffered significant financial losses, including declining box-office revenues blamed on television. Warner, for example, saw net profits fall from $22 million to $2.9 million (Anderson, 1994), which translated into idle sound stages, unused equipment, fewer jobs for film workers, and less need for films – especially for low-budget movies that filled out the double features. In economic terms, the studios had more capacity to produce films than they needed. Ironically, this surplus capacity provided the studios with a new source of revenue: renting sound stages and equipment to newly organized television production companies (Seldes, 1956; Cantor, 1980; Barnouw, 1990). Because the studios reserved their best facilities for movies, this relationship also fostered television's status as inferior to film. From the mid-1940s to the mid-1950s, this ancillary market gave film studios an important role in the television industry, albeit as landlords rather than program producers.

Obviously the studios had considerable experience in producing visual entertainment and owned vast libraries of old movies. Both should have positioned the studios to be significant providers of programming. But pricing was a contentious issue. In 1950, RCA and CBS offered to pay $25,000 for 30 minutes of programming, but the average film ran two hours and cost a million dollars (Anderson, 1994). With such differences over pricing, the studios demurred while claiming that television was killing film. Eventually, of course, networks and studios would negotiate more equitable pricing structures for films, which would give the studios an ancillary market for the redistribution of theatrical movies.

Despite the studios' criticism, movie-makers explored the market for television programming (Barnouw, 1990; Anderson, 1994). Walt Disney produced two highly rated and critically acclaimed Christmas specials, *One Hour in Wonderland* (NBC, 1950, US) and *The Walt Disney Christmas Special* (CBS, 1951, US). Disney then entered negotiations to secure a spot on network television and an investment in its planned theme park with each of the networks. Only ABC accepted these terms and, in 1954, it premiered the *Disneyland* series (ABC, 1954–61, US). A year later, ABC premiered *Warner Brothers Presents* (ABC, 1955–6, US; subsequently revamped as *Cheyenne* [ABC, 1955–63, US]), which got a major studio into the business of supplying television programming on a regular basis. Thus, Disney and Warner demonstrated that studios could successfully move from renting their surplus capacity to using it in television production. They also showed how studios could use television production to promote upcoming theatrical releases, recycle stock footage, use genres and characters established in films, and try out inexperienced actors at low wages. Programs like *The 20th Century Fox Hour* (CBS, 1955, US) and *MGM Parade* (ABC, 1955, US) soon followed. By 1957, the studios had joined the networks and a handful of independent companies like Desilu and Ziv as major producers of new programming for television.

Eventually television production overtook renting surplus capacity as the main way in which film studios participated in the television industry. In the 1960s and 1970s, the studios used their production capacity to dominate the market for made-for-television movies. They also became major players in the market for new series by building partnerships with independent producers in which the studios provided the production capacity. During that period, the FCC paid them little attention, focusing instead on the networks. As a result, the studios were relatively free to pursue their interests in television programming, whether licensing movies to television for post-theatrical release, or using idle capacity to create made-for-television movies, or constructing partnerships to generate new series given their ownership of idle capacity. In this way, Hollywood made television safe for film.

Media Deregulation: Integrating Film and Television

Starting with the Reagan Administration in 1980 and continuing to the present day, neoconservative deregulation has facilitated a radical reorganization of media industries and operations (Streeter, 1996; McChesney, 1999; Kunz, 2006; Meehan, 2006). Undergirding that reorganization has been the FCC's dismantling of regulations designed to keep television a separate industry and the Department of Justice's gutting of antitrust regulation, including the Paramount decree. As a result, media companies have restructured themselves to expand beyond their traditional operations, often restructuring as conglomerates that stretch across media industries with operations in as many kinds of media as possible. Thus film studios have acquired television networks and vice versa. Deregulation has also fostered vertical and horizontal integration within each industrially based operation such that media conglomerates may own multiple studios or networks.

Managing such huge, multi-focused entities is challenging to say the least. One solution has been corporate synergy: the practice of coordinating operations so that a product can move smoothly across multiple internal markets and thereby feed as many operations as possible. For example, Time Warner's synergizing of *Batman Begins* (Christopher Nolan, 2005, US) included a novelization, CD, DVD, video-cassette, soundtrack, and comic book, thus feeding Time Warner operations in book publishing, recorded music, home entertainment, and comic book publishing. Synergy encourages media conglomerates to expand their holdings into ancillary markets.

Currently, the Hollywood film industry is controlled by six firms: Disney, General Electric, National Amusements, News Corporation, Sony, and Time Warner. General Electric and Sony are diversified conglomerates in which entertainment operations contribute a very small portion of overall revenues. But like Disney, National Amusements, News Corporation, and Time Warner, General Electric's and Sony's entertainment operations stretch across the film and television industries, among others. However, each firm's particular situation and structure means that the process and extent to which entertainment operations contribute will vary by conglomerate. Recognizing that, we will review each of the Big Six in turn with special attention to how they deal with film's ancillary markets in home entertainment (DVDs and videocassettes), pay-per-view, premium cable channels, television networks or basic cable channels (first run), and subsequent syndication to networks or cable channels. (Information is drawn from each firm's most recent 10-K report, which is cited in the references.)

A Wonderful World: Disney

Disney positions its films in the theatrical market by using various imprimaturs: Walt Disney Pictures, Touchstone Pictures, Hollywood Pictures, Caravan Pictures, Miramax Films, Dimension Films (Wasko, 2002, 2003) and in May 2006 acquired the computer animation studio Pixar (Sikora and Harrison, 2006). While the Walt Disney, Miramax, and Pixar labels have had distinct identities, the others have been more generic. Yet all Disney films are routinely repackaged onto videocassette and DVD via the company's Buena Vista imprint.

The company treats the Walt Disney movies differently from movies issued under its other labels. Under Walt and Roy Disney, the company had released feature-length animations to theaters, then taken them out of circulation for years before re-releasing for another theatrical run. This practice cultivated impressions of specialness for the animations and encouraged intergenerational viewing of Disney "classics." Now Disney uses this pattern of release, moratorium, and limited re-release when it moves Walt Disney films onto DVD and videocassette. After an initial release to the home entertainment market, the Walt Disney films move through the Disney Channels, including premium digital channels and the Disney cable channel, which is premium on some systems and offered as an enhanced basic service on others. Infotainment programming on the Disney Channels uses "making of" or "behind-the-scenes" materials to promote films in theatrical or home entertainment release. Disney uses theatrical films to generate direct-to-video movies as well as television series. For example, *Lilo and Stitch* (Dean DeBlois and Chris Sanders, 2002, US) generated the direct-to-video movie *Lilo and Stitch 2: Stitch has a Glitch* (Michael LaBash and Anthony Leondis, 2005, US) and the television series *Lilo and Stitch: The Series* (Disney Channel, 2003, US).

Less family-oriented fare from Touchstone Pictures, Hollywood Pictures, Caravan Pictures, Miramax Films, or Dimension Films will not run on the Disney Channels. In the ancillary market for pay-per-view distribution, Disney licenses such films to the pay-per-view service owned by Showtime Networks, ultimately owned by National Amusements through its CBS operations, or to iN DEMAND (also known as oN DEMAND), a joint venture run by Time Warner, Cox Communications, and Comcast Communications, which each own one of the top four multiple cable systems in the United States. In the ancillary market where premium cable channels buy films, Disney has a long-term contract with National Amusement's Showtime Networks. That contract routinizes Disney's circulation of films carrying its other labels so that every movie is guaranteed its cable premiere on a premium channel.

Rounding out Disney's available venues for recirculating its films are its wholly owned basic cable channels (ABC Family, Toon Disney), co-owned cable channels (E!, ESPN, History, Lifetime, Lifetime Movie Network), and the ABC broadcast network. Disney also contracts with other firms for family-friendly movies, most notably the once independent DreamWorks SKG and most recently with Time Warner (Dempsey, 2006). Overall, then, Disney integrates the ancillary markets for VHS/DVD repackaging, family-oriented premium cable channels, basic cable channels, and network broadcasts into its structure, licensing films to itself and also from other companies. Only in the pay-per-view market does Disney act as a seller but not also a buyer.

New Kid on the Block? General Electric

Although its interest in broadcasting stretches back to the early 1900s (Barnouw, 1966, 1990), General Electric (GE) only entered television networking in 1986 and theatrical film in 2004. In 1986 GE acquired RCA, selling off most of its operations but retaining the NBC television network and television production and distribution units. Between that acquisition and 2004, GE built a media empire that included full ownership of the NBC and Telemundo networks; 30 percent ownership of Paxson Communications and its generic Christian network PAX; full ownership of the Bravo, Telemundo Internacional, MUN2, and Universal HD cable channels; a 31 percent stake in the world's largest provider of satellite services, SES Global, with clients in the broadcasting, cable, and telecommunications industries; and co-ownership of cable channels A&E (Disney), CNBC (Dow Jones), History (Disney and Viacom), MSNBC (Microsoft), National Geographic (News Corporation and the National Geographic Society), and ShopNBC (Value Vision Media). By 2004, GE was the only major corporation in television networking, production, and cable channels that did not own a film studio.

On May 11, 2004, GE finalized a $134 billion deal with the highly diversified French conglomerate Vivendi to acquire the media holdings from Vivendi Universal, including Universal Studios. Although not all of Vivendi's media holdings, the deal included Universal Studios, Universal Television, Universal Home Entertainment, basic cable channels (Trio, Sci-Fi, USA), and Universal Parks and Resorts. GE and Vivendi organized the deal as a joint venture, with GE owning 80 percent of the new NBC Universal and Vivendi agreeing to a timeline that would transfer full owner-ship to GE.

The deal set up a pathway for NBC-Universal films to move from theatrical release to NBC-Universal VHS/DVD and eventually to NBC-Universal cable channels and to network runs on NBC and Telemundo. In this way, GE built internal markets in film's ancillary industries of VHS/DVD, basic cable channels, and network broadcast. The only ancillary market in which GE could not license its films to itself was pay-per-view.

The Corporation Behind the Thrones? National Amusements

In 2005, discussions of film's Big Six or television's Big Five generally noted that Viacom owned Paramount Pictures as well as the CBS and UPN television networks, among other media properties. Viacom itself was controlled by National Amuse-ments, which held 71 percent of the voting rights and 11 percent of Viacom's equity. This made National Amusement's owner, Sumner Redstone, the power behind Viacom. Indeed, on December 31, 2005, Redstone broke Viacom into two firms to be traded separately in stock markets: the new Viacom and CBS Inc. Redstone's announced intent was to increase shareholder value, which started rumors that he might be preparing to sell or getting ready to go on a buying spree (*Economist*, 2005; Fabrikant, 2005). Headed by Thomas E. Freston, the new Viacom focused mainly on film, basic cable channels, music, and movie theaters. At the new CBS, Leslie Moonves ran operations in broadcasting, pay-per-view, premium cable channels, theme parks, book publishing, and outdoor advertising. Both firms were connected via a series of agreements regarding taxation, programming, and other matters (Fabrikant, 2005; CBS, 2006; Viacom, 2006).

Despite their titular separation, Viacom and CBS remained under National Amusements' control. Filings from Viacom and CBS with the Securities Exchange Commission note that Redstone and three other directors from National Amuse-ments sit on their boards. As the Viacom filing puts it, National Amusements could thus "control the outcome of corporate actions that require stockholder approval, including the election of directors and transactions involving a change of control" (Viacom, 2006, I-25; CBS, 2006, I-33, 34).

By coordinating and synergizing its holdings in theatrical film, gaming, charac-ters, etc., with Viacom and CBS, National Amusements could function as both seller

premium and basic cable channels, and television networks. National Amusements could produce films under its Paramount, Paramount Classics, BET, MTV,
Nickelodeon, and, as of 2006, DreamWorks labels. It could book those films into
its theaters, license them to Paramount Home Entertainment for release as videos
and DVDs, run them on Showtime's pay-per-view service, and recirculate them on
the Showtime pay or digital channels. National Amusements could then match the
film's targeted audience with the primary audiences targeted by its basic cable
channels: MTV for youthful music fans; VH1 for older music fans; Nickelodeon
for children and families; Spike and Comedy Central for young men; and Black
Entertainment Television for African Americans. Through CBS' Showtime Networks, National Amusements is also part owner of the Sundance Channel, rooted
in Robert Redford's Sundance Film Festival and an appropriate venue for independent-
style movies. A similar matching process was made possible by National Amusements'
strategy of orienting its CBS and UPN television networks for different audiences.
While UPN targeted various minority audiences including women, African
Americans, and "tweens," CBS went after the general commodity audience for
television, with emphasis on the demographic most prized by advertisers and targeted for films: 18–34-year-old white males in upscale households subscribing to
cable (Meehan, 2006). In January 2006, National Amusements and Time Warner
announced the merger of their niched networks, respectively, UPN and WB, to form
a new network, CW. According to CBS' Moonves, the CW would be "a strong competitor to the Big Four" (*TVRules*, 2006), presumably serving as an outlet for films
as well as television productions.

This pipeline between film and television carried traffic both ways. For example,
National Amusements built three films from its cable television program *Rugrats*
(NIK, 1991–2004, US): *The Rugrats Movie* (Igor Kovalyov and Norton Virgien, 1998,
US), *Rugrats in Paris* (Stig Bergqvist and Paul Demeyer, 2000, US), and *Rugrats Go
Wild!* (John Eng and Norton Virgien, 2003, US).

Striding into the Twenty-First Century: News Corporation

Controlled by Rupert Murdoch through ownership of nearly 29 percent of the
voting shares, News Corporation generated films through its Blue Sky Studios
(animation), 20th Century Fox Animation, 20th Century Fox Films, 20th Century
Fox, Fox Searchlight (independent-style films), Fox Studios (Australia, Baja, Los
Angeles), and Fox 2000 labels. Regardless of label, all News Corporation-owned films
can be found on video or DVD through 20th Century Fox Home Entertainment.

They can also be found on News Corporation's DirecTV, BSkyB, and other
satellite systems. Among its cable channels offering films are Fox Movie Channels,
FUEL, FX, and SPEED. For its Fox Kids operations in the United States, News
Corporation relies on Disney as part of the deal in which News Corporation
sold the Fox Family cable channel to Disney. Overseas, News Corporation controls
its Fox Kids operations. The various News Corporation studios, then, have a
quasi-internal market for their family-friendly movies. The FOX network filled

FIGURE 5.1 Viacom's *Rugrats* franchise, here honored on the Hollywood Walk of Fame, June 28, 2001. Photo by Associated Press

out the bottom of this hierarchy, ready to broadcast films, and occasionally feeds material into film production as when *The X-Files* television series (FOX, 1993–2002, US) was brought to the big screen in the movie *X-Files: The Movie* (Rob Bowman, 1998, US). Augmenting this hierarchy was the firm's "special relationship" with Viacom's UPN.

FIGURE 5.2   Rupert Murdoch. Photo by Associated Press

   That changed in 2006 with the announcement of the UPN–WB merger forming CW. Previously, News Corporation had owned ten broadcast television stations that it had affiliated with UPN. These were located in markets where News Corporation already owned a station affiliated with its FOX network. In creating CW, National Amusements and Time Warner excluded News Corporation's stations that had been affiliated to UPN. Having been cut out of the CW deal, News Corporation announced the launch of My Network, noting that My Network would run films from its "sister companies" (News Corporation, 2006).

An Exemplar of Convergence: Time Warner

Despite initial difficulties with AOL, Time Warner's corporate structure effectively converged media technologies including print, radio, television, satellites, telephony, internet, film, and cable systems. This set up pathways for synergizing films across multiple media including infotainment coverage in Time Warner's *Entertainment Weekly*, novelizations published by Warner Books, websites on Time Warner's AOL, etc. Let us trace the pathways from film to television.

Time Warner released films under the Warner Bros. Pictures, Castle Rock Entertainment, New Line, Fine Line, Warner Independent Pictures, and Warner Bros. Animations labels. Movies were repackaged as videos and DVDs under Warner Home Video. Time Warner was a co-owner of the largest pay-per-view service in the United States, along with fellow cable multiple system operators Cox, and Comcast (respectively, 30.3 percent, 15.6 percent, and 54.1 percent). Besides giving Time Warner a pay-per-view outlet, this arrangement united the three largest multiple system operators in support of a single pay-per-view platform, variously called iN DEMAND or oN DEMAND. For Time Warner, this also fostered relationships with Disney, GE, National Amusements, and Sony, which had films to license for pay-per-view.

Time Warner owned the Home Box Office (HBO) and Cinemax premium channels and their digital derivatives (for example, HBO2, HBO Signature, HBO Comedy, MoreMAX, ActionMAX, ThrillerMAX, etc.). Among Time Warner's cable channels that use recent films to fill their schedules are TBS, TNT, and Cartoon Network. As live action and animated films age, Time Warner shifts them to its "classic" channels – Turner Classic Movies for live action, Boomerang for animation. While Time Warner ran some films on the WB, the new CW may be better positioned to run Warner Bros.' blockbuster films. It should be noted that Time Warner occasionally generates television series from its blockbuster franchises, e.g., the Batman franchise's *Birds of Prey* (WB, 2002–3, US) live action series and the animated series *Batman: The Animated Series* (FOX, 1992–5, US).

Underdog? Sony Corporation of America and Sony

As a major innovator of technologies, manufacturer of home and mobile electronics, and provider of financial services and computer-based information systems, Sony has a commitment to invention and innovation that rivals General Electric's. However, not every new technology succeeds in the marketplace, as Sony's superior Betamax videocassette recorder demonstrated in the late 1970s when it was defeated by Mashusita and JVC, whose victory was aided by aggressive licensing of their VHS technology and the greater number of titles available on VHS than Beta. To protect its "hardware" operations (Sony, 1990), Sony began acquiring "software" operations like CBS Records (1988), Columbia Pictures (1989), and Guber-Peters Entertainment, which had produced the original *Batman* film (Tim Burton, 1989, US) for Time Warner. In order to operate more easily in the United States, where anti-Japanese sentiment can be whipped up easily, Sony created Sony Corporation of America. That subsidiary now owns Sony Pictures Entertainment, Columbia TriStar, Sony Pictures Classics and Screen Gems. Given this heritage, Sony Corporation of America may seem an unlikely candidate for the term "underdog."

However, the subsidiary's film and television operations have been disadvantaged in the markets for recirculating film and for network television series (Kunz, 1998, 2006). Sony has had to contend with an oligopoly in cable and broadcast television that is controlled by its rivals in film: Disney, General Electric, National

Amusements, News Corporation, and Time Warner. To get onto one of the two major pay-per-view systems, Sony has had to deal with either National Amusements or the consortium formed by Time Warner, Cox, and Comcast. To get movies onto a major pay cable channel, Sony had to negotiate with National Amusements or Time Warner. Accessing basic cable channels means dealing with Disney, General Electric, National Amusements, News Corporation, or Time Warner – the same companies that control the broadcast networks. As a result, Sony has had to accept unfavorable pricing with regard to films, and to cede copyrights for television series to these oligopolists.

The obvious solution would be to start or acquire television venues of one's own. However, Sony America is barred from owning television stations because it is controlled by a foreign entity and US law requires that station owners be American citizens. Owning stations is crucial to the creation of a national network. With a direct solution apparently blocked, Sony sought other ways into film's ancillary markets.

In 2005, Sony finalized a deal with Comcast, the largest US provider of integrated cable and broadband services, co-owner of eight cable channels, and co-owner of iN DEMAND (*Global News Wire*, 2005; Sony Corporation, 2005). For Sony, the deal meant expanding its properties by acquiring MGM's film library, guaranteed access to Comcast's existing channels, including the iN DEMAND pay-per-view channels, and an agreement that Comcast would create, manage, and carry cable channels featuring movies created or owned by Sony. Through these arrangements, Sony gained some influence over ancillary markets in pay-per-view and presumably premium as well as basic cable. The flows of product created by these arrangements might encourage Sony to favor recirculation of films over cable channels rather than broadcast networks. For Comcast, the deal linked it with a powerful creator and owner of content, perhaps alleviating the rebuff of its hostile bid to take over Disney in 2004 (Sorkin, 2004).

Sony also used this deal to expand its holdings in film by adding MGM and United Artists to Sony Pictures Entertainment, Columbia TriStar, Sony Pictures Classics and Screen Gems. Both Sony and MGM had routinely repackaged movies for sale or rental on VHS/DVD. While the acquisition of MGM and United Artists fed Sony's operations in film and VHS/DVD repackaging, the alliance with Comcast seems to have secured Sony's access to ancillary markets in pay-per-view and cable channels. Sony's ability to own a broadcast network has been stymied to date by federal regulations limiting such ownership to native-born or naturalized US citizens.

From Corporate Structure to Industrial Structure

Looking back to the era immediately after World War II, we can see how changes in Federal economic and regulatory policies have fostered changes in the relationship between the film and television industries. The FCC's decisions favoring the radio establishment's control of television networking effectively blocked the

Hollywood studios from innovating television as home theater. But the studios were not cut out of markets for programming. Despite their complaints about television killing film, the studios rented out their unused capacity for production to television makers, eventually negotiated acceptable prices with networks for films, and launched their own television production units. For decades, film studios used network television as a lucrative ancillary market for premiering theatrical films and local stations as a rerun market for aging movies. In those markets, the studios functioned as sellers and the networks or stations as buyers. The advent of cable television, multiple system operators, and satellite distribution expanded the number of ancillary markets, as did the swift adoption of videocassette recorders.

Technology, then, has been a major force in the film industry's proliferation of ancillary markets. But technology has not been the determining factor in how the studios have structured and restructured those markets. Starting with the Reagan Administration, federal economic policies shifted from support for antitrust law to disregarding such laws. The FCC deregulated television, opening the way for companies to reorganize themselves as transindustrial conglomerates and thereby integrate as many media as possible within a single firm. This allowed companies to internalize ancillary markets such that a company could function as both buyer and seller.

By analyzing the Big Six's corporate structures, we have seen how each company has constructed its own blend of the five ancillary markets for film. When that blend is used synergistically, the owning firm uses its movies to feed its television operations. However, the Big Six are not equally strong in all operations, as is indicated by National Amusements' and Time Warner's decision to merge UPN and WB. As the Sony-Comcast and iN DEMAND arrangements indicate, the Big Six may require the assistance of external partners to meet their goals. Over time, such arrangements may chafe, fostering unease among partners, as is indicated by the exclusion of News Corporation's UPN stations from the CW deal. These and other examples discussed above suggest that we need to better integrate the structural and industrial approaches in order to fully capture how ancillary markets operate both as internal elements of media conglomerates and external markets that companies enter in order to transact their business. However, overall, the analysis does raise questions regarding the future usefulness of our traditional distinction between the television and film industries: are film's Big Six on the way to complete integration of film and television?

REFERENCES

Anderson, C. (1994) *Hollywood TV: The Studio System in the Fifties.* Austin: University of Texas Press.

Balio, T. (n.d.) "Ancillary Markets," Encyclopedia of Television. Chicago: Museum of Broadcast Communications online at <http://www.museum.tv/archives/etv/A/htmlA/ancillarymar/ancillarymar.htm> (accessed July 17, 2007).

Barnouw, E. (1966) *A History of Broadcasting in the United States: A Tower in Babel*, vol. 1. New York: Oxford University Press.

Barnouw, E. (1990) *Tube of Plenty: The Evolution of American Television*, 2nd revised edn. New York: Oxford University Press.

Cantor, M. G. (1980) *Prime Time Television: Content and Control.* Beverly Hills: Sage.

CBS (2006) Form 10–k for 2005, online at <http://www.sec.gov/Archives/edgar/data/813828/000104746906003576/a2168282z10–k.htm> (accessed February 12, 2006).

Dempsey, J. (2006) "ABC Reels in WB Pix," *Daily Variety*, March 17, online at <http://80–web.lexis nexis.com.libezp.lib.lsu.edu/universe/document?_m=c36d7b4a11f54f71906ec254d9ee54e6&_docnum=3&wchp=dGLzVlz-zSkVA&_md5=3c2e18fdd789c0d1c5420d09afd55a2d> (accessed March 19, 2006).

Economist (2005) "Old and New Media Part Ways; Viacom," June 18, online at <http://web.lexisnexis.com.libezp.lib.lsu.edu/universe/document?_m=3de2cac14eec27a32667ecda74ffdc89&_docnum=1&wchp=dGLbVtb-zSkVA&_md5=9deac54b231fdae4c31586e19f92abd7> (accessed July 5, 2006).

Fabrikant, G. (2005) "Viacom Comes to the Great Divide, and Calls It a Path to Growth," *The New York Times*, December 26, online at <http://select.nytimes.com/search/restricted/article?res=F30915FF39540C758EDDAB0994DD404482> (accessed February 21, 2006).

General Electric (2006) Form 10-k for 2005, online at <http://www.sec.gov/Archives/edgar/data/40545/000004054506000009/frm10k.htm> (accessed February 10, 2006).

Gitlin, T. (1983) *Inside Prime Time.* New York: Pantheon Books.

Global News Wire (2005) "Sony, Comcast, and Others Complete MGM Acquisition," April 11 online at <http://80web.lexisnexis.com.libezp.lib.lsu.edu/universe/document?_m=6113e432198f3bfcc3b44ed61b590649&_docnum=1&wchp=dGLbVzbzSkVb&_md5=4426041e49111b3c8a67b3a1611c4469> (accessed February 12, 2006).

Hilmes, M (1990) *Hollywood and Broadcasting: From Radio to Cable.* Urbana: University of Illinois Press.

Kunz, W. M. (1998) "A Political Economic Analysis Of Ownership and Regulation in the Television and Motion Picture Industries." Unpublished Ph.D. dissertation, University of Oregon.

Kunz, W. M. (2006) *Cultural Conglomerates: Consolidation and Concentration in the Motion Picture and Television Industries.* Lanham, MD: Rowman & Littlefield.

McChesney, R. (1999) *Rich Media, Poor Democracy: Communication Politics for a Dubious Times.* Urbana: University of Illinois Press.

Meehan, E. R. (2006) *Why TV Is Not Our Fault.* Lanham, MD: Rowman & Littlefield.

Mosco, V. (1979) *Broadcasting in the United States: Innovative Challenge and Organizational Control.* Norwood, NJ: Ablex.

News Corporation (2005) Form 10–k for 2005, online at <http://ccbn.tenkwizard.com/filing.php?repo=tenk&ipage=3667542&doc=1&total=&attach=ON&TK=NWS&CK=0001308161&FG=0&CK2=1308161&FC=000000&BK=FFFFFF&SC=ON&TC=FFFFFF&TC1=FFFFFF&TC2=FFFFFF&LK=0000FF&AL=FF0000&VL=800080> (accessed February 24, 2006).

News Corporation (2006) "Fox to Launch My Network TV: New Station-Friendly Prime-time Option Set for September," February 22, online at <http://www.newscorp.com/news/news_277.html> (accessed February 24, 2006).

Seldes, G. (1956) *The Public Arts.* New York: Simon & Schuster.

Sony (1990) *Annual Report 1990.* Tokyo: Sony Corporation.

Sony Corporation (2005) "Acquisition of Metro-Goldwyn-Mayer Completed; MGM Names New Senior Management Team," online at <http://www.sony.net/SonyInfo/ IR/news/2005/20050421.html> (accessed January 10, 2006).

Sony Corporation (2006) *Annual Report*, online at <http://www.sony.net/SonyInfo/IR/> (accessed February 20, 2006).

Sorkin, A. R. (2004) "Sony Wins MGM: Comcast Throws in with Group Buying Studio Holdings," *San Francisco Chronicle*, September 14, online at <http://www.sfgate.com/cgi-bin/article.cgi?f=/c/a/2004/09/14/BUGQ08OAVA1.DTL> (accessed October 20, 2004).

Streeter, T. (1996) *Selling the Air: A Critique of the Policy of Commercial Broadcasting in the United States.* Chicago: University of Chicago Press.

Time Warner (2006) Form 10-k for 2005, online at <http://www.shareholder.com/Common/Edgar/1105705/950144–06–1556/06–00.pdf> (accessed February 12, 2006).

TVRules (2006) "TVNews: The WB & UPN Announce Merge Fall Of 2006," January 24, online at <http://www.tvrules.net/modules.php?name=News&file=article&sid=9766> (accessed March 24, 2006).

Viacom (2006) Form 10–k for 2005, online at <http://custom.marketwatch.com/custom/nyt-com/html-secfilings.asp?symb=VIA&sid=2174901&guid=4282066> (accessed February 11, 2006).

Walt Disney Company (2006) Form 10-k for 2005, online at <https://clients.moulton-commerce.com/disney/pdfs/2005_10–K.pdf> (accessed February 9, 2006).

Wasko, J. (1994) *Hollywood in the Information Age: Beyond the Silver Screen.* Austin: University of Texas.

Wasko, J. (2002) *Understanding Disney: The Manufacture of Fantasy.* Cambridge: Polity.

Wasko, J. (2003) *How Hollywood Works.* London: Sage.

CHAPTER 6

ANCILLARY MARKETS – VIDEO AND DVD: HOLLYWOOD RETOOLS

FREDERICK WASSER

The home video revolution is easily the biggest thing to happen to movies since sound. Home video in its successive forms – first the VCR, and now the DVD – contributes more revenue to Hollywood than any other market. This has been true for more than two decades. Its effects are easily measured in the economic sphere; however, the effects in other spheres are less obvious. Home video was the imported revolution, exotic to Hollywood and America. Sony's Betamax, the first successful consumer video device, was greeted with either hostility or chilling indifference from the movie industry. Therefore the most decisive leaders of the revolution were the individual consumers. They determined the use of the machines; they bought them as additions to their TV sets and then transformed them into home movie theaters. Slowly and then more astutely the American film industry adapted to these transformations. By now film executives accept the video revolution as a surprisingly rewarding gift to Hollywood. In order to understand these transformations, it is helpful to look at three groups: manufacturers, audiences, and media industries.

VCR Rollout

The possibility of magnetic recording was first demonstrated by Valdemar Poulsen in 1898, a few years after the invention of cinema. However, the use of magnetic tape to record visual signals was not explored until television had become a mature technology in the 1950s. While the American electronic giant RCA first engaged this problem, it was an upstart, Ampex, that demoed video recording in 1956. Subsequently it was the Japanese company Sony that did the most to bring video recordings to the public. Its half-inch Betamax cassette launched the video revolution in 1975. Another Japanese company, JVC, introduced the Video Home System (VHS) within a few months of Betamax. The system was manufactured by the biggest Japanese electronics firm, Matsushita, and marketed in the US by the still formidable RCA. Collectively Betamax and VHS became known as video-cassette recorders (VCRs).

In 1978 a rival videodisc system from MCA (in partnership with Philips) and another one from RCA three years later were placed on the consumer market. Sony and Matsushita's VCRs were able to match videodisc systems on purchase price and the VCR also had a formidable sociological advantage over videodisc. While the videodisc systems were a play-only technology, the VCR allowed consumers to record programming from television. The entire television broadcasting industry was premised on set schedules that tried to match its audience schedule but the audience was increasingly not able to adhere to such schedules. People in the US and other affluent countries were working more, and as their jobs shifted from manufacturing to services, their schedules became less dependable. Both Sony's chairman, Akio Morita, and Kenjiro Takayanagi (the prime mover behind VHS) had a hunch that the VCR would help with the leisure-time crunch. Morita launched the home video revolution when he emphasized Betamax's ability to "time-shift," which is to say that users could record a TV show at the time it was broadcast and play it back later when it was more convenient to view it.

Morita and Takayanagi were vindicated when, in the US and Japan, consumers embraced VCRs in order to time-shift. The VCR adoption rate was unprecedented. It is important to note that the VCR was not initially viewed as a new market for theatrical movies. The development of a market for pre-recorded video movies was not sought out by Hollywood or the VCR manufacturers but arose, without much forethought, as the market reached a critical mass.

Technologists such as Ruth Schwartz Cowan have tried to model the intersection of the various forces – technology, industry, and consumers – that drives technology adoption. She coined the term "consumption junction," which Joshua Greenberg has more recently applied to the video revolution. Greenberg has demonstrated that there was a pent-up demand for a machine such as the Betamax that would allow users to manipulate the TV schedule and even to eliminate commercial breaks. Other uses emerged and changed the market. People were soon swapping tapes of television shows, mainstream movies, and adult films, even before the Hollywood film studios allowed official transfers of their movies to tape. In 1976 Jim Lowe started *The Videophile's Newsletter* to facilitate and advise about such grassroots activities (Greenberg, 2004: 33–4). By the following year, George Atkinson, Erol Oranan, and other "storefront" entrepreneurs set up the first rental and exchange shops for pre-recorded video tapes.

Due to better distribution by RCA and Matsushita, VHS had a slight initial advantage over the rival Betamax format in the hardware market, and stores therefore tended to stock more VHS copies of a tape. Consumers responded by buying more VHS machines through the 1980s until even the diehard Beta people had to get a VHS machine in order to rent tapes. By the late 1980s Betamax dropped out to become strictly a professional standard while the videodisc systems remained a distant third. However, Philips took its key patents from the laserdisc technology it had developed with MCA and, working in partnership with Sony, in 1983 introduced the compact disc (CD) for playback of music recordings.

Hollywood Reacts

The Hollywood film studios had largely been absorbed into bigger companies by the time the VCR was launched, but their operations were still relatively autonomous. There was no company that owned both a broadcast network and film division in the mid-1970s. Therefore the film executives rarely thought to anticipate new markets or cross media opportunities as the new video technologies were developed for consumers. The major studios were more interested in the expansion of cable channels leasing their film products. In that time period there were several fully independent film companies handling both production and distribution. Some of these were big enough to be known as "mini-majors." These companies did not have the resources to participate in video manufacturing, but they were the first to explore new video market opportunities.

While most large studios were agnostic in their attitude to video, at least two decided to fight the Betamax. Universal and Disney brought a copyright infringement lawsuit against Sony in 1976. Universal made a lot of television shows and was concerned that recording TV programs would lessen the value of these shows. Disney continually recycled their children's classics and was fearful that video copies of their films would destroy their business model for reissuing gems such as *Snow White and the Seven Dwarfs* (David Hand, 1937, US) for each new generation. The court case went on for eight years. Initially Sony won in the United States District Court (1979), before Universal et al. won in the US Court of Appeals (1984), and finally Sony won the final decision by the US Supreme Court in 1984 by a vote of 5 to 4 (464 US 417).

Universal had made two arguments. One was that videotaping was not covered by fair use. This argument collapsed when Universal failed to demonstrate that it suffered substantial economic harm from home taping of TV shows. The second argument was that the VCR contributed towards copyright infringement. This was a somewhat novel elaboration of an issue that had arisen in the early film industry. In 1911, the Supreme Court had ruled that making a film of a copyrighted stage play contributed to the infringement of copyright since the film would be eventually shown to a paying public (222 US 62-63). In this case the "contributory infringement" argument did not convince the judges, who accepted the counterargument that copyright infringement was not the primary use of the VCR. The use of the contributory argument is interesting, since more recently it has been used again successfully in cases against music download facilitators such as Napster and Grokster (Goldstein, 2003: 165–9). In addition, the contributory argument was accepted in West Germany and other European countries, and therefore copyright royalties are collected in these countries from the sale of both video machines and blank videotapes.

As the lawsuit progressed, VCRs continued to be sold and the market for swapping tapes grew. At first the major studios did not move. It was an entrepreneur in Michigan who finally led them into the new world. Andre Blay of Magnetic Video approached the Hollywood film companies for the license to transfer and sell their films on tape in 1977. 20th Century Fox was the only one to respond to Blay's proposal. Their caution was expressed by restricting Blay to older film titles and by forcing him to take on most of the financial risk. He therefore set the videotape price high, at over $50. Since single consumers balked at this pricing, rental stores became the primary customers. Studios (in particular Warner and Disney) resented the rental business, because they could not command a share of the revenues from rental transactions. All they got was the initial sale revenue. While they fretted, the releasing of films on pre-recorded videocassette became a viable market and no one could ignore the new revenue stream. In 1979 20th Century Fox bought out Magnetic Video, and that same year Paramount and Columbia started their own video distribution divisions. In 1980 all the remaining major studios became active in video distribution, except for MCA, the parent company for Universal, which stalled for one more year before becoming the last of the major Hollywood studios to become a video distributor.

In the early years Warner and Disney led the way in trying to force rental stores to share revenue on every rental. At first they asserted it as their legal right, but Atkinson and other rental store owners quickly found out that this was nonsense. Case law had long established the "first sale" doctrine of copyright law. This doctrine upholds the right of purchasers to do whatever they want with the physical copy of the copyrighted material they buy. First sale is the same rule that allows people to sell used copies of their book, to lend out their records, and engage in other common activities. When rental store owners asserted their legal rights, Warner switched tactics and offered a leasing deal that charged a weekly fee of $8.25 (Lardner, 1987: 193). The studio argued that stores could build up their inventory quickly if they leased the tapes for a fraction of the purchase price. However, store owners balked at this deal when it was proposed at a boisterous trade convention in 1982. The studios gave up the leasing programs at that time.

New distributors such as Vestron and LIVE were springing up to distribute films to rental stores even as the Hollywood studios hesitated. Businessmen such as Stuart Karl and Noel Bloom started producing new types of shows such as workout tapes or reviving the moribund genre of children's animation for video. More people were buying VCRs to view pre-recorded video than to time-shift. The greatest jump in the percentage of Americans owning VCRs was in 1988, when 62 percent of all US TV households had one (MPAA, 1995). By the early 1980s a videotape distribution system had evolved modeled on the record business. Suppliers or distributors used duplication services to mass produce pre-recorded cassettes, which were then sold to wholesalers who shipped cassettes to retailers. In this system, distributors (i.e. Hollywood) typically earned about 40 percent of the wholesale price (Wasser, 2001: 143–52).

The Movie Video Market Matures

In 1982 5 million households had VCRs, and Paramount decided to show some initiative by lowering prices in the hope of "selling through" directly to the consumer. While *Star Trek: The Movie* (Robert Wise, 1979, US) had been sold at $80, *Star Trek II: The Wrath of Khan* (Nicholas Meyer, 1982, US) was priced at $40. *Star*

FIGURE 6.1   Boldly going – when Paramount released *Star Trek II: The Wrath of Khan* (1982) on videocassette priced at $40, it became the first "sell-through" release from a Hollywood studio. Produced by Robert Sallin; distributed by Paramount; directed by Nicholas Meyer.

Trek II sold in large enough volume to offset the lower margin. "Sell-through" pricing was born. However, lower prices did not work for every movie. Some movies everyone wanted to own, other movies only some wanted to rent. Studios had to decide whether films would attract high enough volume sales outside the usual rental stores. They usually released the biggest films and children's titles ("kidvid") at the lower sell-through prices while most films, even very popular ones, were released at the higher prices and were bought predominantly by the rental stores. This system was called two-tiered pricing.

The Walt Disney Company would soon take advantage of two-tiered pricing. It had initially expressed its caution about home video by joining the Universal lawsuit and by unsuccessfully trying to force revenue sharing. As new media evolved in the 1980s, the stockholders grew tired of a lackluster management and made Michael Eisner (formerly at Paramount) the CEO in 1984. Within a year his team decided to release old classics such as *Pinocchio* (Hamilton Luske and Ben Sharpsteen, 1940, US) at sell-through prices to recapture the children's video market. Disney has dominated the sell-through market in video products ever since. This domination financed the expansion of Disney through the late 1980s and 1990s and led the studio's Head of Production, Jeffrey Katzenberg, to revive the production of full-length animation films, a policy he continued during the second half of the 1990s after he became a founding partner in the new studio DreamWorks SKG. Disney emerged the biggest winner in video through the early 1990s, and other studios shook off the dust to develop their own libraries into goldmines.

Independent producers and mini-major studios such as Orion, Vestron, DeLaurentiis, Carolco (allied with LIVE), and Cannon did not have big libraries and therefore expanded their production through the mid-1980s in anticipation that the global video market would pay for more new movies. In contrast the

Hollywood majors did not substantially increase the number of productions (they already had libraries of popular titles) but instead increased the money spent on making and marketing their films. These costs went up almost fourfold between 1980 and 1994. The attempt by the independents to match the marketing campaigns of the major studios meant that even successful films had lower profit margins. Thus when there were inevitable flops and disappointments the independents had no financial cushion, and all of the above had gone out of business by the 1990s. Other independents such as Miramax and New Line allowed themselves to be absorbed by the majors (Disney and Time Warner respectively).

The story was different for major studio executives, who found out that the video market was just right for the "blockbuster." Just on the cusp of the video revolution, Steven Spielberg and George Lucas had demonstrated that movies could be very big with their respective hits *Jaws* (1975, US) and *Star Wars* (1977, US), but these films had cost a lot of money to produce and market. This became the blockbuster formula. However, the risks were demonstrated by the big-budget movie, *Heaven's Gate* (Michael Cimino, 1980, US), which ruined United Artists when no one went to see it in the theater. But starting in 1982, the video market returned enough substantial money to the major studios to give them effective ability to cross-collaterize reversals. Cross-collaterizing means that the movie industry takes the money it makes from hits to write off the losses it sustains from flops. Since video and other ancillary markets – non-theatrical markets such as video, cable, etc. – would ultimately return enough money to cover the flops, the studios could continue to make blockbuster movies. *Heaven's Gate* did not stop the big-budget trend; instead the lesson was that it had come two years too early. Through the next two decades, the studios began to operate at lower profit margins on higher volumes of revenue returns (Vogel, 1994: 45).

Big media corporations (with operations in news, magazines, television, cable) liked how video had enhanced the value of film libraries. Starting with the purchase of 20th Century Fox by News Corporation in 1985, every major film division was absorbed by larger media conglomerates. A graphic illustration of the power of video was demonstrated when in February 1994 Viacom paid $9.85 billion to purchase a 74.6 percent stake in Paramount. Viacom was able to finance the deal with the money it raised from its ownership of the video rental giant Blockbuster, which it had acquired only the previous month for $8.4 billion. A different motivation led to Sony and Matsushita getting into the movie business. The Japanese electronics manufacturers purchased film studios to ensure content for their videos, CDs, and other hardware. Undoubtedly, Sony wanted to have an advantage if there was ever another format war. It purchased Columbia Records in 1988 and Columbia Pictures the next year. Matsushita bought MCA/Universal at the end of 1990 but sold it in 1995 after failing to maximize the value of the studio's assets and demonstrating how film companies belong more properly to media conglomerates than to electronics manufacturers. Indeed, since its entry into the music and film businesses, Sony has changed itself into a media conglomerate to the point where its entertainment divisions are now more profitable than its electronics divisions.

Movie theaters were naturally apprehensive about their new rival market. The development and spread of the multiplex theaters in the early 1980s can be explained as a defensive response to the video revolution. The multiplex could either show many different movies at the same time or one movie with several different overlapping times. They were offering audiences some semblance of the flexibility of home video. The spurt of rebuilding and reconditioning theaters helped maintain constant box-office ticket sales even as video rental grew in size. Theaters continually had to fight off threats from the movie studios to release videotapes while the movies were still in the theaters. The threat continues, although in most cases the movie theaters have managed to hold on to an exclusive window of four to six months before the video or DVD is released. Exhibitors have also increased their revenues throughout the video revolution. The money that the major studios earned from video was therefore new money, not money that replaced lost theatrical earnings.

This new money gave studios the courage by 1985 to increase production budgets beyond the upper limit of US theatrical revenues (Cohn, 1987; Wasser, 2001: 169–71). The new mega-media strategy now was to prepare film and television shows for "repurposing" across various media platforms. The strategists had learned from video that the key to staying ahead of subsequent technological innovations was to have libraries, and the people who had libraries were the old film studios. The conglomerates of the 1980s and 1990s wanted to maximize exploitation by making sure that they controlled distribution divisions in all delivery systems from analog video to broadband digital. The strategy was labeled "synergy" or "cross-media marketing" depending on which Wall Street analyst was speaking. The numbers show how singularly important video was for this strategy. By 1987 Goldman Sachs reported that videocassettes provided the single largest market for films, contributing $3.1 billion or 43 percent of worldwide revenues for US films and surpassing the theatrical, cable, and broadcast television segments.

Video opened up international markets for the new owners of Hollywood. The popularity of home video revealed audiences that wanted more on their TV sets, and governments felt that they had to respond. In Europe the countries that most quickly embraced the VCR were often those countries, such as in Scandinavia, where people felt that TV was not varied enough. The popularity of the VCR implicitly pressured governments to create more television. Everywhere regulations that once hindered the development of new broadcast networks were dropped. New networks were formed from the British Isles to the Korean peninsula. In each case the new programmers filled up their new channels with television and films from Hollywood.

A similar "deregulating" effect occurred in the United States. In 1976 the American media had a few regulations in place such as: the prevention of cross-ownership of movie studios and movie theaters (Paramount consent decree); the obligation for television stations to broadcast programs of "public interest" (fairness doctrine); the prohibition on networks owning shows they distributed (Fin-Syn). In each case the justification for the rules was to enhance competition and diversity of voices in the movie and television industries. The Reagan Administration (1981–9) was hostile to all these rules, and in its briefs and papers cited the VCR and cable as new technologies that had increased competition and diversity, thus eliminating the need for government regulation of media industries. They announced that they would stop enforcing the Paramount consent decree in 1985 and rescinded the fairness doctrine in 1987, while the Fin-Syn rules stayed in place until 1995.

Home video did not, however, open up new competition. Its revenues helped major studios and too few others. In addition on the retail and wholesaling level, its structure favored oligopoly. Blockbuster Video started buying up other rental stores in 1985 and grew to become the largest chain by 1987. In the 1990s mass merchant Wal-Mart became the biggest sell-through outlet for videos and DVDs. Both consolidations favored the Hollywood studios since these companies only dealt with the top suppliers. Currently, no independent producer/distributor tries to enter the video market without forming expensive alliances with a Hollywood studio that has the clout to deal with such retailers. For example, in 2004, Newmarket distributed the very successful *Passion of the Christ* (Mel Gibson, 2004, US) to the theaters. Although the company could anticipate high DVD sales, it had to turn over video distribution to 20th Century Fox, which pocketed the standard 20–30 percent distribution fee from video revenues. Video does not enhance competition; it just allows the big to get bigger (Wasko, 1994: 249–52).

Through the 1990s, there was a drift towards more direct sales of videos to the consumer. The price of manufacturing pre-recorded videos had dropped to below $2. Video direct sale prices fell accordingly, below the price of going to the theater if transportation and other costs were factored in. Studios refined the fine art of pricing video releases, generally issuing family fare and mega-hits at low prices for direct sales while reserving high prices, ranging over $70, for all other titles. In this same time, chain rental stores became more interested in leasing titles rather than buying them, in contrast to the early days when they refused to lease. This arrangement is referred to as "revenue sharing" since the studios receive a portion of every rental charge. From 1998 the largest renters such as Blockbuster have negotiated their own leasing arrangements with the Hollywood studios, while video wholesaler Rentrak has become the biggest middleman operation for leasing tapes to various small and mid-level stores. By the late 1990s the roll-out of DVDs was putting additional pressure on stores to revenue share in order to provide a sufficient inventory of hits.

DVD

As the market for VHS became saturated, several media executives and manufacturers became interested in other home video technologies (Hettrick, 2005). By 1993 moves were afoot to improve on laserdisc and CD technology by using new digital compression methods. This led to the creation of several new formats including the DVD (signifying either "digital versatile disc or digital video disc, depending on whom you ask": Parker, 1999: 80).

To facilitate development the DVD Forum was created between electronics manufacturers – seven Japanese (Hitachi, JVC, Matsushita, Mitsubishi, Pioneer,

Sony and Toshiba) and two European (Philips and Thomson). Media conglomerate Time Warner was the only non-manufacturer in the forum and the only American member. At that time three members of the forum – Matsushita, Sony, and Time Warner – owned movie studios and extensive film libraries. In 1995 Matsushita sold its Hollywood studio to the Canadian company Seagram and reverted to its core business of electronics manufacturing. Time Warner's participation was key since Warner Home Video's President Warren Lieberfarb believed in the DVD and effectively pressured the Hollywood studios to back it (Hettrick, 1997: 65). Because of Hollywood solidarity there was a smooth launch of the DVD system in the US during March 1997, followed by rapid success (Parkes, 1999). DVD built upon the lessons learned from the VCR launch about cooperation between the manufacturers and the film studios, which led to all parties agreeing a universal standard and avoiding the format battles which afflicted the introduction of the VCR.

Lieberfarb anticipated correctly that DVD sell-through would yield better financial results than the saturated videotape market. When DVD was introduced in 1997, discs sold at the low price of $20, for which the consumer received a higher-quality image and the supplementary features of director commentaries, additional footage, and clips about the making of the film. The studios were able to earn 58–60 percent of the DVD wholesale retail price (Kirkpatrick, 2003: 1). By 1999 all the studios were releasing DVD and VHS copies of titles simultaneously (Lieberfarb, 2002). The audience responded with enthusiasm, and DVD consumer sales overtook VHS sales in 2002. Customers liked the added features of a DVD, and the studios invested money in placing commentaries and alternate versions on the discs. One pleasant surprise was that since the DVD took up less shelf space, people would buy entire seasons of TV shows. TV releases had been a small part of the videotape sales, but with DVD up to 15 percent of 2004 DVD sales were accounted for by TV titles which were considered by many to be one of most exciting categories of sales in the market (Netherby and Hettrick, 2005: 1).

As of this writing there is a new format war looming over the next generation of DVDs which deliver high-definition images. Standard DVD does not take advantage of the increased image resolution of the HDTV sets, but the United States government is pressuring broadcasters to switch over to HD broadcasting and consequently most US TV viewers will soon start buying HDTV sets. High-definition DVD has split Hollywood into two camps: Blu-ray Disc (developed by Sony and backed by 20th Century Fox, Lions Gate, and Disney) and HD-DVD (New Line and Universal). At this time the split is unresolved, with some studios (Paramount, Warner) releasing in both formats. Hardware for both formats was released in late spring of 2006 at prices ranging from $500 to $1,000 (Pogue, 2006: C1).

The Big Picture: Audience/Hollywood

The brief history of the video revolution inspires several further questions about why it took the path it did and its impact on the cultural status of Hollywood feature films. The success of consumer video suggests a sea-change in mass media audiences. Throughout the twentieth century the percentage of disposable income that Americans spent on mass media remained constant, as suggested by Charles Scripps and proven by Maxwell McCombs (see McCombs, 1972). By the end of the 1980s, Wood and O'Hare (1991) were able to prove that since the video revolution, the relative amount of media money Americans were spending had gone up. The DVD format only pushed the amount of spending further. By 2004, 90 percent of all US households owning TV sets had a VCR (98.9 million) and 60 percent had DVD players (MPAA, 2005). In that same year they spent $27 billion on DVD software while overseas consumers spent $24.6 billion (Johnson, 2005). Meanwhile consumer spending on the box office was roughly half that amount ("US Film," 2005). The revenue that Hollywood collects from these various markets is hard to tabulate since studios use the catch-all category of "filmed entertainment" (which includes all of TV). In this enlarged category it is estimated, for the most recent tabulated year, that home video contributed 47 percent of total 2004 global revenue of $44.8 billion for major US film studios (Hollinger, 2005: 1).

There are many other reasons beside the increase in spending to suppose that video has altered the global audience. The most obvious change is that "going to the movies" is no longer the primary way to consume a film. Home video thereby becomes part of a larger trend towards privatizing life. It is part of "mobile privatization" – a term originally coined by Raymond Williams (1992) in 1974 on the cusp of the VCR age. He described a century-long trend of centering life inside the home and looking out at the world from the domestic space. Home video has become another technology facilitating such "cocooning."

Video may have also contributed to a downgrading of the status of films, about which industry types and academics have complained (an example can be found in Allen, 1999). While still a top executive at Disney, Jeffrey Katzenberg issued a memo warning that home video lessens the movie experience ("The Teachings of Chairman Jeff," 1991). Spielberg famously resisted releasing E.T. The Extra-Terrestrial (1982, US) on video for four years because he wanted everyone to experience it on the big screen first. It has also been argued that video has loosened the ties between films and linear narrative coherence, and certainly viewers can now control video and watch it in a state of domestic distraction, consuming scenes outside of their scripted order. Thus scenes and effects can be more important to this audience than character development and other hallmarks of classic narratives. Certainly video has contributed to the loss of specialty theaters that once devoted themselves to art and foreign films.

On the other hand there continues to be hope that video will empower the grassroots filmmaker. I have already discussed how the US video market only contributed to the big getting bigger. But this is not a universal experience. In Nigeria cheap video equipment has sparked a decade-long boom in small-time filmmaking. Even in the United States there is more use of video equipment to get films on the internet, though it remains hard to distribute self-made tapes/DVDs on a level that earns profits. Video led to higher production and marketing costs and raised very high entry barriers for new studios. There are instances of the video market allowing the audience to declare effective support for some films and TV shows despite lack of corporate support. A recent example is the 2005 revival of *Family Guy* (Fox, 1999–2002, 2005 to present, US), which after cancellation was placed back on the air due to its strong DVD sales after 2002.

Authentic diversity in production and distribution is a perennial problem in a mass-media-dominated culture. Does home video enhance or obstruct diversity? The access to a library of current and former titles changes filmmaking practices. Right now there is an excess of cultural self-referencing. But it may lead to a genuine interest in diverse ways of making films for diverse reasons. The Hollywood film is currently a multi-purpose commodity, equally suited to the big or small screen, for private as well as public viewing, for merchandising as well as video gaming. But the use of technology is not determined by the industry only; it is negotiated by the triad of viewers, industries, and artists.

REFERENCES

Allen, R. (1999) "Home Alone Together: Hollywood and the 'Family Film'," in M. Stokes and R. Maltby (eds.), *Identifying Hollywood's Audience: Cultural Identity and the Movies*. London: British Film Institute, pp. 109–31.

Cohn, L. (1987) "Pics Payback Keeps On Perking," *Variety*, March 4, pp. 1, 40.

Cowan, R. S. (1987) "The Consumption Junction: A Proposal for Research Strategies in the Sociology of Technology," in T. Pinch, W. Bijker, and T. Hughes (eds.), *The Social Construction of Technological Systems*. Cambridge, MA: MIT Press, pp. 261–80.

Goldman Sachs (1991) *Movie Industry Update*.

Goldstein, P. (2003) *Copyright's Highway: From Gutenberg to the Celestial Jukebox*, revised edn. Stanford: Stanford University Press.

Greenberg, J. M. (2004) "From Betamax to Blockbuster." Ph.D. dissertation, Cornell University.

Hettrick, S. (1997) "WHV on Platform for DVD," *The Hollywood Reporter*, January 9, pp. 1, 65.

Hettrick, S. (2005) E-mail to the author from the editor-in-chief of *DVD Exclusive*, June 27.

Hollinger, H. (2005) "DVD Rocking Studios' World," *The Hollywood Reporter*, May 3, pp. 1, 67.

Johnson, R. (2005) "Good News in Hollywood, Shhh," *The New York Times*, January 31, p. 1.

Kirkpatrick, D. (2003) "Action-Hungry DVD Fans Sway Hollywood," *The New York Times*, August 17, p. 1 (downloaded from Lexis Nexis on May 1, 2007).

Lardner, J. (1987) *Fast Forward: Hollywood, the Japanese and the Onslaught of the VCR*. New York: W. W. Norton.

Lieberfarb, W. (2002) "2001: The Breakout of DVD," DVD Entertainment Group Press Reception, International Consumer Electronics Show, January 8, online at <http://www.dvdinformation.com/News/press/WLCESfnl.ppt> (accessed December 23, 2005).

McCombs, M. (1972) "Mass Media in the Marketplace," *Journalism Monographs*, 24, August.

MPAA (1995) *US Economic Review*. Encino, CA: Motion Picture Association of America.

MPAA (2005) *US Entertainment Industry: 2004 MPA Market Statistics*. Los Angeles: Motion Picture Association of America.

Netherby, J., and S. Hettrick (2005) "Disk Bliss for Biz," *Daily Variety*, January 5, p. 1.

Parker, D. J. (1999) "Defining DVD," *IEEE Multimedia*, 6(1), pp. 80–4.

Parkes, C. (1999) "Disc World Crusader," *Financial Times*, February 8, p. 13.

Pogue, D. (2006) "Which New DVD Format? Neither Just Yet," *The New York Times*, June 22, pp. C1, C12.

"The Teachings of Chairman Jeff" (1991) *Variety*, February 4, pp. 5, 24.

"US Film" (2005) *Screen Finance*, March 23, p. 7.

Vogel, H. L. (1994) *Entertainment Industry Economics: A Guide for Financial Analysis*, 3rd edn. Cambridge: Cambridge University Press.

Wasko, J. (1994) *Hollywood in the Information Age*. Cambridge: Polity.

Wasser, F. (2001) *Veni, Vidi, Video: The Hollywood Empire and the VCR*. Austin: University of Texas Press.

Williams, R. (1992) *Television: Technology and Cultural Form*. Hanover, NH : University Press of New England.

Wired (2005) "The Big Picture," September, p. 109.

Wood, W. C., and S. L. O'Hare (1991) "Paying for the Video Revolution: Consumer Spending on the Mass Media," *Journal of Communication*, 41(1), pp. 24–30.

CHAPTER 7

ANCILLARY MARKETS – VIDEO GAMES: PROMISES AND CHALLENGES OF AN EMERGING INDUSTRY

RANDY NICHOLS

Ties between the video game and film industries have existed for more than 30 years. The early video game industry actively modeled itself on the film industry, attempting to emulate its structures and controls (*People*, 1985; Brandt, 1987; Wasko, 2003). Video games were seen as a technology that could expand upon all that was great in film – immersive storytelling, emotional response from an audience, and, of course, profit. Such a beginning may seem surprising to us 30 years down the line when press coverage of video games seeks to place them as the hot, new idea even in relation to film.

In part, the current interest in video games by the film industry owes to the scare caused when video game profit exceeded US box-office ticket sales (Bloom, 2001; Hein, 2002; *USA Today*, 2003; Grover et al., 2005). Figure 7.1 compares the revenues from software sales and Hollywood's box office from 1995 through 2001. By 2004, video games had consistently surpassed Hollywood box-office revenue. Moreover,

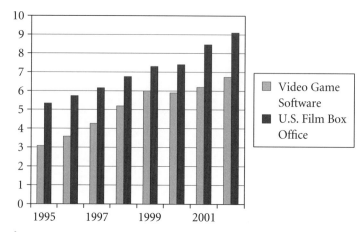

FIGURE 7.1   US video game software sales and film box-office receipts ($ billion)
Source: ESA, 2002a; MPA, 2005.

a number of major media and communication companies began to use video games for branding and advertising, and Hollywood franchises benefited from integrating video games, for instance, "Harry Potter," "Lord of the Rings," and "James Bond" (Bloom, 2001; Bloom and Graser, 2002). Cross-industry licensing has cut both ways, and the video game industry has begun to look for inroads into Hollywood's territory. When Microsoft's *Halo 2* broke sales records, prompting the game producer's decision to produce its own movie rather than go through Hollywood channels, it was seen as a sea-shift for the two industries, leaving analysts to wonder who would come out on top (Fritz, 2004; Brodesser and Fritz, 2005; Holson, 2005a).

In spite of the tremendous profitability of video games, it seems unlikely that video games will supplant Hollywood anytime soon. A comparison of the two industries reveals a number of areas the video game industry will have to master before truly threatening film. But Hollywood is no longer the 800-pound gorilla; particularly in matters of technology and production, the video game industry is holding its own.

Birth of a Notion: The Early History of Film and Video Games

Hollywood's interest in video games as an ancillary market goes back almost as far as video games themselves. The film industry's involvement with video games has worked in one of two ways: either the film industry is seeking active control – and hence, ownership – in the video game industry, or the industry is content to license products to video game producers. When video game profits are up, Hollywood seeks control. When profits are down, Hollywood licensing is the order of the day.

Hollywood's forays into the video game industry have always been problematic at best. To some extent, this has been due to Hollywood's uncertainty about how video games should be developed. Typically, the film industry has seen video games as a promotional ploy for a movie, with video games being little more than ways for players to re-enact what was on screen. But Hollywood isn't completely to blame. In the early years of the video game industry, it became common practice for video game developers to license movies and superficially redesign an existing video game to match up with a Hollywood film. Why make a new game based on *Raiders of the Lost Ark* (Steven Spielberg, 1981, US) when you already had *Pitfall?* Because of this, it may come as no surprise that it is a video game based on a hit movie, *E.T. The Extra-Terrestrial* (Steven Spielberg, 1982, US), that marks the first decline of video games in the early 1980s, and with it, Hollywood's first major distancing from the industry (Kent, 2001). The 1984 failure of the game resulted in 5 million cartridges being sent to a landfill, representing the biggest failure of the Hollywood/video game attempts at crossover (Grover et al., 2005).

The video game industry took a sharp decline in the early 1980s. Hollywood would not take an active interest in the creation of video games until the mid-1990s, though licensing was still common. The industry's resurgence led companies like

DreamWorks SKG, Time Warner, and Disney, as well as other media giants, to build their own game development units. Ultimately, these developments faltered due to high development costs and to Hollywood's continued video game blindspot (Holson, 2005a).

By the late 1990s, Fox and DreamWorks had all but abandoned their game units, preferring instead to license content and allow the video game industry to risk the high costs of development (Grover et al., 2005). But it was during this period that the video game industry made its first inroads into converting its properties into film (table 7.1). In 2003, Hollywood entered its most recent foray into the video game industry, with Hollywood majors restructuring their franchise models to better allow game development of a variety of properties from the extensive libraries of content owned by the major Hollywood players (Diamante, 2005). Table 7.1 details the top ten video games made into films.

Halo, Hollywood; Video Games Come of Age

As an emerging cultural industry, the video game industry has worked towards developing its own unique "logics of production" (Miege, 1989). These logics include the rules of the distinct markets in which video games are made and sold, labor patterns, and methods of production, distribution, marketing, and retail practices which bring video games to the point of consumption. In order to understand these logics, one must understand how production is organized (Wasko, 2003).

As noted previously, the video game industry has modeled itself on Hollywood, organizing itself into hardware manufacturers, game developers, game publishers, and retailers. Licensing arrangements, marketing deals, and production specifications are all negotiated through either software publishers or hardware manufac-

FIGURE 7.2 Grossing over $131 million at the North American box office, *Lara Croft: Tomb Raider* (2001) proved commercial success can be found with the transfer of game properties to the big screen. Produced by Lawrence Gordon, Lloyd Levin and Colin Wilson; distributed by Paramount; directed by Simon West

TABLE 7.1   US video game software sales and film box office receipts ($ million)

Film	Studio	Game publisher	Adjusted gross ($ million)	Release date
Lara Croft: Tomb Raider (Simon West, 2001, US)	Paramount	Eidos	$131.2	2001
Pokemon: The First Movie (Michael Hagney and Kunihiko Yuyama, 1999, US)	Warner	Nintendo	$95.5	1999
Mortal Kombat (Paul W. S. Anderson, 1995, US)	New Line	Midway	$91.7	1999
Pokemon: The Movie 2000 (Michael Hagney and Kunihiko Yuyama, 2000 , US)	Warner	Nintendo	$45.9	2000
Street Fighter (Steven E. de Souza, 1995, US)	Universal	Capcom	$45.3	1994
Mortal Kombat: Annihilation (John R. Leonetti, 1997, US)	New Line	Midway	$44.3	1997
Final Fantasy: The Spirits Within (Hironobu Sakaguchi and Moto Sakakibara, 2001, Japan)	Sony	Square/Nintendo	$32.1	2001
Super Mario Bros. (Annabel Jankel and Rocky Morton, 1993, US)	Disney	Nintendo	$28.6	1993
Resident Evil (Paul W. S. Anderson, 2002, US)	Sony	Capcom	$17.7	2002
Pokemon 3: The Movie (Michael Hagney and Kunihiko Yuyama, 2001, US)	Warner	Nintendo	$17.1	2001

Source: ELPSA, 2003; Wasko, 2003.

turers, allowing power within the industry to concentrate in these sectors (Williams, 2002; Nichols, 2005). The industry is highly concentrated in both hardware manufacture and software publishing. In 2004, global revenues for the top 17 companies in the industry topped $24.5 billion, with the top four companies – Sony, Microsoft, Nintendo, and Electronic Arts – earning between $16.7 and $18 billion on their own (*Gamasutra*, 2005b).

Like the film industry, the video game industry is transnational in nature, though not to the same extent as film. Currently, there are three main product markets – North America, Europe, and Japan (Dyer-Witherford, 2002). Products in these markets are regionalized, so that a game from one region cannot be used on a machine from another region. In Japan, almost 80 percent of households own and play video games (Aoyama and Izushi, 2004). Japan is the second largest market for video games behind the United States and has served as the first market for a number of games (Guth, 2001). Moreover, it is home to two of the biggest companies in the industry, Sony and Nintendo, both producers of hardware and software. The Japanese market is also notable because it has proven to be a remarkable test of which games will be successful globally (Nelson, 1990). In contrast, the European market has tended to be treated as the least consequential, and has been often the last market for new hardware to be deployed (*Gamasutra*, 2005a; Ip and Jacobs, 2004).

While this may suggest a strong similarity to the logics of film production, video games draw on two other industries to define themselves: the toy industry and the computer industry. And it is from these areas that many of the disputes between video games and film arise. Like the toy industry, video games work on a distinct production schedule. A majority of video game profits come in the fourth quarter – the Christmas buying season. In 2003, for example, the industry sold roughly $7 billion in goods during the holiday quarter alone (Richtel, 2004).

Similarly, from the computer industry, video game production has come to rely on a system of planned obsolescence, with new hardware systems produced roughly every two to three years. In turn, this requires new games to be produced and new purchases to be made by consumers. The industry has also drawn its system of labor organization from computer production, which has resulted in an industry that has relied on work incentives such as stock options to ensure worker satisfaction. While these incentives were effective, it enabled the industry to resist attempts at unionization. However, following the burst of the dot.com bubble, such incentives became less effective and employee dissatisfaction resulted in attempts at unionization which the video game industry resisted (Dyer-Witherford, 1999; Nichols, 2005). However, as technologies have advanced, increasing production times are often longer than those for Hollywood blockbusters. Development for Triple-A games, the video game equivalent of a blockbuster movie like *Titanic* (James Cameron, 1997, US) or *Star Wars* (George Lucas, 1977, US), can now take between 18 and 24 months (Levine, 2005b).

Finally, the video game industry has worked to draw in larger adult audiences, which has helped to keep the industry profitable. While conventional wisdom holds that video games are a children's medium, there is ample evidence that, both in its early history and currently, video games rely heavily on adult use as a means to profitability (ESA, 2002b, 2004; Nichols, 2005). Conservative estimates suggest that as many as 50 percent of Americans over the age of 6 play video games and approximately 17 percent of computer-owning households include someone who plays online games (Bulkeley, 2003; ESA, 2005b). Not surprisingly, video games are also tremendously popular with college-age individuals, an audience that also is one of the key demographic groups for moviegoers. In the US, more than 65 percent of students indicate that they play video games regularly (Carlson, 2003). But games are also popular with an older crowd. In the US, the average player age is 29 years old, and at least 17 percent of all gamers are over the age of 50 (Emeling, 2004;

ESA, 2005a). Studies show that already as many as 39 percent of all gamers are women (Grover et al., 2005). The ages of female players are striking: girls aged 6 to 17 make up roughly 12 percent of the total video games market, while women over 18 make up 26 percent (Loftus, 2003). It is the older audience that has best supported the industry's growth, allowing video games to draw increasing numbers of not only males over the age of 20 but women as well.

The New Odd Couple: Cross-Industry Benefits

With the video game industry again appearing highly profitable, it is not surprising that Hollywood is again trying to figure out its relationship to video games. In spite of the high profitability of the video games industry, which has surpassed US box-office sales, Hollywood is still the stronger industry (Diamante, 2005). Not only does the film industry have a more extensive catalog of established intellectual properties, but it also has more ways to ensure profit from a concept. By marketing the idea for a film or a video game through all of film's ancillary markets, profitability is much more certain for a company than it is with just a single commodity.

In contrast, video game revenues depend primarily on sales with a small amount coming from game rentals. Moreover, video games typically have a shelf-life of roughly three months, unlike films which can be released and re-released over a longer period of time (Grover et al., 2005). But increasingly, video games and film are becoming an integral part of the film industry's synergy strategy. In 2002, more than 100 games were being developed based on movies and video releases (Tramain, 2002). And in 2005, when Sony scheduled the launch of its PlayStation Portable platform, United Pictures International released a number of movies specially formatted for the device (Dawtrey, 2005). The most successful games tend fit the Hollywood action formula, which has been so successful internationally (Wasko, 2003). Table 7.2 shows the most successful games based on movies from 2001 to 2005. Among these are games based on the Spider-Man, Matrix, and Lord of the Rings franchises.

For the video game industry, drawing on Hollywood's catalog makes sense. The rights to older films are much cheaper than developing a new concept. Estimates suggest that the rights to an older film can run between $150,000 and $400,000 – much cheaper than the $1 million and more for a new release. But unlike releases based on current movies, such games don't receive the benefit of the marketing provided by the promotion of new Hollywood films. Because major games can now cost more than $10 million to produce, without the benefit of Hollywood's marketing dollars, a licensed game may need to sell as many as half a million copies in order to be profitable, which very few titles can manage (Levine, 2005b).

By relying on Hollywood licensing, the video game industry has started to free itself from the production constraints of the toy industry. While typically video games have been released on or close to the release date of major films, in order to benefit from the marketing of films, increasingly the release date is being pushed back to coincide with DVD releases and other film promotions (Elkin, 2002; *USA Today*,

TABLE 7.2   Successful video games based on movies, 2001–2005

Film	US box-office gross	Video game revenue
Spider-Man (Sam Raimi, 2002, US)	$403,706,375	$149,544,132
Spider-Man 2 (Sam Raimi, 2004, US)	$373,595,825	$116,123,491
Lord of the Rings: The Two Towers (Peter Jackson, 2002, New Zealand)	$341,786,758	$102,031,678
Lord of the Rings: The Return of the King (Peter Jackson, 2003, New Zealand)	$377,027,325	$92,559,581
The Matrix Reloaded (Andy Wachowski and Larry Wachowski, 2003, US)	$281,576,461	$91,193,922
Star Wars: Episode III – Revenge of the Sith (George Lucas, 2005, US)	$380,270,577	$80,841,742
Harry Potter and the Chamber of Secrets (Chris Columbus, 2002, US)	$261,988,482	$77,362,255
Finding Nemo (Andrew Stanton, 2003, US)	$339,714,978	$76,368,870
The Incredibles (Brad Bird, 2004, US)	$261,441,092	$72,315,486
Harry Potter and the Sorcerer's Stone (Chris Columbus, 2001, US)	$317,575,550	$67,875,142

Source: Gamedaily.biz, 2006.

2003). This has allowed the video game industry to begin producing games to be released year-round, freeing the game business from some of the difficulties of not only its long production schedule, but also the increasing production and advertising costs associated with major releases (Nichols, 2005).

Mortal Kombat: Tensions Between the Industries

Though ties between the two industries seem to offer numerous benefits, there are also a number of conflicts. A majority of these are unrelated to licensing, but instead focus on questions of production and labor. When the film *Final Fantasy: The Spirits Within* was released in 2001, it was seen as a watershed moment not only because it was a blockbuster based on a video game, but also because developers used tools to create video games to create the film itself. This resulted in discussions about computer-generated stars supplanting the Hollywood star system (Bloom, 2001). While little has come of this debate, the use of game-design tools to aid in film production has been increasing.

A number of games include built-in movie-making tools that allow players to make and modify their own animation (*Economist*, 2004). This animation, termed "machinima," can rival the graphical capabilities used to create movies like *Shrek*

FIGURE 7.3   *Final Fantasy: The Spirits Within* (2001), from game to film. Produced by Jun Aida, Chris Lee, and Hironobu Sakaguchi; distributed by Columbia; directed by Hironobu Sakaguchi and Moto Sakakibara

(Adam Adamson, 2001, US) or *Finding Nemo* (Andrew Stanton, 2003, US) (*Economist*, 2004; Levin, 2005a). Machinima has been used by Spike TV to help create shorts for its 2003 video game awards program, and by Steven Spielberg to help storyboard his movie *Artificial Intelligence: A.I.* (*Economist*, 2004). It has also become a staple of video game marketing campaigns and has influenced the development of a number of television shows and internet shorts based on video games (Levin, 2005a). Surprisingly, the type of Hollywood companies seemingly best capable of making the leap to producing their own video games – animation studios – have preferred to sign outside licensing deals. Among those companies seeking outside game production are Pixar, DreamWorks Animation, and Fox's animation studios (Fritz, 2005c). Recent plans by Microsoft to work around Hollywood and develop its own movie for the "Halo" franchise have raised eyebrows in the film industry (Fritz, 2004; Grover et al., 2005). Though not directly a response, a number of Hollywood companies are considering tightening policies on video game production. The head of Warner Bros.' new game division, Jason Hall, stirred the hornets' nest by insisting that licensed games that do not meet minimum quality standards set by Warner will receive decreased royalties (Holson, 2005b).

Labor and unionization have also become a problem for the two industries. As noted previously, the video game industry, like most computer and high-tech industries, has been reluctant to unionize. However, as video games have come to increasingly rely on Hollywood talent there has been more pressure for the industry to incorporate unions. In 2004, almost 2,000 unionized actors found work in video games, including such notables as Ewan McGregor, Tobey Maguire, and Willem Dafoe (Gentile, 2005). As the profits in the video game industry have risen, actors have started to demand a bigger share of the pie. Recent contract negotiations between the industry and the Screen Actors Guild (SAG) and the American Federation of Television and Radio Artists (AFTRA) focused heavily on ensuring that voice actors for video games received compensation including health care, pensions, and residuals (Brodesser and McNary, 2005). However, because the profitability of video games is less than that of films, residuals were a hotly contested issue in the negotiations. The previous contract provided minimum pay rates with no provision for residuals, in part because so much of video game voice work has always been done in-house (Brodesser, 2005). The video game industry is also wary of residuals because currently only 10 to 15 percent of all games involve unionized workers.

Eventually a contract was ratified between the representatives of the industry and AFTRA, calling for a 36 percent pay hike but still granting no residuals (Fritz, 2005a). SAG's negotiating committee endorsed the same deal, but the general membership voted it down. This will likely limit future negotiations with SAG, making AFTRA the powerhouse union to deal with the video game industry (Fritz, 2005b). Moreover, the video game industry is still unhappy about the presence of unions and thus there will likely be increased skirmishes over the issue.

To Infinity and Beyond? The Future of Hollywood and Video Games

What is clear is that the future of film and video games has become entwined. One is gaining increasing access to coveted audiences, while the other has both more experience and a great amount of content ready to be exploited. Despite the benefits to both of cross-licensing, technology and labor practices have caused both industries some uncertainty about how best to work with each other.

While it is uncertain how well the video game industry will take to Hollywood labor practices, the current interest in games by the Hollywood majors, combined with the reliance on both Hollywood's talent and its tremendous catalog, makes clear how vital each industry is to the other. As with most other cultural industries, what does seem assured is the continued concentration of ownership. Whether this concentration will involve cross-industry mergers between film and video games or a continued hesitancy based on past failures, it does seem likely that the film industry will try to find ways to enforce its control over video games as content.

REFERENCES

Aoyama, Y., and H. Izushi (2004) "Creative Resources of the Japanese Video Game Industry," *Cultural Industries and the Production of Culture 33*, pp. 110–29.

Bloom, D. (2001) "Final Fantasy Goes to Hollywood," *Red Herring*, May 9, online at <http://www.redherring.com> (accessed July 18, 2007).

Bloom, D., and M. Graser (2002) "H'Wood Game to Cash in on Licenses," *Variety*, May 27–June 2, p. 10.

Brandt, R. (1987) "Trip Hawkins Wants to be the Walt Disney of Software," *Business Week*, November 9, p. 134.

Brodesser, C. (2005) "Gamers' SAG Snag: Deadline Looms for Producers Unions," *Daily Variety*, April 13, p. 1

Brodesser, C., and B. Fritz (2005) "Halo, Hollywood," *Daily Variety*, February 3, p. 1.

Brodesser, C., and D. McNary (2005) "Vidgame Biz and Thesps Extend Pact a Third Time," *Daily Variety*, April 17, p. 2.

Bulkeley, B. W. M. (2003) "Sony Plays a Videogame Grid," *Wall Street Journal*, February 27, p. B5.

Carlson, S. (2003) "Video Games Can Be Helpful to College Students, a Study Concludes," *The Chronicle of Higher Education*, August 15, p. 32.

Dawtrey, A. (2005) "U Has an Int'l Game Plan," *Daily Variety*, June 23, p. 6.

Diamante, V. (2005) "E3 Report: New Practices in Licensing and Ancillary Rights," online at <http://www.gamasutra.com/features/20050523/diamante_pfv.html> (accessed May 26, 2005).

Dyer-Witherford, N. (1999) "The Work in Digital Play: Video Gaming's Transnational and Gendered Division of Labor," *Journal of International Communication*, 6(1), pp. 69–93.

Dyer-Witherford, N. (2002) "Cognitive Capital Contested: The Class Composition of the Video and Computer Game Industry," online at <http://multitudes.samizdat.net/article.php?id_article=268> (accessed March 15, 2005).

Economist (2004) "Deus ex machinima?," September 16, online at <http://www.economist.com> (accessed July 18, 2007).

Elkin, T. (2002) "Video Games Try Product Placement," *Advertising Age*, May 20, p. 73.

ELSPA (2003) *The Cultural Life of Computer and Video Games: A Cross Industry Study*. London: Entertainment and Leisure Software Publishers Association.

Emeling, S. (2004) "Seniors Taking to Computer Games," *Salt Lake Tribune*, December 30.

ESA (2002a) "Historical Sales Figures," online at <http://www.idsa.com/ffbox7.html> (accessed February 14).

ESA (2002b) "Who Plays Computer and Video Games," online at <http://www.idsa.com/ffbox2.html> (accessed February 14).

ESA (2004) "2004 – Sales Demographic, and Usage Data: Essential Facts about the Computer and Video Game Industry," (accessed March 31, 2005).

ESA (2005a) "2005 – Sales Demographic, and Usage Data: Essential Facts About the Computer and Video Game Industry," (accessed March 31, 2005).

ESA (2005b) "Top Ten Industry Facts," online at <http://www.theesa.com/facts/top_10_facts.php> (accessed March 10, 2005).

Fritz, B. (2004) "Hot Vidgames Snub H'wood," *Daily Variety*, December 21, p. 1.

Fritz, B. (2005a) "SAG Rejects Vidgame Deal," *Daily Variety*, June 21, p. 1.

Fritz, B. (2005b) "SAG Revisits Vidgame Agreement," *Daily Variety*, June 23, p. 5.

Fritz, B. (2005c) "Sony Takes Page for Ubisoft's Game Plan," *Daily Variety*, January 26, p. 8.

Gamasutra (2005a) "European PlayStation 2 Users Base to Exceed U.S." <http://www.gamasutra.com/php-bin/news_index.php?story=5258> (accessed April 24, 2005).

Gamasutra (2005b) "Survey Shows Top Game Businesses Make $25 Billion," <http://www.gamasutra.com/php-bin/news_index.php?story=5166> (accessed March 23, 2005).

Gamedaily.biz (2006) "Games and Movies: A Hollywood Marriage?" online at <http://biz.gamedaily.com/industry/advertorial/?id=11536> (accessed January 15, 2006).

Gentile, G. (2005) "Actors Weigh Strike Over Video Game Voices," *USA Today*, May 25, online at <http://www.usatoday.com/tech/news/2005-05-25-voice-actor.protest_x.htm> (accessed July 18, 2007).

Grover, R., C. Edwards, I. Rowley, and M. Ihlwan (2005) "Game Wars: Who Will Win Your Entertainment Dollar, Hollywood or Silicon Valley?" *Business Week*, February 29, online at <http://www.businessweek.com/magazine/content/05_09/b3922094.htm?chan=search> (accessed July 18, 2007).

Guth, R. A. (2001) "Sony Game Unit Invests in Square, Preparing for Fight With Microsoft," *Wall Street Journal*, October 10, p. A13.

Harris, D. (2004) "Boll Scores $47 Mil.," *Daily Variety*, January 4, p. 6.

Hein, K. (2002) "EA Games Star Potter, Bond," *Brandweek 43*, October 28, online at <http://www.brandweek.com/bw/search/article_display.jsp?vnu_content_id=1749488> (accessed July 18, 2007).

Herold, C. (2003) "Amid the Fighters, a Few Winners," *New York Times*, December 25, sect. G, p. 5.

Holson, L. M. (2005a) "Blockbuster with a Joystick," *New York Times*, February 7, sect. C, p. 1.

Holson, L. M. (2005b) "A New Hollywood Player Pushes A Different Game," *New York Times*, May 16, sect. C, p. 1.

Ip, B., and G. Jacobs (2004) "Territorial Lockout – an International Issue in the Video-games Industry," *European Business Review*, 16(5), pp. 511–21.

Kent, S. L. (2001) *The Ultimate History of Video Games: From Pong to Pokemon and Beyond – The Story Behind the Craze that Touched Our Lives and Changed the World*. New York: Prima Publishing.

Levine, R. (2005a) "A Spartan Warrior with a Sense of Humor," *New York Times*, March 21, sect. C, p. 7.

Levine, R. (2005b) "Story Line Is Changing for Game Makers and their Movie Deals," *New York Times*, February 21, sect. C, p. 1.

Loftus, T. (2003) ". . . and a Jedi Knight in 'Star Wars Galaxies': The Year in Gaming," *MSNBC.com*, December 22, online at <http://www.msnbc.msn.com/id/3703850/p1/0/> (accessed July 18, 2007).

Miege, B. (1989) *The Capitalization of Cultural Production*. New York: International General.

MPA (2005) *US Entertainment Industry: 2004 MPA Market Statistics*: Motion Picture Association.

Nelson, R. (1990) "A Video Game that Tracks Stocks, Too," *Popular Science*, 237, p. 93.

Nichols, R. (2005) "The Games People Play: A Political Economic Analysis of Video Games and their Production." Unpublished dissertation, University of Oregon.

People (1985) "How a Computer-Game Maker Finesses the Software Slow-Down," June 10, p. 72.

Richtel, M. (2004) "Game Sales Thrive Thanks to the Big Kids (in their 20's)," *New York Times*, December 27, sect. C, p. 1.

Tramain, S. (2002) "Game Tie-Ins with Films on the Rise," *Billboard*, June 15, p. 114.

USA Today (2003) "Video Games Go to the Movies," July 11, p. 11e.

Wasko, J. (2003) *How Hollywood Works*. London: Sage.

Williams, D. (2002) "Structure and Competition in the U.S. Home Video Game Industry," *JMM – The International Journal on Media Management*, 4(1), pp. 41–54.

CHAPTER 8

ANCILLARY MARKETS – RECORDED MUSIC: CHARTING THE RISE AND FALL OF THE SOUNDTRACK ALBUM

JEFF SMITH

The history of Hollywood's interactions with the recorded music industry is nearly as old as the studio system itself. Although the relationship between the two industries has undergone many changes, Hollywood has utilized the market for recorded music to fulfill several broad goals. These include the cross-promotion of films, theme songs, and soundtrack albums; the minimization of economic risks; and the development of ancillary revenue streams that defray the costs of production. For its part, the record industry has also enjoyed certain economic benefits from its relationship to Hollywood. The soundtracks for *Saturday Night Fever* (John Badham, 1978, US), *The Bodyguard* (Mick Jackson, 1992, US), and *Titanic* (James Cameron, 1997, US), for example, are among the best-selling albums of all time. Moreover, film soundtracks themselves offered exposure to emerging artists, provided ancillary revenues through the negotiation of synchronization and master licensing fees, and enhanced the value of music publishing and record companies' back catalogs.

Generally speaking, Hollywood film history can be divided into three periods that are distinguished by the predominant types of interactions found between these two industries:

1 1927–1957: recorded music as a form of promotion
2 1957–1977: recorded music as cross-promotion and ancillary revenue
3 1977–1997: recorded music as cross-promotion, ancillary revenue stream, and means of spreading risk

While Hollywood's interest in the recorded music market remained fairly consistent throughout its long history, the specific nature of that relationship has been fairly fluid and dynamic, often changing in response to shifts in technology, market structure, and audience tastes. These three periods, then, should not be viewed as distinct and discrete eras, but rather as times bounded by watershed moments that crystallize broader tendencies within these industries. 1927 marked the film industry's innovation of synchronized sound for feature filmmaking, an event that

would have myriad effects on both film technology and Hollywood's market structure. 1957 saw the completion of Hollywood's acquisition and creation of recorded
music subsidiaries, a development that signaled the film industry's growing interest in music as a form of cross-promotion and ancillary revenue. 1977 witnessed
the debut of the disco classic *Saturday Night Fever*, a film that indicated both the
ascendance of popular music on film soundtracks and the emergence of new cross-
marketing schemes and industrial synergies. Soundtrack albums, theme songs, and
music videos have played a vital role in making audiences aware of upcoming films
while films themselves have provided a vivid, and often memorable, showcase for
both new and classic recordings.

1927–1957: Recorded Music as a Form of Promotion

Hollywood's first foray into the recorded music business occurred when Warner
Bros. purchased Brunswick Records in 1926. Warner made this investment, however, not because they were interested selling records, but rather because they needed
a physical plant to press the records used in their Vitaphone synchronized sound
technology. Not surprisingly, after the Vitaphone "sound on disk" system was
replaced by competing "sound on film technologies," Warner Bros. sold their stakes
in Brunswick Records in 1932 (Millard, 1995: 161–7).

During the early 1930s, Hollywood showed little interest in recorded music,
preferring instead to develop its interests in music publishing houses as a way of
maintaining copyright control over the songs and scores that appeared in its films.
The late 1930s and early 1940s, though, saw the emergence of the first "movie music"
albums. In 1938, Victor Records released the soundtrack from Walt Disney's *Snow
White and the Seven Dwarfs* (David Hand, 1937, US) on three 78 rpm discs as a
tie-in to the film's release (Burlingame, 2000: 2). Later, in 1942, RCA Victor commissioned composer Miklos Rosza to rework his score for *The Jungle Book* (Zoltan
Korda, 1942, US) into a 28-minute suite that featured narration by the film's
putative star, Sabu (Burlingame, 2000: 3–4). Marketed as a three-disc "recordrama,"
The Jungle Book was the first original film score to be circulated in a recorded
format (Karlin, 1994: 227).

However, it was not record sales, but rather the vast reach of radio that spurred
Hollywood's initial interest in recordings as a form of film promotion. The great
showman David O. Selznick pioneered the "exploitation" potential of original film
scores during the mid-1940s through a series of radio tie-in albums made for *Since
You Went Away* (John Cromwell, 1944, US), *Spellbound* (Alfred Hitchcock, 1945,
US), and *Duel in the Sun* (King Vidor, 1947, US). Ted Wick oversaw the campaigns
for these films as Selznick's director of radio advertising and exploitation, and for
the most part, Wick's job entailed writing and producing radio spots for Selznick
pictures. When Wick heard Max Steiner's score for *Since You Went Away*, though,
he suggested creating a promotional record that could be played by disk jockeys as
part of a 15-minute program and would function as a "free plug" for the film. Working
with the film's music editor, Lou Forbes, Wick hired a 77-piece orchestra to record

a 14-minute suite of the score's various cues onto a 16-inch transcription platter that functioned as the master. Over a thousand copies of the album for *Since You Went Away* were pressed and sent to radio stations across the country. Within a month of the film's premiere, stations were playing either all or part of Steiner's score, and announcers were not only mentioning the film's title, but its producer and cast as well (Wick, 1976). As the example of *Since You Went Away* indicates, however, the function of these movie music albums was primarily promotional. By and large, recorded music helped to sell films; the reverse, however, was not true.

1957–1977: Recordings as Cross-Promotion and Ancillary Revenue

During most of the 1950s, only two of Hollywood's studios had any investment in the recorded music industry: MGM, who had started up their own label in 1946; and in 1952 Decca Records became the major shareholder in Universal before the two companies were consolidated ten years later by Lew Wasserman's talent agency, MCA. Beginning in 1957, however, all of the major studios began buying or starting up their own record subsidiaries. Paramount Pictures, for example, purchased Dot Records in early 1957, while United Artists launched a new record label and a new music publishing company in October of that same year. While this shift in strategies was consistent with a broader move toward horizontal integration following the Paramount decree, it was further motivated by two important changes in the 1950s: (1) records had replaced sheet music as the major form of musical home entertainment for consumers, and (2) studios recognized that records were an untapped market for the musical properties that appeared in their films.

The studios enjoyed varying degrees of success with their record subsidiaries, but they all recognized that theme songs and soundtrack albums were excellent vehicles for circulating the name and imagery of their films among potential moviegoers. Although the studios' chief interest was in the music's promotional value, they also realized that a chart success was an effective way of generating additional revenue for their companies, both in terms of publishing and performance royalties and, of course, in outright sales. During the early 1960s, soundtrack albums and theme songs became the fastest-growing segment of the record market, with music from films like *Exodus* (Otto Preminger, 1960, US), *Never on Sunday* (Jules Dassin, 1960, Greece), *Breakfast at Tiffany's* (Blake Edwards, 1961, US), *Goldfinger* (Guy Hamilton, 1964, UK), and *A Hard Day's Night* (Richard Lester, 1964, UK) achieving unprecedented exposure on radio and in record stores. The title theme for *Never on Sunday*, for example, spawned more than 400 recordings worldwide, which in turn accounted for sales of more than 14 million copies of the single (*Variety*, 1961).

Of all the new film-owned labels, United Artists Records proved to be the most innovative in marketing their soundtrack albums and theme songs. To some degree, this was motivated by necessity; as a start-up company, United Artists lacked the extensive roster of artists and repertoire found at other labels. Instead, they relied heavily on their film music properties to provide their schedule of releases. Focusing on their music's promotional possibilities, UA Records developed a number of strategies designed to interest radio disk jockeys and record store owners in their upcoming releases. They invited retailers and radio station personnel to special advance film previews. They worked with local stations in organizing contests and publicity stunts that typically involved programming United Artists albums. They also encouraged theater owners to install racks in their lobbies, which were then used to display and sell soundtrack albums for the film currently shown at that theater (Smith, 2004).

Yet, while this era saw greater emphasis on the sales of soundtrack albums and theme songs, cross-promotion remained the most important objective for these film-owned record subsidiaries. When radio airplay was combined with television performances, sheet music racks, in-store display art, and record sales, the cumulative promotional value was staggering. As one record executive put it in 1961, "A film company *must* have a record arm. It could lose money, and it would still come out way ahead on the promotion of basic product" (quoted in Gross, 1961: 46).

Perhaps the era's most important change, though, was the emergence of rock, soul, funk, and rhythm & blues as viable stylistic options for film scoring. Coinciding with a "youthquake" in Hollywood film production, these commercial music styles achieved enormous popularity in films like *The Graduate* (Mike Nichols, 1967, US), *Easy Rider* (Dennis Hopper, 1967, US), *Midnight Cowboy* (John Schlesinger, 1969, US), *Zabriskie Point* (Michelangelo Antonioni, 1970, US), *Shaft* (Gordon Parks, 1971, US), *Superfly* (Gordon Parks Jr., 1972, US), and *American Graffiti* (George Lucas, 1973, US). While Hollywood's older composers complained that pop music was often inappropriate for many of the films in which it was used, the commercial potential of these scores and their value as cross-promotional tools sometimes outweighed these aesthetic considerations. Hit films yielded hit albums, which in turn fueled further revenues for both industries.

Perhaps more importantly, when an individual song was featured in a film, the film also served as a means to promote that song to hit status. The Proclaimers' "I'm Gonna Be (500 Miles)" offers a particularly potent example of this phenomenon. Although the song first appeared in 1988 on the Scottish duo's album, *Sunshine on Leith*, it did not reach *Billboard*'s charts until it was included in the 1993 Johnny Depp film, *Benny and Joon* (Jeremiah S. Chechik, 1993, US). Featured in the film's opening credits, "I'm Gonna Be" was certified gold and reached number 3 in *Billboard*'s "Hot 100" charts nearly five years after its initial release.

1977–1997: Recorded Music as Cross-Promotion, Ancillary Revenue Stream, and Means of Spreading Risk

Due to major structural changes within Hollywood and a slack sales period for soundtracks in the mid-1970s, studios such as United Artists and 20th Century Fox began to sell off their record labels as dead weight on their balance sheet. Those studios that remained in the record business – Warner Bros., Universal, Columbia

FIGURE 8.1 "Stayin' Alive" – Tony Manero (John Travolta) struts to the sound of the
Bees Gees in the opening of *Saturday Night Fever* (1977). Produced by Robert Stigwood;
distributed by Paramount; directed by John Badham

– became highly diversified entertainment corporations that enjoyed oligopoly
status within both the film and record industries. In 1994, for example, Time Warner,
Sony, and Matsushita would account for approximately 47 percent of an estimated
$11 billion in recorded music sales (*New York Times*, 1995).

More importantly, perhaps, massive sales of the soundtrack for *Saturday
Night Fever* encouraged producers, both large and small, to seek cross-promotional
synergies within the film and record markets. According to *Billboard*, the proto-
typical ingredients for such synergies included "Commercially viable music.
Timing. Film cooperation on advance planning and tie-ins. Music that's integral
to the movie. A hit movie. A hit single. A big-name recording star. A big-name
composer" (Peterson, 1979: ST-2).

The emergence of music video and MTV in the early 1980s added still another
outlet to the studios' arsenal of promotional strategies and techniques. As several
record executives pointed out, MTV's target audience was essentially the same demographic sought by film producers during this period, and since a music video included
actual footage from the film, it gave a much better idea of the film's stars, plot, genre,
and visual style than an accompanying album or single would. *Flashdance* (Adrian
Lyne, 1983, US) provided the initial model for film and music video cross-promotion.
Paramount released the video for Michael Sembello's "Maniac" to MTV about four
weeks before the film's initial playdates, which enabled it to play a key role in the
cross-promotion of *Flashdance* as film, soundtrack album, and title song. The video
contained no footage of Sembello, and essentially functioned as a four-minute
musical trailer for the upcoming film. With its sleek visual style, its dance
sequences, and sexy subject matter, *Flashdance* was tailor-made for the MTV audience.

FIGURE 8.2   Film and music cross-promotion – the "Maniac" sequence from *Flashdance* (1983). Produced by Jerry Bruckheimer and Don Simpson; distributed by Paramount; directed by Adrian Lyne

It went on to earn some $185 million at the box office and its soundtrack sold more than 17 million copies (Denisoff and Romanowski, 1991: 360). Undoubtedly, music video played a key role in the film's success, as both "Maniac" and the title song spent several weeks in heavy rotation on MTV. After *Flashdance*, the network became sensitive to charges that it offered free advertising to Hollywood, and thereafter stipulated that future film-inspired videos must include the recording artist in at least 50 percent of the video's footage (Gold, 1984).

Not surprisingly, the studios' active interest in such synergy led to exponential growth in sales of soundtrack albums and music licensing revenues, both of which quadrupled between 1985 and 1995. By 1995, the soundtrack album had become an important enough commodity that most major record labels had specific divisions devoted to their production and exploitation (Browne, 1998: 31).

The growing demand for popular recordings in film, television, and advertising drove up licensing revenues at a comparable rate. EMI-Capitol Music, for example, saw its master licensing business nearly quintuple between 1989 and 1997 (Waldman, 1997: S-12). Likewise, according to one label executive, by 1997 the costs of using a particular recording over a film's opening credits were now five to ten times higher than the decade before (Waldman, 1997: S-66). Although several factors govern the price tag on an individual song, including its narrative importance, its prominence on the soundtrack, and the length of the musical excerpt used, synchronization fees for a popular title ran anywhere from $150,000 to $750,000.

Besides providing ancillary revenues and cross-promotional opportunities, soundtrack albums and theme songs offered an additional economic benefit during this period, namely minimizing risks. For example, when Thom Mount, Universal's head of film production, agreed to greenlight *The Wiz* (Sidney Lumet, 1978, US), he did so only after consulting the record sales of the film's star, Diana Ross. According to Mount, the thinking was that, with a $13 million budget for *The Wiz*, Universal would break even on sales of the film's soundtrack regardless of whether or not it succeeded at the box office. When *The Wiz*'s budget swelled to approximately $37 million, though, the cost overruns negated the studio's efforts to minimize financial risks, and the film went down in history as one of the biggest flops of its time. A similar phenomenon was evident in low-budget films, whose soundtracks enjoyed exceptional sales exceeding the box office performance of the films they accompanied. For example, the albums for *Above the Rim* (Jeff Pollack, 1994, US) and *Set It Off* (F. Gary Gray, 1996, US) enjoyed long stretches in *Billboard*'s Top Ten that extended well beyond their films' theatrical runs. The tepid box office figures for these films suggested that many of those who bought the albums never bothered to see the films that they accompanied. Thus, although the *Above the Rim* and *Set It Off* themselves were flops, their negative costs of production were nonetheless counterbalanced by the strong sales of their respective soundtrack albums.

By the mid-1990s, soundtracks were established as an important source of corporate synergy for companies both large and small, and were packaged according to two very different philosophies, depending on the types of films they accompanied (Jolson-Colburn, 1996). For "tent-pole" or "franchise" films, soundtracks often grouped together several different styles of music in an effort to break into as many different radio formats as possible. Warner Bros.' *Twister* (Jan De Bont, 1996, US), for example, lumped together hard rock bands, like Van Halen and the Red Hot Chili Peppers, with country singers Shania Twain and Alison Krauss. The same company's *Batman & Robin* (Joel Schumacher, 1997, US) featured an eclectic mix of performers that included R.E.M., the Goo Goo Dolls, Smashing Pumpkins, Jewel, and R. Kelly. With such a variety of different artists, the *Batman and Robin* soundtrack was featured in modern rock, adult contemporary, and urban music formats respectively.

In contrast, for smaller, independent productions the soundtrack was often organized around a particular music genre or marketing concept in order to sharpen the film's appeal to its intended demographic. *Singles* (Cameron Crowe, 1992, US) attempted to exploit the "grunge" zeitgeist of the early 1990s while *All Over Me* (Alex Sichel, 1997, US) capitalized on the burgeoning "riot grrrl" phenomenon that surrounded bands like Bikini Kill and Babes in Toyland. Moreover, films that explicitly addressed race or gender issues frequently utilized similarly themed soundtracks. *Waiting to Exhale* (Forest Whitaker, 1995, US), for example, exclusively featured female soul and hip-hop artists to enhance the film's appeal to women.

Conclusion: After the Gold Rush

While soundtracks have long been used as a promotional tool and source of ancillary revenue within the film industry, their function in the latter regard is

TABLE 8.1   Bestselling soundtrack albums of all time (total units sold in US)

---

 1   *The Bodyguard* (17 million, Arista)
 2   *Saturday Night Fever* (15 million, RSO)
 3   *Purple Rain* (13 million, Warner Bros.)
 4   *Forrest Gump* (12 million, Epic)
 5   *Dirty Dancing* (11 million, RCA)
 6   *Titanic* (11 million, Sony Classical)
 7   *The Lion King* (10 million, Disneyland)
 8   *Footloose* (9 million, Columbia)
 9   *Top Gun* (9 million, Columbia)
10   *Grease* (8 million, RSO)
11   *Waiting to Exhale* (7 million, Arista)
12   *O Brother, Where Art Thou?* (7 million, Lost Highway)
13   *Flashdance* (6 million, Casablanca)
14   *Space Jam* (6 million, Warner Bros.)
15   *The Big Chill* (6 million, Motown)

Source: Recording Industry Association of America website, <http://www.riaa.com>.

increasingly uncertain. While sales of all recorded music have declined (down 12 percent since 1999), sales of soundtracks have dropped even more precipitously (down 34 percent since 1999). In 1998, buoyed by the success of *Titanic*, soundtracks accounted for 8.6 percent of the domestic market as retailers sold more than 61 million albums; by 2004, that figure had shrunk to 4.2 percent and sales of 27.4 million (Hay, 2004: 10; Fiore, 2005: 15). Similarly, between 1996 and 1999, about 25 to 30 soundtracks each year exceeded the 500,000 mark in sales; in 2004, only two albums reached that figure (Kipnis, 2002: 8; Hay, 2004: 93).

A number of factors have contributed to the decline in soundtrack sales, most of them related to its function as a kind of sampler album that brings together a number of songs from different artists. In many instances, these soundtrack samplers offered consumers an overview of a particular musical style. *The Crow* (Alex Proyas, 1994, US), for example, featured several goth and heavy metal bands while *200 Cigarettes* (Risa Bramon Garcia, 1999, US) includes several songs by classic punk and New Wave artists. Perhaps the biggest industry "bogeyman" is music file-sharing, a phenomenon that garners most of the blame for the overall downturn in recorded music sales. Another factor affecting soundtrack sales was increased competition from other collections, like the *NOW That's What I Call Music!* franchise (Fiore, 2005: 14). Capitol and Sony have released more than 20 of these hit collections in the United States, many of them reaching number 1 on *Billboard*'s sales charts, while EMI has issued more than 60 albums in its *NOW* series in the UK. Finally, soundtrack sales have been affected by MP3 technology and its ability to store a vast library of recorded music within a highly mobile and interactive format. In the era of iTunes and iPods, there is little need to purchase the latest

FIGURE 8.3 *Wedding Crashers* (2005) partying to the sound of the Isley Brothers' "Shout." Produced by Peter Abrams, Robert L. Levy, and Andrew Panay; distributed by New Line; directed by David Dobkin

soundtrack collection when consumers can simply make up comparable "playlists" themselves.

Studios appear to be retrenching in an effort to preserve the soundtrack's promotional function, but to minimize its costs (Kipnis, 2004: 7). To be sure, we can expect future soundtrack packages for music-savvy auteurs like Quentin Tarantino and Wes Anderson, but music divisions will exercise more discerning judgment and will not reflexively release an album simply because the accompanying film is on its parent company's production schedule. Likewise, studios are tightening their budgets in order to scale production costs for soundtrack albums to the current market. For example, by keeping the budget for the soundtrack of *The Wedding Crashers* (David Dobkin, 2005, US) under six figures, it only needed to sell 100,000 copies in order to turn a profit (Fiore, 2005: 15). For its part, the music industry will continue to explore other visual media besides film as a means of giving exposure to breaking artists. That Polyphonic Spree track that once might have been featured on a Miramax indie-rock package is now playing in a Volkswagen commercial beamed directly into your living-room. It is in this very fluid and dynamic market that soundtrack albums must find their niche if they hope to continue to be the economic and cultural force that they have been for the past 50 years.

REFERENCES

Browne, D. (1998) "Star-Ship Enterprise," *Entertainment Weekly*, March 13, p. 31.

Burlingame, J. (2000) *Sound and Vision: 60 Years of Motion Picture Soundtracks*. New York: Watson-Guptill Publications.

Coniff, T. and Hay, C. (2002) "Labels, Studios Rethink Soundtrack Strategy," *Billboard*, October 12, pp. 1, 63, 65.

152 JEFF SMITH

Denisoff, R. S., and Romanowski, W. (1991) *Risky Business: Rock in Film*. New Brunswick: Transaction Publishers.

Fiore, R. (2005) "Sound Waves: Battling a Slump, Movie Soundtracks Get Remixed," *Entertainment Weekly*, August 12, pp. 14–15.

Gold, R. (1984) "Hollywood Majors Spinoff Videos from Youth Pix," *Variety*, February 22, p. 108.

Gross, M. (1961) "Pix Promotion's Cuffo Ride," *Variety*, September 6, pp. 45–6.

Hay, C. (2004) "The State of Soundtracks," *Billboard*, November 20, pp. 10, 93.

Jolson-Colburn, J. (1996) "Making Tracks," *Hollywood Reporter*, August 27, p. S-19.

Karlin, F. (1994) *Listening to Movies: The Film Lover's Guide to Film Music*. New York: Schirmer Books.

Kipnis, J. (2002) "Film & TV Confab Addresses Visual Path to Musical Exposure," *Billboard*, October 26, p. 8.

Kipnis, J. (2004) "Budget Talk Rules Film & TV Confab," *Billboard*, November 27, pp. 1, 64.

Millard, A. (1995) *America on Record: A History of Recorded Sound*. New York: Cambridge University Press.

New York Times (1995) April 10, pp. D1, D8.

Peterson, S. (1979) "Selling a Hit Soundtrack," *Billboard*, October 6, pp. ST-2–4.

Sanjek, R. (1983) *From Print to Plastic: Publishing and Promoting America's Popular Music (1900–1980)*. Brooklyn: Institute for Studies in American Music.

Smith, J. (1998) *The Sounds of Commerce: Marketing Popular Film Music*. New York: Columbia University Press.

Smith, J. (2004) "Linking the Film and Music Industries: Cross-Promotion, the Soundtrack Album, and the Case of United Artists," in C. Gorbman and W. Sherk (eds.), *Film Music 2: History, Theory, Practice*. Sherman Oaks, CA: The Film Music Society.

Variety (1961) "'Never on Sunday' Racks Up 10-Mil Sales Worldwide in Over Thirty Disk Versions," August 9, p. 1.

Waldman, A. (1997) "Going for a Song," *Hollywood Reporter*, August 26, pp. S-12, S-66.

Wick, T. (1976) "Creating the Movie Music Album," *Hi Fidelity*, April, pp. 68–70.

PART II
INDUSTRY DYNAMICS

CHAPTER 9

LABOR: THE EFFECTS OF MEDIA CONCENTRATION ON THE FILM AND TELEVISION WORKFORCE

SUSAN CHRISTOPHERSON

The 1990s and early 2000s should have been a golden age for the US media entertainment industry workforce. Global demand for films and television programming continued to increase and the venues for entertainment product distribution expanded to include DVD, cable TV, and the internet, potentially creating new markets. According to both public data and industry-supported research, US-based television and film production increased in the 1990s and continued to expand into the 2000s (Monitor, 1999; State of California Employment Development Department, 2005). Within the US, Los Angeles maintained and enhanced its dominant role in industry production, as evidenced by the region's ability to capture the majority share of new production (EEI and the PMR Group, 2004; Christopherson et al., 2006).

For much of the workforce, however, this period of industry expansion has been marked by heightened anxiety over their income expectations, and anger over a loss of creativity and pressure to produce too much too fast. Even in this historically high-risk industry, the recent period has been one in which the rewards of working in media entertainment are more elusive than ever.

One result of workforce anxiety has been a search for scapegoats to blame for deteriorating employment and working conditions. In this "blame game," the growth of media production centers outside of the US, particularly in Canada, has been singled out as the reason for increased insecurity among US media workers. In addition to production outsourcing, changes in film and television work have been attributed to a set of factors, including new production and distribution technologies and an expanding workforce. Increased insecurity has, in turn, fostered internecine conflicts among unions and between the unionized and non-unionized workforce over both the causes of and solutions to the changing fortunes. What connects these factors – but is rarely mentioned in conjunction with changes in work and bargaining power – is increasing concentration among firms dominating product distribution and production since the mid-1980s.

In this chapter I examine some indicators of how work in the media entertainment industry has changed under industry conglomeration, particularly in film and television, and how conglomeration is related to changes in labor force bargaining power. Although I describe the patterns occurring in feature film, it is impossible to separate those patterns from the broader picture of industry employment. Because of the consolidation and integration of entertainment media now more than ever media workers are working across film and television. So, whereas in the 1980s we still might have been able to speak of the film industry workforce, we now have to look at a workforce that finds employment across both media.

I then look at the labor politics that have emerged in response to the challenges produced by conglomeration and at how the powerful media unions are responding to changing employment conditions. Obviously, at the most basic level, changes in labor supply and labor demand underlie changes in labor bargaining power. What I argue, however, is that the political reconstruction of industry governance, particularly the deregulation of the industry that began during the Reagan Administration in the 1980s, has concentrated control over distribution, and, as a result, power over what is produced and how it is produced. Concentrated power has, in turn, affected the bargaining strength of the highly skilled workforce that makes film and television products and, perhaps most unfortunately, limited the ability and willingness of their unions to take on the real source of their problems.

This chapter draws on recent research by two groups of media entertainment industry researchers, at the Entertainment Economy Institute (EEI and the PMR Group, 2004) in Los Angeles and Cornell University in New York, who have attempted to track and make sense of changes in employment and work patterns in media entertainment. This is a daunting task given the project-oriented nature of work in the industry, the tendency of producers to see every product as a one-off event, and the absence of industry interest in documenting long-term production trends, employment patterns, and working conditions. Unlike many US industries, film and television cannot be easily understood by looking at publicly available statistics. They capture only a semblance of employment patterns that are typically very volatile week to week, season to season, and year to year. An adequate understanding of these project-based industries requires long-term analysis of industry patterns, the use of multiple sources of data, including proprietary data provided by the industry, and the application of industry knowledge to interpret what might appear to be contradictory trends and tendencies. Through great effort and long experience in working with labor and management in media entertainment, both Cornell and EEI have managed to construct a picture of media entertainment employment in the 1990s and into the early 2000s that, in turn, provides a basis for interpreting the fractious labor politics that have emerged during this period.

Labor Expansion, Peripheralization, and Deprofessionalization

Questions concerning employment in the entertainment industries have always been difficult to answer because of the project-oriented character of production.

Even the most successful entertainment industry worker has multiple employers during the course of the year, spells of intense work, and spells of unemployment. Using ES202 or social security payment reporting data, the EEI (EEI and the PMR Group, 2004) found that a very broadly defined entertainment industry workforce grew at a rate of 35 percent in California between 1991 and 2002, more than twice as fast as the overall California workforce. And the core workforce, those whose incomes were continuously made from entertainment industry employment at least 75 percent of the time, grew 17 percent between 1991 and 2002. What is more significant than this growth rate, however, is that core workers declined as a *share* of the total workforce, from 38 percent in 1991 to 33 percent in 2002. So while the workforce was expanding, a smaller portion of the total workforce was able to derive a full-time income from work in the entertainment industries.

With concentration in the film and television industries, employment in firms in film and television production has also concentrated in Los Angeles, with 63 percent of total employment in 2004 (Christopherson et al., 2006: 14). Employment in firms in the second largest center of production, New York, has stagnated and there are indications that the proportion of the New York workforce that is made up of independent contractors has increased (Keegan et al., 2005). This shift in employment patterns is especially significant in television, which historically has employed more people in medium-size and large firms.

As in many other industries, in the US, media firms are paring down their production workforces to an essential core and using temporary workers and self-employed workers on an as-needed basis. However, increased use of a flexible labor supply is only part of the story; changes in labor supply are another important dimension. The expansion of the labor supply has been stimulated, in part, by the success of higher education media training programs. In these programs, which have proliferated in Los Angeles and New York as well as in other cities, students learn a wide variety of production skills and are introduced to new technologies that cross conventional union jurisdictions. They learn how to produce on "shoestring" budgets and to work very rapidly and under severe time constraints. They learn to work in efficient, multi-functional production teams. When they graduate, they make up a flexible, independent contractor workforce perfectly suited to the high-growth segment of the media industry – production for cable television. In some respects, the members of this workforce have more in common with their young colleagues in New Media than they do with their elders who work in network television and medium- to high-budget film (Batt et al., 2001).

Working style, expectations, and a cultivated amateurism separate this "free agent" workforce from the establishment professionals that populate the traditional guilds and unions. Although there is still considerable intersection (and even some merging) between the professional worker with a defined role and the multi-functional media production team member, the workforce appears more segmented and differentiated than it did in the 1980s, when the major divide in the US workforce was defined by union or non-union status.

Changing Media Firm Strategies in a Concentrated Industry

The recent growth in media entertainment industries in the US and particularly in its "capital city," Los Angeles, took place in a production and distribution environment very different from that which existed in the early 1980s. A small number of media conglomerates have acquired ownership of entertainment media distribution channels – cable networks, commercial broadcast networks, DVD rentals, and theaters – and are now also legally permitted to produce their own products for those outlets. As one member of the Creative Coalition – a group of actors, writers, directors, and producers concerned with the effects of vertical integration on creativity – described the new market, "There's multiple voices, but there are very few ventriloquists" (Pingree and Hill, 2004: 20).

The control of multiple distribution markets by a handful of firms has spawned strategies to squeeze more profits out of products, both old and new, by multiply-

FIGURE 9.1   Militant mouse – mock fighting during a demonstration by the National Association of Broadcast Employees and Technicians and Communications Workers of America outside the gates of Disney's headquarters at Burbank, California, November 6, 1998. Photo by Associated Press

ing the venues in which they can be distributed and increasing their value through cross-market advertising. Films produced by Universal are advertised on NBC, the conglomerate's broadcast television network, and hyped through its news and information programming. Theaters owned by the conglomerates advertise its other media products before films. Libraries of old television programs and films are mined to find anything that could attract an audience, fill cable hours, and attract even small advertising dollars.

The impact of changes in ownership has become apparent in both film and television production. A Directors Guild representative, testifying before a US Federal Communications Commission hearing in Los Angeles in October 2006, described the impact of concentration on television production. In his testimony he noted that, in 1993, about 66 percent of network television programs came from independent producers while 44 per cent were produced by the networks. In 2006, only 22 per cent of network television was produced by independent producers while 76 percent was produced by the networks themselves using subcontractors. As competition has declined, the power of producers to realize an independent vision has also declined. Key decisions once made by the producer regarding casting and location are now made by the network (Reardon, 2006).

In another example of the transformation in the role of media conglomerates into merchandising platforms, the US television networks have adopted the strategy of demanding a financial stake in pilots that are picked up for the primetime schedule. Even advertisers have noted the implications of this shift, warning that "broadcast networks are more interested in financial deals than putting the best shows they can find on the air" (*Advertising Age*, 1999, cited in Bielby and Bielby, 2003). This strategy reflects both the increased power over distribution access held by the conglomerates and their ability to shift risk for project development. According to Bielby and Bielby (2003: 590), "to reach the prime-time schedule, the supplier has to agree to forgo a share of the future revenues."

As Tom Schatz lays out in chapter 1 above, ownership concentration also has been associated with changes in types of films produced and distributed. Production has become bifurcated into big-budget blockbusters, distributed by "The Majors," costing an average of $100 million to produce and market, and a lively and growing independent film sector with films typically costing less than $10 million. The independent films comprise over half of the total film output (though only 5 percent of total revenue), and account for much of the total growth in production numbers. What has been declining is the middle-budget film.

The reasons for shifts in film production are complex. As the entertainment media industries have concentrated, the cost of producing and distributing a feature film has increased dramatically (Jones, 2002; MPAA, 2006). Among the reasons for this increase are accounting rules for the industry, which were changed in 1981 as new distribution venues for entertainment products emerged (Fabrikant, 1992). These rules permit the (now) conglomerate owners of multiple distribution venues to distribute the costs of marketing among theatrical release, network television, and cable and to rapidly write off the cost of a product while at the same time increasing their bottom line (in current profits) by longer-term estimates of future revenues from these multiple outlets. This accounting strategy encourages the conglomerates to extract high advertising and marketing costs from their distribution outlets and raises the overall cost of marketing and advertising the product. This strategy, not coincidentally, raises barriers to entry for non-conglomerate-controlled producers.

Together, the bifurcation of the film market and cost-cutting by network television have limited the number of mid-range productions that have traditionally composed the "bread-and-butter" jobs in film and television. The combination of these trends in historically unionized major employment venues, along with the expansion of the labor supply and the emergence of cable television, have created a new bargaining climate for the media industry workforce. They, too, have become multi-media.

How Labor Demand Reflects Conglomeration and Product "Repurposing"

Possibly the most important change on the labor demand side over the period of the 1990s was increasing demand for low-budget productions to fill endless cable networks. Many programs for cable networks are produced within small "turn-key" budgets by producers whose profit margin depends on saving on labor costs, for example using crews not working on standard union contracts.

The character of production for cable is significant because television production has outpaced film production in Los Angeles and New York since the mid-1980s and much of the recent growth has been concentrated in low-cost production for cable television networks (Scott, 2004). So, while the number of productions has increased in Los Angeles and New York, much of this increase appears to be in low-budget productions for cable distribution.

At the same time there is a larger supply of labor vying for a pool of less remunerative or reliable jobs. And the opportunities for employment in higher-budget, unionized productions have been eroded by slow growth in feature film production, the tendency of filmmakers to shoot outside the US in order to obtain financing through co-productions, and a decrease in the proportion of the more expensive and labor-intensive scripted productions (such as dramatic series) for television (Epstein, 2005). So, while the number of marginal productions for television is increasing, producers of medium- to high-budget feature films have also been under pressure to cut costs. The pressure to reduce total expenses (emanating from rising star salaries and product marketing costs) has focused particularly on "below-the-line" or skilled craft labor costs because this work is perceived as less important in adding value to the product and acquiring necessary financing.

When we look at information from New York on changes in employment by occupation, those occupations connected with television production have seen increased work hours. So, for example, members of the American Federation of Television and Radio Artists (AFTRA), who work primarily in television, have experienced a 33 percent increase in workdays over the period 2000–2003. There has also been more work in television for background actors (formerly called "extras"), with an 80 percent growth in workdays between 1995 and 2003 in television productions shot in New York. Work in television has also increased for members of the Directors Guild, with increased workdays in television production in the 2000–2005 period. Since cable production work is more frequently done in studios than on location, there has, not surprisingly, been a significant increase in working hours by studio mechanics. Their work hours in television production increased 40 percent between 2000 and 2003.

Another "craft" group benefiting from increased television production are editors, whose work hours in New York doubled between 2002 and 2003 and increased 25 percent between 2003 and 2004. Editors are extremely important in growing production types such as reality television, which use editing to produce a story from hours of shooting with only a minimal script. The number of editors employed actually declined during this period, indicating that those editors who are employed are working more but that the risk of unemployment may have increased.

Although below-the-line or entertainment industry craft workers are most affected by the restructuring of the industry and the ability of entertainment conglomerates to squeeze producers in order to extract higher profits, the changes wrought by industry concentration affect even the most creative segments of the industry. According to one veteran filmmaker, "in cable, residuals (payments for each showing of the product) for writers, actors, and directors are a percent of the producer's gross. But if that producer is a network who self-deals the rights to their cable company . . . there is no compensation for that. Suddenly you discover that the eleven or twelve per cent gross residual among the three guilds that has been fought over for so many decades is virtually meaningless, as rights are simply self-dealt among related entities" (Pingree and Hill, 2004: 20).

Anne-Marie Johnson of the Screen Actors Guild described the impact of these changes in her testimony at the Federal Communications Commission Hearings:

> As actors, we find the continued consolidation of media companies has drastically limited our ability to individually bargain our personal services agreements . . . the networks decide what the top-of-the show rates are, in a parallel practice. Some networks will even tell you they only pay 50 per cent of the going rate. Take it or leave it. This salary compression cripples the middle class actor's ability to make a living. (SAG, 2006)

Increasing employment in television has combined with two other patterns: (1) increasing bifurcation in the incomes of above-the-line talent, indicated by data on SAG members in both Los Angeles and New York, and (2) a narrowing of the income gap between people employed in the entertainment media and the median income of all people employed in California (EEI and the PMR Group, 2004). Although these trends are only suggestive and require more definitive research, they point to changes in the relative position of media entertainment workers and to a relative diminution of their income advantage relative to other occupations.

The expansion of low-budget production for cable, the growing labor pool, and slow growth in the more lucrative (for labor) production segments, such as feature film and broadcast network television series, partially explain why increased employment and production numbers in Los Angeles and more recently in New York City are combined with high levels of worker dissatisfaction and a sense of increased risk.

Hourly wages in the media industries remain high, but reports from the unions indicate that the work has become harder and less predictable than it was in the early 1990s. One common complaint is that producers attempting to cut costs will reduce shooting days by requiring overtime work from the production crew. While long working hours are legendary in the media entertainment industry, the boundaries that circumscribed abuse appear to have broken down as unions have lost power over industry practices, and with an increase in the proportion of productions made on "shoestring" budgets.

Labor Politics Emerging from the Big Squeeze

The labor politics emerging in the wake of the restructuring of the media entertainment industry have been influenced by three major tendencies: (1) an increasing labor supply across occupations and an increase in the proportion of industry workers employed as independent contractors (Keegan et al., 2005); (2) changing labor demand, especially increasing demand for a flexible, inexpensive production workforce for cable television; and (3) pressure on producers from media distributors to identify production strategies that will substantially reduce costs and directly finance productions.

With these changes the still powerful media unions have faced significant challenges. An already complex union and guild terrain has become more difficult to interpret because of shifts of power among unions. Unions representing the workforce for television have experienced growth and increasing work hours for their membership. In unions whose members work in both television and film, such as the Director's Guild, it is television employment that is contributing more to total income. This shift has caused old rivalries between film and television-based unions such as SAG and AFTRA to re-emerge, as well as talk of mergers.

Because they generally continue to operate as conventional US unions – that is, by representing their current membership rather than serving as a *labor* movement, the unions appear to be losing touch with a younger generation that does not perceive union membership as an indicator of "having arrived" in the media industries. Instead, unions are perceived more than ever as gatekeepers for a labor aristocracy whose goals and working style are not relevant to the younger generation of multi-skilled independent contractors.

To the extent that they have become more inclusive of the larger peripheral media workforce (referred to as "wannabes" among industry insiders), guilds and unions,

FIGURE 9.2   Actor Charlton Heston joins the picket outside Paramount Studios during the strike by SAG members in August 1980. Photo by Associated Press

such as SAG, are suffering from the deprofessionalization of their membership. This deprofessionalization applies both to their skills, experience, and career potential and to their roles as union members. The new "peripheral unionists" are potentially more militant because they are distanced from employers in a way that was not the case in the past. They also have little to lose from strikes and excessive demands.

The craft unions have, for the most part, attempted to carve out and capture the proportionally smaller, high-end segments of media production. They have focused on retaining the "good jobs," those still controlled by union contracts, in bigger, more lucrative, and (in the case of television) longer-term projects. Medium-budget ($20–$50 million) film and multi-episode television series are at the core of the "good jobs" category. It is the unionized higher-budget segments of media production, those requiring sophisticated facilities and a skilled workforce, that have become the focus of union efforts to mitigate the effects of consolidation in the industry.

Although researchers and press accounts have provided evidence that changes on the production side are attributable to a decreased number of corporate customers for media products (Bielby and Bielby, 2003) and thus increased pressure on producers to shave costs, the unions have chosen to place the blame for their plight on the outsourcing of production, particularly to Canada. In essence they have delinked outsourcing from its originating causes – in conglomerate strategies that encourage and sometimes require producers to carry out production in lower-cost locations. Although union accounts acknowledge that production location decisions have shifted from a product-differentiation to a cost-reduction strategy, they rarely examine the sources of that shift: the fact that the conglomerates and their lobbying organizations have made long-term investments in facilities in British Columbia enabling the development of a satellite center, frequently referred to as "Hollywood North" (Elmer and Gasher, 2005).

Instead the controversy focused on the hot-button issue of American jobs being stolen by "the Canucks." As the controversy evolved, however, splits emerged among talent and craft unions as to what policy measures should be undertaken to address what was being portrayed as unfair competition.

The media conglomerates, along with labor allies, such as the Directors Guild, whose members are most susceptible to pressure from their conglomerate employers, *support* the Canadian government's rationale for subsidies. These subsidies encourage what the Canadian government refers to as "service production," based in the "cultural exception," a provision of international trade law that allows governments to provide subsidies to encourage the production of media products that sustain cultural identity.

According to Bonnie Richardson, head of government relations at the Motion Picture Association of America, the trade association that represents the media conglomerates in the US and in Canada, trade action against Canada "threatens to further sour US–Canada relations already strained by tariffs on Canadian lumber, as well as hurt efforts to dismantle barriers abroad to US movies . . . It's a 'dagger-to-the-heart challenge to very sensitive cultural subsidies,' said Richardson, whose group represents Hollywood Studios including the Walt Disney Co., Sony Corp.'s Sony Pictures and AOL Time Warner's Warner Brothers" (Pethel, 2002).

Despite the emphasis on the Vancouver–Los Angeles competition, the impact of media conglomerate ability to ratchet up its bargaining power with skilled labor and exercise a cost-based location strategy is most apparent in US production centers outside Los Angeles. These locations formerly benefited from location shooting for the purposes of product differentiation and have been the big losers in an environment in which cost (and state subsidies) trump "look" in making location decisions.[1]

By the end of the 1990s, states such as Texas, North Carolina, Florida, and Illinois, which had developed a small media industry base by providing technical assistance to filmmakers shooting on location, some studio facilities, and modest incentives, suffered dramatic declines in production shooting (Jones, 2002; Lee, 2002).

Again, the interpretation of this trend has not focused on firm strategies or on changes in what was produced and how it was produced, but rather on the ability of places and regions to supply the needs of a global industry. The increasing cost-based character of production location decisions was attributed to the rise of *international* competition based on the ability of regions in the US and abroad to provide both the physical and human infrastructure that supports the industry (Weinstein and Clower, 2000).

As a consequence, states and cities in the US were pressured by regional economic development coalitions, including local media industry unions, to find ways to "level the playing field": to move beyond the public service incentives they offered in the 1980s to provide direct subsidies, studio facilities, a skilled labor force, and production financing to media producers in order to keep them in the United States

(Monitor, 1999; EIDC, 2001; Jones, 2002). The media conglomerates have been major beneficiaries of these subsidy programs. They have encouraged the shaping of subsidy programs in their interests (as opposed to those of small-scale, independent producers, for example) and have played one region off against another. In New York, for example, the major recipient of state and city subsidies is NBC Universal (owned by General Electric), which has been producing television series in New York for many years.

Beyond the subsidies, however, industry lobbyists have focused significant attention on the issue of labor flexibility and labor cost. There is continuous discussion of direct and indirect labor costs in conjunction with lobbying for subsidies. This sub rosa discussion and its implication that regions (including Los Angeles) are losing production because of demands by organized labor ignores the impact of concentration and production restructuring on what is produced and how it is produced and places attention squarely on inter-regional differences in craft worker below-the-line labor costs.

Conclusion

The sense of crisis felt by many members of the entertainment media industry is different from that experienced by manufacturing workers upon the restructuring of their industries in the 1970s and 1980s. For one thing, people in the entertainment industry generally accept that they are in a high-risk business. As Jon Stewart noted in his introduction to the Academy Awards in 2006, "People in this industry are not in it for the health benefits." That being said, the career aspirations of the workforce have undoubtedly changed. The opportunity for employment in the most prestigious arena of media entertainment, the feature film, has declined. Even for stars, continuous employment in studio-distributed feature films is an increasingly unattainable goal. At the same time, a wide variety of more risky, entrepreneurial opportunities for employment have opened up with the expansion of the independent film sector and low-cost television production.

What is perhaps most significant about the changes in film and television work is the link that can be drawn between politics and policies (particularly deregulation) and the changing fortunes of the labor force. While these policies have been attacked because of their effects on access, freedom of expression, and creativity, they have not been tied to changes in what is produced and how it is produced and thus, to the squeeze on producers, the workforce, and the media unions. It is this story that needs to be told.

NOTE

1   Independent filmmakers continue to make films with the look and feel of particular places, but these films are a very small segment of total film production and, if successful, serve the prestige needs of the media conglomerates rather than their profit goals.

REFERENCES

Batt, R., S. Christopherson, N. Rightor, and D. Van Jaarsveld (2001) *Net Working: Work Patterns and Workforce Policies for the New Media Industry*. Washington, DC: Economic Policy Institute.

Bielby, W. and D. Bielby (2003) "Controlling Prime-Time: Organizational Concentration and Network Television Programming Strategies," *Journal of Broadcasting and Electronic Media*, 47(4), 573–96.

Christopherson, S., M. Figueroa, L. S. Gray, J. Parrott, D. Richardson, and N. Rightor (2006) *New York's Big Picture: Assessing New York's Position in Film, Television and Commercial Production*. New York: Cornell University.

EEI and the PMR Group (2004) *California's Entertainment Workforce: Employment and Earnings, 1991–2002*. Los Angeles: The Entertainment Economy Institute.

EIDC (2001) *MOWs – A Three Year Study*. Los Angeles: Entertainment Industry Development Corporation.

Elmer, G., and M. Gasher (eds.) (2005) *Contracting Out Hollywood: Runaway Productions and Foreign Location Shooting*. Lanham, MD: Rowman & Littlefield.

Epstein, E. J. (2005) *The Big Picture: The New Logic of Money and Power in Hollywood*. New York: Random House.

Fabrikant, G. (1992) "Blitz Hits Small Studio Pix," *The New York Times*, July 12, p. 7.

Jones, M. (2002) *Motion Picture Production in California*. Report Requested by Assembly Member Dario Frommer, Chair of the Select Committee on the Future of California's Film Industry. Sacramento: California Research Bureau.

Keegan, R., N. Kleiman, B. Siegel, and M. Kane (2005) *Creative New York*. New York: Center for an Urban Future, Mt. Auburn Associates.

Lee, K. (2002) "Remaking the Geography of Southern California's Film and Television Industry," paper presented at the Annual Meeting of the American Association of Geographers, March 19–23, Los Angeles.

Monitor (1999) *US Runaway Film and Television Production Study Report*. Santa Monica, CA: Monitor Company.

MPAA (2006) *US Entertainment Industry: 2005 MPA Market Statistics*. Los Angeles: Motion Picture Association of America.

Pethel, B. (2002) "Canada's Movie, TV Subsidies under Fire," *Toronto Star*, July 4, p. A23.

Pingree, C., and L. Hill (2004) "Can Media Artists Survive Media Consolidation?," *The Journal of the Caucus of Television Producers, Writers and Directors*, 22, 17–21.

Reardon, M. (2006) "Hollywood Bashes Media Consolidation," online at <http://news.com.com/2100-1026_3-6122447.html?tag=item> (accessed October 15, 2006).

SAG (2006) "Entertainment Industry Group Testify at FCC Public Hearing on Media Ownership in Los Angeles on Tuesday Oct. 3," online at <http://www.sag.org/sagWebApp/Content/Public/fcc_hearing2006.htm> (accessed July 15, 2007).

Scott, A. J. (2004) "The Other Hollywood: The Organizational and Geographic Bases of Television-Program Production," *Media, Culture and Society*, 26(2), pp. 183–205.

State of California Employment Development Department (2005) *Biennial Report on the Motion Picture and Television Industry in California*. Sacramento: State of California Employment Development Department.

Weinstein, B., and T. Clower (2000) "Filmed Entertainment and Local Economic Development: Texas as a Case Study," *Economic Development Quarterly*, 14(4), pp. 795–819.

CHAPTER 10

THE STAR SYSTEM: THE PRODUCTION OF HOLLYWOOD STARDOM IN THE POST-STUDIO ERA

PAUL McDONALD

Stars may be high-profile individuals but Hollywood film stardom is always conditional upon the collective effort required to make and circulate the mediated identities of stars. It is for this reason that the production of stardom in Hollywood has frequently been spoken of as a system.

A star system emerged in Hollywood as talent scouts, coaches, and publicists were involved with finding performers and making them into stars. In the vertically integrated Hollywood film industry of the 1920s, 1930s, and 1940s, these responsibilities were all undertaken in-house by the studios themselves. The studios made the stars and, due to the notoriously restrictive terms imposed by exclusive services contracts, the studios also owned the stars (McDonald, 2000). Remnants of this system survived into the 1950s and 1960s, but as vertical disintegration and the post-World War II decline in cinema-going forced the industry to restructure, the studios cut back on production and reduced costly overheads by releasing expensive talent from their contracts. Stars gained independence, becoming part of a large freelance labor market in Hollywood, and although they worked for the studios they were no longer the property of the studios.

Reflecting on this situation, William Fadiman, a literary consultant to Warner Bros., asked in 1972, "Does the star system exist in the New Hollywood?" (1972: 82). Fadiman's question was a reasonable one, for as stars became independent and the production of stardom moved outside of the studios, it was debatable whether Hollywood still systematically produced stars. Yet the answer to Fadiman's question must be yes, for today film stardom continues to be produced through an organized and restricted network of professional functions. By examining the production of Hollywood stardom in the 1980s and 1990s, this chapter explores what can be described as the post-studio star system. To propose that Hollywood stardom entered a post-studio phase is not to suggest that the studios became irrelevant to Hollywood stardom: although the studios were no longer central to making film stardom, they remained the key employers of stars. Instead, Hollywood stardom entered a post-studio era as independent firms undertook the tasks necessary for cultivating, directing, and sustaining the images of leading performers. When film stars belonged to the studios, they had hired agents, personal managers, and press agents or publicists to act on their behalf, but as stars became independent these roles assumed greater importance. Agents, managers, and publicists became vital intermediaries, procuring employment on behalf of performers, guiding their careers with creative, professional, or business advice, and dealing with the press, broadcasting organizations, and web content providers vital to dispersing the visibility of Hollywood film stardom beyond cinema itself. Stars have also employed the services of entertainment attorneys to draw up the contracts which define the terms of their employment and their economic value for the studios.

Agents: Representing Talent

As the studios shed talent, so agents became the key mediators between the studios and the supply of stars, writers, or directors. In Hollywood any practicing talent agency must be licensed under special sections of the California Labor Code, which defines an agent as any "person or corporation who engages in the occupation of procuring, offering, promising, or attempting to procure employment for an artist or artists" (ATA, 2005).

Over successive decades the talent agency business has been topped by groupings of three or four major firms. In the mid-1970s, the William Morris Agency (WMA) continued to be the traditional face of talent representation in Hollywood, but was rivaled by the new firms International Creative Management (ICM) and Creative Artists Agency (CAA), formed respectively at the end of 1974 and start of 1975. New agencies appeared in the 1980s as Triad Artists and InterTalent were launched, and in 1991 Bauer-Benedek merged with Leading Artists Agency to form the United Talent Agency (UTA). However, a period of consolidation followed. In one week during October 1992, InterTalent collapsed after its partners moved to ICM and UTA, and Triad was sold to WMA. Only UTA survived to join WMA, ICM, and CAA as the fourth major agency in Hollywood. The Endeavor Talent Agency (ETA), established in March 1995 after four agents left ICM, remained predominantly a literary and television agency, but represented a limited number of star performers. From the late 1990s these agencies were representing the overwhelming majority of leading performers in Hollywood, with CAA displaying the strongest client roster (table 10.1).

As CAA rose to prominence during the 1980s and 1990s, it came to define the modern Hollywood talent agency. When Bill Haber, Ron Meyer, Michael Ovitz, Rowland Perkins, and Mike Rosenfeld left WMA to form CAA, they replaced the venerable tradition of WMA with an assertive and aggressive dynamism that rapidly lifted their new agency to the forefront of the business. To build a star client roster, in October 1976 CAA merged with Martin Baum Associates, who represented

TABLE 10.1 Leading agencies and star clients, 2006

CAA	Endeavor	ICM	UTA	WMA
Drew Barrymore	Ben Affleck	Michael Caine	Jack Black	Russell Crowe
Sandra Bullock	Matt Damon	Jodie Foster	Johnny Depp	Clint Eastwood
Jim Carrey	Vin Diesel	Andy Garcia	Harrison Ford	Scarlett Johansson
Nicolas Cage	Michael Douglas	Richard Gere	Wesley Snipes	Tommy Lee Jones
George Clooney	Paul Giamatti	Mel Gibson	Ben Stiller	Lucy Liu
Sean Connery	Dustin Hoffman	Samuel L. Jackson	Owen Wilson	Jennifer Lopez
Tom Cruise	Hugh Jackman	Diane Keaton		Kevin Spacey
Penelope Cruz	Jude Law	Steve Martin		Kiefer Sutherland
Cameron Diaz	Mark Wahlberg	Brittany Murphy		Catherine Zeta-Jones
Jamie Foxx		Susan Sarandon		
Hugh Grant		Sharon Stone		
Gene Hackman		Christopher Walken		
Tom Hanks		Denzell Washington		
Ed Harris		Sigourney Weaver		
Angelina Jolie				
Nicole Kidman				
Demi Moore				
Julianne Moore				
Mike Myers				
Gywneth Paltrow				
Sean Penn				
Michelle Pfeiffer				
Brad Pitt				
Keanu Reeves				
Tim Robbins				
Julia Roberts				
Meg Ryan				
Will Smith				
Meryl Streep				
Hilary Swank				
Billy Bob Thornton				
Uma Thurman				
Naomi Watts				
Robin Williams				
Bruce Willis				
Kate Winslet				
Renée Zellweger				

Source: ATA, 2006.

Sidney Poitier, Julie Andrews, Richard Harris, and Joanne Woodward amongst other star names. CAA also aggressively poached clients from its competitors: Sylvester Stallone, for example, was approached in person while he holidayed in Hawaii with an offer to leave WMA for CAA (Singular, 1996: 78). With a mixture of bold tenacity and financial incentives, CAA was able to build a premium talent roster, and by 1989 represented 134 actors, including Cher, Sean Connery, Kevin Costner, Dustin Hoffman, Paul Newman, Robert Redford, Barbra Streisand, and Robin Williams, alongside directors, writers, and music artists such as Michael Jackson, Madonna, and Prince (Davis, 1989: 11).

If CAA represented the modern agency, Ovitz characterized the modern agent, becoming emblematic of the new status and power of agents in Hollywood. By controlling the supply of talent, Ovitz influenced the production schedules and budgeting of the studios, and his manner of conducting business attracted respect, reverence, fear, and loathing in equal measure. By the time Ovitz left CAA in 1995 to become President of the Walt Disney Company, he had transformed the conduct of the agency business. As Michael Wolff observed, "The paradigm shift is that pre-Ovitz, talent was dependent on agents; post-Ovitz, *purchasers* of talent were dependent on agents, too" (1999; emphasis in original).

At WMA, CAA's founders had all become acquainted with the practice of agencies receiving a packaging fee for combining actors, directors, producers, and scripts for projects sold to the television networks. Carrying the practice over to films, at the start of the 1980s CAA packaged stars Bill Murray and Harold Ramis with director Ivan Reitman for *Stripes* (1981, US). The trio were teamed again for *Ghostbusters* (1984, US) while CAA clients Hoffman, Teri Garr, and director Sydney Pollack were brought together on *Tootsie* (1982, US). No packaging fee was paid to the agency for providing these combinations of talent; instead, CAA's income came from commissions on its clients. On *Legal Eagles* (1986, US), CAA supplied the stars, director and writing team. Stars Redford and Debra Winger were paid $5million and $2.5million respectively, with Reitman earning in the region of $2.5million and the writers $750,000. Approximately one-third of the estimated $32 million budget was therefore spent on CAA clients, and while *Legal Eagles* failed at the box office, the agency nevertheless profited from commissions (Davis, 1989: 11). CAA was not alone in packaging clients: InterTalent teamed director Geoff Murphy with actors Emilio Estevez and Kiefer Sutherland on *Young Guns II* (1990, US), while also partnering John Travolta with Linda Fiorentino on *Shout* (Jeffrey Hornaday, 1991, US).

Packaging became widely regarded as one of the clearest demonstrations of agents extending their powers by assuming a role in the development of projects which formerly would have been undertaken by the studios. Yet at the start of the 1990s, industry executives held the view that if packaging existed at all in Hollywood, it happened with perhaps only one out of every 200 films made and was something largely confined to the mid-1980s (Natale and Fleming, 1991). The genesis of some projects also raised questions over the extent to which packaging really happened or had any actual influence over the greenlighting of projects. On the face of it, *A League of Their Own* (1992, US) seemed a CAA package: clients Tom Hanks and Madonna starred alongside Geena Davis, who took a role originally intended for Winger. Yet it was director Penny Marshall who was responsible for the casting decisions, and rather than leverage the project into production, the concentration of talent did not prevent 20th Century Fox rejecting the project, and the film was

FIGURE 10.1   CAA packaging – Harold Ramis (left) and Bill Murray (right) together in *Ghostbusters* (1984). Produced by Ivan Reitman; distributed by Columbia; directed by Ivan Reitman

finally made by Columbia. The significance of packaging therefore exceeded actual practice: it became an evocative industry mythology encapsulating the newfound status of agents in their dealings with the studios.

Personal Managers: Engineering Careers

Agents played a key role in forming the careers of their star clients, but during the 1990s their role was partly encroached upon as many stars hired personal managers alongside or instead of an agent.

A manager does not represent a direct substitute for an agent as several differences distinguish the roles. Agents procure work for stars while managers provide career guidance or business advice, day-to-day counseling, and networking services. As manager Bernie Brillstein commented: "An agent's agenda is to get talent jobs and it's our job to advise, consult and recommend to the client whether it's enough money, whether the billing is correct, if the script and director are right and if the release date is right. It's our job to take the whole picture into account, not just the particular job" (quoted in Eller and Marx, 1993: 260). Where an agent is conventionally paid 10 percent of a client's income, the commission paid to managers is more variable, usually falling between 8 and 15 percent.

Personal managers had been present from the earliest years of the film industry, but their rise to importance in the 1990s was a response to the contemporary state of the agency business. Following the consolidation of the agencies in the early 1990s, the dominance of the major agencies presented obstacles to breaking new and mid-level talent. Only by keeping large client rosters and poaching clients from competitors could the major agencies retain their status. At the larger agencies, an agent might therefore oversee dozens of existing clients while inter-agency competition placed pressure on the agent to hire or steal new clients. In comparison a manager could be looking after only one client or a smaller stable of maybe ten clients. While the backing of a large roster gave the major agencies the muscle to bargain on behalf of individual clients, stars valued the greater dedicated personal attention and all-round career coaching they could receive from a manager. For example, Bresler Kelly and Associates represents 13 actors but only one star client, Jack Nicholson. Even the largest management companies did not grow to the same scale as the major agencies in terms of their client rosters. Large management companies such as Brillstein-Grey, Management 360, or 3 Arts Entertainment emerged during the 1990s, yet unlike the four dominant agencies, the management business was populated by a broader collection of medium- and small-scale enterprises.

Managers also proudly presented their business as free of the dirty dealing in talent poaching. Due to the internal pressures of sustaining a large client list, the boom in personal management was also fed by many agents leaving the major firms to become managers. These included Howard Klein, who departed ICM in 1990 to become a partner in 3 Arts, while Brian Medavoy left ICM to become co-founder with Erwin More of More Medavoy Management (Brodie and O'Steen, 1995: 1).

Stars like Tom Cruise, Mel Gibson, Julia Roberts, and Arnold Schwarzenegger did not hire managers because they had high-powered agents at the top companies dedicated to looking after their individual interests. In contrast, a few stars declined the services of agents to be solely represented by a manager backed by the services of an entertainment attorney. In the 1990s, Harrison Ford and Sharon Stone, for example, were amongst the stars opting for representation through managers alone, although both later signed to major agencies.

The rise of personal managers created tensions in the production of Hollywood stardom. As managers assumed a more central role in determining the career choices of star clients, agents were angered by regulatory conditions which offered unequal benefits to managers. While the 1986 Talent Agency Act requires all agents be licensed and regulated by the state, the same conditions do not apply to managers. Although the act prohibits managers from negotiating deals or procuring work on behalf of their clients, by exploiting ambiguities in how negotiation and procurement may be understood and defined, it was widely acknowledged within Hollywood that some managers have acted illegally by obtaining work for clients.

According to the Act, agents cannot engage in production, yet the same restriction does not hold for managers. By bridging the roles of representation and production, producer-managers play an important role in mediating the supply of star talent to film projects. Access to star talent gives managers considerable leverage to enter production: many have negotiated arrangements for either directly producing films featuring their star clients or otherwise gaining an executive producer credit, frequently for their role in bringing stars to a project. While managing Sharon Stone during the 1990s, Chuck Binder received executive or co-producer credit on seven of the star's 13 films between 1994 and 2000, including *The Specialist* (Luis Llosa, 1994, US/Peru), *The Quick and the Dead* (Sam Raimi, 1995, US/Japan), *Last Dance* (Bruce Beresford, 1996, US), and *Beautiful Joe* (Stephen Metcalfe, 2000, US/UK).

Similarly, after his rise to stardom in the late 1970s, John Travolta's career waned, but from the late 1980s it experienced a renaissance through the intervention of producer-manager Jonathan Krane. Krane financed and produced *Look Who's Talking* (Amy Heckerling, 1989, US) for TriStar, with Travolta in the lead role, and the success of this film generated two sequels featuring the star. Krane's partnership with Travolta continued throughout the 1990s, with the manager assuming producer or executive producer responsibilities on nearly a dozen films featuring the star, including *Phenomenon* (Jon Turteltaub, 1996, US), *Face/Off* (John Woo, 1997, US), *The General's Daughter* (Simon West, 1999, US/Germany), *Battlefield Earth: A Saga of the Year 3000* (Roger Christian, 2000, US), and *Basic* (John McTiernan, 2003, US/De). Yet such manager–star relationships did not represent a widespread trend. Most managers engaged in production worked on television projects and, where they did work on film projects, generally these involved mid-range and relatively unknown performers rather than major stars.

The involvement of managers in production also resulted in some of the larger management companies gaining first-look deals with studios for the consideration of projects featuring star clients. For example, in the 1990s Keanu Reeves was managed by Erwin Stoff at 3 Arts. Stoff had co-produced *Bill and Ted's Bogus Journey* (Peter Hewitt, 1991, US) starring Reeves, and after becoming a founding partner in 3 Arts, Stoff secured a first-look deal with Fox. The immediate outcome of this was *Chain Reaction* (Andrew Davis, 1996, US) starring Reeves, and the producer-manager and star teamed on over a dozen subsequent projects, including the specialty feature *Feeling Minnesota* (Steven Baigelman, 1996, US), together with the Warner productions *The Devil's Advocate* (Taylor Hackford, 1997, US/De), *The Matrix* (Andy and Larry Wachowski, 1999, US), and *Constantine* (Frances Lawrence, 2005, US/De).

Producer-managers were frequently criticized for the conflict of interest caused by their dual role: as one commentator noted, "where *does* a producer-manager's loyalty fall when there's a conflict between a client's needs and a project's needs?" (Fleming, 2005: 67; emphasis in original). When delivering star talent for a production, some managers may forgo their usual commission in favor of a producer's fee. While this practice lessens the deductions made from a star's earnings, it can raise the costs of production as the manager's remuneration is effectively passed on from client to studio.

Publicists: Controlling Visibility

In-house publicity departments had been a feature of the vertically integrated studios, but as the industry restructured these departments were either downsized or the publicity function outsourced to external independent publicity firms. Compared to channels of paid advertising, publicity generates exposure which is relatively "free." Whenever stars make personal appearances at press conferences or film premieres, give television interviews, are displayed on magazine covers, or grant the press access to cover a private event such as a marriage, publicity is at work. Although costs are attached to hosting a premiere for example, the presence of a star or stars may gain front-page coverage in the next day's press at no direct cost, and in space which cannot be formally bought: "Publicity is designed to turn advertising into news. Its value is that you gain media space without paying for it and that its positioning as news rather than advertising gives it greater credibility" (Turner, Bonner, and Marshall, 2000: 31).

Hollywood publicists create and manage relationships between film stars and the array of other media channels through which the identities of stars are circulated. Stars have a dual relationship with publicity, for they publicize films but also, and importantly in the freelance market, have an interest in self-publicity. It is for the latter reason that while many stars continue to regard managers as an optional luxury, today the majority of stars in Hollywood hire publicists to manage their media visibility. Instead of a percentage, publicists are retained on a monthly fee, averaging in the region of $3,000 per month.

As part of the public relations business, independent publicists include Hollywood stars and studios as their clients, alongside corporations and individuals from the worlds of entertainment, sports, finance, technology, retailing, and other business sectors. For example, after its formation in 1950, the firm Rogers & Cowan (R&C) became the leading name in Hollywood public relations and played a decisive role in transforming the importance of PR for the studios and the stars. Founding partner Henry Rogers had made his name as a press agent to Rita Hayworth and Claudette Colbert, but looking after star visibility represented a high-maintenance and relatively low-income revenue stream. By the early 1990s, corporate billings had become the main profit center, as stars paid fees averaging $2,000–$3,000 per month, while medium-sized corporate accounts attracted $15,000–$20,000 each month (Brown, 1992: 79). Today R&C maintains 11 different divisional groupings, covering personalities, music, film, television, fashion/beauty, sports, promotions, product placement, special events, corporate and consumer marketing, and convergence. Film stars, directors, and producers, together with supermodels, authors, and fashion designers, are handled by the Personalities Group, which "work[s] on a highly personalized basis, building and maintaining favorable images for our clients through strategic counsel, media campaigns and solid relationships with reporters and editors . . . advis[ing] producers, directors and film and television personalities on all media and marketing decisions" (Rogers and Cowan, 2006).

Rogers & Cowan was not only successful in its own right but also provided the breeding ground for some of the key figures who emerged at the forefront of Hollywood PR in the 1980s and 1990s. After working at R&C, in 1989 Michael Nyman became a founding partner in Bragman, Nyman and Cafarelli, Inc. (BNC). Pat Kingsley joined R&C as a secretary in 1959 and progressed to become a planter before leaving in 1971 to form Pickwick Public Relations with Lois Smith. Nine years later, Pickwick merged with Maslansky-Koenigsberg to establish PMK and from the 1980s the company became the leading name in Hollywood PR. Amongst PMK's clients,

Kingsley handled Tom Cruise, Sharon Stone, Richard Gere, Jodie Foster, and Al Pacino, while Smith represented Michele Pfeiffer and Robert Redford, and a third partner, Leslee Dart, looked after Tom Hanks and Denzel Washington (Seabrook, 1994: 215).

When the studios managed star publicity, Hollywood desperately courted exposure by using elaborate stunts to gain the attention of the press. But by the 1980s, the relationship between the publicists and the media had reversed. With gossip tabloids and glossy magazines all clamoring for coverage of the stars, the media competed for access to stars and other popular figures. Rather than the stars and studios depending on press coverage, the press needed stars and other celebrities to gain a popular readership. By controlling access, publicists increased their importance and influence, becoming "gatekeepers" between the stars and the media (Walls, 2000).

Kingsley and PMK represented this new relationship between Hollywood stardom and the US media. Anecdotes abounded over the manipulative and abrasive manner with which Kingsley controlled the media's access to her star clients, particularly Tom Cruise. After working on the historical drama *Far and Away* (Ron Howard, 1992, US), Cruise insisted Universal hired Kingsley and PMK to publicize the film instead of the studio's own staff. Kingsley organized a weekend junket at the Four Seasons hotel in Los Angeles and journalists were corralled into groups for their interviews with stars. Teaming with Nancy Seltzer, the publicist for Cruise's co-star Nicole Kidman, Kingsley demanded journalists sign a consent agreement stipulating quotes from the two stars could only be used at the time of the immediate theatrical release of the film (Walls 2000: 251). In 1993, when *Los Angeles* magazine profiled Cruise, Kingsley required the publication to submit "fact-checking questions" in return for written answers which could not be verified as originating from the star (Bart, 1993: 5). Kingsley became infamous for the demands she made on journalists by exacting approval on writers, questions, quotes, and sometimes copy in relation to interviews with her clients. Kingsley and PMK were therefore representative of a climate in which publicists not only rigorously guarded access to Hollywood stars but also wrested control away from magazine or newspaper editors by effectively pre-editing coverage of their clients.

Between 1997 and 2001 the power of public relations firms in shaping Hollywood stardom increased as a succession of acquisitions changed the ownership of major PR companies. In April 1987 the London firm Shandwick became the owner of R&C as part of an extensive acquisition program which made the London firm one of the world's leading PR groups. After Shandwick was acquired in 1998 by Interpublic, the advertising and communications conglomerate made further acquisitions in Hollywood PR. In February 1999 Momentum, a marketing subsidiary of the Interpublic's McCann-Erickson WorldGroup, acquired PMK. Two years later Interpublic's subsidiary Weber Shandwick bought Bragman, Nyman and Cafarelli, whose clients included Cameron Diaz, Whoopi Goldberg, and Kate Hudson, and in May that year Momentum bought Huvane Baum Halls, which handled Gwyneth Paltrow and Russell Crowe. A new merged entity was created, PMK/HBH. With R&C, BNC, and PMK/HBH, Interpublic took ownership of nearly all the leading

Hollywood PR firms. A similar move occurred in October 1999 as the PR firm Baker Winokur Ryder (BWR), who counted Ben Affleck, Leonardo DiCaprio, Brad Pitt, Chris Rock, Adam Sandler, and Renée Zellweger amongst its clients, was acquired by the New York company Ogilvy Public Relations Worldwide, a subsidiary of the marketing and communications group WPP.

Criticism was expressed by the press that Interpublic's acquisition program concentrated access to the stars, potentially restricting editorial freedom. Although Kingsley dismissed such concerns, in the *New York Post* Michelle Gotthelt responded to the PMK/HBH merger by speculating that journalists could be blacklisted for asking the wrong questions of stars, or otherwise have their access to other stars curtailed: "Who dare ask [Russell] Crowe why he really dumped Meg Ryan when they could be jeopardizing future access to Cruise or Paltrow? . . . Nobody dares ask [Matt] Damon for the true lowdown on Winona Ryder because they may be refused [Johnny] Depp" (quoted in O'Dwyer, 2001).

The production of stardom therefore became the ground for greater interaction between Hollywood and the PR business. By manipulating access to stars, PR firms influenced the editorial coverage of stars, and while companies such as ID Public Relations and Wolf-Kasteler also handled media relations for Hollywood stars, the acquisition programs of Interpublic and Ogilvy consolidated the channels through which the media could gain access to the stars.

Entertainment Attorneys: Sealing the Deal

In Hollywood, entertainment attorneys work in conjunction with agents to finalize the deals which contract star talent. The agent will obtain work for the star and conduct the up-front negotiation of terms concerning the star's fee, rendering of services, and granting of rights. Only after the basic deal has been agreed does the attorney step in, liaising with the agent and the buyer of the star's services to refine the detail of the deal, particularly regarding matters of compensation and profit participation (Garey, 2006: 186).

Although the broad role of the entertainment attorney can be described, the workings of the Hollywood lawyer are for ever shrouded in confidentiality. What attorneys actually do on behalf of whom is not open to public disclosure or scrutiny. However, it is only in the fixing of contractual terms that the economic value of film stardom is formalized and documented. Possibly more than agents, managers, or publicists, the work of entertainment lawyers demonstrates how the production of Hollywood stardom rests on a paradox created in the tension between wanting to keep private and secret the operations by which the publicly exhibitionist show of film stardom is created and maintained.

The LA-based law firm Ziffren, Brittenham, Branca, Fischer, Gilbert-Lurie, Stiffelman and Cook occupies a prominent place amongst the leading legal representatives in Hollywood. Formed in 1978 by Ken Ziffren and Harry M. 'Skip' Brittenham, television has remained at the center of Ziffren Brittenham's business, but the company has included DirectTV, DreamWorks, Microsoft, and Pixar amongst the corporate clients it has worked for. Alongside star clients, including Sandra Bullock, Tom Hanks, Keanu Reeves, Bruce Willis, and Catherine Zeta-Jones, the firm also represents film directors (Tim Burton, Barry Sonnenfeld) and producers (Scott Rudin). Ziffren was personally credited with bringing both sides together to reach a resolution during the 1988 strike by the Writers Guild of America (WGA), and his influence in Hollywood earned him the title amongst those in the entertainment business of "the pope." By representing talent but also executives who head the studios which hire the talent, Ziffren Brittenham have prompted the question, "Should any one lawyer represent both the fish and the bait?" (Eller, 2005). In the 1990s, Ziffren Brittenham faced three cases of litigation over conflict of interest, including accusations that the more powerful party was favored in deals between clients. However, for the clients the advantages of representation by a company dealing with valuable talent or high-level decisionmakers is cherished "as a sign you're really connected" (Eller, 2005). Instead of charging an hourly fee for their services, Brittenham and Ziffren take 5 percent of a client's earnings, which some critics argued meant they'd gone into business with his clients (Citron and Welkos, 1992).

Barnes, Morris, Klein, Mark, Yorn, Barnes and Levine represent a younger breed of entertainment attorney. In January 1996 Kevin Morris established his company, representing Matt Stone and Trey Parker who later became the creators of the lucrative animated television series *South Park* (1997–). An association with comedy saw Barnes build his client list, and the firm expanded as new clients joined and as further new partners brought clients with them. Alongside the film stars it represents, the client list also includes television performers (Kim Cattrall, Ellen DeGeneres) and film directors (John Singleton, Keenan Ivory Wayans). In 2000 Deborah Klein joined as a partner from another firm, bringing with her star clients including Jim Carrey, Will Ferrell, Samuel L. Jackson, and Vince Vaughn. Klein is representative of the gains which strong legal representation can offer for stars. She

FIGURE 10.2   A $20 million performance – Jim Carrey in *Cable Guy* (1996). Produced by Judd Apatow, Andrew Licht, and Jeffrey A. Mueller; distributed by Columbia; directed by Ben Stiller

acquired a reputation for helping clients to secure major leaps in star salaries after her role in raising the price of Carrey's services. Carrey was paid $300,000 for *Ace Ventura: Pet Detective* (Tom Shadyac, 1994, US), but his fee increased to $7 million for *Dumb and Dumber* (Peter Farrelly, 1994, US), and with *Cable Guy* (Ben Stiller, 1996, US) he became the first star to receive $20 million for a role.

The modern entertainment attorney does not see his or her role as confined simply to dealing with the legal paperwork of clients. Attorneys also take a hand in making the careers of their star clients. Kevin Yorn joined Barnes Morris in the first months after the company was formed, and has represented Scarlett Johansson since she was 16. Yorn has occupied a key role in the building of Johansson's career as she has worked across films for major studios and independents, together with contracts with advertising clients. By building a long-term relationship with clients and intervening in steering the careers of star talent, attorneys now perform a role comparable to that of the agent, manager, or publicist.

The Post-Studio Star System

Stars are a form of capital and a resource of great value to the commerce of Hollywood, and the production of stardom is a vital part of the film industry. As John Belton observes, "The industry that makes motion pictures also manufactures, with the aid of the press and other media, movie stars" (1994: 85).

Vertical disintegration in the contemporary Hollywood film industry has produced a stratified structure divided between the oligopoly of the major studio financier-producer-distributors and an array of specialized firms who provide services to the studios and other users. This situation has defined the context in which film stardom is produced in contemporary Hollywood. As stars became part of the freelance labor market, responsibility for the production of stardom shifted to independent agencies, managers, publicists, and attorneys. Although the studios remain the main employers of Hollywood film stars, and while appearances in the films made by the studio are essential to performers achieving the level of visibility necessary to distinguish them as stars, the studios are no longer central to the making of stars. Instead talent agents, personal managers, publicists, and legal representatives have become the leading specialized service providers in the making of Hollywood stardom.

While agents, managers, publicists, and attorneys belong to the scattering of independent services feeding the major studios, and while their rise has come as the result of limited disintegration amongst the studio oligopoly, nevertheless there remains a strongly discernible core of participant firms in the production of Hollywood stardom. At the start of 2006, the four major agencies and Endeavor represented the majority of film stars in Hollywood. Leading management companies were handling the careers of stars, offering bespoke services and generally handling fewer clients. Six independent PR companies, three of which were owned by Interpublic, were responsible for generating coverage for most of the stars in Hollywood. Finally, despite

TABLE 10.2   Who represents whom? Leading Hollywood agents, managers, publicists, attorneys and selected film star clients, 2006

Agents

Creative Artists Agency	Endeavor Talent Agency	International Creative Management	United Talent Agency	William Morris Agency
Tom Cruise	Ben Affleck	Jodie Foster	Jack Black	Russell Crowe
Tom Hanks	Matt Damon	Mel Gibson	Johnny Depp	Clint Eastwood
Julia Roberts	Vin Diesel	Samuel L. Jackson	Harrison Ford	Reese Witherspoon
Will Smith	Michael Douglas	Sharon Stone	Ben Stiller	Catherine Zeta-Jones

Personal Managers

Brillstein-Grey Entertainment	The Firm	Management 360	3 Arts Entertainment
Nicolas Cage	Robert De Niro	Kirsten Dunst	Matthew Broderick
Andy Garcia	Cameron Diaz	Meg Ryan	Keanu Reeves
Brad Pitt	Samuel L. Jackson	Reese Witherspoon	Chris Rock

Independent Publicists

Bragman Nyman Cafarelli	PMK/HBH	Rogers & Cowan	Baker Winokur Ryder	ID Public Relations	Wolf-Kasteler
Cameron Diaz	Russell Crowe	Mel Gibson	Ben Affleck	Dustin Hoffman	Nicolas Cage
Kate Hudson	Tom Hanks	John Travolta	Brad Pitt	Mike Myers	Samuel L. Jackson
	Nicole Kidman	Denzel Washington	Reese Witherspoon	Ben Stiller	Michelle Pfeiffer
	Demi Moore	Bruce Willis	Renée Zellweger		

Entertainment Attorneys

Barnes, Morris, Klein, Mark, Yorn, Barnes & Levine	Bloom, Hergott, Diemer	Greenburg Glusker	Hirsch, Wallerstein, Hayum, Matlof & Fisherman	Jackoway, Tyerman, Wertheimer, Austen, Mandelbaum & Morris	Ziffren, Brittenham, Branca, Fischer, Gilbert-Lurie, Stiffelman & Cook
Will Ferrell	Brad Pitt	Tom Cruise	Jennifer Lopez	Cameron Diaz	Tom Hanks
Samuel L. Jackson	Sylvester Stallone		Julia Roberts	Nicole Kidman	Keanu Reeves
Vince Vaughn				Hilary Swank	Bruce Willis

Sources: ATA, 2006; assorted news stories; <IMDbpro.com>.

the secrecy surrounding the star–attorney relationship, legal representation of major stars could be identified as concentrated in the hands of just a few firms.

With each category of participant serving a particular role in the making of stardom, and with the number of significant participants remaining relatively restricted over a period of time, Hollywood has retained a star system, but one revised by and responsive to the structural transformation of the Hollywood film industry. Numerous other agencies, managers, publicists, and law firms exist in Hollywood, and indeed the growth of these services has resulted in many individuals and companies crowding into the business. Despite the multiplication of entrants, a nucleus of dominant firms remains at the center of Hollywood stardom (table 10.2). As this cluster of firms also handles clients from the fields of television, music, and sports, so the production of Hollywood film stardom has become part of the more general production of celebrity, and, rather than a product of the film business, Hollywood stardom today is created across a broad-based entertainment industry.

While the structure of the star system may have changed over the last few decades, its purpose has remained the same: to generate and disseminate the images of stars as signs of commercial value in cinema and popular culture. Since stars sell things – films, magazines, tabloid papers, etc. – stardom is a form of resource or capital used by Hollywood. The value of stardom partly relies on its rarity, for only a very few lead performers achieve star status, and the star system also manages the deployment of stardom, determining who will be recognized as a star and controlling the contexts in which stardom will be used. The small cluster of companies that form the contemporary star system therefore make, manage, and control the capital of stardom in Hollywood cinema.

REFERENCES

ATA (2005) "Laws Relating to Talent Agencies," online at <http://www.agentassociation.com/frontdoor/agency_licensing_detail.cfm?id=273> (accessed January 3, 2006).
ATA (2006) "Actors' Agent Search," online at <http://www.agentassociation.com/frontdoor/actors_agent_search.cfm> (accessed November 1, 2006).
Bart, P. (1993) "Buzz," *Variety*, November 29, p. 5.
Belton, J. (1994) *American Cinema/American Culture*. New York: McGraw-Hill.
Brodie, J., and K. O'Steen (1995) "Antsy Agents Make Mutant Managers," *Variety*, March 20, p. 1.
Brown, C. (1992) "The Stunt Men & the Brat Flacks," *Premiere* (US) May, pp.76–83.
Citron, A., and R. W. Welkos (1992) " 'The Pope of Hollywood': Ziffren's Representation of Studios, Stars Is Challenged," *Los Angeles Times*, p. D-1.
Davis, L. (1989) "Hollywood's Secret Agent," *Daily Telegraph*, November 25, p. 11.
Eller, C. (2005) "He Reels in the Big Deals," *Los Angeles Times*, p. A-1.
Eller, C., and A. Marx (1993) "H'wood: Under New Management," *Variety*, May 10, pp. 1, 260.
Fadiman, W. (1972) *Hollywood Now*. New York: Liveright.

Fleming, M. (2005) "How Are Producers Managing?," *Variety*, December 5, pp. 11, 67.

Garey, N. H. (2006) "The Entertainment Lawyer," in J. Squire (ed.), *The Movie Business Book*, 3rd edn. Maidenhead: Open University Press, pp. 184–93.

McDonald, P. (2000) *The Star System: Hollywood's Production of Popular Identities*. London: Wallflower.

Natale, R., and C. Fleming (1991) "Pic Packaging: H'wood's Near Myth," *Variety*, October 7, pp. 3, 217.

O'Dwyer, J. (2001) "Celebrity Publicist Raps Article," *Jack O'Dwyer's Newsletter*, 34(23), p. 2.

Rogers and Cowan (2006) "What We Do," online at <http://www.rogersandcowan.com/rc-2.html> (accessed January 3, 2006).

Seabrook, J. (1994) "Kingsley's Ransom," *The New Yorker*, March 21, pp. 215–21.

Shprintz, J. (2002) "Shakeup for Legal Eagles," *Daily Variety*, December 17, p. 1.

Shprintz, J. (2006) "Pact Mentality," *Daily Variety*, October 17, p. A1.

Singular, S. (1996) *Power to Burn: Michael Ovitz and the New Business of Show Business*. Secaucus, NJ: Birch Lane Press.

Turner, G., F. Bonner, and P. D. Marshall (2000) *Fame Games: The Production of Celebrity in Australia*. Cambridge: Cambridge University Press.

Walls, J. (2000) *Dish: How Gossip Became News and the News Became Just Another Show*. New York: Perennial.

Wolff, M. (1999) "He'll Manage," *New York Magazine*, March 8, online at <http://www.newyorkmetro.com/nymetro/news/media/columns/medialife/155/> (accessed November 23, 2005).

CHAPTER 11

HOLLYWOOD AND THE STATE: THE AMERICAN FILM INDUSTRY CARTEL IN THE AGE OF GLOBALIZATION

MANJUNATH PENDAKUR

Monopolist capitalist combines, cartels, syndicates and trusts divide among themselves, first of all, the home market, seize more or less complete possession of the industry of a country. But under capitalism the home market is inevitably bound up with the foreign market. Capitalism long ago created a world market. As the export of capital increased, and as the foreign and colonial connections and "spheres of influence" of the big monopolist combines expanded in all ways, things "naturally" gravitated towards an international agreement among these combines, and towards the formation of international cartels.

(V. I. Lenin, *Imperialism, the Highest Stage of Capitalism*, p. 79)

Lenin made these observations about monopoly capitalism almost a hundred years ago and they are useful to understand the historic development of Hollywood as an industry dominated by a small number of oligopolistic corporations with monopoly power whose tentacles have spread widely, and in many cases penetrated deeply, into the global markets (see Wasko, 2003; Miller, et al., 2005). As discussed earlier in this volume, these corporations, also known as the majors, monopolize the lion's share of revenues and profits from the film industry. While these corporate giants compete fiercely with each other for talent, capital, and access to markets around the world, they also collaborate under the benevolent umbrella of the Motion Picture Association of America (MPAA) in trying to achieve some common goals. The MPAA also actively seeks collaboration and support from the US and other governments, often resulting in positive gains for the Hollywood majors. Due to the intense rivalry and conglomeration in the entertainment industry in the last 20 years, the MPAA appears to have doubled its efforts to address the issues and concerns the member companies face in the global markets. This chapter sketches those intra-industry relationships in the context of the current phase of globalization and examines the close relationship between the MPAA and the US government.

Cartelization and Power

A cartel's principal goal is to contain inter-capitalist rivalry and the antagonisms that develop out of the contradictions within capital. Cartels engage in anti-competitive trade practices such as fixing prices of the commodities its members buy and sell, and gaining exclusive access to markets (and thereby monopoly profits) for its members.

A cartel also presents a united front to external forces that may pose a threat to the structure of the industry; its policies benefit the member companies who form this exclusive "club." The external forces may be the various regulatory bodies of a state (domestic and foreign), consumers of the products that are produced by cartel's members, certain technologies that challenge corporate control and their monopoly profits, and religious organizations and other civil society groups who may have collective concerns about the products sold by the cartel's members.

The motion picture industry cartel, the MPAA's predecessor, the Motion Picture Producers and Distributors of America, was organized in 1922 in specific circumstances to fend off such external threats by uniting the competing major motion picture producers and distributors under one umbrella (see Ulf-Moller, 1998: 51). In other words, from its inception the organization's project was both political-economic and global in scope, and not, as claimed by Gomery, purely political ("the main activity of the Association has been political": 2004: 1). He correctly notes, however, that "the companies have always hired well-connected Washington insiders to represent their interests in the capital."

Very astutely, the industry leaders decided to hire Will H. Hays, a politically connected former US Postmaster General, who knew the ways in which Washington worked, and who ran the organization from 1922 to 1946. Hays was rewarded with the high position of Postmaster General after he headed the presidential campaign of Warren G. Harding, who won the presidential election in 1921. Equally importantly, Hays was one of the Republican leaders who was instrumental in crafting the US economic/foreign policy in that period to promote exports. Herbert Hoover, who was then Secretary of Commerce and an important player in formulating and implementing the US economic policy, was a staunch ally of big business and promoter of a corporatist state that facilitated close collaboration between big capital and public administration.

The early patterns established by Will Hays – of building relationships with centers of power, including the Catholic Church, self-censorship to fend off the possibility of federally imposed censorship, and building alliances with foreign governments, owners of theatrical networks abroad, individual politicians, retired generals, etc. – continue to this day. In the more than 80 years of its operation, the MPAA has had only five presidents, all appointed by the member companies: Will Hays (1922–45), Eric Johnston (1945–63), Ralph Hetzel (1966), and Jack Valenti (1966–2004). Not much is known of Hetzel, but Johnson was head of the US Chamber of Commerce. Valenti, who ran the organization for the longest period, with 38 years of service to the majors, was on the staff at the White House during the Lyndon

B. Johnson presidency. Dan Glickman, the most recently appointed president and CEO, is also a Washington insider. He served President Bill Clinton as his Secretary of Agriculture from 1995 to 2001 and then directed the Institute of Politics at Harvard University before assuming the presidency of the MPAA in 2004. The majors pay a share of their gross revenue annually to the MPAA towards its operating expenses.

The MPAA issued a media release on July 1, 2004, when Valenti announced his decision to resign, and noted the following as one of the accomplishments during his nearly four decades of tenure:

> When he assumed leadership of MPAA [sic], its member companies were mainly involved in a domestic operation centering on theatrical movies and TV programming. The international market had yet to soar to its current heights. When Valenti came to the MPAA, Hollywood's major studios' worldwide revenues in 1967 were $1.26 billion, of which international markets comprised 33% or $418 million. Since then, there has been an exponential growth and upheaval, with the MPAA/MPA organization asserting itself as a global entertainment, cultural and economic phenomenon. In 2003, the MPAA's Cember [sic] Companies' global revenues were some $41.2 billion with international revenues at 40% or $16.6 billion. (MPAA, 2004b: 1)

As discussed later in this chapter, such phenomenal growth in exports has been facilitated by the MPAA's sustained diplomacy around the world, and also by pressure tactics and, when necessary, the whole weight of the American presidency being brought to bear on that process. MPAA's international counterpart, the Motion Picture

FIGURE 11.1   Jack Valenti (left), with President Bill Clinton, addressing television executives at the White House, February 29, 1996. Photo by Associated Press

Export Association (MPEA) was established as a sister-corporation in 1945. In 1994 the MPEA was renamed as the Motion Picture Association (MPA).

Constituted as a trade association under US law (the Export Trade Act 1918), the president of the MPAA also presides over the MPA. Better known as the Webb–Pomerene Export Trade Act, named after the co-sponsors Senator Pomerene and Congressman Webb the law

> grants an exemption under US antitrust laws to American exporters who are permitted to group together under its protection to cope with foreign export cartels that operate in all developed countries. This limited immunity applies only to marketing abroad and requires strict adherence by American Webb–Pomerene companies to antitrust laws both within domestic US markets and with respect to the export trade of non-member US competitors. (Valenti, 1980: 26)

The US Congress passed the Sherman Antitrust Act in 1890 as a response to the fact that monopoly was endemic to capitalism, and because preserving competition was seen as a public good. The Sherman Act made it illegal for corporations to "monopolize, or attempt to monopolize, or combine or conspire with any other person or persons, to monopolize any part of the trade or commerce among the several states, or with foreign nations."

The Clayton Act, passed in 1914, exempted non-profit organizations and also labor unions because Congress found that "The Labor of a human being is not a commodity or article of commerce." Congress also clarified through the Clayton Act that certain specific discriminatory and anti-competitive actions by capitalists, such as price-fixing, block-booking, and tied sales, would be illegal because they would have the effect of reducing competition in the marketplace.

When it came to the foreign markets, however, it was a different story: Congress appeared to turn its attention away from preserving competition for the good of society to privileging US-based corporations. The Webb–Pomerene Export Trade Act exempted US companies from certain provisions of the Sherman and Clayton Acts that address the critical issue of defining the monopolization of trade as a felony as long as such monopolization was limited to their trade practices abroad and did not impinge on competition in domestic trade. For example, collusion and price-fixing were not illegal, as long as they were practiced abroad. Valenti (1980) emphatically states how vitally important the law has been to the cartel's exports:

> Without the embrace of Webb–Pomerene, the US film and television industry would have been seriously, perhaps fatally, crippled in its efforts to win the admiration and the patronage of foreign audiences for the creative programming which we license to almost 120 nations beyond the rim of our shores . . . The crucial point is that without Webb–Pomerene the American film industry would be an invalid, and we would not be able, as we are now, to return to the United States each year some $800 million in a surplus balance of trade. In fact, we provide some 47 percent of all the export trade earnings reported by the 36 Webb–Pomerene associations now in existence.

Valenti goes on to assert that there would be more cartels from other industries "except that, in my judgment, the Damoclean threat of anti-trust action by the Justice Department and Federal Trade Commission frightens potential users of this magnificent export trade asset." It is a baffling statement because at no time in the history of the MPAA has the Justice Department or the Federal Trade Commission challenged the cartel for violations of the antitrust laws. There have been numerous court cases, however, against the majors, and the Justice Department has intervened in relation to market abuses in the domestic film industry, most notably in relation to the majors' vertical control of theaters under the Paramount consent decree in 1948. The Webb–Pomerene law is still in force in an amended version under the title of the Export Trading Company Act 1982. The meetings and documents of both the MPAA and MPA are not accessible to the public, except for what they themselves decide to reveal. In fact, only representatives of the member companies are invited to attend their meetings.

It is believed that MPA meetings are held outside the US, at Cannes in France, to avoid the possibility of independent film companies accusing the cartel of conspiring to fix prices and thereby restrain domestic trade (Frank, 1987). To give some credence to that possibility, *Variety* releases global prices for US feature films and television serials once a year around the time when the MIPCOM festival and market take place in Cannes ("Global TV Price Guide," 2006: B12). The MPAA's website (<www.mpaa.org>) tells us little about how the organization works. In 1994, the organization decided to change its name to the MPA in order, according to the website, to "more accurately reflect the global nature of audiovisual entertainment in today's international marketplace" (MPAA, 2004a). However, this statement doesn't appear to reflect reality because the organization's primary goal has never been to bring global entertainment made by different companies (who could be potential competitors) in various countries to the international marketplace but to export products that are owned or licensed by the MPAA's member companies worldwide (see Guback, 1969; Pendakur, 1985, 1990). At the very core of their rhetoric lies US nationalism. Jack Valenti, President and CEO, spoke in his usual bombastic style to identify who it is that the MPAA/MPA serves in his testimony to the Senate Foreign Relations Committee in 2004: "The spread of theft of America's creative works flows like a swiftly running river in every nook and cranny of this planet . . . It is thievery that our country cannot afford to tolerate" (Valenti, 2004: 1).

Valenti is not suggesting that his organization or the US government provide copyright protection to all films in the world or that all films (such as films produced and distributed by independent filmmakers in the US) should carry the banner "American" – only those films produced, licensed, or distributed by the members of MPAA/MPA. More will be said on intellectual property issues later, but renaming the Motion Picture Export Association of America simply the Motion Picture Association clearly is an attempt to mask its country of origin.

The MPAA/MPA is headquartered in Washington, DC, a couple of blocks from the White House, and it maintains another office in Los Angeles. This two-headed organization operates from these two cities, along with offices in Brussels, New Delhi,

Rio de Janeiro, Singapore, Mexico City, Toronto, and Jakarta. It has had the support of the US government in various ways. The Department of Commerce, the US Trade Representative, the US embassy diplomatic staff, and the Department of State stand ready to help. This pattern of support to a US cartel, conjoining commercial policy with foreign policy, was first established under Secretary Herbert Hoover and became a significant part of US government strategy after World War II. According to one scholar:

> Hoover took the lead as Secretary of Commerce in intensifying the US trade competition with the Europeans. By sending out a corps of commercial attachés from the Department of Commerce, he complemented the diplomatic and consular service of the Department of State. The job of Hoover's attachés was to return information about the opportunities for American businesses, look for foreign firms which might like to trade with the US, and spot changing markets where the Americans could introduce new products. (Ulf-Moeller, 1998: 52)

The President of the MPAA and its other officials travel the world preaching the mantra of "free" enterprise as opposed to regulated markets, while at the same time their member companies can indulge in regulating markets in their own favor. For example, at least since the 1970s, Paramount and Universal have combined their distribution operations worldwide to form the Cinema International Corporation (renamed United International Pictures in 1981). Warner Bros. used to market all of Disney in India. This is done in order to contain operating costs in certain markets and arrogate market dominance. Clearly they are anti-competitive because the biggest suppliers of film can control the screen time and put theater owners at a disadvantage. One could argue that such limits imposed on the market by combinations in, let us say, Japan would prevent independently owned US corporations and those based in other countries from competing freely in that market. There are, however, no legal challenges to the MPAA's activities by US-based independent producers or distributors. The Webb–Pomerene Export Trade Act does not prevent such combinations of power, but they may be illegal under specific laws of certain countries.

The MPAA had an exclusive deal with the Indian government limiting the import of English-language pictures to only those films marketed by the member companies of the cartel (Pendakur, 1985). Under this agreement, MPAA companies imported approximately 100 feature films annually into the Indian market and the total profits were in the range of $5 million. This meant that independently made films from the US or other parts of the world could not find entry into the Indian market unless the US majors distributed them. Because the French and Soviet governments complained about this unfair situation, the government of India signed agreements with Sovexport Film and Francefilm. While the market size and the profits were negligible at the time, the MPAA's exclusive deal in the Indian market was advantageous because having access to a potentially large market for English-language imports was beneficial in the long term.

In Canada, MPAA companies pursued a different strategy consisting of direct distribution, direct ownership of theaters, and aggressive diplomacy in Ottawa and in Washington to keep the Canadians from passing any legislation that would limit the power and profits of its member companies (see Pendakur, 1990). Ever since World War II, Canada has had the dubious distinction of being one of the top five markets in the world for US film imports. Thanks to the diplomatic efforts of the MPAA, the US Congress, and occasionally the US President, not only is the lion's share of revenues and profits from the theatrical market in Canada controlled by MPAA companies, but, barring some exceptions, Canadian-made films by companies unaffiliated with MPAA members cannot get distribution in their national market.

Numerous attempts have been made by Canada to work out an agreement with the MPAA, but none has produced any results that would solve the structural problems. There was one heroic attempt in February 1987 to pass the federal distribution bill, which would have attempted to restructure the market, into law. The bill was never passed by Parliament, however, because Jack Valenti mounted a powerful offensive against it by getting the US President Ronald Reagan to lobby Prime Minister Mulroney. The US House of Representatives and the Senate sent a letter to Mulroney registering the "strongest objections" to the bill. The Senate at the time was considering the Free Trade Agreement between the US and Canada and decided to pass a resolution that caused shock waves in Ottawa:

> Resolved by the Senate of the United States of America –
>
>   (1) that proposals by the Government of Canada to impose discriminatory limitations on the ability of foreign companies to distribute motion pictures in Canada reflect a highly protectionist trade policy aimed primarily at US motion picture distributors, and
>
>   (2) such measures are totally at odds with concepts of free trade between nations and could result in an absolute bar to the successful completion of negotiations and Senate approval of a Free Trade Agreement between the US and Canada. (quoted in Pendakur, 1990: 231)

The potential loss of the trade deal with the US on which the Mulroney government had staked its future was too big a scare. The distribution bill died and has not been reconsidered by successive governments since then.

The Hollywood Lobby since the 1990s

Hollywood stars, talent agents, producers, directors, corporate bosses, and even labor leaders have cultivated individual politicians and political parties for a long time, and even presidents have courted the leaders of the industry for one favor or another, including fundraising for their political campaigns. This is all part of the political process at work in the US and there is nothing unusual about it. The corporate media closely scrutinized and criticized President Clinton's close association with some of the Hollywood "liberals" because it fed the frenzy to demonize the "decadent liberals" in an America that was being transformed into a fundamentalist Christian state. In contrast, President Regan was not chastised by the corporate media for his ties with the conservative elements in the Hollywood industry. The actor Reagan, who had been president of the Screen Actors Guild, had also been an FBI informant against his own friends who were sympathetic to communism. MCA's Lew Wasserman, known as the power broker in the industry, had made Reagan a well-paid, General Electric lobbyist to pacify labor in the 1950s, for which his talent company won specific concessions from the existing SAG rules that prevented talent agencies from becoming producers of films that featured their own clients (Moldea, 1986). President Reagan went on to dismantle the public service responsibilities of US broadcasters in his eight years at the White House, thereby helping his friends in the radio and television broadcasting industries amass bloated profits.

Such patterns of relationships can be observed in spite of the institutional process of the MPAA, the National Association of Broadcasters (NAB), or the Recording Industry Association of America lobbying the government for one reason or another. A brief look at what was at stake in the 1990s for the Hollywood majors and how much money was spent in that lobbying process will make this historic process clear.

Life for the President of MPAA and his branch officers around the world became a little easier because the structure of the world economy and certain critical national policies in most countries began to change. This process of liberalization and privatization of national economies began in earnest with the arrival of Ronald Reagan and Margaret Thatcher on both sides of the Atlantic, but picked up momentum after the collapse of the Soviet Union. While "free" trade acts between the US, Canada, and Mexico set the pattern of things to come around the world, multilateral agencies pushing for the unimpeded global flow of capital got intensely busy. The IMF and the World Bank formed the broad institutional umbrella that reshaped these relationships in the "new" world economic order favoring private capital in this period that continues unabated to this day. Liberalization and privatization policies were not simply imposed on national governments; they were actually embraced by comprador capitalists and their governments. The push that the MPAA had made since World War II was to keep the markets open for Hollywood cinema, lower tariffs, eliminate censorship, and oppose any attempt by national governments to create national cinemas as a competitive force vis-à-vis Hollywood. That seemed to change with this new mood in most parts of the world to liberalize and privatize local economies. The MPAA's push now was to ensure all nations had a policy against piracy and some way to implement and enforce it.

The MPAA's attempt to eliminate censorship in India and China, for example, has not worked. Rupert Murdoch of News Corp made a deal with the Hindu fundamentalist-led regime in New Delhi to self-censor his music television network, V, in order to gain market access for his STAR TV network which he acquired from Li-Ka Shing in Hong Kong. The MPAA also succeeded in having all import restrictions in India lifted. Repatriation of profits in hard currency, which had been a contentious issue, is not an obstacle any more for the majors. A more compliant regime in New Delhi was willing to collaborate with international monopoly capital and gave in to the long-standing pressure from the MPAA. China, however, still has more stringent rules regarding importation and diplomatic efforts continue on that front.

On the domestic front, much was at stake for the Hollywood majors in the 1990s with the impending reform of the Communications Act of 1934. President Clinton signed the Communications Act 1996, which allowed significant changes to the structure of the communication industries and helped the media giants to expand their market control even more by relaxing limits to ownership of broadcast outlets. The oligopolies had cleverly made the argument that bigness was needed in order for them to compete with British, Italian, and other corporations. This led to another wave of mergers and acquisitions, and the media giants such as AOL-Time Warner became possible. Even information technology giants such as Microsoft began setting up joint ventures such as MSNBC (Kunz, 2006: 15–54). Recently, Google Corporation has entered the content venue by acquiring YouTube, and News Corp extended its reach into the World Wide Web by buying MySpace. Such combinations have not been challenged under the antitrust laws but they create anti-competitive pressures on the market.

The Financing and Syndication Rules were dropped. These rules existed to demarcate clear lines between the television networks, which were principally distributors of content, and the production companies, which churned out the television serials, promos, television movies, dramas, etc. With the changes in the 1996 law, the dominant television networks (NBC, ABC, CBS, and Fox) could demand ownership of the shows that they aired on their stations. As a result, hundreds of unaffiliated production companies and ancillary service providers went out of business (Glick, 2003). The economic model that had existed for nearly 50 years in television production collapsed, which clearly hurt a number of independent corporations that had much to do with television production. One scholar has concluded, "The nature of conglomeration has changed to a dramatic degree, however, as the studios have been engulfed within conglomerates with vast holdings in the motion picture, broadcast television, and cable television industries" (Kunz, 2006: 51). What has been sacrificed in this process is competition between the majors and unaffiliated independent corporations that are often the fertile ground for innovation and creativity. Competition in the film and television industries clearly became scarce.

The National Association of Broadcasters, which represented all the broadcasters in the country and lobbied on their behalf, was weakened. Rupert Murdoch of NewsCorp and Sumner Redstone of CBS/Viacom declared that they would not pay NAB dues and withdrew their companies from that organization. In other words, they did not need them in the new economic environment fostered by the 1996 Communications Act. The Hollywood majors got into joint ventures with each other and the state looked the other way as they re-entered the theatrical exhibition industry by buying chains. These were reversals of historic policy in the US since the 1948 Paramount consent decree.

Lobbying picked up from all quarters, as figures 11.2 and 11.3 indicate. It is customary in lobbying to spread the money to leading politicians in both political parties in the US. The goal is to be able to get the particular company's or industry's perspectives well understood by legislators who have the power to decide which rules to keep and which rules to eliminate in governing an industry; on some occasions, drafted legislation would formally be sponsored by a member of Congress. To accomplish such a critical task, and benefit industry, friendships are crucial. Consider the welcoming comments made by a senior Senator, Joseph Biden (Democrat, Connecticut), at a hearing of the Senate Foreign Relations Committee, where Jack Valenti provided testimony regarding the committee's evaluation of international intellectual property piracy:

> Hey, Jack. It's great to see you. You guys are important, but not as important as Jack. Jack, it's hard to believe they're talking about you leaving. You know, I mean you're taking off. You're going to be – I'm here to find out where you're going to live. That's the real – when we get to you, I'm going to put you under oath and find out where you're going to be living, 'cause I want to know where to hang out. (US Senate, 2004)

The MPAA companies, as shown in the figures, contribute donations to politicians as individual corporations and also as a cartel (figure 11.2). The NAB, however, represents the interests of over-the-air broadcasters, including those companies unaffiliated with the vertically integrated networks which depend on their supply of programs from syndication. If the four major television networks (Fox/NewsCorp, CBS/Paramount/Viacom, NBC/Universal/GE, Disney/ABC) control

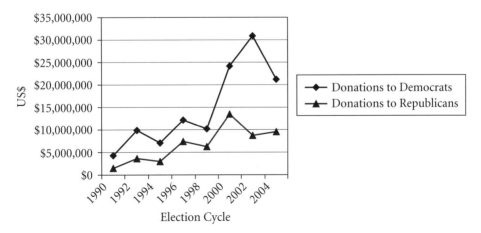

FIGURE 11.2   Donations of TV/music/movie industries to Democratic and Republication politicians
Source: adapted from opensecrets.org, 2007b.

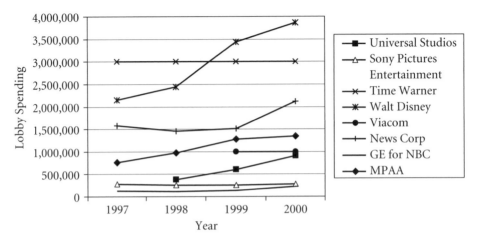

FIGURE 11.3   Lobby spending by majors and MPAA, 1997–2000
Source: compiled from opensecrets.org, 2007a.

the product supply, competition is limited to those four and in such a situation prices go up. Clearly, in this dynamic the majors gain and the hundreds of smaller networks and single-station owners lose.

An astounding amount of money is being spent annually to lobby the politicians in Washington. More money in their hands means more money in the hands of the major TV networks. Much is at stake, not only in the realm of copyright protection and compliance by the community of nations worldwide, but also in regard to issues such as cross-media ownership, which are under discussion in the domestic regulatory agencies. Having a chummy relationship with the leaders of the Senate and the House clearly has been beneficial to the MPAA member companies.

Conclusions

The MPAA and its sister organization the MPEA (now MPA) have successfully contained inter-capitalist rivalry in the motion picture and television industries in the US at a time when those industries have experienced remarkable changes in their structure, growth, and expansion abroad. The limited competition that exists among the majors is well contained within the oligopolistic structure that has lasted nearly 100 years. It is amazing to witness not only its continuation but its further entrenchment into the way the film and television industries function at a time when the internet could open the market by lowering the barriers and allowing new entrants.

In the new structure, film and television industries are far more integrated than after the Paramount consent decree in 1948. US theatrical revenues have reached a plateau of $10.5 billion, but foreign market revenues have doubled since the 1980s and they are larger than domestic market revenues. The DVD, television, and other ancillary markets have also grown abroad given privatization and liberalization of national economies. The fastest-growing markets are in Asia, particularly India and China, with their populations of over a billion people in each nation. Even though the governments of those countries are friendly to direct foreign investment, joint ventures, etc., due to the changed political-economic environment in the post-Soviet period and the fact that they have signed deals with the World Trade Organization, the MPAA's ambitions to widen its market penetration into those countries will illuminate the industry–state relationships in the globalized context in the next few years.

The US government, its laws, and its institutions have clearly facilitated the creation and functioning of cartels abroad. Herbert Hoover's corporatist state through its various apparatuses (Departments of State, Justice, Commerce, the Trade Representative, etc.) will continue to provide diplomatic and political support to the Hollywood cartel because of the historic benefits accruing to those industries and the positive contribution they make to the balance of payments. The aggressive strategies for market expansion that individual capitalists pursue – for instance Murdoch and Redstone in China – may occasionally run up against the collective interest of the majors as a group. The MPAA steps into such situations to sort out their differences. Dan Glickman's work in the future is not going to be any less challenging than that of his predecessors because there are many skeptics and activists poised against globalization despite the frequent compliance of nation-states in the process. The Chinese government, for instance, still insists on an annual quota of 20 to 25 imported films which are supposed to be from diverse sources (meaning Europe as well as America). The rumblings in Venezuela, Mexico, Brazil, and India against globalization and Hollywood dominance may not go away because the nation-state has to respond to those pesky communists and other opponents to capital's voracious appetite to turn everything into a commodity and humans into markets.

NOTE

I would like to thank Young Cao, a doctoral student in the College of Mass Communication and Media Arts, Southern Illinois University, for his research assistance in preparing this chapter.

REFERENCES

Frank, Richard H. (President, Walt Disney Studios) (1987) telephone interview, July 17, Los Angeles.
Glick, S. (Davis–Glick Productions) (2003), interview, December 11, Los Angeles.
Gomery, D. (2004) "Motion Picture Association of America," online at <http://www.museum.tv/archives/etv/M/htmlM/motionpictur/motionpictur.htm> (accessed February 24, 2004).

Guback, T. (1969) *The International Film Industry: Western Europe and America Since 1945.* Bloomington: Indiana University Press.

Guilder, Elizabeth (2007) "Global TV Price Guide," *Variety*, April 16, online at <http://www.variety.com/article/VR1117962951.html?categoryid=1714&cs=1> (accessed July 21, 2007).

Kunz, W. M. (2006) *Culture Conglomerates: Consolidation in the Motion Picture and Television Industries.* Lanham, MD: Rowman & Littlefield.

Miller, T., N. Govil, J. McMurria, and R. Maxwell (2005) *Global Hollywood 2.* London: British Film Institute.

Moldea, D. E. (1986) *Dark Victory: Ronald Reagan, MCA, and the Mob.* New York: Viking.

MPAA (2004a) "About the MPAA," online at <http://www.mpaa.org/about/content.htm> (accessed February 24, 2004).

MPAA (2004b) "Jack Valenti Announces Resignation after 38 Years as Head of MPAA/MPA," *Media Release*, July 1, 2004, p. 1.

opensecrets.org (2007a) "Lobbying Databases," online at <http://www.opensecrets.org/lobbyists/index.asp> (accessed July 21, 2007).

opensecrets.org (2007b) "TV/Movies/Music: Long-Term Contribution Trends," online at <http://www.opensecrets.org/industries/indus.asp?Ind=B02> (accessed July 21, 2007).

Pendakur, M. (1985) "Dynamics of Cultural Policy Making: The U.S. Film Industry in India," *Journal of Communication*, 35(4), pp. 52–72.

Pendakur, M. (1990) *Canadian Dreams and American Control: The Political Economy of the Canadian Film Industry.* Detroit: Wayne State University Press.

Ulf-Moller, J. (1998) "The 'Film Wars' Between France and the United States: Film-Trade Diplomacy, and the Emergence of the Film Quota System in France, 1920–1939." Unpublished Ph.D. dissertation, Brandeis University.

US Senate (2004) Hearing of the Senate Foreign Relations Committee, June 9. Chaired by Senator Richard Lugar, Federal News Service, Inc.

Valenti, J. (1980) "Webb–Pomerene: The Great U.S. Ally in the Battle for World Trade," *Vital Speeches of the Day*, 47(1), p. 26.

Valenti, J. (2004) Testimony, Senate Foreign Relations Committee.

Wasko, J. (2003) *How Hollywood Works.* London: Sage.

CHAPTER 12

HOLLYWOOD AND INTELLECTUAL PROPERTY

RONALD V. BETTIG

This chapter explores the essential role of intellectual property, copyrights, trademarks, and patents in shaping the structure and performance of the motion picture industry. It begins with a brief review of the history of intellectual property rights, then looks at their role in the development of the industry, and concludes with an analysis of how these rights remain essential to Hollywood's global presence and economic power. It follows the historical method of political economy, using the past to understand the present.

A Brief History of Copyrights, Trademarks, and Patents

The origins of patent and copyright are bound up with the rise of capitalism, liberalism, and industrialization (Bettig, 1996; Vaidhyanathan, 2001). The first patents were issued by city-state governments in Italy in the fifteenth century. Their purpose was to promote the growth of infant industries by giving manufacturers exclusive rights to their trade in the form of monopolies. The patents sought to protect publishers from piracy of books by unlicensed competitors taking advantage of the low costs of reproducing published works. From this moment on, copyrights and patents have been about the control of intellectual and artistic creativity by the owners of the means of production and communications. For example, in Britain, a handful of licensed book publishers controlled the industry from the late sixteenth century through the seventeenth century. In exchange for exclusive rights to publish certain titles or categories of books they agreed not to publish seditious or heretical works. The result, as with any oligopolistic industry, was works that were low in number, high in price, and poor in quality.

In the United States, founders added a clause to the Constitution giving Congress the power to pass laws "to promote the progress of science and useful arts by securing for limited times to authors and inventors the exclusive right to their respective writings and discoveries" (Constitution, Art. I, para. 8). The first copyright law passed in 1790 gave authors or owners of maps, charts, and books the sole rights to their works for a period of 14 years. Congress extended copyright laws in the nineteenth century to cover works such as engravings, etchings, prints, musical compositions, and photographs. During the heyday of vaudeville (roughly, 1880–1920), producers used trademarks, copyrights, and negative publicity as mechanisms to protect their live acts (Segrave, 2003). Motion pictures did not receive copyright protection until 1912. Until then, film producers incorporated trademarks into motion picture sets to identify the owner of the motion picture. Although piracy of motion pictures remained rampant until the beginning of World War I , copyrights, trademarks, and patents ultimately became a means for the appropriation of works in the motion picture industry by the owners of the means of production. Since then they have been used to create industrial power, as illustrated by the history of the motion picture industry.

One of the earliest efforts to establish industrial power in the motion picture business involved the control of patents. In 1896, Thomas Edison introduced a patented motion picture viewer called the Kinetoscope, and by 1897 he was using his patent rights to file infringement suits "against nearly everyone of consequence that had entered the business" (Balio, 1985: 10). This set off more than a decade of "patent wars" that ended when the cost and burdens of defending against litigation made it cheaper to join than to fight Edison. The Motion Picture Patents Company (MPPC), formed in 1909, was the result of a pooling arrangement converging 16 patents that covered everything from raw film stock supplied by the Eastman Kodak Company through film production, distribution, and exhibition. The company generated revenues from licenses and royalties, and helped bring stability to the industry with standard practices. Like all monopolies, it stifled creativity by making the product scarce and refusing to innovate. At the same time, it invited competition and new sites of creativity since there were monopoly profits to be earned (Anderson, 1985). This competition, along with private and federal antitrust action, led to the demise of the MPPC trust by the mid-1910s (Litman, 1998: 10).

Usually the making of a theatrical motion picture is a collective endeavor involving work for hire. In fact, the first Edison films starred Edison's own employees. Under US law, copyright to a motion picture belongs to the production company. However, when Edison was making his early films Congress had not yet conferred copyright status on the medium. As with patents, Edison used available law by submitting both negative and positive prints of his films to the US Copyright Office, registering them as photographs, which had been copyrightable since 1865. With a major revision of US copyright law in 1909, the groundwork for corporate ownership of motion pictures was established, and in 1912 Congress added "motion picture photoplays" to the list of copyrightable works. Motion picture copyright owners sought strict protection of "their" works and fought against authors of original works who sought compensation for adaptations. Nonetheless, the practice of paying authors became standard by the middle of the twentieth century, and by the end the price of literary rights had escalated into the realm of millions of dollars. The use of star authors was one way for owners to reach pre-constituted audiences and minimize risks. And the high costs of the rights raised barriers to entry that favored the core oligopolistic firms.

The patent wars over sound motion pictures in the late 1920s were also significant as they helped determine the major players in the industry and recruited bankers to the scene (Gomery, 1985). First, the introduction of sound gave rise to two new major players that would round out the Big Five: RCA's Radio-Keith-Orpheum (RKO), created in 1928 to allow RCA to promote its sound technology, and Warner Bros., which had joined with Western Electric. The others were Loews/MGM, 20th Century Fox, and Paramount. Second, the conversion to sound production and exhibition was very costly and, along with the Depression, helped wipe out independent producers and exhibitors. The majors, with their guaranteed audiences for copyrighted works and their patented sound systems, were helped with the conversion to sound by banks, but at the cost of making movies from the 1930s to the 1950s that were more homogenous, conformist, and conservative, since the investment capitalists insisted on being rewarded for their risks. This brief history of copyrights, trademarks, and patents in motion pictures illustrates the central role of intellectual property in forming the structure of the filmed entertainment industry.

First Challenges to Filmed Entertainment Copyrights: Cable TV and Videocassette Recorders

Copyright became the main mechanism through which the filmed entertainment industry controlled the use of its intellectual property. The turnstile served as the primary means of exclusion, and exhibitors were subject to license agreements based on runs, zones, and clearances. However, with the arrival of television in the 1950s, the industry faced a new competing medium that threatened its centrality amongst the culture industries. Hollywood's initial response was to withhold its product through the control of copyright and at the same time to make filmgoing a more unique experience. In the end, cinema and television became partners, highlighted by the inauguration of *Saturday Night at the Movies* on NBC in 1961 (Belton, 2005: 316). By the 1990s, worldwide television rights generated 20 percent of the industry's revenues and with the relaxation of restrictions on network ownership of prime-time programming a wave of mergers gave Hollywood control of 70 percent of the market (Bettig, 1999). The film industry was able to build its partnership with broadcast television based on existing copyright practices, established by the music recording and broadcast radio industries in the 1920s. The rise of cable television in the 1960s challenged these accepted practices, and for over a decade, from 1965 to 1976, Hollywood, television broadcasters, and cable operators fought over who should profit from this new concept for delivering television signals called "distant signal importation" (DSI) (Bettig, 1996: 117–50).

Cable television operators began setting up hilltop antennas in the early 1960s to receive television broadcasts from distant areas that they then delivered to the valley communities below. By the mid-1960s local broadcasters began to feel threatened by DSI, as it undermined the exclusive access they had to audiences in their area and cut into advertising revenues as viewers migrated toward channels imported from distant cities. This in turn reduced the fees that film and television copyright owners could charge for their programs. At the same time, cable operators were essentially getting their programming for free. Broadcasters appealed to the Federal Communications Commission (FCC) and the courts in *US v. Southwestern* (1968), while the filmed entertainment industry turned to Congress and the courts in *United Artists v. Fortnightly* (1967). In 1966, the FCC sought to protect broadcasters by prohibiting DSI in the top one hundred television markets, roughly 90 percent of US households. The Supreme Court added to the confusion by first upholding the FCC's right to regulate DSI in 1968 but then ruling in the same year that cable delivery of broadcasts was not a "performance" and therefore not covered by copyright (*Fortnightly v. United Artists*, 1968).

Congress addressed the issue as part of a long discussed revision of the seriously outdated 1909 Copyright Act. While Hollywood sought to extend its copyrights to cable television, broadcasters sought a copyright that covered their entire programming schedule. Congress eventually agreed that cable operators were making money from the use of copyrighted programming carried in broadcast signals and that they should pay intellectual property owners. A compulsory license was built into the Copyright Act of 1976 to deal with the extraordinarily high transaction costs involved in licensing each broadcast program on each cable system, at a time when the cable industry was still quite fragmented. Since then, cable operators have paid a royalty fee that is in turn distributed to copyright owners. Thus, while the cable industry briefly challenged the filmed entertainment industry, the logic of copyright was on the side of copyright owners and the compulsory license became the means for protecting the integrity of their intellectual property. Following this logic, in 1988 Congress extended the compulsory license to include satellite retransmission of superstation and network signals.

In the fall of 1975 Sony Corporation introduced the Betamax VCR, posing a new threat to filmed entertainment copyrights. The Betamax was marketed as a device for taping television shows for later viewing. In November 1976 Universal Pictures and the Walt Disney Company filed suit against Sony for engaging in contributory copyright infringement on the grounds that Sony knew the Betamax would be used for infringing purposes. Home taping of television programming also threatened the value of advertising revenues, as viewers could zip (fast-forward) or zap (delete) commercials, reducing audience ratings. The VCR also enabled home tapers to create their own libraries of television programming to be watched in lieu of broadcast TV. The plaintiffs sought damages and an injunction against the manufacture and marketing of the Betamax within the US. Three years later, a US district court found in favor of Sony, but the decision was reversed by the US Court of Appeals in 1981. While Sony appealed to the Supreme Court, both the consumer electronics and filmed entertainment industries turned to Congress for legislative relief. Political cartoons with images of "video police" breaking into homes,

Gestapo-like, confiscating tapes and Betamaxes, put the issue in the spotlight (Bettig, 1996: 162).

The Motion Picture Association of America (MPAA) sponsored bills seeking to defend the integrity of its members' copyrights by declaring home taping an infringement but exempting the practice in return for a compulsory license to be imposed on importers and manufacturers of recording devices and videocassettes. The royalty fee on VCRs and tapes, in turn, would be distributed to the copyright owners of television programs and movies, not the actual broadcasters. The consumer electronics industry sponsored legislation that sought to exempt all private, noncommercial videotaping from copyright liability. While Congress held hearings, the Supreme Court brought closure to the matter in 1984 by ruling that Sony was not responsible for contributory infringement and that home taping of television broadcasts for the purposes of time-shifting was a fair use. The court also recognized a First Amendment dimension in copyright law, finding that home taping increased public access to television programming. The economic impact of the ruling on the filmed entertainment industry was minimal, but the Sony case would return when the movie and music industries began litigating illegal downloading. Disney, meanwhile, had quietly dropped out of the case after realizing there was more revenue to be made from prerecorded videocassettes (at first mostly to video rental outlets) than there was to be lost from home taping. Videocassette pirates realized the potential as well.

The global proliferation of VCRs in the 1980s spawned massive global piracy. The film industry estimated that it was losing $1 billion per year in revenues and enlisted the US government to help combat video pirates in foreign markets, beginning with western Europe and then moving to the Middle East and Southeast Asia. In Europe, Hollywood worked with local industries and governments to pass laws and strengthen enforcement. By the early 1990s, videocassette piracy had significantly declined in primary markets and the Hollywood majors were well on their way to dominating European home video rental and sales. In the Middle East, the problem of video piracy was rooted in the lack of copyright agreements between the US and Middle Eastern nations. Beginning in the mid-1980s, the US government moved to correct this problem by pressuring Middle Eastern governments to pass copyright laws and protect US intellectual property. By the early 1990s, several countries in the Middle East had enacted the first intellectual property laws in their history. The situation in Southeast Asia was much the same, but since there were no oil fields, the US government used more stick than carrot: the threat of trade sanctions to force these governments to enact and enforce intellectual property laws. Prodded by the MPAA, Congress passed legislation that made privileged access to the US market for countries such as Taiwan, Singapore, and South Korea contingent upon the trading partner's protection of US intellectual property rights. For China, the US held out the carrot of membership in the World Trade Organization (WTO) in exchange for enacting its first copyright law in 1991. Despite these efforts, videocassette piracy remained rampant due to lack of enforcement and punishment. The war between Hollywood and pirates escalated as video went digital.

Copyright in the Digital Era

Hollywood's concerns over videocassette piracy diminished as the VCR gave way to DVD players and recorders. The digitalization of the industry's property – the ability to make perfect copies to share or sell – became the new front in the war on piracy. The MPAA termed the illegal manufacture, distribution, and sale of motion pictures in digital disk formats "optical disc piracy" engaged in by "hard-goods" traffickers (MPAA, 2005). The disks were sold online via the web or auction sites, by street vendors, and in flea markets around the world. Hollywood reported global revenues of $84 billion in 2004; of that about $56 billion, roughly two-thirds of annual earnings, came from DVDs (O'Brien, 2005: 1, 7). The industry estimated that annual losses in 2003 and 2004 to optical disk piracy ranged from $3 billion to $4.5 billion (IFPI, 2004; MPAA, 2005). Such estimates are generally self-serving and based on the assumption that each pirated disk supplants the sale of a legitimate one. Nevertheless, in Russia, China, Southeast and central Asia, and parts of South America, 75 percent or more of the DVDs sold in 2004 were illegal copies (O'Brien, 2005: 7). Most were produced in industrial DVD factories, but easy access to DVD recorders made it possible to forge copies in smaller operations more difficult to detect.

Looming large by 2005 was the specter of rampant online movie file-sharing through peer-to-peer (P2P) networks. Hollywood was determined not to replay the music industry's failure to anticipate the rise of P2P culture. Technological limits also gave the film industry a head start on limiting movie file-sharing. In 2005, illegal movie downloads through P2P could take hours even through broadband connections. Still, unauthorized copies of movies flowed over the internet, sometimes days after they were released. They could be copied anywhere in the world and reproduced as pirated disks or recirculated on the internet. The original copies came from sources within the industry (employees at labs or theaters, or members of the Academy of Motion Picture Arts and Sciences and media critics who are sent personal copies or "screeners," for review), and from "cammers" using digital video cameras to record movies at the theater. Industrial pirate operations also had specialists who were able to decode encryptions of previously released DVDs.

Hollywood's response to global disk and internet piracy involved four basic strategies: (1) securing legislation and trade agreements to strengthen copyright protection; (2) managing digital rights through encryption and watermarks; (3) enforcing copyright through litigation, intimidation and police action; and (4) entering and expanding markets for legitimate product (Bettig, 2003). US copyright owners initiated their enclosure of cyberspace through legislation in 1997 when Congress passed the No Electronic Theft Act (NETA) that criminalized the distribution of copyrighted works over the internet. The Digital Millennium Copyright Act of 1998 (DMCA) further protected copyright owners by making internet service providers (ISPs) responsible for policing the distribution of copyrighted materials. To get the ISPs to go along, Congress exempted them from copyright liability when they followed "notice and take down" procedures, basically the purging of unauthorized works. The DMCA also criminalized encryption decoding and watermark washing despite protests by librarians, universities, and computer programmers, who argued that encryption technologies violate both fair use and First Amendment principles by inhibiting access to intellectual and artistic works. For example, film history teachers who routinely use pre-dubbed video sequences of movie excerpts to illustrate lectures now face the task of compiling new teaching tools – impossible or impractical if they include rare footage, and illegal if they disable encryptions. To stop cammers, the MPAA pushed through the Family Entertainment and Copyright Act in 2005, which made camcording in a theater a federal felony (literally, a serious crime such as murder that is punished more severely than a misdemeanor) and established new penalties for pirating films before their commercial release.

As copyright owners sought to extend protection of their works to encompass digital video, some of their most valuable copyrights were set to expire, including those covering Disney characters such as Mickey Mouse and Donald Duck. In 1998, Congress offered a quick fix by passing the Sonny Bono Copyright Term Extension Act, often referred to as the "Mickey Mouse Extension Act" because of Disney's heavy lobbying efforts. The Act extended copyright for an additional 20 years for cultural works, protecting them for a total of 70 years after the death of an individual author or 95 years from publication in the case of works created by or for corporations. Underlying Congressional intellectual property legislation was the necessity of bringing US law into compliance with international law. Parts of the DMCA were specifically designed to bring the US into accord with new standards set by the World Intellectual Property Organization and the WTO. These are organizations, especially the latter, where multinational corporations hold sway. Once global standards are set, intellectual property owners can use them to force domestic legislation to advance and protect their interests.

The NETA and DMCA legislation provided copyright owners with the laws they needed to proceed with the development and deployment of encryption technologies. Encryption raises the industry's costs, as well as the likelihood of decryption by those so inclined. With legislative protection, however, copyright owners knew they had the support of the state. Encryption of videocassettes and DVDs became standard practice. Watermarking is a related strategy designed to prevent unauthorized copying of digital video. Watermarks prevent the transfer of copyrighted works from one source to other devices, and they help track the flow of copyrighted materials on the internet and aid the identification of infringers. As early as 2002 the film industry was deploying "bots" to scour internet websites, chat rooms, newsgroups, and P2P networks in search of unauthorized copies of movies (Ahrens, 2002). So as copyright owners cracked down on piracy, they also opened the door to insidious invasions of privacy. Watermarks on theatrical prints allowed the industry to trace the exact time, date, and venue where a camcorder copy was made. At the same time, the MPAA began working with the camcorder industry to develop jamming technologies to disable camcorders within theaters.

FIGURE 12.1   Former record producer and Republican politican Sonny Bono (left) (here pictured in February 1996 with the then President of the MPAA Jack Valenti (center) and House Speaker Newt Gingrich (right)) campaigned for revisions to legislation which led to the passing in 1998 of the controversial Copyright Term Extension Act. Photo by Associated Press

Hollywood learned from its war on videocassette piracy that copyright laws are useless unless they are enforced by the police and the courts. With the backing of the state and the implementation of digital rights management systems in place, the industry turned to the courts to defend its property through litigation. In 1999, the MPAA successfully sued the publisher of a hacker website, forcing him to take down links publicizing a DVD decryption program that enabled Linux users to play encrypted DVDs on their home computers. The first claim was that the program violated the DMCA, but the industry's main concern was that it could serve as a platform for massive sharing of movies online. In addition to attacking the source of encryption, MGM Studios with the backing of the MPAA and the Recording Industry Association of America (RIAA) filed suit against Grokster and Streamcast (makers of Morpheus), two P2P file-sharing services, for contributing to copyright infringement, testing the Supreme Court's decision in the *Sony* case. Following *Sony*, both the district and appeals courts decided that P2P networks had legitimate uses and the defendants were not liable for contributory infringement.

In the summer of 2005 the Supreme Court weighed in with a unanimous ruling in favor of MGM that Grokster and others could be held liable for copyright infringement since they functioned, and indeed willfully marketed themselves, as sites for illegal downloads. While the decision was unanimous, the court issued three separate majority opinions, not overturning *Sony*, but inviting Congress to outlaw technology aimed at circumventing copyrights. Such legislation was already pending in Congress in the form of "inducement acts." Any producer of technologies that facilitated the unauthorized copying of intellectual property could be held liable for contributory infringement. In the end, *MGM v. Grokster* therefore did not overturn *Sony*, but the opinions were confusing enough to intimidate future software and hardware developers of copying technologies. Grokster announced in 2006 that it would return as a legitimate file-sharing site. Meanwhile, illegal music downloads moved to new sites and private networks as movie file-sharing picked up speed.

In addition to attacking the source of internet piracy, the film industry, following the lead of the music industry, initiated lawsuits against P2P users. The lawsuits were backed up by an intimidation campaign. For example, in November 2004 the MPAA took out full-page advertisements in college newspapers in the form of a movie poster. *Star Wars*-style ISP addresses warned students that they were traceable. In 2003, the MPAA convinced the Academy of Motion Picture Arts and Sciences to stop sending DVDs of Oscar-eligible films to screeners. Independent distributors called foul, claiming that distribution of DVDs to screeners was one of the few ways in which Academy members were exposed to their films. The Academy backed down, distributing only encoded videocassettes. It extended the intimidation factor by sending the FBI after an Academy member who sent copies of screener tapes to a friend, who then shared them. Highly publicized lawsuits were supplemented by police action around the globe, usually with the help of the copyright industries who ran their own investigative units. The war on piracy sought to legitimize foreign markets. At the same time illegal copies of Hollywood films whetted the world's appetite for its products.

Legislation, encryption, and litigation are complemented with a strategy of market penetration. One explanation for the rise of a music downloading culture was that the recording industry failed to provide a legitimate alternative and music fans were tired of paying for overpriced CDs. While Hollywood bided its time on releasing films for legal downloading, Apple's iTunes proved that a pay-per-song service, with a carefully managed rights system, could work. In 2005, Apple's introduction of Video iPods led Hollywood to release television shows for downloading. The film industry had dabbled with digital downloads since the mid-1990s. In 2005 Movielink, a joint venture including Sony/MGM, Paramount, Fox, Warner Bros., and Universal, began providing movies for download that could be owned, although the task of transferring a film from the computer to the television screen remained onerous (Hansell, 2005). In July 2006 both Movielink and CinemaNow announced their intention to offer download-to-burn services. However, many of the most valuable movies remained in the copyright owners' vaults.

Both the internet and video-on-demand (VoD) disrupted the major distributors' usual schedule for releasing movies, from theaters to video to television. Hollywood had already anticipated the new order when Warner Bros. released *The Matrix*

Revolutions in 2003 for theatrical exhibition around the world at the exact same time. Theatergoers in China paid $10 and were required to pass through metal detectors to prevent camming. In January 2006 Steven Soderbergh, with the backing of Mark Cuban and Todd Wagner, released *Bubble* (2005, US), a $1.5 million film, simultaneously to theaters, high-definition cable, and DVD, in a signal that the windows on Hollywood's distribution system were closing. While theater owners protested, the consumer electronics industry sat poised to pounce on the opportunity to bring theatrical films to the in-home theater venue. Wagner predicted that the studios would come around, since they could tap non-theater audiences generating extra revenue (Smith, 2006). Meanwhile, independent film producers remained hopeful, like garage bands before them, that the internet and VoD would magically transform their lives, in seeming denial of the vital role the majors' deep pockets play in marketing and promoting unknown works.

This brief history of patents, trademarks, and copyrights in the motion picture industry illustrates the centrality of intellectual property to Hollywood's dominance of US and global cinema. From the very beginning, control of intellectual property has been used to establish and maintain concentration in the movie business. The technologies have changed over the years – from Kinetoscope peepshows to digital downloads – but the pattern of enclosure and concentration through control of intellectual property, with the ultimate goal of amassing profits rather than facilitating the production and distribution of diverse endeavors, remains the same. The system is inherent to capitalism and consistently works against freedom of artistic and intellectual creativity. Perhaps it is time to envision what a cinematic landscape freed from the logic of capitalism might look like.

REFERENCES

Ahrens, F. (2002) "'Ranger' vs. the Movie Pirates: Software Is Studios' Latest Weapon in a Growing Battle," *Washington Post*, June 19, p. H1.

Anderson, R. (1985) "The Motion Picture Patents Company: A Reevaluation," in T. Balio (ed.), *The American Film Industry*. Madison: University of Wisconsin, pp. 133–52.

Balio, T. (ed.) (1985) *The American Film Industry*. Madison: University of Wisconsin.

Belton, J. (2005) *American Cinema/American Culture*, 2nd edn. Boston: McGraw-Hill.

Bettig, R. (1996) *Copyrighting Culture*. Boulder, CO: Westview.

Bettig, R. (1999) "Who Owns Prime Time? Industrial and Institutional Conflict over Television Programming and Broadcast Rights," in M. Mander (ed.), *Framing Friction*. Urbana: University of Illinois, pp. 125–60.

Bettig, R. (2003) "Copyright and the Commodification of Culture," *Media Development*, 45(1), pp. 3–9.

Gomery, D. (1985) "U.S. Film Exhibition: The Formation of a Big Business," in T. Balio (ed.), *The American Film Industry*. Madison: University of Wisconsin, pp. 218–51.

Hansell, S. (2005) "Forget the Bootleg, Just Download the Movie Legally," *New York Times*, July 4, pp. C1, C4.

IFPI (2004) "MPAA Studios Take Actions Against Major P2P Operators to Stem Global Movie Piracy," online at <http://www.ifpi.org/site-content/press/20041214a.html> (accessed January 21, 2006).

Litman, B. (1998) *The Motion Picture Mega-Industry*. Boston: Allyn & Bacon.

MPAA (2005) "Optical Disk Piracy," online at <http://www.mpaa.org/piracy_OptDisk.asp> (accessed January 21, 2006).

O'Brien, T. (2005) "King Kong vs. the Pirates of the Multiplex," *New York Times*, August 28, pp. 1, 7.

Segrave, K. (2003) *Piracy in the Motion Picture Industry*. Jefferson, NC: McFarland.

Smith, S. (2006) "When the 'Bubble' Bursts," *Newsweek*, January 23, online at <http://www.msnbc.msn.com/id/10853264/site/newsweek/> (accessed January 23, 2006).

Vaidhayanathan, S. (2001) *Copyrights and Copywrongs*. New York: New York University.

PART III
INTERNATIONAL TERRITORIES

CHAPTER 13

HOLLYWOOD AND THE WORLD: EXPORT OR DIE

JOHN TRUMPBOUR

From Hicks to Hottentots: The Birth of Planet Hollywood

Since the early decades of the twentieth century, critics of Hollywood feared the film industry precisely because of its global reach. "The movies of today are a vast industry supplying the nations of the world with a standardized, machine-made entertainment," wrote the Russian-born film commentator Alexander Bakshy in a 1928 edition of *The Nation*. "The standards are those demanded by the world market which the industry serves." While convinced that "the American 'hick' is the arbiter of taste who dictates the fashions of Hollywood," Bakshy speculated that

> The time does not seem far off when this proud position will be held probably, by the humble Kaffir or Hottentot of the movie-civilized kraals of Africa, whose intellectual and moral reactions to the unhappy ending, for instance, will then be carefully studied, with the help of charts and diagrams, in the selling and producing offices of Hollywood. (Bakshy, 1928: 360)

Emitting Menckenesque tones of disdain for the American "hick" and the African Hottentot, Bakshy held out hope that "cultured people all over the world" would eventually clamor for "standards of quality, and not those demanded by the world 'boobery.'" In 1926 the *Berliner Zeitung am Mittag* had similarly blamed the country bumpkin and rural idiocy for Hollywood's global success, what the newspaper called a strategy of "flabbergasting the farmer":

> The Americans count on the innocence of the farmer, who is removed from civilization by many days' travel out on his prairie. All these masses of gold, silver, cut-glass chandeliers, thick carpets, pages in fancy costumes, all this carries a farmer into fairyland, while it turns our stomach. (United States Embassy Berlin, 1926)

Though individual foreign officers sometimes shared these dismissive attitudes concerning Hollywood's output, the US State Department backed the film industry partly on the grounds that it was helping to sell US goods while promoting something more precious, "the American way of life." Well before he became US Secretary of State for the Eisenhower Administration, John Foster Dulles auditioned for the role of a lifetime by once declaring: "If I were granted one point of foreign policy and no other, I would make it the free flow of information" (quoted in Knight, 1946: 476). Dulles's own brother Allen provided the US film industry legal representation concerning trade issues – that is, before he left the law firm Sullivan & Cromwell to assume leadership of the fledgling Central Intelligence Agency (CIA).

For the Dulles brothers and their postwar successors, "free flow of information" at times served as a high-minded principle and an inspiring light to shine upon governments seeking to limit the US film industry's domination over foreign cultural markets. Still, John Foster Dulles developed a wary eye when looking at the opulence depicted in many Hollywood productions. In an article from April 1950 for *Life* magazine entitled "How to Take the Offensive for Peace," he pondered whether Americans should be so fond of displaying "the marvels of mass production and . . . the number of automobiles, radios, and telephones owned by our people. That materialistic emphasis makes some feel that we are spiritually bankrupt. It makes others envious and more disposed to accept Communist glorification of 'mass effort' " (Dulles, 1950: 136).

Once in power, the Dulles brothers made many compromises with "free flow" absolutism, as the US Secretary of State would admit that even loyal US allies faced acute pressures to avert Hollywood's total obliteration of domestic film industries. Indeed a few allies noticed that, despite its commitment to "the free flow of information," the United States banned foreigners from owning broadcast outlets. Meanwhile, some US film distributors exhibited a reflexive refusal to bring overseas product to North American screens.

Often reluctantly, as they hammered out broad trade agreements, US policymakers learned to live with what later became known as "the cultural exception." This meant that cultural products could be exempted from the relentless pursuit of open markets. Nevertheless, Washington frequently served notice that this would not stand as a permanent feature of global trade policy. Even so, "the cultural exception" has had some tenacity over the decades. Pointing out that "the cultural exception" in the GATT (General Agreement on Trade and Tariffs) accords negotiated in 1993 still permits nations such as France to maintain trade barriers that prevent the unimpeded influx of Hollywood films, Fritz Pleitgen, director of the Westdeutschen Rundfunks (WDR) broadcasting service, received sustained applause at the third annual German–French co-production summit held in Cologne during November 2005 when he roared, "The 'cultural exception' clause is the only reason the economic ceasefire between the US and the EU hasn't broken out into a trade war" (quoted in Roxborough, 2005: 23). In October 2005, during the UNESCO General Conference, France and Canada co-sponsored the Convention on the Protection and Promotion of the Diversity of Cultural Expressions, which gave renewed support to the cultural exception in winning a crushing 148–2 victory, with the United States and Israel casting the twin dissenting votes.

How and why Hollywood came to dominate global cinema remains at the center of a variety of inquiries into the film industry. While most accounts begin with the sheer size and affluence of the US domestic audience as distinctive market advantages, there have been other prominent features that played critical roles in securing US supremacy in the global film trade, whether through state–industry cooperation (Guback, 1969), the building of new distribution networks and procedures (Thompson, 1985), or mastery over a process called the New International Division of Cultural Labor (NICL, sometimes pronounced "nickel") that mobilizes the spatial mobility of capital, a globalized workforce, and the longstanding US leadership in developing "the legal codification of film as intellectual property" (Miller et al., 2001: 24; Miller et al., 2005). Reflecting on the work of historian Victoria De Grazia on the US culture industry, political scientist Donald Sassoon mixes these organizational triumphs with a brief foray into content analysis: "Much of Hollywood's genius lay in recasting European culture for a new modern mass society, and then re-exporting it back to Europe and the rest of the world. Its strength was its capacity to attract so many talents, organize them, and furnish them with the largest market in the world" (Sassoon, 2005: 145; see also De Grazia, 2005).

Patterns of Trade in Cultural Commodities

When it comes to the world trade in cultural commodities such as films, music, and literature, Sassoon (2002) discerns the following four major patterns:

1 Culturally dominant states – commanding a large domestic market, these nations are able to use local strength to achieve prodigious export of cultural goods. Since World War I, the United States has often stood alone with this distinction. But it is sometimes forgotten that Britain and France attained significant hegemony over the export trade in world literature during the nineteenth century, while Italy in opera and Germany in symphonic production held a certain preeminence in music on a few continents. Raising the specter of "the Red Rooster scare," France overwhelmed rivals in the film trade for the first twenty years of the medium's invention (ca. 1895–1915). Were it not for the United States' rampant flouting of copyrights throughout much of the nineteenth century, the export trade in cultural commodities would have been substantially more lucrative for these European competitors.

2 Protectionist states – these nations achieve control over the national market; but they are not serious exporters on global markets, and they impose tight to draconian restrictions on imports. The USSR, North Korea, and Maoist China are probably among the more dramatic examples of this pattern.

3 States with thriving domestic industries and room for foreign importation, though with a checkered performance in export – in Sassoon's judgment, India and Japan fit these criteria. In 2004, according to the annual survey of *Screen Digest* (June 1, 2005), India supplied 92.5 percent of the films for its domestic market, even

though Hollywood manages to reach a significant swath of the South Asian public through television. In Japan, domestic producers provided 37.5 percent of its screened movies. The latter figure is actually high compared to most of the advanced industrial world, with EU lands such as Spain (13.4 percent), Italy (20.3 percent), the UK (22 percent), and Germany (23.4 percent) trailing significantly. Of the EU lands, only France, able to hold 39 percent of its domestic market, could stake a claim to outperforming the Japanese. Supplying 93.9 percent of the movies in its local market for 2004, the United States shares the distinction with India of having the least foreign penetration among film-trading nations (*Screen Digest*, 2005).

Surveying performance in exports, Sassoon is probably less impressed than other commentators over Japan's triumphs in *animé*, which he calls "a niche market" containing Western content and sometimes conscious suppression of Japanese themes. His third category may underestimate the regional impact of India and Japan. Indian films play to packed theaters in Sri Lanka, Bangladesh, and Mauritius. In Bangladesh, some nationalists complain about how the Dhaka-based film industry has so aped Bollywood that it has come to be known as Dhallywood. War correspondent Jason Burke adds that in Afghanistan "it seemed that the greatest bulwark against the resurgent Taliban was not the US-led 'Operation Mountain Thrust' but the extraordinary popularity of Bollywood soundtracks." He expressed the frustration of Afghan fighters in Tora Bora when their shortwave radios tuned into "the drums and flutes of local traditional music" and their utter "joy if they found Bollywood soundtracks" (Burke, 2006: 37). Certainly, Japanese exports of popular culture have made a mark in East and Southeast Asia: beyond *animé*, there is Pokémon, J-pop music, and television drama. South Korea still has high quotas insuring the display of local films, but it has softened censorship regulations that were once used to prevent the entry of many foreign films, particularly those from Japan. While the craze for Japanese pop has been weaker in Indonesia, Malaysia, and Thailand, its very strength in Taiwan, Hong Kong, South Korea, and Singapore encouraged the *New Straits Times* to ask youthful Chinese Singaporeans in 1999 whether they would prefer to be Japanese: over 8 percent agreed to this most politically incorrect proposition (Iwabuchi, 2002: 208)! Long recognized as a commercial cinematic dynamo, Hong Kong saw production plunge between 2000 and 2005. In contrast, South Korean cinema is gaining accolades as one of the more formidable national film industries, with mounting success in the home market as well as in Japan and much of East Asia.

4   Culturally dominated states – this is probably the status of the majority of the world's nations, though there are variations. Sassoon provides the examples of Bulgaria and Belgium, with the latter nation only supplying a meager 1.3 percent of the films for the local market in 2004. However, there are some tiny nations able to escape from abject domination: for example Denmark, with a population of under 3 million, has in recent years produced 20–25 percent of the films shown in Danish theaters. With vibrant film schools and public support

for domestic cinema, Danish filmmakers have secured a market share outpacing many large countries in western Europe.

Hollywood and the Export Imperative: Then and Now

The British empire spawned many proponents of the doctrine "Export or Die." Harold Wilson, former president of Britain's Board of Trade and a future Prime Minister, carried this idea into the early postwar period: " 'Export or die' was a maxim which applied as much to the film industry as to the nation" (quoted in Guback, 1969: 14). As will be seen, this has also been the guiding principle of those responsible for representing the worldwide aspirations of the US film industry. In the first half of the twentieth century, Hollywood counted on overseas markets to provide approximately 20–40 percent of its revenues. Calling on the US State Department to keep overseas markets open, Will H. Hays, the first president of the Motion Picture Producers and Distributors of America, explained in 1943 that this foreign revenue "is the margin by which the supremacy of United States pictures is financed and maintained" (Hays, 1943; Trumpbour, 2002: 91–2).

Today, for Hollywood productions, the foreign box office is significantly greater than the domestic US market. In 2004, the Motion Picture Association of America (MPAA) boasted that the foreign box office, with $15.7 billion in revenues and a 44 percent leap over 2003, was well outpacing US box-office receipts, which finished at $9.54 billion (Glickman, 2005). No longer surrounded by "gold, silver, cut-glass chandeliers, thick carpets, [and] pages in fancy costumes," movie theaters and their owners are smelling doom from the new technologies for delivering entertainment. The typical US consumer goes to the movie theater around five times per year, but purchases approximately ten DVDs (Parkes, 2005). In the harsh assessment of Ty Burr of the *Boston Globe*,

> Hollywood doesn't care, since the studios make almost three times as much money from DVDs than from movie theaters; while the box office has been sagging. DVD sales and rentals have increased 676 percent since 2000. In effect, the big-screen version now functions as an ad to raise brand awareness for the home-video release. (Burr, 2005: N12)

Disney in particular had a brief but nasty row with theater owners when its CEO Robert Iger lobbed the idea in August 2005 that the gap needed to be narrowed or possibly eliminated between the time of a film's theatrical release and its sales in DVD or pay-per-view formats. Iger beat a hasty retreat, but all of this may have significance for the future of the global film trade. Disney wants theaters to convert to digital distribution of films, which the *Wall Street Journal* estimates could save the major studios "some $1 billion a year in film print and distribution costs" (Marr, 2005: A6). While some theater owners are resisting this and harbor doubts that the digital format can deliver larger audiences, the major studios may increasingly finance the conversion costs to digital, which runs around $80,000 to $100,000 per auditorium.

Now some futurists, such as the entertainment lawyer Bert Fields, talk about the day when a new film can be simultaneously delivered digitally to theaters around the globe and perhaps even to millions of home video systems, a scenario he calls "the billion dollar opening." He also recognizes that containing labor costs has been a significant agent for change in Hollywood history, including launching the transition to sound, which became a means of overcoming the musicians' unions of the 1920s. Fields anticipates the rise of cyber-thespians, and he believes the studios could eventually use new technologies to create the ultimate actor for the twenty-first century, a computer-created combination of Brad Pitt and Tom Cruise who might be christened "Brock McNally" (Fields, 2004 and 2005). In terms of the foreign film trade, Hollywood might be able to tweak the editing of pictures by adjusting cyber-thespians to some of the cultural specifications of certain regional or national markets.

One of the more difficult challenges for tracking the global film trade is identifying the national origins of production. Films are increasingly created in firms owned by globalized media conglomerates. As recently as 1998, according to the statistics of the European Audiovisual Observatory, all 20 of the world's leading films at the box office had US national origins, though one film, *Tomorrow Never Dies* (Roger Spottiswoode, 1997), was a UK–US co-production. In 2005, all 20 films at the top of the global box office had US involvement in their production, but fully eight were co-productions (see tables 13.1 and 13.2).

Increasingly films can claim myriad national origins. André Lange, the Head of Department on Markets and Financing Information for the European Audiovisual Observatory, admits that the primary source of investment has taken precedence in his institution's assignment of national origins, but he explains the dilemmas in the *Focus 2005* annual report:

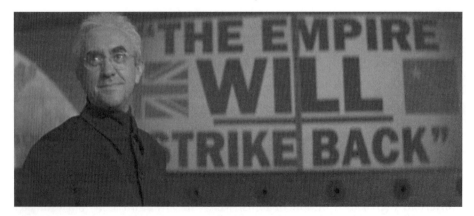

FIGURE 13.1 *Tomorrow Never Dies* (1997), $186 million at the international box office. Produced by Barbara Broccoli and Michael G. Wilson; distributed by MGM; directed by Roger Spottiswoode

TABLE 13.1   World box office Top 20, 1998* ($ million)

	Nationality	US box office	International box office	Total
1. *Titanic*	US	488	1,209	1,697
2. *Armageddon*	US	201	263	464
3. *Saving Private Ryan*	US	191	235	426
4. *Godzilla*	US	136	240	376
5. *Deep Impact*	US	141	209	350
6. *There's Something about Mary*	US	174	154	328
7. *As Good As It Gets*	US	124	166	290
8. *Lethal Weapon 4*	US	130	155	285
9. *Doctor Dolittle*	US	144	133	277
10. *Mulan*	US	121	149	270
11. *The Truman Show*	US	126	119	245
12. *Good Will Hunting*	US	134	88	222
13. *The Mask of Zorro*	US	94	112	206
14. *Tomorrow Never Dies*	UK/US	52	134	186
15. *The Horse Whisperer*	US	75	109	184
16. *The X-Files*	US	84	100	184
17. *City of Angels*	US	79	105	184
18. *The Man in the Iron Mask*	US	57	123	180
19. *Rush Hour*	US	136	26	162
20. *Six Days, Seven Nights*	US	74	84	158

* Some of these films collected additional receipts in the previous and subsequent year.
Source: EAO, 1999: 41; *Variety*.

For example, what nationality should be given to the Oliver Stone film *Alexander*, which was shot in Thailand and Morocco at Warner's initiative? It was partly financed thanks to European, Japanese and Korean pre-sales organized by the British subsidiary of a German group. Some of the cast are European (including Alexander, who speaks with an Irish accent!) and the post-production phase took place in France. (EAO, 2005: 4)

Throughout the twentieth century, Hollywood carried out many productions with an overwhelming international presence. To take an example regularly cited in film literature, *Casablanca* (Michael Curtiz, 1942, US) had a director and cast of entirely foreign background, with the notable exception of Humphrey Bogart and the keyboard-playing Dooley Wilson (Pells, 2004: 149). While Hollywood from its early history may have developed a better grasp of globalization than many other industry sectors, there are new frontiers expanding the global reach of media conglomerates.

Though sometimes facing counter-measures from authoritarian social orders, satellite broadcasting and the internet are increasingly delivering entertainment content

TABLE 13.2   World box office Top 20, 2005* ($ million)

	Nationality	US box office	International box office	Total
1. *Star Wars III: Revenge of the Sith*	US	380	468	848
2. *Harry Potter and the Goblet of Fire*	UK/US	277	531	808
3. *War of the Worlds*	US	234	357	591
4. *Madagascar*	US	193	340	533
5. *Charlie and the Chocolate Factory*	UK/US	206	266	472
6. *Mr. & Mrs. Smith*	US	186	282	468
7. *The Chronicles of Narnia*	US/NZ	226	202	428
8. *King Kong*	US/NZ	175	213	388
9. *Batman Begins*	US/UK	205	166	371
10. *Hitch*	US	178	189	367
11. *Meet the Fockers*	US	117	230	347
12. *Fantastic Four*	US/Germany	155	175	330
13. *Wedding Crashers*	US	209	76	285
14. *Robots*	US	128	133	261
15. *Constantine*	US	76	154	230
16. *Million Dollar Baby*	US	99	121	220
17. *Chicken Little*	US	132	84	216
18. *Kingdom of Heaven*	UK/Germany/ Spain/US	47	163	210
19. *The Pacifier*	US/Canada	113	85	198
20. *Flightplan*	US	89	105	194

* Some of these films collected additional receipts in the previous and subsequent year.
Source: EAO, 2006: 9, and *Variety*.

FIGURE 13.2   *Alexander* (2004), a production with international credentials. Produced by Moritz Borman, Hans De Weers, Jon Kilik, Thomas Schühly, and Iain Smith; distributed by Warner Bros.; directed by Oliver Stone

to markets once relatively closed to Hollywood's penetration. Today China, via Hong Kong, has welcomed a Disney theme park, and the Hollywoodization of Sino-communism is now referred to as the rise of Mouse Zedong. Commentators call attention to the harmony between the conservative pro-family, pro-market celebrations of Disney and those values trumpeted by the Communist Party elite. As economist Francis Lui of the Hong Kong University of Science and Technology explained to the *Guardian* (September 12, 2005): "Ideology is totally unimportant in China now. All that matters is business. And Disney is no threat to the Communist party. Both are very conservative in their outlook" (quoted in Watts, 2005). If the Hong Kong experiment takes off, there are further plans to add another Disney theme park to Shanghai around 2012.

The Film Trade and the Future for Global Culture

China's embrace of the market and gradual opening to Hollywood is raising questions about the cultural transformation of the developing world. In the post-war social sciences there is a long-simmering debate between (1) those who regard societal convergence and cultural homogenization as the ascendant thrust of modernity, and (2) others testifying to amplified cultural conflict and fragmentation. For the first tendency, sociologist Alex Inkeles, in his writings on the convergences between capitalist and communist industrial societies, provided the most pronounced version of the homogenization thesis. In stark contrast, political scientist Samuel P. Huntington, with his vision of a clash of civilizations without end, repudiates scenarios of incipient cultural harmonization.

While theorists of industrial society welcomed homogenization for heralding the triumph of modernity and the peaceful coexistence of different social orders, cultural activists feared that industrial Hollywood and Americanization might deliver a bland world of McDonaldized sameness and a hollow public space resembling "the geography of nowhere." In *The Geography of Nowhere* (1993), James Howard Kunstler speculated that the United States had become "a nation of overfed clowns living in a hostile cartoon environment" and added for good measure: "Indeed, the relentless expansion of consumer goodies became increasingly identified with our national character as the American Way of Life. Yet not everyone failed to notice that the end product of all this furious commerce-for-its-own-sake was a trashy and preposterous human habitat with no future" (Kunstler, 1993: 10, 108).

Assuredly, evidence mounts of the persistence of cultural variety that might repudiate the most lugubrious forecasts of cultural pessimists about a bland and enveloping homogenization. The literary historian and tracker of world culture Franco Moretti notes that "The diffusion of American comedies is low almost everywhere, children's films tend to prefer wealthy areas, action films South and East Asia" (Moretti, 2001: 98). Cultural geography studies show that comedy travels poorly to most outside cultures, which indicates that the global village may not be as Americanized as once foretold in works such as W. T. Stead's *The Americanization of the World*

(1902). Meanwhile, audience reception theorists have shown that *Dallas*, the world's most popular television show of the 1980s, provoked widely divergent interpretations based on the national culture of viewers (Liebes and Katz, 1990).

Nevertheless, the ongoing celebrations of cultural resiliency and the postmodern findings of flourishing *différence* have probably contributed to an absence of urgency about promoting alternative media and cinematic institutions. Nowadays academic social science seems content to mock the concept of cultural imperialism as a grotesque and strident simplification. There are many assurances that the internet and other technological wonders are creating a buzzing beehive of micro-resistances and cultural ferment. Alas, this critical complacency may be leaving the Fortune 500 goliaths freer from democratic challenge as they work to solidify their reign over globalized media and the expanding visual entertainment universe.

REFERENCES

Bakshy, A. (1928) "The Future of the Movies," *The Nation*, October 10, pp. 360–4.

Burke, J. (2006) "Louder than Bombs: Every Conflict Has its own Soundtrack," *The Observer Music Magazine*, July 16, pp. 34–39.

Burr, T. (2005) "Are the Movies Dying?," *Boston Globe*, June 26, pp. N9, N12.

De Grazia, V. (2005) *Irresistible Empire: America's Advance through Twentieth-Century Europe*. Cambridge, MA: Belknap Press of Harvard University Press.

Dulles, J. F. (1950) "How to Take the Offensive for Peace," *Life*, April 24, pp. 120–36.

EAO (1999) *Focus 1999: World Film Market Trends*. Strasbourg/Cannes: European Audiovisual Observatory/Marché du Film.

EAO (2005) *Focus 2005: World Film Market Trends*. Strasbourg/Cannes: European Audiovisual Observatory/Marché du Film.

EAO (2006) *Focus 2006: World Film Market Trends*. Strasbourg/Cannes: European Audiovisual Observatory/Marché du Film.

Fields, B. (2004 and 2005), Annual lecture for the course "Entertainment, Media, and the Law," Harvard Law School.

Glickman, D. (2005) Remarks Prepared for Delivery by Dan Glickman, President and Chief Executive Officer, Motion Picture Association of America, to ShoWest 2005, Bally's Paris Las Vegas, March 15.

Guback, T. (1969) *The International Film Industry: Western Europe and America Since 1945*. Bloomington: Indiana University Press.

Hays, W. H. (1943) Letter to Cordell Hull, October 21, and memorandum, October 18, US National Archives Record Group 59, 800.4061, 1940–1944 Motion Pictures.

Iwabuchi, K. (2002) *Recentering Globalization: Popular Culture and Japanese Transnationalism*. Durham, NC: Duke University Press.

Knight, J. S. (1946) "World Freedom of Information," *Vital Speeches of the Day*, 12(15), May 15, pp. 472–7.

Kunstler, J. H. (1993) *The Geography of Nowhere: The Rise and Decline of America's Man-Made Landscape*. New York: Simon & Schuster.

Liebes, T., and E. Katz (1990) *The Export of Meaning: Cross-Cultural Readings of Dallas*. New York: Oxford University Press.

Marr, M. (2005) "Better Mousetrap: In Shakeup, Disney Rethinks How It Reaches Audiences – Iger Seeks High-Tech Delivery of Movies, TV Shows; Theater Owners Worry – 'Housewives' on a Handheld," *Wall Street Journal*, October 1–2, pp. A1, A6.

Miller, T., N. Govil, J. McMurria, and R. Maxwell (2001) *Global Hollywood*. London: British Film Institute.

Miller, T., N. Govil, J. McMurria, and R. Maxwell (2005) *Global Hollywood 2*. London: British Film Institute.

Moretti, F. (2001) "Planet Hollywood," *New Left Review*, 9, 2nd series, May–June, pp. 90–101.

Parkes, C. (2005) "Hollywood Dreams Crumble as the Silver Screen Loses its Shine," *Financial Times*, September 17–18, p. 11.

Pells, R. (2004) "From Modernism to the Movies: The Globalization of American Culture in the Twentieth Century," *European Journal of American Culture*, 23(2), pp. 143–55.

Roxborough, S. (2005) "Germans Hail French Films," *Hollywood Reporter*, November 21, pp. 6 and 23.

Sassoon, D. (2002) "On Cultural Markets," *New Left Review*, 17, 2nd series, September–October, pp. 113–26.

Sassoon, D. (2005) "From Buddenbrooks to Babbitt?," *New Left Review*, 36, 2nd series, November–December, pp. 141–8.

Screen Digest (2005) "World Film Production/Distribution," June, pp. 173–80.

Thompson, K. (1985) *Exporting Entertainment: America in the World Film Market, 1907–1934*. London: British Film Institute.

Trumpbour, J. (2002) *Selling Hollywood to the World: U.S. and European Struggles for Mastery of the Global Film Industry*. New York: Cambridge University Press.

United States Embassy Berlin (1926) "Agitation Against American Films," National Archives RG59 862.4061/49 despatch #1118, May 25.

Watts, J. (2005) "Mouse Zedong? Disney Opens its Gates in Hong Kong," *The Guardian*, September 12, p. 25.

CHAPTER 14

BRITAIN: HOLLYWOOD, UK

PAUL McDONALD

Hollywood is internally part of the very substance of the film industry in Britain. So deep and long-standing are the interactions between Britain and Hollywood that any sense of a cinema industry or industries in Britain can only reasonably be defined as the collection of commercial actions and reactions by which British producers, distributors, exhibitors, and cinemagoers have embraced, willingly collaborated with, unwillingly collaborated with, or actively resisted the involvement of Hollywood in the film culture of the UK.

Britain's relationship to Hollywood cinema was largely fixed in the first decades of the twentieth century as Britain became an attractive operational base and market for American film companies in the international film trade. Failures to establish a successfully integrated UK industry, the skepticism of financial institutions about investing in the film business, and the reluctance of successive governments to sufficiently aid a sustainable domestic industry have also produced internal weaknesses which have made the UK amenable to Hollywood. At the same time, those weaknesses have meant that film production, distribution, and exhibition in Britain have all relied on Hollywood to retain any semblance of a domestic industry.

As a way of understanding these interactions, this chapter takes five points at which the presence of Hollywood has registered in the contemporary mediascape of Britain, towards exploring how the involvement of the Hollywood studios is firmly woven into the commerce and culture of the nation.

Hollywood Films, British Screens

UK subsidiaries of the major studios – UIP (part of Universal and Paramount's joint international distribution venture), Buena Vista International (Disney), 20th Century Fox, Columbia TriStar (Sony) and Warner Bros. International – are at the forefront of film distribution in Britain. During the period 1993 to 2003, US-produced films accounted for 52–62 percent of all films shown in the UK (table 14.1).

TABLE 14.1 Number of films shown in the UK, 1993–2003

	All films	US films	US films as % of total
1993	236	135	57
1994	297	175	59
1995	300	182	61
1996	316	189	60
1997	336	192	57
1998	351	186	53
1999	360	190	53
2000	364	189	52
2001	321	186	58
2002	350	216	62
2003	403	226	56

Source: author's analysis of data from annual editions of the BFI Film and Television Yearbook.

TABLE 14.2 Split of UK box office revenues, US and other distributors, 1991–2000

	Total box office £	US distributors		Other distributors	
		Box office £	Share %	Box office £	Share %
1991	294,936,145	194,873,762	66.07	100,062,383	33.93
1992	290,973,394	231,882,045	79.69	59,091,349	20.31
1993	318,719,874	261,477,957	82.04	57,241,917	17.96
1994	381,781,334	282,336,069	73.95	99,445,265	26.05
1995	384,742,356	301,368,355	78.33	83,374,001	21.67
1996	426,052,115	321,860,226	75.54	104,191,889	24.46
1997	506,257,828	395,974,180	78.22	110,283,648	21.78
1998	514,733,325	426,672,540	82.89	88,060,785	17.11
1999	570,506,363	482,781,813	84.62	87,724,550	15.38
2000	577,280,342	458,925,555	79.50	118,354,787	20.50

Source: author's analysis of data from annual editions of the BFI Film and Television Yearbook.

Year-on-year feature films released by and wholly or partly funded by the studio-distributors top the British box office. Over the decade 1991 to 2000, films released by the Hollywood studios annually gained between a 66 percent and an 85 percent share of gross box-office revenues (table 14.2). In 2004, distribution divisions of the six major studios handled 136 of the 445 films released in the UK, which accounted for 80.5 percent of box-office revenues (author's analysis of data in Adler, 2005). In 2004, there were 3,342 cinema screens in the UK. During the summer season that year, Warner opened *Harry Potter and the Prisoner of Azkaban* (Alfonso Cuarón, 2004, UK/US) on 535 screens (16 percent of the total), while UIP's release of *Shrek 2* (Andrew Adamson, 2004, US) began on 512 screens (15 percent) and Fox launched *I, Robot* (Alex Proyas, 2004, US/Germany) across 447 screens (13 percent). Only the major distributors are capable of organizing the large-scale supply to feed a wide national release, and their films take a disproportionate share of the annual box office.

However the influence of the Hollywood distributors is not merely confined to the circulation of studio productions. Hollywood studio distributors also handle some UK-financed domestic productions: Columbia TriStar released *S Club: Seeing Double* (Nigel Dick, 2003, UK/ Spain); UIP handled *Long Time Dead* (Marcus Adams, 2001, UK), *The Parole Officer* (John Duigan, 2001, UK), and *Beautiful Creatures* (Bill Eagles, 2000, UK); and Buena Vista distributed *High Heels and Low Lifes* (Mel Smith, 2001, UK). Occasionally the studios distribute a few foreign-language productions to UK screens: Buena Vista released the Brazilian feature *Cidade de Deus* (*City of God*) (Fernando Meirelles, 2002, Brazil/France/US) while Warner Bros. released the German production *Der kleine Eisbär* (*The Little Polar Bear*) (Thilo Rothkirch, 2001). Distribution divisions of the Hollywood majors have therefore displayed an opportunistic tendency for selecting titles from international producers.

Amongst British distributors, the largest, Entertainment Film Distributors, predominantly releases titles from US producers. In particular, Entertainment's major releases have come from New Line Cinema, the producer-distributor which is part of Time Warner, the parent company of Warner Bros. Amongst the films from New Line which Entertainment has handled in recent years are *Final Destination 2* (David R. Ellis, 2003, US), *Blade: Trinity* (David S. Goyer, 2004, US) and, most profitably, the *Lord of the Rings* trilogy.

In the video market VHS/DVD rental and retail is also dominated by divisions of the studios. Paralleling their theatrical distribution operations, Disney (Buena Vista), Columbia TriStar, Fox, and Warner all operate video subsidiaries, while Universal and Paramount departed from their theatrical distribution co-venture to operate separate home entertainment divisions. Since 1991, the value of video retail in the UK has exceeded video rental, with the difference becoming more pronounced after 1998 following the introduction of DVD. While recently released features from the studios have topped the weekly charts from the earliest years of consumer video in the UK, the popularity of these new features can only partly explain the dominance of the studios. Drawing on their valuable film libraries, the studios can feed the inventories of major retailers, providing an extensive list of titles from their back catalogs. This capacity became particularly important as DVD initiated a new collecting mentality amongst consumers. Between 1993 and 1998, the Hollywood studios accounted annually for around 68 to 76 percent of retail units sold. But as the impact of DVD was felt and the studios re-released titles from their libraries, over the period 1999 to 2004 the whole retail market nearly trebled in value and the studios increased their annual share to between 77 and 87 percent of units sold. In 2004, the studio distributors accounted for 72 percent of the total 234 million VHS/DVD units sold in the UK and 82 percent of the feature films sold. Similarly, studio distributors accounted for 82 percent (including the partnership between

Fox and domestic distributor Pathé) of the 153 million rental transactions that year (BVA, 2005).

This state of play invites a range of contradictory responses. Hollywood films clearly dominate British screens and do inhibit the space in which other modes of film can be shown, but they also prevent the formation of a viable indigenous film industry outside of Hollywood's influence. In this sense Hollywood is a threat. That threat can be perceived in economic terms, but also in cultural terms as an assault on national cultural forms and preoccupations. Yet, by their widespread visibility and commercial success, Hollywood films define popular cinema for British cinemagoers. So long-standing is the presence of Hollywood film in Britain that it would be simplistic to regard this impact in terms of an alien imported culture threatening a notional national culture. Rather, the presence of Hollywood entertainment is just one example of how the popular imagination of UK residents is continually formed through transnational flows of symbolic goods. Hollywood film is today as much a part of British culture as fish and chips or warm beer.

The British Hollywood Film

Notting Hill (Roger Michell, 1999, UK/US) is a romantic comedy. Hollywood film star Anna Scott, played by Hollywood film star Julia Roberts, is in London to publicize her new film, where she meets lowly bookshop owner William Thacker, played by British actor Hugh Grant. They fall in love but, in the best tradition of the genre, the course of true love does not run smooth: it is a relationship that mixes attraction with rejection. Resolution can only be reached once William realizes that despite his desire for independence, he simply cannot do without Anna.

Notting Hill is not only a film about an American in London: it is symptomatic of Hollywood's relationship with Britain. With its title, *Notting Hill* is precisely

FIGURE 14.1   Hollywood and Britain reach a harmonious understanding – Julia Roberts and Hugh Grant together at the end of *Notting Hill* (1999). Produced by Duncan Kenworthy; distributed by Universal; directed by Roger Michell

situated in the London suburb of W11, and the film mixes real-life locations with studio work shot at Shepperton. Produced by Working Title, the film was made by the leading company in British film production. After achieving popular and critical recognition for the British productions *My Beautiful Launderette* (Stephen Frears, 1985, UK) and *Wish You Were Here* (David Leland, 1987, UK) in the 1980s, Working Title became emblematic of contemporary British film. In 1991 the company was bought by PolyGram, at the time the world's largest recorded music company, which was expanding its own film operations. PolyGram was sold in 1998 to the Canadian drinks company Seagram, which also owned the Hollywood studio Universal, and PolyGram's entire film operation was folded into the Universal Pictures division.

In North America *Notting Hill* was distributed through Universal's domestic distribution division, while UIP handled the film in many international territories, including the UK. By the end of 1999, *Notting Hill* had grossed £30.7 million at the UK box office, while in North America the film took $116 million. With a total global box office of $363 million, *Notting Hill* ended the twentieth century as the highest-grossing British production of all time, surpassing the previous holder of that title, *Four Weddings and a Funeral* (Mike Newell, 1994, UK), also starring Grant and also made by Working Title. Following on the heels of *Four Weddings* but also of other films such as *Bean* (Mel Smith, 1997, UK/US), *Johnny English* (Peter Howitt, 2003, UK/US), and *Bridget Jones's Diary* (Sharon Maguire, 2001, UK/France), *Notting Hill* belonged to the category of "Britcoms" which had become the face of popular British films in the US film market.

As product and metaphor, *Notting Hill* is therefore representative of the intricate and deep relationships which have characterized interactions between Hollywood and British cinema. An almost exclusively British cast, together with a British writer and director, worked on a film set and shot in identifiably London locations. Although using UK production facilities and locations, the film created a little fantasy world that was both London and not London. Made by a UK-based production company, a subsidiary of Universal's film division, the film received financial backing from the studio and was released through Universal's international distribution network. For its commercial success, *Notting Hill* depended on the North American box office, and to sell the film internationally the film narrative contrived to import a Hollywood star. Shortly after its release, Universal was sold to the French utilities and communications group Vivendi, who three years later sold on the studio to the US network NBC, owned by General Electric. The rights to *Notting Hill* have now therefore changed hands several times until they now reside with the US electronics company.

Notting Hill is a common form of hybrid, the British Hollywood film. Other films, such as the *Harry Potter* films or long-running James Bond franchise, also belong to this category. These are films made with a majority of British creative input but which integrate US talent in leading performance and/or production roles. They receive funding from UK sources but only commence production and reach completion through financing from the Hollywood studios, who distribute the films around the world. As these films become the highest grossing of any of the films made with British backing or talent, the British Hollywood film therefore defines contemporary British filmmaking, not only in the domestic but also in the international markets.

Globalization and Industrial Agglomeration: Hollywood in London

Use of the label "Hollywood" to denote the American film industry links business to place: it is a convention born of the historic concentration of production and distribution activities in Los Angeles. Yet the interpenetration of Hollywood and the film industry and market in Britain results from foreign direct investment by the major US studios for establishing overseas subsidiaries and creating geographically extended distribution networks for selling films to international territories. These globalizing tendencies appear to disembed Hollywood from any attachment to a particular place. But as Allen J. Scott has emphasized, rather than eliminating the specificities of place, the globalized cultural economy is continually characterized by geographically concentrated clusters of creative and economic activity: "Despite the claims one sometimes hears to the effect that . . . globalization represents a sort of universal deterritorialization/liquefaction of world capitalism, modern flexible production activities remain firmly anchored in durable regional clusters of capital and labor" (2000: 24). For Scott, cities play a key role in the global cultural economy as the concentration of skilled labor, industry knowledge, and resources in particular places enhances both competitive performance and creative possibilities.

Globalization has not therefore removed the importance or efficacy of place in the conduct of the film industry. Instead, since the formation of a global film market at the start of the twentieth century, localized centers of creative and commercial activity have formed industrial agglomerations fundamental to sustaining such a market. In the film business, this is evident in how the cities of Los Angeles, London, Paris, or Mumbai, for example, have not only provided commercial centers for national film industries but also become hubs within global networks for the production and distribution of film.

London began to emerge as a hub in the global film market after the French studio Pathé set up a UK office in 1904, and two years later Vitagraph became the first American company to establish an office in the city for the sale of films. With other US studios opening London offices over the next decade, the pattern was established of the American film industry entering the UK market through direct investment rather than by forming leasing arrangements with local agents. As the US industry commenced a concerted push into foreign markets from 1909 onwards, London achieved strategic importance, as the center not only for managing national distribution but also for coordinating releasing to European markets and accessing territories of the British empire (Thompson, 1985). Although the years of World War I and the imposition in 1915 of an import duty on American films saw London wane after 1916 as a center for American distribution, in subsequent decades the city remained a base for the distribution and production activities of the Hollywood studios.

Today London continues to operate as the center for the cinema business in Britain, which is part of a more widespread agglomeration of cultural industries formed by the concentration of West End theaters, national museums, broadcast industries, and new media businesses. According to a report by Oxford Economic Forecasting (2005: 2) commissioned by the UK Film Council and the studio company Pinewood Shepperton, in 2004 of the 31,000 jobs in the UK film industry, approximately 50 percent were located in London. In the city the dynamics of geographical concentration are focused further inwards, for a significant majority of businesses involved with the film industry converge within the single, tightly demarcated area of Soho. In Soho and the suburb of Hammersmith, the major studios maintain offices for their production and distribution subsidiaries. Soho is home to some of the major providers of services to the film industry, including the post-production house De Lane Lea, which has recently completed work on Miramax's *Cold Mountain* (Anthony Minghella, 2003, US) and *King Arthur* (Antoine Fuqua, 2004, US/Ireland) from Disney's Touchstone division. Soho based post-production houses such as the Moving Picture Company (owned by French electronics giant Thomson), Double Negative, Cinesite (owned by Kodak), and Framestore CFC have all supplied digital visual effects for films from Fox, MGM/Sony, and Warner in recent years (Glover, 2006). Before they can be released theatrically or on video, all films shown in Britain, including Hollywood titles, must receive certification from the British Board of Film Classification (BBFC), whose office is based in Soho Square. Other significant industry organizations are also located in the area, including the Film Distributors' Association (FDA), of which the Hollywood studios are the leading members. Central London sites are used as locations for Hollywood productions: for example, in recent years the Farmiloe Building, National Portrait Gallery, and Draper Hall featured respectively in Warner's *Batman Begins* (Christopher Nolan, 2005, US), Columbia's *Closer* (Mike Nichols, 2004, US), and MGM's *Agent Cody Banks 2: Destination London* (Kevin Allen, 2004, US). The presence of Hollywood spills out regionally to the counties surrounding London. Just outside the city at Isleworth in Middlesex, the Federation Against Copyright Theft (FACT) operates as part of the MPAA's sponsored network of national anti-piracy agencies and includes the major studio-distributors amongst its members. Around the periphery of London, in the 'home counties' of Buckinghamshire and Middlesex, the Pinewood and Shepperton studio sites have provided facilities in recent years for Warner's *Charlie and the Chocolate Factory* (Tim Burton, 2005, US/Australia), Universal's *The Chronicles of Riddick* (David Twohy, 2004, US) and Columbia's *The Da Vinci Code* (Ron Howard, 2006, US), amongst other US-financed productions.

London represents in microcosm the intricate array of interactions that pertain between Britain and Hollywood. In the international film market, the city has remained an operational and creative cluster for the studios to work through. Although demonstrating the global extension of the studio operations, the presence of Hollywood in London ties business to place. As Lilach Nachum and David Keeble (2000) observe

FIGURE 14.2   Sohowood – the De Lane Lea post-production house in Dean Street, London. Photo by the author

FIGURE 14.3   The Farmiloe Building, London, masquerades as Gotham City police station in *Batman Begins* (2005). Produced by Larry Franco, Charles Roven, and Emma Thomas; distributed by Warner Bros; directed by Christopher Nolan

in their study of transnational companies – including the Hollywood studios – in the London film industry, the clustering of economic activity in close proximity offers such companies a range of ownership, location and internalization (i.e., conducting transactions within the company rather than the market) advantages. In

many ways Hollywood's relationship to Britain is therefore filtered through a relationship between LA and London, for the UK capital and surrounding counties
provide a necessary and advantageous infrastructure for the production and distribution of Hollywood films. London represents the global diffusion of Hollywood
but also shows how that dispersal remains firmly rooted to the concrete importance of place.

Multiplexing Britain: The Changing Exhibition Infrastructure

At the start of the 1980s, film exhibition in Britain was dominated by the long-
standing domestic duopoly of the ABC and Odeon chains. Both had arrangements
by which they were aligned with the two largest distribution companies in the UK,
Cinema International Corporation (CIC) and Columbia-EMI-Warners Distributors
Ltd (CEW), which together handled films from six of the leading Hollywood studios.
   However the UK exhibition sector was radically transformed as multiplex cinemas
opened. In 1985 the first multiplex opened in Britain, operated by American Multi-
Cinema (AMC), the exhibitor who had pioneered the multiplex concept in the US.
At the time theaters were closing across the US due to over-screening while the UK
remained under-screened. North American exhibitors and the Hollywood studios
therefore invested in UK exhibition, resulting in the boom in multiplex construction which occurred in the late 1980s and early 1990s. In 1988, Canadian exhibitor
Cineplex established a subsidiary to open UK multiplexes, and that same year National
Amusements opened its first Showcase site. Of the Hollywood studios, United Cinemas
International (UCI), a joint venture between Universal and Paramount, began developing new sites from 1987 and acquired the small chain AMC had built. Two years
later Warner Bros. International Theaters (WBIT) commenced their own development
program and in 1997 formed a partnership with the vertically integrated Australian
studio, Village Roadshow, to jointly develop and operate a national chain of sites.
   As these new operators entered the sector, the old ABC/Odeon duopoly was displaced and subsidiaries of the Hollywood studios became part of the new oligopoly
which emerged in UK exhibition. The involvement of the Hollywood studios had
three effects on the UK exhibition sector. With their combination of production
activities together with distribution and exhibition entities in the UK, Universal,
Paramount, and Warner effectively created a vertically integrated structure of
operations overseas. Secondly, the UK multiplex chains were just divisions of
studios which themselves belonged to larger corporate entities with diversified
assets. UCI was a division of Universal Studios, which itself belonged, through
successive ownership changes from the 1990s onwards, to the Japanese electronics
manufacturer Matsushita, Canadian drinks company Seagram, and French utilities
and media company Vivendi. Paramount's stake in the UCI partnership belonged
to Paramount Communications, which was taken over in 1994 by Viacom, while
Warner commenced UK multiplex development in the same year that Warner
Communications was acquired by Time Inc. Leading chains in the UK exhibition

sector therefore became part of the diversified assets owned by the large media and communications conglomerates formed from the late 1980s. Finally, as UCI and WBIT expanded further into international territories, the UK sites became components of globally extended theater chains which included sites in parts of western Europe, Latin America, East Asia, and Australia. Through the Hollywood studios, UK exhibition was therefore transformed in its ownership structure and was folded into the dynamics of conglomeration and globalization shaping not only the film industry but the whole media environment.

Those same dynamics would also lead to further change. As part of globalized conglomerates, the studio-owned multiplex chains were vulnerable to the fate of their parent companies. After the mega-mergers of 2000 which formed Vivendi Universal and AOL Time Warner, the UK multiplex chains were included in the assets disposed of by these media conglomerates as they attempted to ease the heavy debt burdens created by those mergers. In May 2003 the Warner Village chain was bought by SBC International Cinemas for $402 million as the parent company sold various businesses and non-strategic assets to reach a net debt reduction target of $20 billion. In October the following year the European operations of UCI were sold off to UK private equity company Terra Firma as Vivendi looked to refocus on its core businesses before selling the whole of Universal's remaining film and television operations to NBC.

During the multiplex era the changes caused to the UK exhibition sector by the entry and subsequent withdrawal of the Hollywood studios indicate how the shaping of the cinema industry in Britain can no longer be attributed to a single force such as Hollywood cinema, for Hollywood itself now belongs to, and is fashioned by, the larger diversified and globalized media marketplace.

Premium Content: Hollywood Film and the Pay-Television Economy in Britain

During the 1990s, all western European nations developed their pay-television (PTV) offerings. In Britain, satellite broadcaster Sky launched in 1989, and the following year rival satcaster British Satellite Broadcasting (BSB) commenced services. For these new platforms, films and sports became the premium content for persuading a British public familiar with license fee- and advertising-supported television about the merits of paying directly for additional television services. As part of the News Corporation media conglomerate, Sky had easy access to the film library of 20th Century Fox, owned by the same parent company. Both Sky and BSB worked to secure deals with the remaining Hollywood studios for films to supply their premium movie channel offerings. Movie content was used as bait to attract subscribers, but also to battle the ground in the nascent satellite market. Consequently, both satcasters overpaid for this prized content, and as the subscriber base grew slowly, both operators hemorrhaged funds and quickly agreed to merge as British Sky Broadcasting (BSkyB).

Hollywood films became popular currency in the UK's PTV market, permeating all pay options. Films received their first showing in pay-per-view and video-on-demand windows, showing on Sky Box Office and the cable service Front Row. A secondary window was created by the Sky Movies premium subscription suite of nine channels. Meanwhile archival titles were shown on the Turner Classic Movies (TCM) and Sky Cinema channels bundled as part of some basic satellite or cable packages. One sign of the value placed on films in the PTV market is that in fiscal year 2004, BSkyB spent £393 million, or 23 percent of its total programming budget of £1.7 billion, on film acquisitions (Wynn, 2004).

According to a 2004 study by the research agency Informa Media, Europe's PTV windows were principally supplied by Disney, Sony, Fox, Universal, and Warners, who leased between 10 and 20 new films each year, followed by Paramount, MGM, and DreamWorks. Amongst the five leading western European nations, in 2003 Britain was the most valuable PTV market for the licensing of Hollywood films: an estimated $580 million was paid in licensing fees to show Hollywood films in premium-pay windows (i.e. pay windows excluding basic packages), compared to $220 million in Spain and $210 million in France (Marich, 2004: 4). Licensing fees were also higher in the UK than in other territories, with single picture deals for premium-pay windows priced at between $1 million and $6 million, against $1 million–$3 million in France, and $0.4 million–$2 million in Germany.

Films are important in the PTV economy not only for attracting payments for additional premium services but also for maintaining the entire appeal of PTV offerings:

> pay-television platforms that skimp on their film offer – meaning cutbacks on top films – risk triggering dissatisfaction from subscribers, who *expect* hit films to also pop up on their pay-television channels. Failing to deliver hit films risks triggering subscriber churn – and also subscribers scaling back on the basic service. (Marich, 2004: 4; emphasis in original)

While a valuable category of content for building the PTV economy, the attraction of sporting events remains limited by national allegiances and gender differentials. Movies, in comparison, provide a more solid foundation for maintaining a subscriber base. As Britain has moved towards the multi-channel economy, Hollywood movies have therefore become vital currency for introducing and sustaining a whole sector of new media provision.

Britain's Hollywood

Hollywood's presence in Britain problematizes notions of a discreet domestic film industry. As film critic Ernest Betts observed, "The most striking fact about the British film industry is that it is not British . . . It is as much American as British, if not more so" (1973: 11). But as Hollywood has become part of the cinema industries in so many territories it would also seem legitimate to ask to what extent Hollywood is American. Certainly the geographical location of senior studio management in the US, or the conceptual division of Hollywood's global market into the categories of "domestic" and "international," are just some of the indicators that could be cited as privileging the US as the home of Hollywood. Yet Hollywood takes place, in the sense that production or distribution is planned and organized, in LA, but also in London and other cities around the world. In the international film market, the most visible face of British filmmaking comes from films made with the creative and financial support of the Hollywood studios. The involvement of Hollywood in aspects of the media industries in Britain, such as film exhibition or pay-TV, reveals the dominance of the major studios, but in turn the workings of those studios are contingent on transnational corporations whose operations are shaped by the performance of assets widely spread across international territories.

The cinema industry in Britain is a long way from being entirely British, and similarly Hollywood cannot straightforwardly be thought of as American. With its global ambitions, Hollywood has basically become too big to be just American. Britain's interactions with Hollywood are therefore a relationship formed not just with an external "American" cinema industry but with a globally scattered form of popular cinema which is both *in* and *of* the cinema industry in Britain. Hollywood represents a part of the cinema industry in Britain, but at the same time Britain is a part of Hollywood, the operations of which have long ago exceeded local or national contexts.

REFERENCES

Adler, T. (2005) "Distributors Increase Marketing Spend by 6%," *Screen Finance* 18(6), March 23, p. 6.

Betts, E. (1973) *The Film Business: A History of British Cinema 1896–1972*. London: George Allen & Unwin.

BVA (2005) *The BVA Yearbook 2005*. London: British Video Association.

Glover, T. (2006) "Hooray for Sohowood," *The Business*, October 21, pp. 28–30.

Marich, B. (2004) "Hollywood Earns £896m from European Pay-TV," *Screen Finance*, July 28, pp. 4–5.

Nachum, L., and D. Keeble (2000) "Localized Clusters and the Eclectic Paradigm of FDI: Film TNCs in Central London," *Transnational Corporations*, 9(1), pp. 1–37.

Oxford Economic Forecasting (2005) *The Economic Contribution of the UK Film Industry*. Oxford: Oxford Economic Forecasting.

Scott, A. (2000) *The Cultural Economy of Cities*. London: Sage.

Thompson, K. (1985) *Exporting Entertainment: America in the World Film Market 1907–1934*. London: British Film Institute.

Wynn, C. (2004) "Sony Renews BSkyB Contract, But Terms Change," *Screen Finance*, October 20, p. 6.

CHAPTER 15

FRANCE: A STORY OF LOVE AND HATE – FRENCH AND AMERICAN CINEMA IN THE FRENCH AUDIOVISUAL MARKETS

JOEL AUGROS

The hands of Robert Mitchum in *The Night of the Hunter* (Charles Laughton, 1955, US) are famous among French film buffs. On one hand is tattooed "love," on the other, "hate." Imagine the words "French cinema" and "Hollywood" instead. Both cinemas have known a tumultuous historical relationship, and the battle is not over. Hollywood has been dominating the French box office on a regular basis for many years. Today roughly 50 percent of revenues collected in movie theaters are returned to US companies. This chapter explores the market for films in France, considering historical trends in the relationship between Hollywood and French films. It also compares the positions occupied by these films across the theatrical, television, and video sectors of the market and their place in the nascent internet market.

A Long History of Rivalry

Though the Red Rooster, Pathé's emblem, was seen on most American screens before 1914, it rapidly disappeared after World War I. Not only did the French cinema lose its biggest foreign market but the domestic market was also swiftly overrun by pictures made in the United States. Even if the first strips of American films were seen in France during the war (Chaplin rapidly became tremendously successful for example), the presence of American films became most noticeable from the 1920s onwards. Unfortunately, figures are quite sparse and incomplete for this period, and due to the lack of box-office data the only information available concerns the supply of movies. By 1925, 70 percent of the movies released in France were coming from the US (Bordat, 1989). Although the percentage declined later – the figure was 63 percent by 1928 – the domination of Hollywood over French theaters was clear. Such a situation was not uncommon in Europe: between 1924 and 1927, 77 percent of films shown in France were American, which compares to 85 percent in Britain, 65 percent in Italy, and 50 percent in Germany (Guback, 1969). Furthermore, one must not forget the large presence of German movies alongside the American titles on French screens during the 1930s. Between 1930 and 1938, 14 percent of foreign films supplied to the French market came from Germany (Montebello, 2005) and 186 films were co-produced by French and German companies during that same period (Courtade, 1978).

From the American major companies there was clearly a strategy. In Joinville-le-Pont, Paramount opened a studio to shoot European-language versions of its movies (after 1933 the studio was used only as a facility for dubbing). Meanwhile, the other majors produced European versions in California. At the same time, in every large national market in Europe, the majors established distribution affiliates. By 1934 in France, all of the majors had their own affiliates which distributed exclusively the output supplied by Hollywood.

As Germany and Britain had done some years or months before, the French government reacted to Hollywood dominance by introducing a quota to cap imports. In 1928 a quota system of Byzantine complexity was established and subsequently amended several times. Certificates for foreign films were issued, but only if a signed reciprocity agreement allowed French movies to enter the opposite country. Any dubbing had to be done in France. But this policy had no effect. For example, the quota established in 1939 was for 188 foreign dubbed movies of which 150 were American, roughly the actual number of foreign movies entering the market in previous years. After World War II, on May 26, 1946, Léon Blum, former head of the Popular Front Government and Foreign Trade Secretary of State, signed a new agreement with James F. Byrnes, the American Secretary of State, in Washington. According to this agreement, in each quarter four weeks were reserved for French movies in theaters (increased to five weeks in 1948 after demonstrations by professionals in the French industry) and 186 dubbing permits were given, 121 of which were for American movies. Of 400 pictures released in France in 1946, 220 were American and 90 French (Courtade, 1978). It is interesting, though, to note that while producers, technicians, and actors were leading demonstrations and signing petitions, the theater owners remained silent. The lack of supervision meant that they didn't have to implement the policy, and as their patrons were eager to see the American movies they had been deprived of during the war, they quietly counted the pennies pouring into the box office.

Theatrical Distribution

The supply of movies

Every year since 1955 roughly 4,000 movies have been exhibited in France at least once, of which 40 percent are French, a proportion that remains quite constant. However the American supply shows more fluctuation: 1,130 American movies were exhibited in 1955 against 1,295 in 2003, with a low in 1961 (1,034) and a high in 1982 (1,485) (unless otherwise stated, figures are from CNC, 2005).

Between 10 and 15 percent of these films are new releases. There were 238 new French movies in 1975 and 239 in 2004, but only 153 in 1984 and 154 in 1996. In the same period the output of new American movies remained stable at 147 to 168 movies. One must observe, nevertheless, a slight increase since 1998 (see below). Meanwhile the distribution of new movies from outside France and Hollywood is constantly decreasing, having dropped from 322 films in 1975 to 153 by 2004.

The majority of box-office revenues come from newly released movies. In 2003, 90.8 percent of box office revenues for Hollywood films were earned by the 156 American movies premiered that year, while the 201 new French movies shown accounted for 86.2 percent of receipts from French movies.

Receipts

In terms of admissions, during 1949 French and Hollywood films were roughly on a par in the French market: 172.2 million tickets were sold for Hollywood films against 164.5 million for French ones. By 1957, ticket sales for French movies had increased to 205.9 million and admissions for Hollywood films had declined. The exact reasons are difficult to grasp. One might be the reduction of the number of movies made each year by the Hollywood studios, leading to a drop in the quantity of A movies exhibited in foreign countries (Montebello, 2005). By 1973 the nadir was reached, with only 34.7 million tickets sold for American movies. At the beginning of the 1960s, attendances for French films declined too. The result of these two trends was that, by the beginning of the 1970s, French cinema was proud of its share in the domestic box office, with more than 50 percent of receipts. Nevertheless, it is important to bear in mind that the overall number of tickets sold had fallen, from the roughly 400 million tickets sold each year during the 1950s to slightly fewer than 200 million during the 1970s (Forest, 2002). But from its historic low point of 1973, Hollywood steadily won back patrons. French cinema had a short upturn at the beginning of the 1980s before a new drop to around 30 million tickets sold at the beginning of the 1990s. More recently, with 76 million tickets sold for French movies and 92.3 million for their Hollywood counterparts in 2004, the two intimate enemies have shown some recovery.

However, it is important to look beyond the quantity to the quality of the pictures released. The blockbuster policy adopted by the majors from around the mid-1970s is certainly one of the main causes of Hollywood's reconquest of the French market. Furthermore, differences in the ways and means of distributing movies determine the performance of domestic and Hollywood films in France. French movies are mostly released by companies with low capital (Goudineau, 2000). For instance, in 1998, 80 percent of the French films distributed were handled by companies which released fewer than 10 movies (of which 40 percent had fewer than five). These companies did not have the influence to negotiate with theater owners and they could not secure the screens and dates they would have liked. Moreover, they were not able to print enough copies or invest in the right amount of marketing. Around this period, each month 10 to 15 new American movies were released. In the meantime, the release of French movies was more irregular: 10 to 20 pictures a month appeared, with a steep decline to 11 in July 1999. Distributors did not therefore have a steady supply of French movies throughout the year.

In France, American movies are mostly released by subsidiaries of the Hollywood studios. These branches are quite often concentrated by joint ventures either between two or more American majors. Universal and Paramount operated United International Pictures (UIP), while the American and French majors Buena Vista and Gaumont formed Gaumont Buena Vista International (GBVI) from 1993 to 2004, and French distributor UGC operated the UFD partnership with Fox from 1995 to 2004.

The quality and steadiness of supply from Hollywood has given the American distributors an advantage over French exhibitors for several reasons. First, the smaller the theater, the bigger is its dependence on the leading distributors. As annual receipts always depend on just a few high-earning titles, it is vital to get the few movies which are going to be the best sellers of the year, and these are usually US productions. Secondly, through maintaining a steady supply, US movies are available all year long. Finally, Hollywood films enjoy large-scale releases. Generally speaking, US movies have more prints than their French counterparts. In 2004, on average, French movies were released on 128 prints (118 in 2003) while US movies benefited from 216 prints (243 in 2004) (CNC, 2005).

As discussed above, the annual number of US films released has been increasing for several years. The reason is quite simple: the Hollywood majors have signed output deals with the main television broadcasters and pay channels in France, such as TF1, M6, Canal Plus, Canal Satellite, and TPS. Broadcasters ask for a theatrical release to help establish these movies as "real movies" and not mere "telepics" because they then get better ratings when they are broadcast. Yet in many cases these films feature lesser-known stars and inferior production values and do not perform well at the box office. So, since 1994, the number of American pictures that sold fewer than 10,000 tickets rose from 10 to 30. At the same time, the number of films attracting fewer than 25,000 moviegoers rose from 20 to 60. As a result, today there are as many American as French pictures with fewer than 25,000 tickets sold.

Television

In France the film market is framed by European Union (EU) regulation, particularly since October 3, 1989, when the "Television Without Frontiers" directive came into effect. According to the directive, "Member States shall ensure where practicable and by appropriate means, that broadcasters reserve for European works . . . a majority proportion of their transmission time" (European Commission, 1989). Moreover, owing to the possibilities opened up by the directive, French regulations

TABLE 15.1   Films on the main five French television broadcasters by nationality

	1998	1999	2000	2001	2002	2003	2004
French	561	571	567	530	558	534	540
Other European	231	278	217	266	242	248	229
US	381	354	344	351	366	363	394
Other countries	64	45	56	51	26	65	46
Total	1,237	1,248	1,184	1,198	1,192	1,210	1,209

Source: CNC, 2005.

are stricter: 60 percent of the fiction broadcast must be European and 40 percent French.

On the whole, the supply of films on television is similar to the pattern found in the theatrical market. There is a marked dichotomy between French and US movies and a diminishing place for films from other countries (table 15.1). Over the last ten years the number of films shown on French television has fallen while the supply of sport, drama, series, and reality TV has increased.

French films receiving their first broadcast represent 36 percent of new programs broadcast, but US films get better exposure, with 41.3 percent aired in stronger scheduling slots during prime time (45 films) against 34.7 percent of French movies. In 2003, on the privately owned TF1 channel and public channel France 2, four out of five of the best-rated movies were French. Meanwhile on France 3 (public) and M6 (private), French films accounted for two and one of the five top-rated movies respectively. All the other top movies came from Hollywood. Meanwhile, on the Franco-German network Arte, reserved for arts and cultural programming, two of the five highest-rated films came from the US: *Modern Times* (Charles Chaplin, 1936, US) and *City Lights* (Charles Chaplin, 1931, US). Previously unbroadcast pictures are the ones which get the best ratings, be they French or Americans. On average the premiere of a US movie attracts 5.3 million viewers against 4.1 million for a French one.

Generally the ratings and shares gained by films broadcast on French television are in constant decline. If we study the case of TF1, the average rating for French films broadcast on primetime fell from 19 percent in 1991 to 12.4 percent in 2003. Meanwhile Hollywood movies declined at a slower rate, from 18.6 percent in 1991 to 13.3 percent in 2003 (Chaniac, 1998; CNC, 2005). One of the main reasons of such a change is that not all French movies can be broadcast on television as many are too violent or abstruse, or are cast with actors who are not sufficiently famous. Consequently the same French movies are shown repeatedly on television and lose all their freshness. At the same time, Hollywood produces new films at a steadier rate, conforming to identifiable generic types, including detective films, a genre almost dropped by French cinema but adopted by French television drama.

Video

Video is widely regarded to be the ultimate free market. Unlike television broadcasting, no quotas are applied and there is no financial backing provided by the Centre National de la Cinématographie (CNC) as there is with the theatrical market. As more than 60 percent of sales come from motion pictures, it is unsurprising therefore that the video market is for the most part captured by Hollywood.

In 2003, 5,135 features were available on VHS or DVD in France. Of these, 51 percent originated from Hollywood and these earned 70.6 percent of revenues against 61 percent in 2004 (CNC Info, 2005). In comparison, 31.6 percent were French features, earning 17.6 percent of revenues. "British" movies ranked third, with 6.2 percent of titles and 4.3 percent of revenues, although this did include films such as *Harry Potter and the Sorcerer's Stone* (Chris Columbus, 2001), a film made with substantial British creative input but financed through the Hollywood studio Warner Bros. Furthermore, American movies often top the bestseller lists: in 2003, 16 of the top 20 sellers came from Hollywood, continuing the pattern seen in previous years: Hollywood was responsible for 16 of the top films in 2002 and 15 in 2001.

In 2003, sales generated by American movies totaled €666 million, an increase of 227 percent over 1994. Over this period, the overall value of the video market grew by 273 percent (from €344.7 million to €943.8 million). US movies therefore remained important for video sales, but the proportion of revenues earned by these films slightly decreased, from an 84.8 percent market share in 1994 to 70.6 percent in 2003) (CNC Info, 2005). Yet in any year, the popularity of just one or two movies can cause ripples in the video market. For example, in 2003 the success of *Lord of the Rings: The Two Towers* (Peter Jackson, 2002, US/New Zealand/Germany) saw New Zealand capture 3.6 percent of revenues (CNC Info, 2005).

The predominance of US movies in the video market can be explained by two main factors. First, Disney's distribution arm Buena Vista is the largest seller in the market due to the company's success with sales of catalog movies, especially "classic" animation. Secondly, the video market is driven by new releases, particularly from Hollywood distributors. In 2003, 566 movies were released on video for the first time, representing 11 percent of the total supply but 47.3 percent of revenues from video sales. Generally speaking US movies are also released on video in higher volumes than French titles: in 2003, an average 84,015 video copies appeared for any new release of a US film, compared to 29,323 copies for French films. Finally, more US films transfer to video than French films. Of the 3,671 new pictures release in theaters from 1996 to 2003, 94.5 percent of US movies were later released on video against only 64.4 percent of French movies (CNC Info, 2005).

Concerning video distributors, the US majors rank highly amongst the 15 leading companies according to market share. Of the five leading distributors, four were US (Buena Vista, Warner, 20th Century Fox, and Columbia). Columbia TriStar operates jointly with one of the major French companies, Gaumont, through Gaumont Columbia TriStar Home Video. French company Metropolitan appears in fifth place, and has a special role in distributing independent US movies on the French market. Moreover, it is important to note that in addition to distributing their own productions on video, the Hollywood majors also distribute French movies. Warner, for example, scored a success in France with the comedy *Chouchou* (Merzak Allouache, 2003, France).

The Internet

Research on the internet as a platform for film distribution is still in its infancy. It is difficult to establish the volume of downloaded movies and even more difficult to discover their nationality.

In October 2005, Canal+ began to operate a legal video-on-demand service over the internet through CanalPlay, starting with 700 titles and increasing to 1,000 by December of that year. Yet this was a rather meager output, and approximately 60 percent of the titles had pornographic subject matter. Among the 280 non-pornographic titles available, 100 came from the US, 112 were French and 68 were from other countries. Films become available to the service nine months after their release in theaters. At the time of writing, the market for internet delivery is still too small to measure its value. Amongst consumers, there is also very little understanding or awareness of how the internet has opened a new window to accessing films: a year after the launch of CanalPlay, a further 25 downloading services were operating, but only 18 percent of French citizens had a rough grasp of what video-on-demand meant, and only 1 percent had actually used one of these services to buy a movie (Deleurence, 2006).

Legal download services face competition from operations which offer illegal, pirated films. It is estimated that of films released in theaters, around 27 percent of French movies are available illegally over the internet, against 72 percent of US movies (Danard, Jardillier, and Delacroix, 2005). Films appear online before they are released in France: in 2004–5, only three French movies were available on the internet before their theatrical release but 53 percent of US movies were pirated before their release in France. In recent years it has been estimated that 52 percent (2003–4) or 46.5 percent (2004–5) of pirated films on the internet have come from the US, but this availability does not provide any indication of how regularly films are accessed, and it remains difficult to gauge the frequency of downloading.

Conclusion

This chapter has provided some of the figures and data necessary to comprehend the relative situations of French and American films in the French market. No simple conclusions can be drawn as the situation varies between the theatrical, television, and video segments of the market. US movies first appeared in French theaters over a century ago, but although they have asserted a dominant presence in the market they have not killed off French cinema. French cinema has developed and maintained its own qualities and economic model to remain firmly in its own marketplace.

REFERENCES

Bordat, F. (1989) "Le Cinéma américain en France: Histoire et bilan," in C.-J. Bertrand and F. Bordat (eds.), *Les Médias américains en France (influence et pénétration)*. Paris: Belin, pp. 90–108.

Chaniac, R., and J.-P. Jezéquiel (1998) *Télévision et cinéma: Le Désenchantement*. Paris: Nathan/Institut National de l'Audiovisuel.

CNC (2005) *Bilan 2004*. May, Paris: Centre National de la Cinématographie.

CNC Info (2005) *Le Marché de la vidéo en 2004*, #293, March, Paris: Centre National de la Cinématographie.

Courtade, F. (1978) *Les Malédictions du cinéma français*. Paris: Editions Alain Moreau.

Danard, B., S. Jardillier, and F. Delacroix (2005) *L'Offre "pirate" de films sur Internet*. Paris: Centre National de la Cinématographie/Association de Lutte contre la Piraterie Audiovisuelle.

Deleurence, G. (2006) "La Vidéo à la demande doit encore se faire un nom," online at <http://www.01net.com/article/327805.html> (accessed September 30, 2006).

European Commission (1989) "Promotion of EU works and Independent Production (Art. 4 & 5)," online at <http://ec.europa.eu/comm/avpolicy/reg/tvwf/implementation/promotion/index_en.htm> (accessed December 25, 2005).

Forest, C. (2002) *L'Argent du cinéma*. Paris: Belin.

Goudineau, D. (2000) *Rapport sur la distribution des films en salles*, à l'attention de Mme la Ministre de la Culture et de la Communication.

Guback, T. (1969) *The International Film Industry: Western Europe and America Since 1945*. Bloomington: Indiana University Press.

Montebello, F. (2005) *Le Cinéma en France*. Paris: Armand Colin.

CHAPTER 16

GERMANY: HOLLYWOOD AND THE GERMANS – A VERY SPECIAL RELATIONSHIP

PETER KRÄMER

The 1970s were a watershed decade in the relationship between Hollywood and the Germans. Before this decade, the success of American films in German movie theatres had been quite limited, whereas afterwards American imports dominated the box office in West Germany and, from October 1990, in the reunified Germany, while also performing strongly on German television, video, and, eventually, DVD. In addition, since the 1970s (West) German investors have provided Hollywood with a significant share of its finance. Furthermore, the 1970s saw the retirement or death of the last remnants of several waves of German-speaking immigrants and refugees (from both Germany and Austria) who, as studio founders, executives, directors, actors, writers, composers, cinematographers, set designers, talent agents, etc., had shaped American cinema ever since the first decades of the twentieth century (Krämer, 2002a). At the same time, a new generation of German filmmakers was getting ready in the 1970s for the move to Hollywood, where some of them met with great success.

This chapter outlines the interactions between Hollywood and the Germans in recent decades. The first section discusses the rapid growth of Hollywood's revenues from the German market since the 1970s, while the second section outlines the attempts of German companies to participate in the success of Hollywood movies, either by buying their distribution rights for Germany or by investing in their production. The third section deals with successful German–American collaborations, ranging from Hollywood's use of German studios and the use of Hollywood stars in German productions to the work of German filmmakers in Hollywood.

The Growth of Hollywood's German Revenues since the 1970s

As one of the three or four largest economies in the world since the late nineteenth century, Germany has always constituted a vast potential market for American films. However, until the early 1970s, several factors restricted the revenues which Hollywood was able to extract from Germany. To begin with, West German cinema audiences largely preferred domestic films and European imports to Hollywood productions (Garncarz, 1994, 1996). As a consequence, the annual market share of American imports in the 1950s and 1960s ranged only from 25 to 40 percent, that is, in individual years American films accounted for between a quarter and two-fifths of all ticket sales; at the same time, these imports typically made up between 30 and 50 percent of annual releases in West Germany (Garncarz, 1996: 444; Waterman, 2005: 158). Thus, Hollywood's share of ticket sales was smaller than its share of releases, which means that, on average, Hollywood films underperformed in the West German market. What is more, for both political and economic reasons, the number of American imports to East Germany was severely restricted (Berghahn, 2005: 31–3).

Secondly, throughout the 1950s and 1960s fewer cinema tickets tended to be sold in West Germany than in other large industrialized countries. For example, the country's postwar record of 818 million admissions in 1956 was exceeded by the sales records in Italy (819 million in 1955), Japan (ca. 1,100 million in 1958) and the UK (1,635 million in 1946); among large industrialized countries only France had consistently lower ticket sales than West Germany during the 1950s and 1960s (Vincendeau, 1996: 466; Waterman, 2005: 185). Thirdly, the diffusion of television, a potentially lucrative secondary market for theatrical releases, proceeded much more slowly in West Germany than, for example, in the UK and Japan; a 70 percent household penetration was achieved only in the second half of the 1960s (Garncarz, 1996: 448; Waterman, 2005: 184). In addition, before the late 1960s, less than 20 percent of all films shown on the two West German networks came from the US (Garncarz, 1996: 433).

Through the 1970s and 1980s these limitations disappeared, and, relative to the film markets of other large industrialized countries, the German film market became more important for Hollywood. First of all, television finally arrived in almost all West German households and Hollywood's share of film broadcasts more than doubled, while its share of the ten top-rated movies exceeded 50 percent in some years (Garncarz, 1996: 433–5). Before 1984, American studios did not deal directly with West German broadcasters but relied on the services of German film trader Leo Kirch, whose profits from the sale of television rights for Hollywood films allowed him to create a media empire with annual revenues in the hundreds of millions (Clark, 2002: 72–80). However, beginning with an $80 million deal between MGM and German broadcaster ARD in 1984, the major studios managed to reduce Kirch's role and thus increased their income from the licensing of German TV broadcasts (Clark, 2002: 82). Further increases came when prices were driven up by the dramatically growing demand for Hollywood product caused by the proliferation of new, commercial (rather than public service) broadcasters in the late 1980s and early 1990s, including Kirch's launch of premium cable channels which mostly showed Hollywood movies (see Clark, 2002).

Secondly, the preferences of German cinema audiences shifted towards Hollywood films to such an extent in the 1970s and 1980s that in most years since 1990 the market share of American imports in Germany has exceeded 80 percent, far surpassing their share in Italy, Japan, and France (Garncarz, 1994, 1996; Waterman, 2005: 158). At the same time, the German market grew in relative importance when compared to Hollywood's other major export markets. The 20-year decline in annual ticket sales in West Germany, which had followed the record year of 1956, slowed down in the late 1960s and finally bottomed out with 115 million tickets being sold in 1976 (Vincendeau, 1996: 466–7). From then on cinema attendance has been some-what erratic, but, broadly speaking, admissions in West Germany – and from October 3, 1990 in a reunified Germany integrating the formerly separate East German market – increased, and also came to exceed those in Italy and the UK, while only slightly lagging behind those in Japan and France in some years (Vincendeau, 1996: 467; *Screen International*, 2001: 8; Squire, 2004: 482; Waterman, 2005: 185).

From the mid-1990s onwards, annual German ticket sales have been in the region of 150 million, with a box-office gross in the region of $800 million, most of which was generated by American films, which in turn were mostly distributed by the German subsidiaries of the major Hollywood studios. In 1998, for example, 149 million cinema tickets were sold in Germany, generating box-office revenues of $829 million, 85 percent of which were spent on American films (*Screen International*, 2000a: 42–4). In 1999 UIP (a joint venture of Paramount, Universal and MGM/UA), Disney's Buena Vista, Fox, Warner Bros., and Columbia together had a theatrical market share of over 70 percent, while in 1998 the German video arms of the major studios had a 67 percent share of the rental market (which generated $374 million) and also dominated sell-through ($505 million) (*Screen International*, 2000a: 45). In addition several majors have been at the forefront of multiplexing in Germany, so that in 1998, for example, UCI (until 2004 jointly owned by Universal and Paramount) was one of the five biggest cinema chains in Germany, with 140 screens at 15 sites (*Screen International*, 2000a: 45).

As a result of these developments, (West) Germany became one of the most import-ant sources of income for Hollywood. In 1990, for example, West Germany gener-ated 10 percent of Hollywood's total foreign feature film revenues from cinemas, free TV, video and pay TV; only Japan (15 percent) and France (13 percent) had a larger share while the UK, Italy, and Canada had the same (*Screen Finance*, 1989: 10). Throughout the 1980s, the share of the American film industry's total income from feature films generated in foreign markets rose from around 30 percent to almost 50 percent (Waterman, 2005: 290–1). Hence, West Germany's 10 percent share of Hollywood's foreign feature income in 1990 accounted for almost 5 per-cent of its total income from features. Figures for 1997 show that Germany accounted for 10 percent of the foreign theatrical income of the major studios, surpassed only by Japan's 12 percent (*Screen International*, 2000b: 6). As far as US independents were concerned, Germany was by far the largest foreign market in 1997, accounting for 17 percent of their foreign income from cinemas, video and television (*Screen International*, 2000b: 6).

Given the importance of the German market for the American film industry, it is conceivable that the types of films which achieved the greatest success in Germany exerted some influence on Hollywood's output. For example, Disney's and Don Bluth's animated films achieved much higher levels of box-office success in West Germany than they did in the US during the 1970s and 1980s, in several years taking one of the two top spots in the annual charts (Garncarz, 1996: 286–91). Thus, the West German market helped to sustain the production of animated features in the US during two decades in which they failed to make it into the annual top ten there (Cook, 2000: 497–503; *Velvet Light Trap*, 1991: 80–2; see Krämer 2002b). However, given the overall size of the world market for Hollywood films, German film preferences can only ever have been a minor consideration for Hollywood executives. The exception to this rule was the few instances in which a major studio set up a production subsidiary in Germany itself so as to cater specifically to the perceived preferences of German audiences. Disney, for example, did this with some success in the late 1990s; its first production in Germany, the German-language comedy *Knockin' on Heaven's Door* (Thomas Jahn, 1997) became the fourth biggest hit of its year at the German box office (Tutt, 2001: 17).

German Participation in Hollywood's Revenues

The fact that, since the 1980s, Hollywood's productions have accounted for the vast majority of film revenues generated in Germany does not mean that these revenues only benefited American companies. For example, German-owned cinemas and video/DVD shops have generated most of their revenues from the Hollywood products they have offered, while German commercial broadcasters have generated advertising revenues from, and German pay TV services have attracted subscribers with, the showing of American films. At the same time, German companies have tried to profit from Hollywood's releases by acting as intermediaries between the American studios and German cinemas and television. Furthermore, German investors have provided Hollywood studios with finance in return for a share of their profits, or for the purpose of tax savings. These last two strategies (distribution and investment) have met with varying degrees of success.

As mentioned in the previous section, there is a long history of German companies – first Kirch and then others – acting as intermediaries between Hollywood and German broadcasters by buying the television rights for films from the former and selling them to the latter. For decades this trade in TV rights generated huge profits which would have gone to the American majors had they dealt directly with German broadcasters. However, the growth of basic and premium cable services in Germany led to a rights-buying "frenzy" from 1996 to 2001, first mainly involving Kirch (labeled Hollywood's "single most important foreign source of finance" in 2001), then, from 1999, also a wide range of established (e.g. Senator) and newly formed (e.g. EM.TV) media companies eager to spend money raised through their recent stock market flotations and bank loans (Dawtrey and Foreman, 1999: 9–10; Guider, 2001: B1, B6; Roxborough, 2004: 18–19). The resulting deals generated hundreds of millions of dollars for the major studios, while also soon causing enormous losses and even bankruptcies for several German companies unable to recoup the money they had spent on Hollywood movies (as well as television series and sports events); the most spectacular financial collapse was that of the Kirch Group (see Lyons and Foreman, 2001: 6, 43; Clark, 2002; Roxborough 2004: 18–19).

In a parallel development, (West) German distributors have long been acquiring the theatrical distribution rights for selected American productions. Since the 1970s, companies such as Tobis and Constantin have scored many major hits at the German box office with Hollywood imports, ranging from re-releases of Chaplin films (e.g. *Modern Times*, 1936; the seventh biggest hit in West Germany for 1972) to contemporary hits such as Orion's *Dances With Wolves* (Kevin Costner; the second biggest hit in West Germany during 1991), Carolco's *Basic Instinct* (Paul Verhoeven; the biggest hit in Germany for 1992) and Universal's *American Pie* (Paul Weitz; the biggest hit in Germany for 2000) (Garncarz, 1996: 286–91; annual German charts post-1990 can be found in the January issues of *Film-Jahrbuch* and *Filmecho/Filmwoche*). By handling Hollywood films as well as other imports, German distributors were able to achieve respectable market shares, which were much higher than the market shares of German productions. In 2000, for example, the top three German distributors Constantin, Kinowelt, and Highlight together had a market share of over 25 percent, and all German distributors combined earned more than a third of all revenues, while German productions had a share of only 14 percent; Constantin had an impressive market share of 14 percent, which was only surpassed in Germany that year by UIP (Blaney, 2001a: 29; Aft, 2004: 482). It is important to note that the bidding wars of the late 1990s drove up prices for theatrical distribution rights, just as they did for television rights, and thus reduced their profitability (Dawtrey and Foreman, 1999: 9–10 *Screen International*, 2000: 44).

At the same time, since the late 1990s, there has been a lot of excitement in the trade press about deals between German investors and Hollywood producers. Once again both established companies and newcomers with money from stock market flotations and bank loans committed hundreds of millions of dollars to buy stakes in Los Angeles-based companies such as Initial Entertainment Group (IEG), to fund the output of leading independent producers such as Arnold and Anne Kopelson, to co-finance individual films, or to engage in any number of other arrangements with American filmmakers and companies (Dawtrey and Foreman, 1999: 10; Foreman, 2000: M6, M16; Harris and Lyons, 2000: 1, 45). As a consequence of these diverse deals, money from Germany has helped to fund a large number of Hollywood films. However, it is unlikely that German investors were able to exert much control over the choice of Hollywood projects to go into production or over their execution, and it is also difficult to determine whether their returns exceeded their initial investments so as to generate profits.

Importantly, the question of profits has been of less concern for those German investors who have exploited German tax legislation so as to generate huge tax savings from their film investments, which allowed them to make money from these investments even if the films in question flopped (see Dale, 1997: 290–5, 301). Since the late 1970s, so-called tax shelters in Germany have provided Hollywood with a major source of finance (Cook, 2000: 13). As with the trade in film rights and the non-tax-related investment deals discussed above, the late 1990s saw an explosion of activity in this field; according to one estimate, German film funds exploiting recent changes in German tax laws raised $4.3 billion between 1997 and 2001, most of which went to Hollywood (Blaney, 2001b: 9). While there has been an ongoing debate in Germany about revoking favorable tax legislation, the first few years of the new millennium saw German film funds investing well in excess of $1 billion annually, mostly in Hollywood (Meza, 2005: 15). In defense of the tax legislation underpinning their activities, representatives of film funds have argued that their Hollywood investments benefit the German economy because many of the films "generated huge grosses here – half of which remained in German theaters," and some of them were shot in Germany, thus stimulating the production sector (Meza, 2005: 15).

Commercially Successful German–American Collaborations

The previous two sections have demonstrated that, since the 1970s, Hollywood has come to depend increasingly on revenues from the German market and, even more so, on finance provided by German investors, while German investors, distributors, exhibitors, and broadcasters in turn have not exerted much influence on Hollywood's production decisions. Nevertheless, German personnel and German production companies have been involved, with varying degrees of control over the production process, in a wide range of internationally successful films which combined German and American resources.

To begin with, while small in comparison with the multitude of Hollywood films shot in the UK, Canada, and Australia, the number of American films shot at German studios has been growing since the 1990s. These productions often draw on German funding – comprising both public subsidies and money from German co-producers – and in some cases deal with German subject matter (Foreman, 2001: 9, 16; Meza, 2001: 29). For example, recent films shot at Babelsberg outside Berlin include the Stalingrad epic *Enemy at the Gates* (Jean-Jacques Annaud, 2001) and the horror film *Resident Evil* (Paul W. S. Anderson, 2002), both generating worldwide grosses of around $100 million, as well as the thriller *The Bourne Supremacy* (Paul Greengrass, 2004), which had a worldwide gross of over $270 million (*Variety* 2004: 10; see Goldsmith and O'Regan, 2005: 124–32).

Furthermore, the output of German production companies includes a number of high-profile English-language films, made with international casts and crews including many Americans. Most prominent among these productions are several bestseller adaptations produced by Bernd Eichinger for the leading German producer-distributor Constantin (see Rauch, 2000). The biggest hits in this series have been *The Neverending Story* (Wolfgang Petersen, 1984; the highest-grossing film of its year in Germany, in addition to which it grossed ca. $20 million in the US), *The Name of the Rose* (Jean-Jacques Annaud, 1985; starring Sean Connery, F. Murray

FIGURE 16.1   Bourne in Berlin – Matt Damon in the lobby of the Westin Grand Hotel, Berlin, from *The Bourne Supremacy* (2004). Produced by Patrick Crowley, Frank Marshall, and Paul L. Sandberg; distributed by Universal; directed by Paul Greengrass

Abraham, and Christian Slater; worldwide gross $124 million) and *The House of the Spirits* (Bille August, 1993; starring Jeremy Irons, Meryl Streep, Glenn Close, and Winona Ryder; worldwide gross $47 million) (Cohn, 1993: C96; Finney, 1996: 250; Dale, 1997: 328). While these films were clearly controlled by a German producer and a German production company, there is also a much larger group of English-language films which have significant organizational and/or creative input from Germans, yet involve Hollywood companies to a greater or lesser extent, with ultimate control of the project in most cases in American hands. An interesting example is *Alexander* (2004), a project initiated by German producer Thomas Schühly in the 1980s, which was only realized when American director Oliver Stone and the Los Angeles-based producer Moritz Borman, also a German, got involved; in the end the film was largely financed by the German Internationale Medien und Film GmbH (IMF) and distributed in the US by Warner Bros. (Kurbjuweit, 2004; Rest, 2004).

Moritz Borman belongs to the large group of Germans who have moved to Los Angeles in recent decades. Partly because the international reach of most German productions has been very limited (for example, in 2000 a list of the 54 all-time top-grossing foreign-language films in the US included only three German productions), while the major American studios have provided both bigger budgets and easier access to all world markets, notably the US itself, Hollywood has always been an attractive destination for German film personnel (Editors of *Variety*, 2000: 67–8; see Blum, 2001: 184–278; Krämer, 2002a: 227–31). In the 1970s and 1980s, several factors made the studios quite receptive to Germans wanting to work in Hollywood (see Krämer, 2002a: 233–4). These factors included the positive critical reception of the so-called "New German Cinema" in the US; a string of German-language films receiving Academy Award nominations for best foreign-language film, with Oscars for *Die Blechtrommel* (*The Tin Drum*, Volker Schlöndorff, 1979) and

Mephisto (Istvan Szabo, 1981; a German–Hungarian co-production); and a series of minor import hits from Germany culminating with the success of *Das Boot* (*The Boat*, Wolfgang Petersen, 1981; US gross $12 million) and *The Neverending Story* (Elsaesser, 1989: 290–303; *Variety*, 1991: 86). In the wake of these successes, a large number of Germans found employment in Hollywood. According to one estimate, by 1997 about 300 German directors, producers, writers, actors, cinematographers, composers, etc. were living and working in Los Angeles, including several Academy Award nominees and even a few Oscar winners such as composer Hans Zimmer (Hansen, 1997: 13; see Blum, 2001).

The Germans in Hollywood have contributed to a wide range of films. Most notable from a commercial perspective are the blockbuster hits directed, and in some cases co-written, by Roland Emmerich or Wolfgang Petersen. Several of their films are ranked highly in the (non-inflation-adjusted) all-time box office charts for the US and for the rest of the world. The non-US chart (IMDb, 2005a) includes *Independence Day* (Emmerich, 1996; $505 million, at no. 10), *Troy* (Petersen, 2004; $348 million), *The Day After Tomorrow* (Emmerich, 2004; $341 million), *Godzilla* (Emmerich, 1998; $240 million), *The Perfect Storm* (Petersen, 2000; $143 million), *Air Force One* (Petersen, 1997; $142 million), *Stargate* (Emmerich, 1994; $125 million,) and *The Patriot* (Emmerich, 2000; $102 million, at no. 287). The US chart (IMDb, 2005b) features *Independence Day* ($306 million, at no. 20), *The Day After Tomorrow* ($187 million), *The Perfect Storm* ($183 million), *Godzilla* ($136 million), *Air Force One* ($173 million), *Troy* ($133 million), *The Patriot* ($113 million, at no. 251) and *In the Line of Fire* (Petersen, 1993; $102 million, at no. 306).

This is an impressive string of hits, by far outstripping the revenues generated by German-produced films and thus confirming that, for maximum audience reach, German filmmakers need to go to Hollywood. Yet, unsurprisingly, Emmerich and Petersen do not appear to have made a unique contribution to American

FIGURE 16.2 President Thomas J. Whitmore (Bill Pullman) takes the battle to the aliens in *Independence Day* (1996). Produced by Dean Devlin; distributed by 20th Century Fox; directed by Roland Emmerich

cinema, participating instead in well-established, successful production trends (thriller, action, science fiction, historical epic, disaster). This also applies to two worldwide hits involving Moritz Borman: *Terminator 3: Rise of the Machines* (Jonathan Mostow, 2003; $150 million in the US, $268 million outside) and the above-mentioned *Alexander* ($34 million in the US, $125 million outside). It has been noted, however, that some of Petersen's and Emmerich's films are unusually patriotic, more so than one might expect from most American directors, and Petersen has explicitly stated that he enjoys venting his suppressed German patriotism through American films (see Krämer, 2004: 135–40).

Conclusion

The relationship between Hollywood and the Germans is a very special one, particularly since the 1990s. Germany has been one of Hollywood's largest foreign markets, and its most important source of foreign finance. Indeed, after the mid-1990s, the revenues Hollywood's features generated in Germany were exceeded by the production finance provided to Hollywood by German investors. Arguably, then, the preference of German film viewers for Hollywood films and the overall size of the German theatrical, televisual and video/DVD markets are of less importance to the American film industry than German tax laws, the banking climate in Germany, and the ups and downs of the German stock market, because favorable tax regulations, generous bank loans, and a buoyant trade in stocks in Germany can release billions of dollars for investments in Hollywood. While German commentators might lament this massive outflow of production capital, German producers and directors have nevertheless been able to participate in big-budget productions that can compete in worldwide markets. They have done so either by staying at home and buying in Hollywood talent (Eichinger's strategy), or by moving to Los Angeles and selling their talent to Hollywood (Petersen, Emmerich, and Borman). Not surprisingly, the latter strategy has been much more successful.

In the light of these complex interactions between Hollywood and the Germans, it is perhaps misleading to speak of "competition" between an American and a German film industry. Instead the relationship between Hollywood companies and personnel on the one hand and German investors, distributors, exhibitors, broadcasters, producers, directors, other film personnel, and indeed audiences on the other might be better understood as a symbiosis – a relationship which, by and large, is mutually beneficial. For Hollywood, the German side provides indispensable finance and revenues as well as often highly valued creative input. For the Germans, Hollywood provides indispensable products for cinema, television, and video/DVD shops, as well as star power for, and creative input into, the country's biggest productions and career opportunities for its most ambitious filmmakers. Of course, the symbiosis does not always work – some films flop, some careers take wrong turns, some investments are lost, some companies go bust – but that, after all, is business as usual.

REFERENCES

Aft, R. (2004) "The Global Markets," in J. E. Squire (ed.), *The Movie Business Book*, 3rd edn. New York: Fireside, pp. 458–82.

Berghahn, D. (2005) *Hollywood Behind the Wall: The Cinema of East Germany*. Manchester: Manchester University Press.

Blaney, M. (2001a) "Downtime," *Screen International*, February 9, p. 29.

Blaney, M. (2001b) "Money, Money, Money," *Screen International*, July 13.

Blum, H. (2001) *Meine zweite Heimat Hollywood. Deutschsprachige Filmkünstler in den USA*. Berlin: Henschel.

Clark, T. (2002) *Der Filmpate. Der Fall des Leo Kirch*. Hamburg: Hoffmann und Campe.

Cohn, L. (1993) "All-Time Film Rental Champs," *Variety*, May 10, pp. C76–108.

Cook, D. (2000) *Lost Illusions: American Cinema in the Shadow of Watergate and Vietnam, 1970–1979*. New York: Scribner's.

Dale, M. (1997) *The Movie Game: The Film Business in Britain, Europe and America*. London: Cassell.

Dawtrey, A., and L. Foreman (1999) "Teutonic Cash Buoys Budgets," *Variety*, October 25, pp. 9–10.

Editors of *Variety* (2000) *The Variety Almanac 2000*. London: Boxtree.

Finney, A. (1996) *The State of European Cinema: A New Dose of Reality*. London: Cassell.

Foreman, L. (2000) "German Dealmakers' Charge Continues," *Variety*, October 23, pp. M6, M16.

Foreman, L. (2001) "Teutons Tout Tempting Location Lures to Pics," *Variety*, January 1, pp. 9, 16.

Garncarz, J. (1994) "Hollywood in Germany: The Role of American Films in Germany, 1925–1990," in D. W. Ellwood and R. Kroes (eds.), *Hollywood in Europe: Experiences of a Cultural Hegemony*. Amsterdam: VU University Press, pp. 94–135.

Garncarz, J. (1996) *Populäres Kino in Deutschland. Internationalisierung einer Filmkultur*. Postdoctoral dissertation (Habilitationsschrift), University of Cologne.

Goldsmith, B., and T. O'Regan (2005) *The Film Studio: Film Production in the Global Economy*. Lanham, MD: Rowman & Littlefield.

Guider, E. (2001) "U.S. Arm Plays Key H'wood Biz Role," *Variety*, October 8, pp. B1, B6.

Hansen, E. (1997) "Germans Launch Blitz on L.A.: Resurgence of Film Scene Back Home Spurs Exodus to H'wood," *Hollywood Reporter*, May 20, p. 13.

Harris, D. and C. Lyons (2000) "Will the Money Tree Wilt?" *Variety*, August 21, pp. 1, 45.

IMDb (Internet Movie Database) (2005a) "All-Time Non-USA Boxoffice," <http://www.imdb.com/boxoffice/alltimegross?region=non-us> (accessed July 17).

IMDb (2005b) "All-Time USA Boxoffice," <http://www.imdb.com/boxoffice/alltimegross> (accessed September 21).

Krämer, P. (2002a) "Hollywood in Germany/Germany in Hollywood," in T. Bergfelder, E. Carter, and D. Göktürk (eds.), *The German Cinema Book*. London: British Film Institute, pp. 227–37.

Krämer, P. (2002b) " 'The Best Disney Film Disney Never Made': Children's Films and the Family Audience in American Cinema since the 1960s," in S. Neale (ed.), *Genre and Contemporary Hollywood*. London: British Film Institute.

Krämer, P. (2004) "Drei Deutsche in Hollywood. Patriotismus, historisches Trauma und 'harmlose' Unterhaltung," in M. Hagener, J. N. Schmidt, and M. Wedel (eds.), *Die Spur durch den Spiegel. Der Film in der Kultur der Moderne*. Berlin: Bertz, pp. 132–45.

Krämer, P. (2005) *The New Hollywood: From Bonnie and Clyde to Star Wars*. London: Wallflower.

Kurbjuweit, D. (2004) "Ritt ins Ungewisse," *Der Spiegel*, December 20, pp. 56–62.

Lyons, C., and L. Foreman (2001) "Teutons Do a Fast Fade-Out," *Variety*, October 29, pp. 6, 43.

Meza, E. (2001) "Pic Production Goes Deutsch," *Variety*, June 18, p. 29.

Meza, E. (2005) "Tax Overhaul Could Ax Funds," *Variety*, March 28, p. 15.

Rauch, A. M. (2000) *Bernd Eichinger und seine Filme*. Frankfurt: Haag+Herchen.

Rest, T. (2004) "Auf dem Level des Wahnsinns," *Süddeutsche Zeitung*, December 3.

Roxborough, S. (2004) "The Leo Effect," *Hollywood Reporter*, July 27, pp. 18–19.

Roxborough, S. (2005) "Germany," *Hollywood Reporter*, May 6, p. 50.

Screen Finance (1989) "Soaring Overseas Demand Creates Studio Upheaval," May 17, pp. 8–10.

Screen International (2000a) "Germany in the New Millennium," special edition.

Screen International (2000b) "Int'l Shrinks for Studios, Boosts Indies," July 28, p. 6.

Screen International (2001) "Growing Steadily," February 2, p. 8.

Squire, J. E. (1992) *The Movie Business Book*, 2nd edn. New York: Fireside.

Tutt, L. (2001) "Foreign Affairs," *Screen International*, August 17, pp. 16–17.

Variety (1991) "Pix from Afar: National Bests in the U.S.," January 7, pp. 86–7.

Variety (2004) "Top 125 Worldwide," January 17, p. 10.

Velvet Light Trap (1991) "The 1980s: A Reference Guide to Motion Pictures, Television, VCR, and Cable," *The Velvet Light Trap*, 27 (Spring), pp. 76–88.

Vincendeau, G. (ed.) (1996) *Encyclopedia of European Cinema*. London: Cassell/British Film Institute.

Waterman, D. (2005) *Hollywood's Road to Riches*. Cambridge, MA: Harvard University Press.

CHAPTER 17

ITALY: THE RISE AND FALL OF THE ITALIAN MARKET

KRISHNA P. JAYAKAR AND DAVID WATERMAN

Introduction

Over the last six decades there have been some striking trends in the receptivity of Italian audiences to Hollywood films. From highs of around two-thirds of the Italian box office in the 1950s, the market share of Hollywood films declined to well below one-third in the late 1960s and the 1970s. Then the relative fortune of American movies began rising again, steadily returning by the early 1990s to a dominating 60 to 70 percent of the Italian box office, and probably as much or more of the video market. These levels of American film prevalence in Italy have generally been sustained through the early 2000s.

It is ironic that the post-1970s return to American film dominance has been accompanied by a fall in the relative significance of Italy among the Hollywood studios' foreign markets. In 1971 Italy was the most lucrative of Hollywood's foreign country markets in terms of the Motion Picture Association of America (MPAA) members' theatrical film rentals. By 1992 Italy had fallen to eighth position, a ranking it retained at least until the end of the century. (Then again, rankings, as well as market share, are influenced by shifts that may partly reflect definitional factors involving trends in Hollywood studio investments in Italian-based productions, a subject discussed in the text below and in Waterman, 2005.) Underlying this apparent paradox has been a turning away by Italians from the paying consumption of all movies, whether exhibited in theaters, on video, or on pay television. This decline in Italian movie consumption from the 1970s to the 1990s was so extreme that it essentially overwhelmed the rise in the American share of that movie spending.

In this chapter, we study these trends, with a focus on the long-term shifts in relative box-office market share of Italian and American films. In the first section below we set out some basic data on box-office admissions, revenues, film production, and market share that document the historical course of the Italian film industry and its patronage. In the context of an economic model of international trade in media products, we then attempt to explain the shifts in box-office market share by relating them to the trends in Italian and American consumer movie spending. We also discuss the possible influence of Italian government audiovisual policies on the Italian industry's international competitiveness, and thus the fortunes of American movies in Italy (see Waterman and Jayakar, 1999 and 2000; Waterman, 2005).

Historical Trends in the Italian Film Industry

Following the great disruptions of World War II, Italian movies were few and American films dominated Italian theaters into the early 1950s, as they did in most of Europe. Steadily, though, domestic Italian productions achieved prosperity. In its heyday of the 1960s and 1970s, the Italian film industry came to be among the world's most robust. Celebrated directors, including Vittorio de Sica, Federico Fellini and Luchino Visconti, and stars such as Marcello Mastroianni, Monica Vitti, and Sophia Loren, reflected the worldwide stature of the Italian industry. Besides receiving accolades at major international film festivals, Italian films were popular with both domestic and international audiences. Italian movies earned a respectable fraction of the filmgoing audience in other European countries, and even in the United States.

Then, in the late 1970s, the Italian industry entered a period of steady economic decline. The number of domestic productions fell, accompanied by steep falls in audiences and revenues. By any economic or cultural measure, the Italian film production industry today retains only a shadow of its former glory.

The economic trends, at least, can be documented in some detail with statistics. The total number of Italian films produced from 1945 to 2004, including both national productions and international co-productions is shown by the solid line in figure 17.1. After a dramatic revival in the immediate postwar years, the Italian industry produced an average of slightly fewer than 240 films per year in the decade and a half from 1960 to 1974, hitting a high of 313 films in 1964. Production began falling in the mid-1970s, reaching a low of 75 total movies in 1995. Since then, a rather weak recovery in production is discernible: in 2004, 138 films were produced.

Italian co-productions – the vast majority of them with France and other west European countries – reflect a similar trend, though it can be seen that co-productions have accounted for higher proportions of Italian films in the past than they do currently (see Thiermeyer, 1994; ANICA, 2004). Guback (1969) estimated that 42 percent of Italian films from 1950 to 1966 were co-produced. There has been a return toward these levels only recently, with international co-productions accounting for 26 percent of all film productions over 2001–4.

Another indication of industry trends is movie theater admissions (figure 17.2), which show current levels of box-office ticket sales to be a small fraction of the levels that prevailed in an earlier era. The decline in admissions, undoubtedly due largely to the diffusion of television, began much earlier than the decline in film production, but also shows a recent, though relatively slight, resurgence in the 1990s.

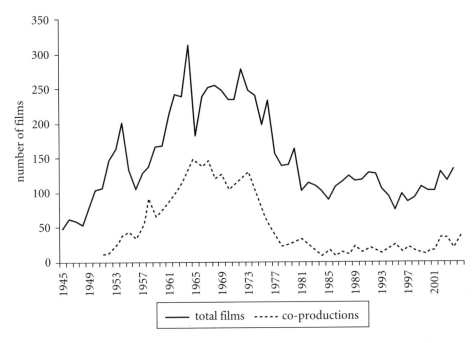

FIGURE 17.1   Number of films produced (national productions and international co-productions) in Italy, 1945–2004

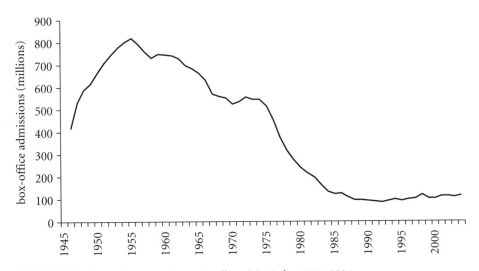

FIGURE 17.2   Box-office admissions (millions) in Italy, 1945–2004

Increases in ticket prices, as well as a shift of movie consumption toward video and other pay media channels since the 1980s (a topic we discuss further below) have mitigated the decline in film producers' revenues. As we shall see in detail, however, a smaller and smaller fraction of movie theater spending, at least, has come back to the producers of Italian films.

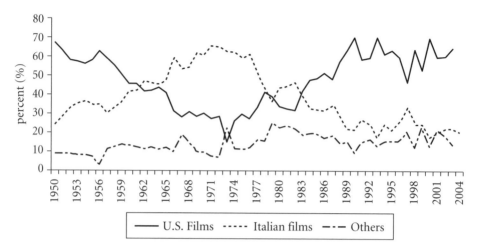

FIGURE 17.3   Market share (%) for Italian and US films in Italy, 1950–2004

Long-term trends in the box-office market share of domestic Italian movies, compared to those of US and all other foreign-produced movies, are shown in figure
17.3. Largely paralleling the historical trends in Italian production levels (figure 17.1),
a steady rise in the domestic Italian market share from 1950 to the mid-1970s is
followed by a steady decline into the 1990s. Notably, a relatively steady share of non-
Italian, non-US films in the 10 to 20 percent range throughout the period shows
that film imports in Italy, as in many other countries, are virtually synonymous
with Hollywood. American movies claimed a major share of the Italian box office
in the 1950s when the domestic Italian industry was recovering from the devasta-
tion of war. Domestic production began to thrive, reaching as much as a 65 percent box-office share in 1971. The reversal of fortunes that began in the mid-1970s
restored American films to at least the dominance they had enjoyed in the unusual
postwar period of the 1950s.

Reasons for the Post-1970s Rise of Hollywood Films in Italy

While the rate of decline of the Italian industry in statistical terms has been relatively extreme in comparison to other European countries, the general pattern of
falling film production levels, movie theater admissions, and domestic market
share since the 1960s or 1970s has been common to many other countries outside
the United States. The worldwide nature of these trends – and their mirror image
of rising market share for Hollywood films in most of the world's markets – means
that an economic explanation of Italian trends cannot be unique to that country.
While we focus on Italy in this chapter, our analysis inevitably has parallels to the
plight of domestic film production in many other countries outside the US.
    Among explanations advanced for the general tendency of American movies to
dominate world markets are so-called "cultural imperialism" (Schiller, 1992); the

ubiquity of American advertising and consumer products, or a general fascination with America and American products (Tunstall, 1977; Tracey, 1985; Sorlin, 1996); the worldwide prevalence of the English language (Wildman and Siwek, 1988); the strong-arm tactics and aggressive behavior of the MPAA in league with the US government (Guback, 1969; Seagrave, 1997); the unique ability of American producers to tune their films to world market tastes (Olson, 1999); and either inadequate trade barriers, or excessive degrees of film subsidy (Hill, 1995; Finney, 1996; Ilott, 1996; Dale, 1997). Other scholars have produced economic models that seek to explain the competitiveness of a country's film industry based on the size of its home market for audiovisual products and the cultural preferences of audiences (Hoskins, Mirus, and Rozeboom, 1988; Waterman, 1988; Wildman and Siwek, 1988).

While these diverse perspectives undoubtedly contribute to understanding the Italian film industry, we argue below that the economic perspective involving the relative size of the home market for films appears to have a compelling relevance to the Italian case.

The basic logic of the "home market" economic model of the film trade that has been advanced is that producers of movies in a given country are assumed to make production investment decisions based on the total potential market of their products, which consists of both the country's domestic market and foreign markets. A key assumption is that audience members are assumed to prefer, other things being equal, films made in their own language, or reflecting their own traditions and culture. Thus, producers confront a "cultural discount" when attempting to market their films in foreign markets (Hoskins, Mirus, and Rozeboom, 1988). The cultural discount assumption essentially means that, other things being equal (notably the level of production investment), movies that are domestically produced, using native actors and actresses and other agents of production, are preferred by that country's audiences over movies with foreign origins. A second assumption is that, other things being equal (notably the film's country of origin), audiences prefer films with higher production values, i.e., films with a greater production investment. Also, audiences will respond to producers investing more in their movies by going to see more of them, with the result that the producers can afford to make a greater number of movies. Finally, it is assumed that there are substantial economies of scale in distributing films to additional audiences: once the "first copy" of a film has been created, the incremental cost of distributing it to consumers in additional theaters, on television, or via other media is relatively low.

The end result of the economic model is that, to the extent that film producers are responsive to economic incentives, domestic films will have a relatively high market share in countries with relatively high spending on films, while those in low-spending countries will have a low market share. The basic logic behind this prediction is that the economies of scale in distributing films worldwide mean that the marginal return to a given producer from investing another dollar in a movie's production rises with the size of that producer's potential market. Since a producer's domestic market is by assumption a disproportionately important part of that potential market, film producers in countries that have relatively large domestic markets have an incentive to invest more in film production. Through market entry, higher product variety will also be offered by the producers in bigger countries. In turn, the larger production budgets will make films from the bigger countries more attractive to international audiences as well, though the cultural discount factor will tend to reduce some of the advantage. Thus, films from bigger countries would tend to do better in international markets as well.

It follows from the economic model of free trade between two countries that trends in domestic movie spending in one country relative to that of another should be reflected by a comparably shifting balance of box-office market share. On the one hand, the international exchange between Italy and the US of feature films for exhibition in theaters has in fact been relatively free of direct trade restraints. Of course, we do not live in a two-country world. Still, the overwhelming combined box-office dominance of Italian plus US films in Italy over the past half-century renders bilateral comparison between movie spending and the box-office market a revealing exercise.

To make these comparisons, we measure the economic size of the domestic movie market as "primary movie spending," the sum of consumer spending on "direct payment" movie media: theater box-office admissions, monthly subscription or PPV television channels, and videocassette rentals and sales. ("Indirect" pay media such as broadcast television are more difficult to quantify. Omitting them may affect the comparison to some degree because the Italian film industry draws a significant share of its revenue from broadcast television. We have discussed this aspect in more detail elsewhere: see Waterman and Jayakar, 1999, 2000; see also the discussion of broadcast television below.)

Italian and American primary movie spending as a percentage of GDP over time are compared in figure 17.4. Up to the mid-1970s, movie spending – in that era

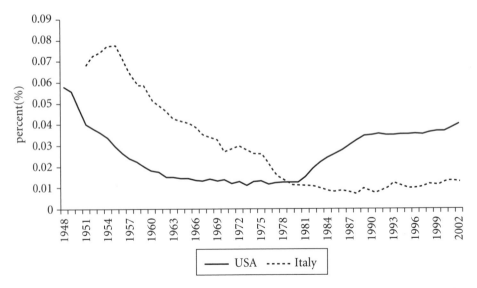

FIGURE 17.4   Primary movie spending as a percentage of GDP in the United States and Italy, 1948–2002

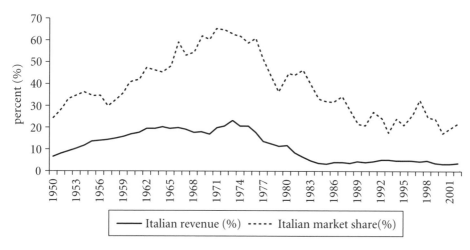

FIGURE 17.5   Comparison of Italian share of US plus Italian primary movie spending vs. market share of Italian films in the home market (%), 1950–2002

consisting entirely of box-office revenues – declined in both countries as television took its toll, but remained consistently higher in Italy than in the US. After the mid-1970s, the situation reversed rather dramatically, with US spending rising rapidly as a proportion of all economic activity, while Italian movie spending languished.

These trends in movie spending are related to trends in box-office market share in figure 17.5. The broken line repeats the Italian domestic market share trend from figure 17.3 above. The solid line below shows the Italian share of primary movie spending (as a percentage of the US-plus-Italy total of primary movie spending). The periods of growth and decline in both graph lines appear to coincide, a relationship documented statistically for the 1950–97 period in Waterman and Jayakar (1999, 2000).

While these comparisons between domestic movie spending and box-office market share over time do not necessarily demonstrate cause and effect, they are generally consistent with the home market economic model. As Italian primary movie spending per capita far exceeded that in the United States during most of the 1960s and 1970s, Italian films maintained their competitiveness in the domestic market. As the trend in primary movie spending reversed, so did the domestic market share.

The broad historical trends in movie spending illustrated in figures 17.4 and 17.5 can in turn be related to the diffusion and use of movie exhibition media in Italy and the United States. The undoubted nemesis of theatrical movie admissions worldwide, broadcast television, diffused much more rapidly in the US, reaching 86 percent household penetration in that country by 1960, while in Italy, penetration had only reached 15 percent by that date. Italian television penetration caught up to 50 percent by 1975 compared to 96 percent in the US, but did not reach 90 percent in Italy until 1985 (*Statistical Abstract of the United States*, various issues; *UNESCO Statistical Yearbook*, various issues).

The relative trends in theater spending illustrated in figure 17.4 thus suggest that the golden age of Italian movie production was made possible in part by a lack of competition from television, along with a diminished flow of competitive films from a weakened American industry. Before the mid-1970s, Italian television was also heavily government controlled, with limited channel options, probably limiting its audience appeal relative to that of the commercially oriented American system.

In 1976, broadcast television was rather suddenly opened up to competition in Italy, and private broadcast channels quickly prospered. The loss of audiences to broadcast television in the subsequent years probably continued to exert a negative effect on theater admissions and thus movie spending, but the widening gap of Italian movie media spending relative to that of the US after the mid-1970s also reflected much lower rates of newer movie media penetration and use in Italy.

While HBO and other subscription TV services quickly prospered after their launch in the United States in the mid-1970s, the first pay television system in Italy, Telepui, was not launched until 1991. VCRs were introduced worldwide in the mid-1970s, but were slow to be adopted in Italy, reaching 26 percent household penetration, compared to 71 percent in the US, by 1990. DVD players, as shown below, have similarly been slow to diffuse in Italy. Meanwhile, annual theater admissions continued to decline in Italy after the mid-1970s, reaching a nadir of 1.5 per capita in 1992, while admissions reached a low point of 4.0 in the US in 1971, before beginning a slow but steady increase since then into the 2000s (Kagan Media Research, 2000: 28; EAO 1996, 2000–1, 2003, 2005).

The economic outcome of these comparative trends is captured in table 17.1, which shows movie media penetration and usage indicators for Italy and the US in 2002. While figure 17.4 above suggests a slow uptrend in Italian movie exhibition markets during the 1990s, they remained far behind those of the US in 2002 on all measures. Diffusion of multi-channel media (cable and DBS) and video exhibition media was well below that of the US. Of most importance from an economic perspective, rates of theater and video usage in Italy were also far below those of the United States.

TABLE 17.1   Primary movie media penetration and usage indicators in the United States and Italy, 2001–2002

	Box-office admissions (per capita)	VCR penetration (% all households)	DVD penetration (% all households)	Multichannel penetration (% TV households)	Video rental transactions (# per year/ household)	Video sales transactions (# per year/ household)
Italy	1.95	60.0 *	3.9	12.0 *	3.3	1.33
US	5.63	89.3	35.5	88.0 *	26.5	9.37

* 2001 data; all other data are for 2002.
Source: Adams Media Research, 2002; Screen Digest, 2002; EAO, 2003; Kagan Media Research, 2003.

The Italian Policy Environment

Besides the economic factors discussed above, the audiovisual policy environment in Italy has affected, directly or indirectly, the market for Hollywood films in that country. To the extent that the slow adoption of movie exhibition media in Italy has contributed to the domestic production industry's stagnation after the 1970s, government policy is relevant. Cumbersome regulations on pay television systems, high taxation of video software, a lack of effective video piracy enforcement, and regulations affecting theater construction have been cited, although it is difficult to distinguish the negative impact of these factors from simple lack of demand (see Waterman, 2005: ch. 5).

Historically, the Italian state has regarded the film industry as an important expression of national culture, and many justifications for why the state should support domestic culture industries have been put forward (see Bagella and Becchetti, 1999). Government patronage of the industry has been available from at least the 1930s, when Benito Mussolini organized state funding for Cinecittà, a self-contained cinema complex that included production facilities, theaters, and accommodation for actors and technicians (Rohdie, 2000; Andreano and Iapadre, 2003).

A significant component of the Italian subsidy system is a minimum quota for "national films" in broadcast television and an "investment quota" for broadcast companies that specifies a minimum share of revenues that should be reserved for the purchase or production of domestic or European works (Andreano and Iapadre, 2003). In themselves, of course, such quotas increase the flow of funds to movie producers. An unintended by-product of these supports, however, may have been excessive film industry dependence on free broadcast television – rather than on revenue-efficient pay media like pay television and video – as a means economic support. By the mid-1980s, free television was contributing a majority of the domestic market's financial support for theatrical films, but perhaps to the exclusion of the more efficient support mechanisms of direct payment media (see Waterman and Jayakar, 1999, 2000).

Until very recently, three types of financing were available through the Fondo Unico per lo Spettacolo (FUS), the United Fund for the Visual Arts: grants (available to commercially successful films based on their box-office revenues, and to a limited number of "quality films"); subsidized loans (soft loans at favorable interest rates, direct credits, and "interest grants" that cover payments up to 6 percent on ordinary loans taken from other lenders); and guarantee funds (for films that have been deemed to be in the "national cultural interest" when ticket revenues do not cover the cost of repaying commercial loans) (Andreano and Iapadre, 2003). Andreano and Iapadre (2003) estimate that film subsidies in recent years have amounted to approximately €86 million annually (around $101 million at 2005 exchange rates). Given a total production investment of €302 million (including both national productions and Italian share of international co-productions) in 2003 (ANICA, 2005), subsidies accounted for approximately 28.5 percent of the annual production budget for Italian films.

A number of studies have addressed the impact of subsidies on the performance of domestic Italian films, and by extension, on the market for Hollywood films (Bagella and Becchetti, 1999; Andreano and Iapadre, 2003; Jansen, 2005). Theoretically, subsidy by means of grants awarded to commercially successful films (by indexing to their box-office revenues) should increase the willingness of domestic film producers to increase their investment in individual films, in turn increasing the production values and audience attractiveness of those movies. Subsidized loans, on the other hand, ensure that movie producers are likely to realize a more predictable return (through the subsidy payments) even before the film is actually released. By appealing to risk-averse filmmakers, this system may encourage production of a large number of small projects with low per-project investments. Indeed, anecdotal evidence suggests that some Italian filmmakers have adopted this low-risk strategy. One Italian trade publication estimated that, from 1994 to 2003, 232 Italian films were made with a total subsidy support of $400 million, but these films earned a total return of just $80 million at the box-office (cited in Vivarelli, 2005). Some of the filmmakers who received state funding apparently did not release their projects in theaters, and in some cases did not even complete them.

Empirical studies also suggest that subsidies have not had as chilling an effect on the Italian market for imported films as some in Hollywood had feared. Andreano and Iapadre (2003) found that the subsidy rate had an impact on domestic market share in Italy with a one-period lag. Another study examined how a number of production variables – including the receipt of government subsidies – affected total admissions, daily revenues and per screen daily admissions for individual Italian movies (Bagella and Becchetti, 1999). These authors found that the receipt of subsidies had no significant effect on the dependent variables, once other factors (notably the popularity of actors and directors) were controlled for. However, subsidized films had significantly lower total admissions than did non-subsidized films when simple group means were compared. In other words, these authors found subsidized films used cheaper production inputs and realized lower returns at the box office – a logical outcome, though one that runs counter to the wishes of government policy planners.

The MPAA and government agencies such as the Office of the United States Trade Representative (USTR) have often addressed the question of subsidies, quotas, and other market barriers in Hollywood's major trading markets. Partly motivated by their persistent complaints, and partly by the desire to scale back subsidies in the wider economy, the Italian government of Prime Minister Silvio Berlusconi in 2003 initiated a partial moratorium on the disbursement of subsidies pending the creation of a new film-financing system (Vivarelli, 2005). Some features of the system eventually adopted include scaled-back state subsidies through FUS; a new "reference system" specifying a number of eligibility criteria for a project to receive state funding; reduced funding limits for individual projects (from 90 to 50 percent of total project costs); permission for product placement in state-supported projects as an alternative source of revenue; and encouragement of public–private funding partnerships coordinated through Cinecittà and other agencies (De Marco, 2005a,

2005b). It remains to be seen whether the new subsidy system, with its greater emphasis on performance and accountability, will help the Italian film industry compete
better against Hollywood imports.

Conclusion

Hollywood's fortunes in the Italian film market have varied remarkably since the
end of World War II. From a postwar dominance of the Italian market, Hollywood's
box-office share plunged to less than a third by the early 1970s, and since then has
revived to the levels witnessed a half-century ago. In the 1950s and 1960s, Italian
filmmakers producing a stream of not only popular, but critically acclaimed films;
as a whole, these overwhelmed Hollywood's products. Not coincidentally, we
claim, broadcast television had reduced the competitiveness of American movies
by diminishing their domestic support base, while the Italian market – and thus
its film producers – remained insulated from TV's ravages until at least the late 1960s.
Beginning in the 1970s, slow adoption and low usage of lucrative pay television
and video movie exhibition media, along with historically very low theater attendance, contributed to the decline of the Italian production industry by diminishing its domestic support base. As the new media grew rapidly in the US and theater
attendance remained remarkably high, Hollywood producers were able to produce
greater numbers of more attractive movies. As in many other countries, but especially in Italy it seems, audiences abandoned their national productions and
flocked to watch American movies.

The Italian government's audiovisual policies have aimed to stem the domestic
decline by injections of money into film production, and by strong support for showing Italian films on broadcast television. An excessive dependence on free broadcast television for film finance, encouraged by these same government policies,
however, may have contributed to the low usage of more efficient direct payment-
supported movie exhibition media. Recent research has also suggested that the Italian
film subsidy system may have had the perverse effect of diminishing the economic
viability of the domestic film industry by distorting producers' incentives.

Certainly, this logic does not provide a full understanding of trends in Hollywood's
dominance. Social, cultural, and political factors have undoubtedly contributed to
the decline of the Italian film industry and the increasing hegemony of Hollywood.
And why, we should also ask, did Italian spending on movies fall so steeply from
the 1970s to the 1990s? Whatever its root causes, that fall was likely accelerated by
the decline in the Italian production industry itself. The growing lack of high-
quality, culturally compatible domestic films, that is, must have discouraged Italian
moviegoers, leading to even further declines in spending, thus fueling Hollywood's
dominance.

Since the 1990s, the Italian film industry, as well as domestic consumer spending on movies, has appeared to be on an uptrend, albeit a slight one. At least in
relative terms, the domestic film production industry should eventually benefit more

than will Hollywood from continuing growth in the domestic consumer market for films. A key factor, however, may be the engineering of the Italian film subsidy system; it could help or hurt the economic prosperity of domestic filmmakers. A rising tide of Italian consumer spending, though, will lift all boats, and that remains the main hope of Hollywood's exporters to restore Italy to among the very top tier of its foreign revenue contributors.

REFERENCES

Adams Media Research (2002) *Hollywood Aftermarket* Newsletter, September 30, p. 3.

ANICA (2004) *Serie Storica* [Historical Series], online at <http://www.anica.it/rassegna/dati.htm> (accessed December 15, 2005).

ANICA (2005) *Dati sul cinema in Italia, 2004* [Data on Cinema in Italy, 2004], online at <http://www.anica.it/rassegna/dati.htm> (accessed December 15, 2005).

Andreano, S., and L. Iapadre (2003) *Audiovisual Policies and International Trade: The Case of Italy*. Hamburg: Hamburgisches Welt-Wirtschafts-Archiv.

Bagella, M., and L. Becchetti (1999) "The Determinants of Motion Picture Box Office Performance: Evidence from Movies Produced in Italy," *Journal of Cultural Economics*, 23, pp. 237–56.

Dale, M. (1997) *The Movie Game: The Film Business in Britain, Europe, and America*. London: Cassell.

De Marco, C. (2005a) "Italian Film, an Experimental Market," *CineEuropa*, June 15, online at <http://www.cineeuropa.org> (accessed December 20, 2005).

De Marco, C. (2005b) "Senate Approves the 'Salvage Cinema' Law," *CineEuropa*, October 20, online at <http://www.cineeuropa.org> (accessed December 20, 2005).

EAO (1996) *Statistical Yearbook 1996: Cinema, Television, Video, and New Media in Europe*. Strasbourg: European Audiovisual Observatory.

EAO (2000–1) *Statistical Yearbook 2001: Cinema, Television, Video, and New Media in Europe, 2001*. Strasbourg: European Audiovisual Observatory.

EAO (2003) *Yearbook 2003: Film, Television, Video and Multimedia in Europe*. Strasbourg: European Audiovisual Observatory.

EAO (2005) *Yearbook 2005: Film, Television, Video and Multimedia in Europe*. Strasbourg: European Audiovisual Observatory.

Finney, A. (1996) *The State of European Cinema*. London: Cassell.

Guback, T. H. (1969) *The International Film Industry: Western Europe and America since 1945*. Bloomington: Indiana University Press.

Hill, J. (1995) "British Television and Film: The Making of a Relationship," in J. Hill and M. McLoone (eds.), *Big Picture Small Screen: The Relations Between Film and Television*. University of Luton Press, John Libbey, pp. 151–76.

Hoskins, C., R. Mirus, and W. Rozeboom (1988) "Reasons for the US Dominance of the International Trade in Television Programmes," *Media, Culture, and Society*, 10(4), pp. 499–515.

Ilott, T. (1996) *Budgets and Markets: A Study of the Budgeting of European Films*. New York: Routledge.

Jansen, C. (2005) "The Performance of German Motion Pictures, Profits and Subsidies: Some Empirical Evidence," *Journal of Cultural Economics*, 29(3), pp. 191–212.

Kagan Media Research (2000) *State of Home Video 2000*. Monterey: Kagan Media.

Kagan Media Research (2003) *Consumer Entertainment Spending*. Monterey: Kagan Media.

Rohdie, S. (2000) "A Brief History of the Italian Cinema," *Metro*, 121/2, pp. 101–12.

Schiller, H. I. (1992) *Mass Communication and American Empire*, 2nd edn. Boulder, CO: Westview Press.

Screen Digest (2002) *European Video, Market Assessment and Forecast*. London: Screen Digest.

Sorlin, P. (1996) *Italian National Cinema, 1896–1996*. New York: Routledge.

Statistical Abstract of the United States (various issues) Washington, DC: US Census Bureau.

Thiermeyer, M. (1994) *Internationalisierung von Film und Filmwirtschaft*. Cologne: Weimer Wein.

Tracey, M. (1985) "The Poisoned Chalice? International Television and the Idea of Dominance," *Daedalus*, p. 114.

Tunstall, J. (1977) *The Media are American*. London: Constable.

UNESCO Statistical Yearbook (various issues). Paris: United Nations Educational, Scientific and Cultural Organization.

Vivarelli, N. (2005) "No More Blank Checks for Italos: New Regime Puts an End to Fly-by-Night Operators," *Variety*, January 17, p. 15.

Waterman, D. (1988) "World Television Trade: The Economic Effects of Privatization and New Technology," *Telecommunications Policy*, 12(2), pp. 141–51.

Waterman, D. (2005) *Hollywood's Road to Riches*. Cambridge, MA: Harvard University Press.

Waterman, D., and K. Jayakar (1999) *Da che parte pende la bilancia della competizione fra l'industria cinematografica italiana e quella statunitense?* [How Will the Competitive Balance between the Italian and American Film Industries Evolve?]. *L'Industria*, 20(3), pp. 393–415; slightly revised as D. Waterman and K. Jayakar (2000) "The Competitive Balance of the Italian and American Film Industries," *European Journal of Communications*, 15(4), pp. 501–28.

Wildman, S., and S. Siwek (1988) *International Trade in Films and Television Programs*. Cambridge, MA: Ballinger.

CHAPTER 18

LATIN AMERICA: HOW MEXICO AND ARGENTINA COPE AND COOPERATE WITH THE BEHEMOTH OF THE NORTH

TAMARA L. FALICOV

The Motion Picture Association of America (MPAA) states that "only one in ten films ever retrieves its investment from *domestic* exhibition" (quoted in Wasko, 2003: 3; emphasis added). The Hollywood film industry, while the most lucrative in the world, is still a risky business in the domestic market. For decades Hollywood has therefore remained dependent on the international arena to recoup its investment. This chapter will focus on two countries in Latin America that Hollywood has penetrated as a viable export market. Mexico and Argentina, which both have developed film industries, will be profiled in terms of their differing finance models as well as their sometimes strained, sometimes accommodating, relationships with the Hollywood industry.

Hollywood films produced in Latin America (principally Mexico) will be explored, in addition to Latin American films financed and/or distributed by the Hollywood studios. In addition to marketing their films throughout Latin America, "the majors" have found ways to cheaply film runaway productions there. According to a 1999 study commissioned by the Directors Guild of America (DGA) and the Screen Actors Guild (SGA), runaways increased from 14 percent of total US film and television productions in 1990 to 27 percent in 1998 (Klein, 2004). Another form of production investment has been via international co-productions.

Historical Overview

In the film business, the relationship between Latin America and the United States begins as far back as the 1920s when Hollywood looked to Latin America to sell its motion pictures, and generated between 80 and 90 percent of box-office receipts in parts of Latin America (Armes, 1987: 47). Data from 2001 show that overall grosses outside the United States account for 55 percent of the total Hollywood studio box-office earnings and that Latin America has accounted for between 12 and 15 percent of foreign theatrical revenue (Toumarkine, 2001).

When European markets – historically the largest buyers of Hollywood films – collapsed during World War I and World War II, Hollywood turned to Latin America to sell its product (see Schnitman, 1984). In 1927–8, Latin America created more revenue for early sound features from Hollywood than Canada, Asia, and Europe combined – about 31.5 percent of the $7.5 million that comprised the annual total foreign return (Usabel, 1982: 80).

During World War II, Mexico's film industry was aided and invested in by the Hollywood studios (the most involved being RKO) and helped train technical crew and actors in Mexico. Mexican actors such as Dolores del Río, Ramón Navarro, and Lupe Vélez crossed the Rio Grande to the US before World War II but then returned to Mexico in the 1930s and 1940s. They became transnational stars in both the US and Mexico and helped popularize what has been dubbed the "golden age" of Mexican cinema from 1938 to 1953. It was also an age of transnational collaboration between the two industries in the fight against communism: the Mexican B-film *Dicen que soy comunista* (*They Say I'm a Communist*) (Alejandro Galindo, 1951, Mexico), among others, perpetuated Cold War propaganda (Fein, 2000: 93).

Argentina, by contrast, paid heavily for its neutrality during World War II. The US government banned the shipping of raw film stock to Argentina amid allegations that the Argentine film industry was producing pro-Axis propaganda. Although one studio, Argentina Sono Film, did produce pro-fascist newsreels, the vast majority of the industry, which at that time was the most industrialized and successful film industry in Latin America, was democratic and supported the Allies (see Falicov, 2007). The US government, at the behest of Hollywood, found a strategic way to distribute US films in the region by severely weakening the Argentine film industry, which had the most developed studio system amongst Spanish-speaking countries at the time (Getino, 2005: 28).

Since the 1950s, both Argentina and Mexico have struggled with the loss of an industrial film studio system and have increasingly had to rely on the assistance of the state to support cultural production in the face of Hollywood's dominance. In the 1990s, Argentina responded with legislation intended to protect the national cinema as an entity that forms part of the cultural patrimony as well as an infant industry in need of protectionist polices. Ten years after production funds were secured via film legislation passed in 1994, a law was passed to strengthen national exhibition in Argentina in response to Hollywood's long-standing film exhibition hegemony. Historically, national films faced discrimination in theater exhibition because Hollywood movies would supplant national ones due to exhibitor preference. Moreover, to this day, the Latin American film market continues to be dominated by Hollywood films, showing on average on between 80 percent (current figures in Argentina) and 98 percent (current figures in Central American countries) of theater screens. For these reasons, in 2004 the Argentine congress enacted a screen quota measure to legally insure that national films would gain equitable screening space. Mexico passed a screen quota designating 10 percent of theater space to be dedicated to national cinema (Article 9 of the 1999 law modified from 1992), but the quota is rarely, if ever, enforced (see Ugalde, 2004).

Although Argentina has attempted corrective measures to wrestle some screen time away from Hollywood, another trend has emerged from Argentina, Mexico, and Brazil (perhaps as a response to the screen quota) where the Hollywood majors have invested in co-production and distribution deals with Latin American film producers. Rather than relying solely on state funding or co-production funding from Europe (usually Spain), more collaboration is taking place between the Hollywood studios represented by the Motion Picture Association (MPA) (the overseas arm of the MPAA) and Latin American producers. While Johnson (2005) has looked at the MPA's relationship to Brazil, this chapter will explore the Mexican and Argentine cases.

The Mexican Film Industry from the Late 1990s to the Present

Mexican cinema has struggled to survive from the 1990s to the present. Unlike other Latin American film industries, especially those of Brazil and Argentina, the industry in Mexico has not been able to push its government to create a strong funding mechanism to work as an incentive for production. Since 1997, production figures have been low (see table 18.1). Although state support exists under the auspices of the Instituto Mexicano de Cinematografía (Mexican Film Institute; IMCINE), there has been increased attention to private film companies who have produced both critically acclaimed films and box-office hits without government funding. From 1997 to 2004, between one-half and one-third of all films produced in a given year were financed with 100 percent private monies. It is these film companies, the majority funded by wealthy entrepreneurs, who are waking up the close-to-moribund film industry. For example, the Mexican conglomerate CIE (Interamerican Entertainment Corporation) has partnered the venture-capital arm of the Grupo Financiero Inbursa (owned by billionaire Carlos Slim Helú) to create Altavista Films (Morales, 2001). Another company, Anhelo, is funded by CEO Carlos Vergara, who made his fortune through Omnilife, a herbal supplement company (Smith, 2003:

TABLE 18.1   Number of Mexican films produced, 1997–2004

Production year	Films
1997	15
1998	11
1999	19
2000	32
2001	18
2002	14
2003	29
2004	36

Source: Vargas, 2003; Cazares, 2006a.

FIGURE 18.1   *Amores Perros* (2000) built the reputation of Mexican director Alejandro
González Iñárritu amongst international audiences. Produced by Alejandro González
Iñárritu; distributed by Lions Gate; directed by Alejandro González Iñárritu

395). These production companies worked with film directors who made films
in Mexico, then became successful in Hollywood (such as Alfonso Cuarón and
Guillermo del Toro), but later returned to their home country to make more personal, quality films. Currently del Toro and Cuarón are based in the US. Alejandro
González Iñárritu has followed the opposite trajectory by making a hit film in Mexico,
and then directing in Hollywood. *Y tu mamá también* (Alfonso Cuarón, 2001, Mexico),
produced by Anhelo, *El espinazo del Diablo* (*The Devil's Backbone*; Guillermo del
Toro, 2001, Mexico), also by Anhelo, and *Amores Perros* (*Love's a Bitch*; Alejandro
González Iñárritu, 2000, Mexico), produced by Altavista, are small, artistic films
that gained critical acclaim in arthouse circles abroad and were equally successful
at the domestic box office. For the most part, lower-budget films such as these get
limited US distribution, if any. In Cuarón's case, however, the independent US distribution company IFC Films distributed *Y tu mamá también* and it became the most
widely distributed foreign-language film in recent US history (Plasencia, 2004).

The three directors of these films are friends and have remarked in interviews that they feel ostracized from the traditional film community for going to
Hollywood (Puig, 2002: 14D). They do not lament the loss of state funding for films:
according to del Toro, private funding signals "that whole fossilized approach has
now been overturned, thank God," and Cuarón states his preference for private investor
finance over what he deems "corrupt Latin American governments," referring to
the 1990s, old-guard ruling-party politics of the once dominant PRI (Institutional
Revolutionary Party) (quoted in Brooks, 2002). This reformist stance is partly
a reflection of the so-called "new" (conservative) government party (National

FIGURE 18.2   *Y tu mamá también* (2001) became one of the most widely distributed foreign-language films from Latin America when released in the US. Produced by Alfonso Cuarón and Jorge Vergara; distributed by IFC Films; directed by Alfonso Cuarón

Action Party) (PAN) that swept to power in 2000, but it is also a defense by these directors following criticisms that some of the film establishment have leveled against them. In the Mexican press *Y tu mamá también* was jokingly renamed "Hombre, Where's My Car?" or "Latin American Pie" likening it to recent Hollywood teen movies. Clearly some in the established film community do not approve of national filmmakers having close ties to Hollywood. Cuarón stated that "Of course, I'm not going to defend America's attitude towards Mexico. Historically it is a very tense relationship. But you have to be pragmatic. Why should I turn down American distribution?" (quoted in Brooks, 2002). These newer directors share similarities with the transnational figures that helped fortify the golden age of Mexican cinema, such as directors Roberto Gavaldón and notably Emilio "El Indio" Fernández, who spent time in Hollywood in the 1920s and 1930s and learned their trade there (Garcia Riera in Tierney, 2003: 227). There is therefore no lack of irony when those in the film establishment criticize the newer directors for working in Hollywood while waxing nostalgic for the bygone days of a more "authentic" Mexican cinema. These current directors represent a new, more youth-oriented film culture that, while not without its controversies, has helped revive Mexico's ailing industry.

The MPA in Mexico

Mexico is the number one market for the US audiovisual industry in Latin America and is ranked tenth by MPA member companies among all foreign markets

(MPAA, 2005). The MPA has played an important role in producing and distributing commercial films made in large part by "industrial auteurs." These directors work with multinational, corporate-owned production companies, and produce television commercials in addition to film. Among the reasons for this involvement, in addition to the desire to diversify the Hollywood portfolio, is the need to respond to nations who demanded cultural exceptionalism during the Free Trade of the Americas (FTAA) agreements. As a way to appease this sector, and as an attempt to simultaneously make a profit, the MPA began to collaborate in cultural production with the three most developed film industries in Latin America (Mexico, Argentina, and Brazil) to demonstrate how "the production and distribution decisions of MPA member countries also reflect this commitment to cultural diversity" (MPA, 2003).

In the case of Mexico, the MPA, via studios such as Disney, Warner Bros., Fox Universal, and Columbia TriStar, has produced, co-produced, and distributed film and TV programs throughout the Americas. The films co-produced with Hollywood studio money generally have very low budgets by Hollywood standards (typically between $1 million and $2 million dollars). The majority of Mexican films that receive co-production funding from Hollywood studios are relatively expensive by Latin American standards, but they tend not to be "quality" productions, but rather popular movies that appeal to younger, upwardly mobile, upper-middle-class audiences who enjoy comedies and trendy urban youth culture (described below). It is these very films that make money at the box office, but which are not being exported to film festivals for world recognition.

Mexican co-producers stand to gain from Hollywood involvement; in addition to money invested, they also receive greater exposure from the wider distribution that the Hollywood studios command. For example, Miravista, the company co-created by Walt Disney Latin America and the Spanish telephone company Admira, signed the Argentine director Gabriela Tagliavini to direct their first Mexican co-production, *Ladies' Night* (2003, Mexico) along with Mexican producers Televisa Mexico and Argos Communication. This film, produced to the tune of $1.6 million, is a comedy about a woman who runs away with a male stripper on the eve of her wedding. According to *Variety*, *Ladies' Night* reached number one at the box office in 2004 and was the second-largest box-office hit in Mexican film history despite receiving little critical acclaim (O'Boyle, 2005). According to Mexican film statistics, the film was the eighth-largest box-office hit from 1999 to 2004, with 2.2 million viewers (Cazares, 2006b).

The Hollywood studios have been willing to distribute films after they have demonstrated success in their home territory. For example, Mexico's largest box-office hit of all time, *El crimen del Padre Amaro (The Crime of Father Amaro*; Carlos Carrera, 2002, Mexico), claimed 5.2 million viewers, before being picked up by Sony Pictures Entertainment. This film outdid the previous record, held by *Sexo, Pudor y Lagrimas (Sex, Shame and Tears*; Antonio Serrano, 1999, Mexico), a film distributed by Fox (MPA, 2003).

Mexico as Hollywood's Backlot

Despite the fact that government subsidies and incentives for film industry investment have not materialized in Mexico (to the same extent as for the private
sector in Brazil for example), there has been an attempt to encourage multinational
investment by legislators. In 2004, Mexico created a 15 percent Value Added Tax
(VAT) rebate on local film production services, provided they contract with a Mexican
production service or a local producer (De la Fuente, 2004: 18), but by September
2005, despite approval from Congress, the government still did not issue the
operating regulations for this tax incentive to draw Mexico's industrial wealth into
filmmaking (O'Boyle, 2005). Anna Marie De la Fuente has argued that international
producers have long been trying to convince Mexico to offer filmmaking incentives. They believe that Mexico, despite its proximity to the United States, has lagged
behind Canada and even New Zealand because it offered nothing, fiscally, to producers. However, in recent years, Hollywood film producers have looked to Mexico
as an affordable place to film high-budget blockbuster movies. Some of these US
film studios have financed runaway productions in Mexico, such as the famous mega-
blockbuster, *Titanic* (James Cameron, 1997, US).

The contemporary history of Hollywood filming in Mexico purportedly began
when *Night of the Iguana* (John Huston, 1964, US) was filmed in the once sleepy
town of Puerto Vallarta. The transformation of the town into a tacky commercial
and tourist destination has been attributed to the film's fame. Restaurants and bars
with the film's name cash in on the tourist market, and in 1999 the set of the film
was resurrected into two theme restaurants based on the film (Koehne, 1999). Big-
budget productions of summer blockbusters didn't return to Mexico until the
mid-1990s when *Titanic*, which for the next decade remained the most expensive
film ever produced ($200 million) was filmed at a huge, custom-built studio in
Rosarito, Baja California Norte (Hawley, 2004). Director James Cameron built a
775 ft. replica of the ship, 10 percent smaller than the real one, and a 17 million
gallon tank in which to sink it within a 40 acre complex Fox set up in Rosarito
(Masters, 1997). The film injected $85 million into the local economy according to
the Mexican government. The facility, now dubbed the Fox Studios Baja, has since
produced *Master and Commander* (Peter Weir, 2003, US), *Pearl Harbor* (Michael
Bay, 2001, US), and other special-effects spectacles.

What are the advantages for Hollywood studios? Wages for Mexican film crews
are about one-quarter of those of their US counterparts, according to Hugo Alonso
Reyes Mejilla, secretary for technicians in the Union of Cinema Production
Workers (Hawley, 2004). Labor costs for the Hollywood studios are cut by one-third
(Tegel, 2002). The Mexican government benefits from a potential influx of money,
including tourism dollars generated by having images of the Mexican landscape projected globally. In addition, the presence of Fox Studios Baja has helped promote
a theme park element to the studio (following the production of *Titanic*), which
has promoted tourism. As Ben Goldsmith and Tom O'Regan note:

FIGURE 18.3   The *Titanic* set constructed at Rosarito, Baja California Norte, Mexico.
From *Building the Ship* (2005), distributed by 20th Century Fox Home Entertainment

> Fox Studio Baja, for example, has clear synergies with efforts to build on the
> tourism potential of the Baja California region, which is acknowledged in the
> development of the "Foxploration" studio tour. The Rosarito site was chosen prim-
> arily for its geographic location – close to the Southern California epicenter of
> English-language audiovisual production – but also perhaps to take best advantage
> of incentives and advantages to locate in Mexico under North American trade rules.
> (2005: 26)

Still, not all was successful in the field of labor relations within Fox Studio Baja
during the filming of *Titanic*. For example, the shooting schedule ballooned from
138 days to 160 and crew members complained about long hours and difficult
working conditions. This was punctuated by a food-poisoning incident with PCP-
laced chowder that sent cast and crew members (including Cameron) to hospital
(Graham, 1997: N1). Union leaders in Los Angeles labeled the Fox studio production nothing more than a "maquiladora" and lamented that "in exchange
for NAFTA [North American Free Trade Agreement]-sanctioned subsidies from
Canada and elsewhere, the studios have turned their backs on their own community and have engaged in the wholesale destruction of the Hollywood jobs base" (Bacon,
1999).

The Argentine Film Industry from the Late 1990s to the Present

Argentina's film industry, which had very low production figures in the early 1990s, saw a revival in production after the passage of the 1994 Ley de Cine 24.377 (Film Law 24.377) which entitled the Instituto Nacional de Cine y Artes Audiovisuales (National Institute of Film and Audiovisual Arts; INCAA) to additional sources of film production funding (table 18.2). Despite the 2001 economic crisis, the biggest to beset Argentina in decades (it was the largest default on an IMF loan in world history), the film industry did not falter. This was in part due to the creativity of newer directors (many of them recent graduates of film schools), who made films on a shoestring which have gained worldwide festival accolades (see Falicov, 2003b). Fifty-one films were produced in 2004, the highest number in decades. Over the second weekend of October 2005, three national films – a police comedy, *Tiempo de valientes* (*On Probation*; Damian Szifron, 2005, Argentina), a Falkland Islands award-winning drama, *Iluminados por el fuego* (*Blessed by Fire*; Tristan Bauer, 2005, Argentina), and the old-age romantic comedy *Elsa and Fred* (Marcos Carnevale, 2005, Argentina) – took nearly 45 percent of the 370,000 total admissions, up from an average 10–15 percent share of the market for the same time period the previous year (Newbery, 2005).

Argentina's film output ranges from low-budget independent films to glossier, more commercial films with budgets of $1.5 million to $2 million. These more mainstream films are produced by industrial auteurs who work with multinationally owned production companies such as Pol-Ka and Patagonik. Both these companies are partially owned by Buena Vista International, the distribution arm of Disney (Patagonik also receives investment funds from Telefónica Media, a massive Spanish telecom company). Pol-Ka produced a popular action film *Comodines* (*Cops*; Jorge Nisco, 1997, Argentina), that was billed as "the first Hollywood blockbuster spoken in Spanish" (*Clarín*, 1997). It utilized television stars, special effects,

TABLE 18.2   Number of Argentine films released, 1997–2004

Production year	Films
1997	28
1998	36
1999	38
2000	45
2001	45
2002	37
2003	46
2004	51

Source: Getino, 2005.

product placement, and the buddy movie genre, and drew record numbers of film-goers. It irked some to know that this film received state subsidies despite being produced by a production company owned by a multimedia conglomerate (see Falicov, 2003a). Buena Vista International/Disney has actively co-produced and distributed films which have commercial potential, such as famed director Marcelo Piñeyro's *Kamchatka* (2002, Argentina/Spain), and the comedy *Cohen vs. Rosi* (Daniel Barone, 1998, Argentina). Two animated films for children were highly successful, and both were distributed by a Hollywood "major": *Patoruzito* (José Luis Massa, 2004, Argentina) was distributed by Buena Vista International, and Columbia distributed *Manuelita* (Manuel Garcia Ferré, 1999, Argentina).

Argentina has witnessed worldwide acclaim with films such as *Nueve reinas* (*Nine Queens*; Fabián Bielinsky, 2000, Argentina) and *El hijo de la novia* (*Son of the Bride*; Juan José Campanella, 2001, Argentina), both which were picked up for US distribution by Sony Pictures Classics. Dylan Leiner, senior vice-president of acquisitions and productions, stated that *Nueve reinas* appealed to Sony since it broke the stereotype of traditional Latin American cinema. "It was very smart and fast-paced. The broader comedies in Latin America don't usually work as well because they feature local television stars or address regional issues. We look for stories that have universal appeal and are easy to understand" (O'Brien and Ibars, 2004: 42). *Nueve reinas* was remade by Hollywood as the mediocre *Criminal* (2004, USA), directed by Gregory Jacobs for Warner Independent Pictures.

SOS (Save our Screens): Enacting the Screen Quota in Argentina

In June 2004, due in part to the left-leaning atmosphere created by current President Kirchner's administration, the INCAA spearheaded the passage of new screen quota legislation to counter Hollywood's hegemony. It stated that movie theaters were obligated to show one national film per screen per quarter: so, for example, a 16-screen multiplex must screen 64 Argentine films per year. Another law called the "continuity average" obligated film exhibitors to continue screening national films if these domestic productions garnered audience attendance of between 6 and 25 percent per theater in a given week. This act ensured that exhibitors could not arbitrarily drop national films mid-week nor change screening times mid-week (Newbery, 2004). By and large Argentine film producers do not have the funds to market their films. A Hollywood blockbuster relies on high-priced "blitz" campaigns for an opening weekend for a film, but an Argentine film usually gains momentum through word of mouth.

Conclusion

Since their inception, both Mexico and Argentina's film industries have struggled to create space for themselves in the shadow of Hollywood. In its current configuration, Mexico has continued to support filmmaking through IMCINE funds, but it has also seen a proportion of films made purely through the private sector – the approach which most closely resembles Hollywood. Moreover, with the emergence of transnational film directors such as González Iñárritu, del Toro, and Cuarón, the transition to private sources of funding has been a system that directors themselves find more efficient and less politically fraught.

Argentina's film industry model has differed from Mexico's in that the state has been relatively successful at distributing grants to both small producers/directors and production houses owned by multi-media conglomerates (including Disney and other transnational companies). Argentina has created film legislation which has strengthened the nation's film development fund, and more recently it passed a screen quota which seems to be functioning well at the time of writing. Rather than the US system, Argentina's film industry is modeled more closely on European film production. However, both Argentina and Mexico are gaining access to markets and funds through new collaborations with MPA member companies. The Hollywood studios have proven thus far to be friendly to both countries' film industries, but it remains to be seen what kind of effect this may have in the long run (for example, one can imagine the effects on the screen quota if eventually the majority of funding comes from the majors). Regardless of these changes, Hollywood, as in the past, continues to maintain a strong foothold in Latin America.

ACKNOWLEDGMENTS

Many thanks to Manuel Pérez Tejada for his invaluable research assistance and feedback on the Mexico portion of this chapter. Heartfelt thanks to Paul McDonald and Stephen Steigman for their astute editorial recommendations and feedback.

REFERENCES

Armes, R. (1987) *Third World Filmmaking and the West*. Berkeley: University of California Press.

Bacon, D. (1999) "Is Free Trade Making Hollywood a Rustbelt?," online at <http://dbacon.igc.org/PJust/22Hollywood.htm> (accessed January 12, 2006).

Brooks, X. (2002) "First Steps in Latin," *The Guardian*, July 19, online at <http://www.guardian.co.uk/arts/fridayreview/story/0,12102,757643,00.html> (accessed January 22, 2006).

Cazares, G. (2006a) "Indicadores por Sector de la Industria Cinematográfica en México, 2000–2004," email from IMCINE's promotion department via email to Manuel Pérez Tejada, January 31.

Cazares, G. (2006b) "Peliculas Mexicanas con mayor asistencia 1999–2004," email from IMCINE's promotion department via email to Manuel Pérez Tejada, January 31.

Clarín (1997) Advertisement for *Comodines*, June 24, p. E4.

De la Fuente, A. M. (2004) "Rebate Boosts Production," *Variety*, November 22–8, p. 18.

Falicov, T. L. (2003a) "Television for the Big Screen: How *Comodines* Became Argentina's First Blockbuster Phenomenon," in J. Stringer (ed.), *Movie Blockbusters.* London: Routledge, pp. 242–54.

Falicov, T. L. (2003b) "Los Hijos de Menem: The New Independent Argentine Cinema, 1995–1999," *Framework*, 44(1), pp. 49–63.

Falicov, T. L. (2007) *The Cinematic Tango: Contemporary Argentine Film.* London: Wallflower Press.

Fein, S. (2000) "Transcultured Anticommunism: Cold War Hollywood in Postwar Mexico," in C. Noriega (ed.), *Visible Nations: Latin American Cinema and Video.* Minneapolis: University of Minnesota Press, pp. 82–114.

Getino, O. (2005) *Cine argentino: Entre lo posible y lo deseable*, 2nd edn. Buenos Aires: Ediciones CICCUS.

Goldsmith, B., and T. O'Regan (2005) *The Film Studio.* New York: Rowan & Littlefield.

Graham, R. (1997) "The Man who Kept Titanic Afloat: James Cameron Steered $200 Million into his Spectacle," *The Boston Globe*, December 14, p. N1.

Hawley, C. (2004) "Hollywood Casts Mexico in Starring Role," *The Arizona Republic*, October 4, online at <www.chateaumanzanillo.com/movies_mexico.html> (accessed December 16, 2005).

Johnson, R. (2005) "TV Globo, the MPA, and Contemporary Brazilian Cinema," in L. Shaw and S. Dennison (eds.), *Latin American Cinema: Essays on Modernity, Gender, and National Identity.* Jefferson, NC: McFarland Press, pp. 11–38.

Klein, C. (2004) "The Hollowing-Out of Hollywood," *YaleGlobal*, April 30, online at <http://yaleglobal.yale.edu/display.article?id=3794> (accessed January 28, 2006).

Koehne, M. A. (1999) "*Iguana* Set Resurrected as a Restaurant," *The Milwaukee Journal Sentinel*, February 28, online at <http://www.findarticles.com/p/articles/mi_qn4196/is_19990228/ai_n10487779> (accessed January 28, 2006).

Masters, K. (1997) "Trying to Stay Afloat: After Endless Crises, Delays and Cost Overruns, the $200 Million *Titanic* Finally Opens This Month. Was All the Misery Worth It?" *Time*, December 8, p. 86.

Morales, E. (2001) "Pulp Nonfiction: *Amores Perros* Leads a Mexican Revival," *Village Voice*, April 3, p. 126.

MPA (2003) "Motion Picture Association: Submission to the Services Workshop," VIII Americas Business Forum, November 17–21, online at <www.sice.oas.org/FTAA/miami/ABF/papers/pMtPicAs_e.asp> (accessed January 12, 2006).

MPAA (2005) "MPA/A Head Glickman Goes to México: Meets with President Fox," March 9, online at <http://www.mpaa.org/press_releases/2005_03_09a.pdf> (accessed January 12, 2006).

Newbery, C. (2004) "Quotas Give Screen Time to Local Pix," *Variety*, July 12, p. 12.

Newbery, C. (2005) "Local Fare Clicks with Argentines," *Variety*, October 10, p. 8.

O'Boyle, M. (2005) "Mexico Looks for a Hit: Local Industry Falters Despite H'wood Help," *Variety*, September 18, online at <www.variety.com> (accessed January 12, 2006).

O'Brien, M., and M. Ibars (2004) "Fame, Glamour, Cash," *Latin Finance*, 156 (April/May), pp. 42–4.

Plasencia, W. (2004) "Is He Acting or Lying?" *Hispanic Magazine.com*, January/February, online at <www.hispaniconline.com/magazine/2004/jan_feb/Features/luna.html> (accessed December 12, 2005).

Puig, C. (2002) "Mexico Still Beckons to these Expat Directors," *USA Today*, April 11, p. 14D.

Schnitman, J. A. (1984) *Film Industries in Latin America: Dependency and Development*. Norwood, NJ: Ablex.

Smith, P. J. (2003) "Transatlantic Traffic in Recent Mexican Films," *Journal of Latin American Cultural Studies*, 12(2), pp. 389–400.

Tegel, S. (2002) "Cue the Governor's Helicopter: Mexico's Film-Hungry States Compete for Tinsel Town Bucks," *Latin Trade*, online at <www.latintrade.com> (accessed December 16, 2005).

Tierney, D. (2003) "Gender Relations and Mexican Cultural Nationalism in Emilio Fernández's *Enamorada/Woman in Love*," *Quarterly Review of Film and Video*, 20(3), pp. 225–36.

Toumarkine, D. (2001) "2001 Showeast Preview: A Challenging Market," *Film Journal International*, November, pp. 140–1.

Ugalde, V. (2004) "Deformaciones," *Etcetera*, November, online at <http://etcetera.com.mx/pag157ne49.asp> (accessed January 29, 2006).

Usabel, G. S. de. (1982) *The High Noon of American Films in Latin America*. Ann Arbor: University of Michigan Press.

Vargas, J. C. (2003) "Mexican Post-Industrial Cinema (1990–2002)," *El ojo que piensa* [The Thinking Eye], online at <http://www.elojoquepiensa.udg.mx/ingles/revis_03/secciones/codex/artic_02.html> (accessed August 3, 2005).

Wasko, J. (2003) *How Hollywood Works*. London: Sage Publications.

CHAPTER 19

EAST ASIA: FOR BETTER OR WORSE

JOHN A. LENT

For nearly its entire history, Asian film has felt the influence of Hollywood, certainly in terms of what was viewed, and often in terms of what was made in Asia. At times, Hollywood's presence was welcomed; at other times, it was fought off or accepted grudgingly.

Nowhere was this love–hate relationship more apparent than in China, one of Hollywood's first and richest foreign markets. By the 1930s, when the average percentage of United States films on the international market was 75 percent, it was 85 to 90 percent in China. For example, of 367 foreign films imported by China in 1936, 328 came from Hollywood, and in the 1930s and 1940s, more than 4,000 American films flooded into China (Ye, 2005).

The US and China already had a joint film venture in 1926 when the American-Oriental Picture Co. was established. The first Chinese movie made with US capital, *Shattered Jade Fated To Be Reunited*, appeared shortly after. Hollywood influences seeped into Chinese films with so many American films available and the existence of joint business operations. In the earliest days of silent films, Chinese directors already were keenly observant of the Hollywood style and techniques, having adopted analytical editing, soft focus, backlighting, and masking from the Americans (Ye, 2005).

Tolerance of US culture (including cinema) ended after the Korean War broke out in 1950; thus, Chinese filmmakers were denied access to Hollywood films produced in the 1950s and 1960s. American films returned when the fourth generation of directors began working in the late 1970s, but it was the fifth generation that thoroughly studied Hollywood cinema. In a few years, however, fifth-generation directors moved away from the Hollywood influence as they were exposed to films from Europe and Japan, began to win awards at international festivals, and became increasingly upset with American arrogance that the fifth generation owed its success to Hollywood. A new term, *haolaiwu zhuyi* (Hollywoodism), was coined to describe Chinese directors' disapproval of American films. It was another of the many changes in the Chinese response to Hollywood (Ye, 2005: 140, 142, 144).

Already in the 1930s, trade disputes flared up between Chinese and Hollywood film companies, with the locals asking Hollywood studios to share in paying taxes, censorship fees, etc. The Americans refused, leading to the Guangzhou exhibitors association boycotting Paramount pictures. After World War II Hollywood "even intervened in contracted exhibitors' operations and limited the release opportunities of Chinese films in these theaters" (Wei, 2002: 134).

Hollywood in Asia: For Better or For Worse

Hollywood, in conjunction with the US government, early on recognized the worth of the huge Asian market for its films and for the consumption of everything "American" that those films depicted. In 1916 Universal Studios opened distribution branches in Japan, India, and Singapore, and by 1928 all seven major film companies had branches in Japan. In Taiwan and Korea, Japanese films held sway because of that country's occupation, but Hollywood films were shown, and by the late 1930s, local and Japanese distribution companies jointly had franchises to distribute them. Actually, US movies began to appear in Taiwan in 1923, and despite strict Japanese control, represented 28 percent of the total five years later.

A number of factors have turned Hollywood's eyes to Asia again in recent years, the most important of which being the fact that Asian governments, banks, and other financial entities have pumped money into film's advancement. In 2006, the South Korean government announced it would channel a fresh $80 million yearly into film, cash raised from a 5 percent levy on cinema tickets. This is in addition to the $50 million the government already contributes to support the Korean Film Council, and other major financial commitments made since 1994–5, when it was acknowledged that film had export potential. Also, the Korean private sector, attracted by the strong local box office and spin-off products sales, bought into the film industry – KTH (part of Korean Telecom) purchased a controlling interest in leading film company Sidus FNH, 22 percent of iHQ.

Similarly, film has become a respectable and lucrative business in other Asian countries. Bank financing of film has been rare in Asia because of mutual distrust; this resulted in most pictures using a combination of equity, "angel" funding, presales, or barter, with some government cash. In less than five years, however, the situation has changed, with Hong Kong's venerable Standard Chartered opening itself to loans for filmmaking, Thailand's investment bank Mullis Capital establishing a film financing arm, and two of the largest US-based completion bond firms hoping to expand in Asia.

Investment in film is popular in India now, as discussed in chapter 20, and in Singapore, film is a large part of the Media Development Authority's ten-year blueprint, Media21, which aims to have the media contribute 3 percent of the country's GNP by 2015. Also catching Hollywood's attention recently has been the sharp increase in regional film exchange. Japanese film and animation have become very popular in East and Southeast Asia, paving the way for a number of pan-Asian ventures. The South Korean, Hong Kong, and Taiwan film industries have definitely been bolstered since the 1990s by regionalization strategies in production and distribution (Shim, 2005). In particular, South Korean films have had a rebirth, accounting for 59 percent of the box office at home, and picking up 30 percent of total revenues from foreign sales. In 2005, South Korean film exports rose for the ninth consecutive year, with 80.3 percent of total exports concentrated in Asia, especially Japan. The regionalization was worrisome for Hollywood as it meant US film revenues were likely to be sliced. Already, the popularity of South Korean films in Japan has dipped into Hollywood's take from that market.

Asia as a Market for Hollywood Films

Hollywood has long cast a shadow over Asia, using bullying tactics engineered by the Motion Picture Association of America (MPAA), in conjunction with the US government, to crack the continent's huge film market. Pressure was applied in 1988, when the MPAA broke South Korea's film quota system – not without tremendous resistance – by threatening to cut trade in other areas if more US film playtime was not made available, and in the late 1990s, when the US dangled World Trade Organization (WTO) membership before China's eyes in order to open that country to Hollywood.

Again in 2006, the MPAA had its way as South Korea prepared to enter negotiations on a free trade agreement with the US. After years of withstanding American nagging, and at a time when Korean film was very successful, the Korean government agreed to cut its screen quota by half, reducing the number of days exhibitors must show local pictures from 146 to 73. The MPAA had long argued that the quota unfairly restricted access to the Korean market. Hollywood had suffered significant losses in Korea, where local picture production surged, Internet piracy reached one of the highest rates in the world, ravaging the DVD market, and popular Korean stars outshone those from the US.

Taiwan began to impose import quotas in 1954, but they never had a significant impact on US films, which continued to control box-office revenues and total screen time with fewer, but bigger-budget and longer pictures. In all matters, Hollywood retained advantages and remained tough in dealing with the Koumintang government. In 1983, in response to the local distributors' lobby, Taiwan reduced the annual import quota for US distributors from 85 to 50, and asked them to pay a special tax on imported films to support local production. The US balked and stopped supplying films for six months; at the same time, Hollywood appealed to the Office of the US Trade Representative. As a result, the 32-year-old quota system was abolished in 1986, and the market share of US films increased so that, by 1999, only 14 Taiwan films were shown in theaters (Wei, 2002).

In other Asian countries, Hollywood's dominance, coupled with the inroads made by new media, nearly decimated once thriving film industries. In their heyday, the

Philippines, Taiwan, and Hong Kong each churned out at least 150 features yearly; now the total for these three states hovers at about 100. Some headway has been made in recent years to revive these film cultures; for example, Taiwanese government subsidies helped the number of local films there to increase from 24 in 2004 to 40 a year later. Filmmakers in some Asian countries do not believe the quota system is the answer to the problem; instead, they are pushing for quality productions, a reduction in piracy, and better theaters.

As its box office in Europe drops, Hollywood is expected to push even harder to gain more playtime in Asia. Countries targeted are Taiwan, with its strong economy, stable political situation, and improved theaters; Malaysia, where multiplexes have grown and piracy has dwindled; Vietnam, where the number of screens is expected to triple by 2010; India, whose awareness of Hollywood has grown through development of suburban multiplexes, the internet, and cable television; South Korea, and China.

Despite the US push, China is not even in the top 25 countries in terms of revenues generated by Hollywood major studios. The yearly quota of foreign films allowed in China is 20 (16 or more of which are American), although through the bilateral agreement made with the US before China's admittance to the WTO, it will be extended to 50. However, the additional 30 films will be on a flat-rate, not a revenue-sharing, arrangement. On this basis, China Film Corporation would pay the foreign filmmaker $50,000 for all Chinese rights to the film (Lent, 2006). Because the quota system is riddled with "exceptions and uneven application," it is difficult for Hollywood to operate effectively in China. As one Hollywood executive complained, "It's not just deciphering the edicts which come down, but figuring out how widely they apply, to whom and for how long, which takes us a lot of time and energy" (Guider, 2005: 6). The China Film Corporation releases foreign films on the criteria of commercial viability, subject matter, and censorship, the latter being the least understood because of lack of published guidelines. Foreign films must also be available at the right time; they are blacked out in high summer and in December to give Chinese films free rein (Frater, 2006b: 8). Compounding Hollywood's difficulties in China is the high degree of piracy, despite crackdowns by SARFT (State Administration of Radio, Film, and Television).

Asia as Production Center for Hollywood Films

Just as automobiles, DVDs, and the whole line of various conglomerates' products are made in Asia, so too are American films. Hollywood has a long history of Asian labor exploitation, particularly in animation. By the 1960s, US animation had begun to outsource the laborious stages of production to Japan, and then South Korea and Taiwan. From these countries, work has been subcontracted to Southeast Asia, southern China, and now India, as it follows the trail of inexpensive labor. Besides its low cost, Asian labor is sought also for its stability (strike-free), low setup costs, high skills, and the workers' strong work ethic and proficiency in English.

Hollywood's use of Asia as a production center operates on a number of levels: the outsourcing of the work itself, location shooting (runaway productions), and co-productions.

As I have said, much of the outsourcing has involved animation and, more recently, special effects. About 90 percent of all American, and high percentages of Canadian and European, animation is made in Asia, where production costs often are one-tenth of those in the US. Throughout the continent, there are huge animation studios whose major (in some cases, only) tasks are completing features and TV series conceptualized in the US – Akom, Dai Won, and Seoul Movie in South Korea; Wang Productions in Taiwan; Fil-Cartoons and pasi in the Philippines; Kantana in Thailand, etc. (see Lent, 1998). In some instances, these studios have converted to domestic animation, especially after Hollywood work orders declined because of a change in taste on the part of American audiences.

For decades India was on the sidelines of international film outsourcing, as discussed in chapter 20. But Hollywood outsources in India and in Southeast Asia now account for $300 million a year, and animation outsourcing in India is growing at 200 percent a year (Govil, 2005: 95).

A clever way of outsourcing increasingly used by Hollywood is the remaking of films already produced and released in Asia. What is outsourced in these instances are the jobs of assistant producers, scriptwriters, supporting crews, marketing teams, and directors. As one writer said:

> Sooner or later, the unions within the Hollywood system will come to realize the outsourcing nature of remaking. But, at least for now, the remaking is making Hollywood leaner, stronger, more efficient, more profitable, and more dominant than ever. This is an irreversible but well-disguised trend. The changed ethnicity serves well to disguise this trend: as much as the glamour of Hollywood star system makes people forget that cinema is a big industry, the Caucasian faces in the remakes cover up the significant contribution of East Asia as the provider of intensive labour required by the film industry. (Xu, 2005: 400)

Location shooting in Asia is favored by Hollywood because of the exoticism and variety of the continent, but especially for the relative inexpensiveness of the outsourcing of studio space, post-production facilities, technical talent, and location hire. It is a simple matter of economics: cheaper labor and weaker (or non-existent) unions (Donald, 2005: 141). For example, China has among the lowest location costs in the world, as does India, although the latter has one of the highest taxation rates (30 percent) for filming.

Hollywood is enticed to do location shooting in some parts of Asia because of the potential spillover to local economies through hiring space and talent and attracting tourists. Some South Korean municipalities forgo taxation of foreign studios, and Hong Kong charges US producers less for location shoots than it does its own filmmakers.

In the past, poor infrastructures to sustain shooting and large amounts of bureaucratic red tape steered Hollywood away from Asia, but some of these problems have been remedied with a growing focus on facilities and services and improved post-production capabilities. In India and Hong Kong, new studios and a $180 million film and post-production facility, respectively, are expected to attract foreign film location. Shanghai has been luring US and British film companies, showing off China's diverse locations, low costs, high production skills, and abundant film crews; however, China also offers much red tape and some rules that interfere with production, such as no filming from helicopters for military reasons. Thailand is an old location site known for its good local talent and lack of bureaucratic interference (Coonan, 2006: C1).

Co-producing with Asian studios and companies has also increased in popularity in Hollywood. One reason is obvious; some Asian film industries (e.g. South Korea) are flush with cash, supported by government subsidies and/or large corporation investments. A second attraction of co-production is that it taps into the creativity of some Asian directors and scriptwriters, who have offered new fare and, in some cases, have reinvented genres. Thirdly, by entering co-production ventures with Asian filmmakers, Hollywood envisions more active involvement in making local-language movies. Warner Bros. has developed, invested in, produced, distributed, and marketed Chinese-language features, animation, and telefilms. Conversely, Korean firms are increasing their number of locally made English-language films, seeking long-term alliances with Hollywood to distribute Korean movies.

Co-producing in China has a number of important benefits for Hollywood, especially as a way to get around the 20-foreign-film limitation put on imports. Also, co-productions get faster distribution clearance from the Film Bureau and have advantages for Chinese filmmakers, such as the possibility of shooting 6–7 days a week and obtaining ready cash from movie conglomerates such as the Huayi Brothers. China is not a complete newcomer to co-productions, having been involved in 247 such ventures between 1990 and 1998, with Taiwan, the US, Hong Kong, and Europe.

After 2000 some restrictions on foreign investment in content production started to be removed, and in 2003 SARFT approved 42 Chinese–foreign joint projects to shoot in China that year. Hollywood has taken full advantage of any leeway the Chinese have given, simultaneously insisting that even more concessions be granted. For example, in late 2004 China began allowing foreign capital in film–TV producing and distributing joint ventures up to 49 percent ownership; Warner Bros., which has the largest investment in Chinese theaters, thought this arrangement was unfair, demanding majority control. Warner entered China's film market in early 2002, and three years later, with four partners, operated 67 screens at eight sites. Warner has also teamed with Beijing's Tom Online to distribute Warner Bros. films on the internet and to mobile phone users; with China Film and the privately owned Hengdian Group to co-produce mostly Chinese-language movies in China; and, earlier, with the Chinese real-estate company Wanda Group, and Guangzhou Jinyi Film and Television Investment Co. to create a total of 40 multiplexes (Lent, 2006: xiv). In April 2006, Warner Bros. announced plans to open 200 studio shops in China to whet the growing consumer appetites of Chinese suburbanites. Disney already has 2,600 Chinese "Disney Corners" (Frater, 2006a).

FIGURE 19.1 With a North American box office gross of over $11 million *Shi mian mai fu* (*House of Flying Daggers*) (2004) has contributed to raising awareness of East Asian films amongst American audiences. Produced by William Kong and Zhang Yimou; distributed by Sony Pictures Classics; directed by Zhang Yimou

The above-mentioned co-productions and remakes have brought a slight improvement in Americans' awareness of Asian film. These and other transnational interactions have provided Hollywood with opportunities to collaborate with Asian films such as *Ying xiong* (*Hero*; 2002, Hong Kong/China) or *Shi mian mai fu* (*House of Flying Daggers*; 2004, China/Hong Kong) and work with Asian directors and stars such as Zhang Yimou, Chen Kaige, John Woo, Ang Lee, Gong Li, Michelle Yeoh, Jackie Chan, Zhang Ziyi, and Vivian Wu. As Asian styles have continued to be popular abroad, Hollywood has increasingly collaborated with Asian filmmakers; in fact, one of the reasons given for the poor state of Hong Kong national film is the talent drain to Hollywood. Previously, the route of popularity was unidirectional: whatever was popular in North America found audiences in Asia. Now, East Asian successes, already well tested in their home markets, are likely to do well in the US in remade versions, if the ethnicity is changed.

Mainly responsible for the remake trend is Roy Lee with *The Ring* (Gore Verbinski, 2002, US) and *The Grudge* (Takashi Shimizu, 2004, US), both originally Japanese films. A series of US remakes of Japanese and Hong Kong movies followed, including *Shall We Dance* (Peter Chelsom, 2004, US/Canada), *Dark Water* (Walter Salles, 2005, US/Japan), *The Departed* (Martin Scorsese, 2006, US/Hong Kong), and others. Remakes are good for Hollywood, as they provide new stories and inexpensive outsourcing possibilities; East Asian filmmakers benefit in that the money they get from the remakes offsets their original production costs (Xu, 2005).

Another twist to the remake phenomenon involves Hollywood studios redoing their own films for Asian audiences. Walt Disney Pictures plans to shoot a live-action, martial arts remake of *Snow White and the Seven Dwarfs* (David Hand, 1937, US) in China, replacing the dwarfs with Shaolin monks. Other US films with a Chinese component are expected.

Despite the deep inroads Hollywood has made into China's film world, SARFT seems to hold its ground, with little intent of liberalizing its market simply to please foreign companies. This may change as the fast-growing, Western-crazed middle class demands more Hollywood films and their assorted paraphernalia. In other parts of Asia not as strong politically and economically as China, there has already been a caving in to the bully tactics of Hollywood and its lobbying arm, the MPAA.

REFERENCES

Coonan, C. (2006) "The Buddy System," *Variety*, January 30, p. C1.

Donald, S. H. (2005) "*The Ice Storm*: Ang Lee, Cosmopolitanism, and the Global Audience," in G. Elmer and M. Gasher (eds.), *Contracting Out Hollywood: Runaway Productions and Foreign Location Shooting*. Lanham, MD: Rowman & Littlefield, pp. 140–55.

Frater, P. (2006a) "Going Over the Wall," *Variety*, April 13, pp. 5, 86.

Frater, P (2006b) "Quota Fix Leaves H'wood Hanging," *Variety*, January 2, p. 8.

Govil, N. (2005) "Hollywood's Effects, Bollywood FX," in G. Elmer and M. Gasher (eds.), *Contracting Out Hollywood: Runaway Productions and Foreign Location Shooting*. Lanham, MD: Rowman & Littlefield, pp. 92–114.

Guider, E. (2005) "Voiceover," *Variety*, July 25, p. 6.

Lent, J. A. (1998) "The Animation Industry and its Offshore Factories," in Gerald Sussman and John A. Lent (eds.), *Global Productions: Labor in the Making of the "Information Society."* Cresskill, NJ: Hampton Press, pp. 239–54.

Lent, J. A. (2006) "Introduction," in H. Kong and J. A. Lent (eds.), *One Hundred Years of Chinese Cinema: A Generational Dialogue*. Norwalk, CT: EastBridge, pp. xiii–xxiv.

Shim, D. (2005) "Globalization and Cinema Regionalization in East Asia," *Korea Journal*, Winter, pp. 233–60.

Wei, T. (2002) "Global Processes, National Responses: Chinese Film Cultures in Transition." Ph.D. dissertation, Loughborough University, Loughborough, UK.

Xu, G. (2005) "Remaking East Asia, Outsourcing Hollywood," in *The Centennial Celebration of Chinese Cinema and the 2005 Annual Conference of Asian Cinema Studies Society Proceedings*. Beijing: Beijing University, Shanghai University, ACSS, pp. 397–402.

Ye, T. (2005) "Hollywood and the Chinese Other," in *The Centennial Celebration of Chinese Cinema and the 2005 Annual Conference of Asian Cinema Studies Society Proceedings*. Beijing: Beijing University, Shanghai University, ACSS, pp. 134–45.

CHAPTER 20

INDIA: HOLLYWOOD'S DOMINATION, EXTINCTION, AND RE-ANIMATION (WITH THANKS TO *JURASSIC PARK*)

NITIN GOVIL

Hollywood undertook this cultural insemination of 400 million people with their most powerful weapon in the world – the movies. Pictures after pictures were sent to India during the two wars – pictures that taught us to dance rhumbas and sambas; pictures that taught us to coo and woo; pictures that taught us to moon and croon; pictures that taught us to kill and steal; pictures that taught us to utter "Hi" and "Gee"; pictures that taught us devilry and divorce and pictures that took us to jinks and drinks.

Baburao Patel, editor and publisher of *Filmindia*, "The Rape of Our Heritage," 1951 (quoted in Wilkerson, 1952)

I really feel there is a marriage to be made between Hollywood and Bollywood. I am meeting with these people to make artistic connections and come up with a new thing.

Actor Will Smith, presiding over the launch of India's third Hollywood-themed cable TV channel (*MX*, 2006)

Baburao Patel and Will Smith suggest a common frame of reference for the sexual politics of transculturation under colonial and neoliberal regimes, but their statements map a shift in the historical deployment of Hollywood as metaphor, from the violence of imperial conquest to the connubial bliss of media synergy. This history is complicated by the twists and turns in Hollywood's passage from abjection to affection: even in 1952, director Frank Capra claimed that "between the largest free nations, one the youngest, the other the oldest, there is a kinship of the spirit. A kinship that can mean only good for all mankind" (*Variety*, 1952). If this Hollywood kinship was neither fully realized nor embraced by the Indian film industries, it nevertheless manifested itself in certain forms of family resemblance which have become more distinctive since the mid-1990s as Hollywood's presence in the South Asian commodity industries has grown.

This growth, however, is relative. For example, in 1928 Paramount noted that India's 0.6 percent share of Hollywood's total foreign income was just a bit higher than "other small places in the world" (Vasey, 1997: 85). Almost 80 years later, Hollywood can muster only 5 percent of the domestic market in India, despite the US Motion Picture Association's (MPA) confidence that Hollywood's Indian box office can grow by 10–15 percent per year. India may be the fourth largest market for Hollywood in Asia (after Japan, Taiwan, and South Korea), yet a film like *Hulk* (Ang Lee, 2003, US) could achieve one of Universal's highest opening weekends with the equivalent of a $214,000 gross from 81 Indian theaters; when *X2: X-men United* (Bryan Singer, 2003, US) took $352,000 on 132 screens during its opening weekend, it accounted for 95 percent of Hollywood's market share (Kay, 2003a, 2003b; Lall, 2005). Of course, ticket returns tell us only part of the story because Indian box-office figures are underreported in order to avoid entertainment and income taxes. A more complete measure of Hollywood's market impact must take into account the large- and small-scale tactics of media piracy in an environment where the boundaries between illegal and legal practices are "porous" at best (Liang, 2005). In addition, Hollywood functions "as a crucial marker of film form" and "the locus of both envy and resentment" in setting the Indian film industries' standards for technical and promotional sophistication (Chakravarty, 1993: 15; Vasudevan, 2000: 123).

The history of Hollywood in India cuts across three overlapping trajectories of consolidation, competition, and collaboration. In the silent and early sound period, American cinema reached a compromise with British colonial cinema to emerge as the dominant foreign player in the subcontinent. However, beginning in the mid-1930s, Hollywood's market share rapidly eroded as regional film industries in the linguistically diverse Indian subcontinent began to adopt and standardize sound technology; the networks of interchange established between these regional language industries helped nurture a commercial cinema – subsumed under the majoritarian category of Indian "national cinema" – that is actually an assemblage of vernacular forms. The collapse of established local distributors of Hollywood film, the consolidation of regional film studios, and a clear preference for local and Hindi-language cinema, coupled with growing protectionist measures limiting film imports after Indian independence in 1947, seemed to seal Hollywood's fate in India. The 1950s saw the beginning of decades of dwindling distribution and tense negotiations between the Indian government and the Motion Picture Export Association (MPEA) the international arm of the MPAA. India's self-proclaimed investment in non-alignment geopolitics and development through import-substitution industrialization, particularly in the 1970s, further restricted Hollywood distribution in India. With the Indian fiscal and political crises of the late 1980s, Hollywood import restrictions were relaxed and a more collaborative relationship with Indian cinema was encouraged. Hollywood's future in the subcontinent is tied to the management of these synergies, particularly in its support of Indian media globalization.

Consolidation and Competition: A Pre-*Jurassic* History

Early American film in the Indian subcontinent was distributed through London-based agencies accustomed to circulating secondhand prints in British colonial territories, but the French company Pathé was the first major foreign player in the Indian market, establishing a direct sales film office in Calcutta in 1907. India as a share of world US film exports doubled to 4 percent through the mid-teens and Hollywood took advantage of World War I European film shortages and stock rationing to consolidate its hold in the area (Thompson, 1985). Universal was the first Hollywood studio to establish an agency in India in 1916 and, by the mid-1920s, was distributing over 150 films. Although Indian film production had risen to 100 films per year, over 85 percent of exhibited films were foreign, the vast majority from Hollywood (Singh, n.d.). Anti-Hollywood censorship quickly emerged as a common ground for comprador guardians of morality and colonial authorities concerned with protecting British film imports in India. Throughout the 1920s and early 1930s, British authorities in India criticized Hollywood films as potential sources of nationalist unruliness; at the same time, the primordialist idea that the nefarious displays of Hollywood film upset the traditional sexual and social foundations of "local culture" was also employed to great effect by advocates of Indian nativism. However, as the advent of sound technology and tightening censorship by fascist European governments threatened to shrink US film exports, Hollywood became more sensitive to the needs of its largest export market and encouraged the production of "empire" films that celebrated British colonial conquest (see Jaikumar, 2006). This genre was capped by the release of *Gunga Din* (George Stevens, 1939, US), whose allusions to Gandhian nationalism spurred Indian officials to call for a national boycott of American film. Still, until the late 1930s and early 1940s, India remained the most lucrative market for Hollywood in South and East Asia and the only market in the region besides the Philippines where an American film could earn four-digit theatrical returns.

The Indian market was one of the few that remained open during World War II; however, as annual Indian sound film production increased to 180 films by the early 1940s, America's market share fell from 80 percent a decade before to 45 percent. By the end of the war, American films earned only 15 percent of India's total box-office revenues (Glancy, 1999), even though there were over a hundred theaters nationwide exclusively dedicated to screening foreign films. Furthermore, a gradual degradation of political relations between India and the US tightened Hollywood's export business during the 1950s. The Central Board of Censors routinely banned films that violated the norms of non-alignment, such as *Cease Fire!* (Owen Crump, 1953, US), which was considered anti-communist, and *The African Queen* (John Huston, 1951, US), for failing "to show the people of Africa in proper perspective" (quoted in *Hollywood Reporter*, 1956). Censorship restrictions, combined with a precipitous decline in Hollywood's market share in India (down to 3 percent by the mid-1950s), inaugurated a period of rising import duties and battles with centralized canalization agencies. Expired trade pacts between the

MPEA and the Indian government lead to multi-year Hollywood embargoes. While the Indian government insisted that the MPEA had reneged on its promise to promote Indian cinema in America, Hollywood's foreign cartel claimed that such promotion would violate US antitrust law.

Despite these tensions, costume and historical spectaculars like *The Ten Commandments* (Cecil B. DeMille, 1956, US) and *Ben-Hur* (William Wyler, 1959, US) were strong draws in India in the 1950s. While there had been some experiments in dubbing Hollywood film, as in the case of *Bambi* (David Hand, 1942, US), American films were almost exclusively screened in English. With the anti-English movements in the north, the adoption of English as an "additional state language" in the southern Indian states helped raise Hollywood's regional revenue to almost twice the national average in the late 1960s. There was also the growing problem of "blocked funds". In 1963, for example, US distributors could claim $1 million in profits but only convert $400,000 of that amount in rupees to foreign exchange, leading to an increasing stockpile of unrepatriable or "blocked" funds. Hollywood came up with innovative ways to spend the blocked funds, from exchanging the monies with British producers interested in location shooting in India to setting location shoots of their own for non-India productions – for example Columbia used blocked funds to film a huge crowd scene outside Bombay for *Close Encounters of the Third Kind* (Steven Spielberg, 1977, US). Under the terms of the MPEA's 1975 trade pact with India, the majors could repatriate 15 percent of their earnings in foreign exchange, up to a limit of $310,000. After covering operational overheads, Hollywood majors could fund US–Indian co-productions, provide interest-free loans to finance theater construction on a small scale, and direct the remainder to blocked funds. However, the use of blocked funds for Indian location shooting was hampered by a clearance system that required script, customs, and foreign equipment approval from a number of different agencies. Not surprisingly, many Hollywood producers simply avoided shooting in India, most notably Steven

FIGURE 20.1   The India sequence in *Close Encounters of the Third Kind* (1977). Produced by Julia Phillips and Michael Phillips; distributed by Columbia; directed by Steven Spielberg

Spielberg, who decided to shoot *Indiana Jones and the Temple of Doom* (1984, US) in Sri Lanka.

Collaboration in the 1990s and Beyond

Faced with a series of political and fiscal crises beginning in the late 1980s, the Indian government "liberalized" the Indian economy by privatizing national industries and encouraging foreign direct investment. In mid-1992, after removing film export tariffs, the government abolished film selection committees and canalization fees for film imports. While liberalization proponents insisted that ending administrative bottlenecks would encourage independent foreign film distribution, Hollywood was galvanized by an increase in repatriation limits to $6 million as well as the rationalization of censorship and other regulatory clearances that consolidated the position of the US majors in India (Pendakur, 1996).

Despite the fact that *Jurassic Park* (Steven Spielberg, 1993, US) had been widely available on pirated video since late 1993, in April 1994 United International Pictures released the film in India with an unprecedented 102 Hindi and 30 English prints (most imported films to that point had six to eight prints) to be released on 117 screens (popular Hollywood films were usually released on 30). *Jurassic Park* was the first Hollywood film to be dubbed into Hindi in a decade, and its $11,000 dubbing costs and $320,000 marketing budget helped generate 4 million admissions after an initial three-week run. Within five months, the film had grossed $5.8 million, compared to the $30,000 average performance of a Hollywood film and $140,000 for a bona fide hit. Soon after these figures were released, Warner Brothers International Theaters announced an agreement with the Maharashtra state government to build a dozen ten-screen multiplexes in key Indian cities at a total cost of $60 million. In a more comfortable regulatory and investment environment, a number of Hollywood companies began preliminary investments in the Indian film exhibition sector, including a United Artists Theaters joint venture to build two dozen multiplexes. Hollywood studios eventually switched their Asian multiplexing attention to China, allowing Australian firms like Village Roadshow to enter India, but *Jurassic Park*'s success greatly bolstered Hollywood's confidence in India. For example, Disney began distributing in India again in 1994 after a two-year hiatus, and a Disney subsidiary, Buena Vista Television International, began to supply programming to the government TV network Doordarshan.

In the mid-1990s, the American film industry made about as much money in India as it did in Israel (and less than it did in Poland). Still, Hollywood's commitment to Asia was clear in its bilateral negotiations with South Korea and China and with the opening of US trade with Vietnam, which was touted as the biggest market for US independent film after Japan and South Korea. Buoyed by the success of action films like *Speed* (Jan de Bont, 1994, US) and special effects vehicles like *Armageddon* (Michael Bay, 1998, US), collaborations between the Hollywood studios, transnational commodity industries, and Indian media firms proliferated in the areas of marketing, exhibition, television, and music.

FIGURE 20.2   When released in India, *Jurassic Park* (1993) became the first Hollywood film dubbed into Hindi for a decade. Produced by Kathleen Kennedy and Gerald R Molen; distributed by Universal; directed by Steven Spielberg

Piracy and Copy Culture

As these institutional affiliations were formalized and US media companies expressed interest in Indian investment, intellectual property emerged as a critical tool in maintaining the integrity of discrete exhibition windows for each horizontally integrated screen product. This presented a problem since, beginning in the late 1980s, Hollywood claimed that it had "lost" $10–15 million per year through video and print piracy in India; with the proliferation of over 40,000 non-legal cable television operators in the country by the mid-1990s, the MPA claimed losses closer to $40 million. In 2001 India was placed on the High Priority Watch List of the International Intellectual Property Alliance (IIPA), the trade coalition representing the major copyright industries in the US, citing $300 million in pirated US intellectual property, including $195 million in pirated business software, and $47 million in lost film revenue.

Hollywood has always had a difficult time responding to everyday copy culture in India. Not only do regional-language cinemas appropriate each other's scripts, formulas, and icons, but Hollywood has been used as a wellspring of themes and plots since the early history of Indian cinema. Given the chaotic state of film financing in India, with most producers interested in short-term investments, and the underdeveloped state of ancillary industries like videocassette and international sales, relying on the proven "pre-sold" success of a Hollywood film to provide script ideas helps manage predictability and risk. Indian remakes have been a sore spot for Hollywood, particularly as the Indian industry grew to become the most prolific in the world in the early 1970s. In the 1980s, the US majors claimed to have lost over $1 billion in royalties and remake fees in India.

FIGURE 20.3   *Deewangee* (2002), borrows from the plot of Paramount's *Primal Fear*
(1996). Produced by Nitin Manmohan; distributed by Spark; directed by Anees Bazmee

Many of the films that Hollywood claims are remakes actually draw on material
familiar to Indian audiences, so that the similarity of *Apoorva Sahodarargai* (S. R.
Singeetham, 1989, India) to *Twins* (Ivan Reitman, 1988, US) can be explained through
the well-worn Indian melodrama of brothers separated at birth. However, with the
wide availability of Hollywood on multiplex screens and cable television, Hindi
cinema remake culture in particular has blossomed in more recent years with films
like *Qayamat* (Harry Baweja, 2003, India) revisiting *The Rock* (Michael Bay, 1996,
US), *Dewaangee* (Anees Bazmee, 2002, India) mirroring *Primal Fear* (Gregory
Holbit, 1996, US), *Humraaz* (Abbas–Mastan, 2002, India) recommitting *A Perfect
Murder* (Andrew Davis, 1998, US), and *Dhund* (Shyam Ramsay, 2003, India)
recalling *I Know What You Did Last Summer* (Jim Gillespie, 1997, US). In some
cases, Indian remakes illustrate the palimpsestic nature of intertextuality; for
example, the producers of *Kaante* (Sanjay Gupta, 2002, India) remade *Reservoir Dogs*
(Quentin Tarantino, 1992, US) in Los Angeles with a crew partially drawn from
Tarantino's "original," itself a remake of *Lung fu fong wan* (*City on Fire*; Ringo Lam,
1987, Hong Kong). While Hollywood has supported the Indian film industries' efforts
to educate consumers on the "civic virtues" of copyright protection, it has been
unable to instantiate a normative distinction between inspiration and plagiarism
in a country where non-legality is not simply "a performative or political stance,
but a functional one" (Sundaram, 2002: 128).

Hollywood, Localization, and the Small Screen

Commonly distributed through neighborhood pirate operators, cable television has
nevertheless opened up new opportunities for Hollywood. While Hollywood had
dubbed India "the market of the future," in 1992 the US majors were paid only

$70,000 a year for Indian television programming. However, with the government unblocking the rupee under new liberalization "reforms," program deals were struck in US dollars and the average price for a syndicated US television series went up from $800 an hour to $1,800 (da Cunha, 1994). By the mid-1990s, transnational media companies involved in Indian cable television found that regional-language programming was cheaper and invited friendlier relations with market control institutions. For example, in early 1994, Rupert Murdoch's STAR acquired Zee Television and then announced plans to launch a 24-hour Hindi channel, while Sony planned to set up Indian film and television production facilities to feed a new joint-venture satellite channel featuring films from the Columbia and TriStar film libraries.

HBO launched in India in September 2000, securing licensing agreements with Paramount, Universal, Warner Bros., and Sony, and distribution through Turner International. HBO then joined Sony Entertainment's bundle of services in 2003 before returning to a Zee–Turner collaboration in 2005. Zee Network launched Zee Movies in March 2000, acquiring over 700 titles from UK and US companies including Warner Brothers International Television and MGM. At the same time that American cable companies were able to leverage Hollywood films on their networks (often in dubbed versions), production of local language television clearly indicated new possibilities for collaboration. Sony received clearance to produce and distribute locally produced films in India in 1998, with Fox and Universal following suit. Nowadays, avenues for institutional and industrial collaboration include outsourcing Hollywood special effects and digital media work to Indian multimedia and graphics firms (Govil, 2005) as well as location shooting and film processing at Indian studios that meet "Western production standards." Shooting at Ramoji Film City in Hyderabad and Yash Raj Studios provides cost savings of 40–60 percent for Hollywood producers and, with the rationalization of script clearance regimes, approvals for location shooting can now be made in three weeks.

How to Avoid Becoming a Dinosaur

Hollywood's market share in India peaked at over 9 percent in 2002; by 2005 it had fallen to its usual 4–5 percent market share as commercial Indian cinemas continued to release crossovers film and experiment with niche and genre cinema after years of bloated budgets, star salaries, and half-empty theatrical premieres. The changing economies of scale in the domestic Indian film industries, alongside the emerging priority of global distribution, suggests that Hollywood's future in India is tied to its role in facilitating the transnational movements of Indian audiovisual media. For example, in 2004, 20th Century Fox became the first Hollywood studio to pick up an Indian film, *The Rising: Ballad of Mangal Pandey* (Ketan Mehta, 2005, India), for wide international release. In a clear indication of these priorities, the following year, Fox actually closed local theatrical operations in India, distributing through Warner instead.

With Indian cinema as the driving force of South Asian popular culture, it is unlikely that Hollywood will be able to increase its Indian box-office revenue beyond a certain threshold. Instead, Hollywood has moved towards an ongoing involvement in the Indian media industries, a transformation that tracks the historical shift from Hollywood as a studio system to "Hollywood" as a strategic singularity in an otherwise thoroughly dispersed set of financing and distribution practices. Hollywood works to facilitate collaboration at all levels, particularly in the field of corporatization and technology, where the American media industries still offer a sense of aspirational possibility for the Indian film industries. That Hollywood has become a signifier of innovation within Indian media, even as it has failed to make significant inroads at the Indian box office, underscores the complex role of influence, exchange, and interoperability in the global media industries today.

REFERENCES

Chakravarty, S. (1993) *National Identity in Indian Popular Cinema, 1947–1987*. Austin: Texas University Press.

da Cunha, U. (1994) "Asia TV Sales: Uphill for US Firms," *Variety*, February 20, p. 35.

Glancy, H. M. (1999) *When Hollywood Loved Britain: The Hollywood "British" Film, 1939–45*. Manchester: Manchester University Press.

Govil, N. (2005) "Hollywood's Effects, Bollywood FX," in G. Elmer and M. Gasher (eds.), *Contracting Out Hollywood: Runaway Productions and Foreign Location Shooting*. Lanham, MD: Rowman & Littlefield, pp. 92–114.

Hollywood Reporter (1956) "India's Ban on African Pictures," May 28, p. 1.

Jaikumar, P. (2006) *Cinema at the End of Empire: A Politics of Transition in Britain and India*. Durham, NC: Duke University Press.

Kay, J. (2003a) "*Hulk* Bulks Up in India," online at <http://www.comics2film.com/ProjectFrame.php?f_id=16&f_page=6> (accessed December 8, 2005).

Kay, J. (2003b) "*X2* Takes Another $5.5m for Fox," *Screen International*, June 3, p. 1.

Lall, B. (2005) "UIP Reorganizes Indian Distribution," *Screen International*, June 24, p. 3.

Liang, L. (2005) "Porous Legalities and Avenues of Participation," in M. Narula, S. Sengupta, J. Bagchi, and G. Lovink (eds.), *Sarai Reader 05: Bare Acts*. Delhi: Sarai/CSDS, pp. 6–17.

MX (Melbourne edition). (2006) "A Touch of Bollywood," February 24, p. 26.

Pendakur, M. (1996) "India's National Film Policy: Shifting Currents in the 1990s," in A. Moran (ed.), *Film Policy: International, National, and Regional Perspectives*. New York: Routledge, pp. 148–71.

Singh, E. (n.d.) *India: A Market for American Products: A Bird's Eye View*. Publisher unknown: *circa* mid-1930s. Pamphlet archived at Special Collections, Margaret Herrick Library, Academy of Motion Picture Arts and Sciences, Los Angeles.

Sundaram, R. (2002) "About the Brazilianization of India," in G. Lovink (ed.), *Uncanny Networks: Dialogues with the Virtual Intelligentsia*. Cambridge, MA: MIT Press, pp. 122–31.

Thompson, K. (1985) *Exporting Entertainment: America in the World Film Market, 1907–15*. London: British Film Institute.

Variety (1952) "H'w'd, India Exchange Pix Views," October 7, p. 1.

Vasey, R. (1997) *The World According to Hollywood, 1918–1939.* Madison: University of Wisconsin Press.

Vasudevan, R. (2000) "National Pasts and Futures: Indian Cinema," *Screen*, 41(2), pp. 119–25.

Wilkerson, W. R. (1952) "Trade Views," *The Hollywood Reporter*, October 9, p. 1.

CHAPTER 21

AUSTRALIA AND NEW ZEALAND: EXPATS IN HOLLYWOOD AND HOLLYWOOD SOUTH

DAVID NEWMAN

During December 2005 the two films which topped the North America box office were films which had been filmed in New Zealand, by New Zealanders, i.e. *King Kong* (Peter Jackson, 2005, NZ/US) and *The Chronicles of Narnia: The Lion, the Witch and the Wardrobe* (Andrew Adamson, 2005, US). At that stage, of the seven directors responsible for the all-time top ten grossing films in the North American market, two were New Zealanders (Peter Jackson and Andrew Adamson) and one was Australian (US-born Mel Gibson) (Internet Movie Database, 2006a). New Zealanders had directed three of the top ten grossing films worldwide – *The Lord of the Rings: The Return of the King* (Peter Jackson, 2003, NZ/US/Germany), *The Lord of the Rings: The Two Towers* (Peter Jackson, 2002, NZ/US/Germany), and *Shrek 2* (Andrew Adamson, 2004, US) – and starred in a fourth, Sam Neill in *Jurassic Park* (Steven Spielberg, 1993, US) (Internet Movie Database, 2006b).

Australians, and to a lesser extent New Zealanders, have been a part of Hollywood since its earliest days. Annette Kellerman and Louise Lovely were but the tip of the iceberg in terms of Australians active in early Hollywood. Several years later, Australian Errol Flynn became a well-known name. A few New Zealand names such as Nola Luxford and Winter Hall can be added to that crowd (Palmer, 1988). But the traffic was not one-way. A number of Hollywood-based Americans found their way down under to use either country as a location, for example Lewis Collins for *The Devil's Pit* (1929, US). The antipodeans were drawn to Hollywood by the dominance of Hollywood films on local screens. Hollywood accounted for approximately 90 percent of the feature films screened in New Zealand and Australia, with Australia being the leading international market for the US films when calculated on a linear foot basis (Way, 1929). Historically, the links with Hollywood were strong.

Since 2001, the Academy Award ceremonies have demonstrated the importance of the "down-under" expatriates in contemporary Hollywood. In the March 2002 Oscar ceremonies, 13 Australians and 11 New Zealanders received nominations, with six Oscars being won by citizens of the two countries. This followed Russell Crowe's Best Actor win for *Gladiator* (Ridley Scott, 2000, UK/US) the previous year.

Over the five award ceremonies from 2002 to 2006, New Zealanders received 49 nominations and Australians were nominated 35 times, with 20 awards going to New Zealand and nine going to Australia. By the end of the 2006 Academy Awards, Richard Taylor, the head of facilities at Weta Workshop and Weta Digital, had accumulated five statuettes, while Peter Jackson had three (Academy of Motion Picture Arts and Sciences, 2006; Licuria, 2006). Following the phenomenal success of the *Lord of the Rings* trilogy (2001–3, NZ/US/Germany), director Peter Jackson emerged as one of the most powerful creators in Hollywood, while still managing to maintain New Zealand as his home and production base. The Oscar successes are not just a recent phenomena however. In 1993 *The Piano* (Jane Campion, Australia/France/NZ) received five nominations and three awards. Australia's first Academy Award was in 1942 for the documentary *Kokoda Front Line!* (Ken Hall and Damien Parer) (Licuria, 2006). New Zealand's first Oscar came much later with Lloyd Phillips' award for the short film he produced, *The Dollar Bottom* (1980, UK) (Cinema.com, 2004).

Explanatory Model

A center–periphery model can be used as a framework of analysis for the relationships between Hollywood and non-Hollywood industries. Center–periphery models have been developed in a number of disciplines and take a variety of forms. For instance, Innis (1962) outlined a metropolis–hinterland theory of social and economic development, while Wallerstein (1974) developed the concept further in world-systems theory to incorporate a third category, the semi-periphery, between the center or core and the periphery. Miller et al. (2005) also make reference to this model. Although this model has fallen out of favor among many scholars as it tends to concentrate only on uni-directional flows, in this instance I am using the concept quite loosely with bi-directional flows.

The relationships between Hollywood and non-Hollywood industries take place on a number of levels, as shown in figure 21.1, with the local industries gaining in recognition and power as an increasing number of variables flow between the Hollywood center and the periphery. The process begins with the flow (or flood) of movies from Hollywood. Viewing the movies in the periphery creates a desire among some of the audience who want to be Hollywood stars (or at least act in Hollywood movies) leading them to physically move to the Hollywood center. Crew, technicians, and writers may also move for career advancement or to be closer to the epicenter of the industry, although having non-Hollywood industry experience is often a necessity. This is more the case for directors, who are more likely to find employment in Hollywood if they have gained international recognition or acclaim for work produced in a non-Hollywood industry. In each of these categories, there may be a flow back into the domestic industry from Hollywood, either with people returning after spending a period of time in Hollywood, or Hollywood people moving out to smaller industries, drawn by the opportunities they present.

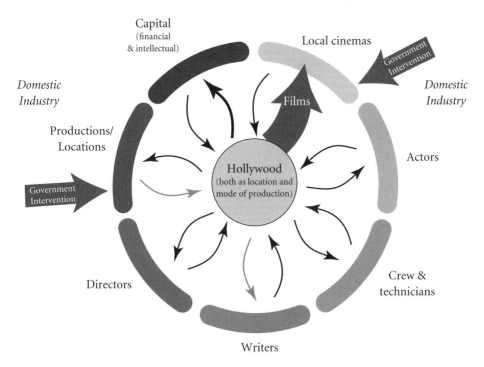

FIGURE 21.1   Center–periphery model for Hollywood/non-Hollywood industries

Hollywood productions may also base themselves in a local industry/location, though this is more likely to happen if there is an existing infrastructure in place with trained (and experienced) crews. As there is frequently a cost differential between Hollywood and non-Hollywood locales/industries, it is unusual to find a non-Hollywood production choosing Hollywood as a production venue. As the local industry develops and becomes more skilled and experienced, it may become possible for it to attract internationally mobile productions looking for unique scenery and cost savings. This may lead to closer relationships between Hollywood and the local industry, with financial capital flowing into the local industry from Hollywood, and ideas or intellectual capital flowing back into Hollywood. Finally, films themselves from the local industry may flow back into the Hollywood market. A final component of the model is government(s) in relation to the non-Hollywood domestic industry, who may intervene to restrict or enhance the flows between Hollywood and the local non-Hollywood domestic industry.

Although the model used here is a two-level center–periphery model, it is evident that there is a semi-periphery in operation (along the lines suggested by Wallerstein, 1974) in some areas of the world, or alternative centers where a local cinema has regional prominence or dominance (such as China, South Korea, and India).

In the early days, Hollywood was a geographical place denoting a style of production, and the center of the production industry. In the contemporary cinema industry, Hollywood continues to be centered in a geographical location, but the label carries more weight as a *mode* or *form* of production as production locations increasingly are situated at a considerable distance from the geographic centre of Hollywood and the US. Although this chapter will focus on the feature film portion of the screen production industry, there are many similarities on the television production side.

Flows of Talent

New Zealanders and Australians are present in all facets of contemporary Hollywood, from technicians and actors through to producers, agents, and directors. Generally they are drawn by similar reasons: career advancement, opportunity, the glamour of working at the epicenter of the industry, and generous salaries. The following discussions of actors and directors are illustrative and can be extended to other roles in the industry.

The recent migration from Australia and New Zealand to Hollywood (the location) followed development in the local industry and subsequent international attention and acclaim for domestically produced films. With the release in Europe of *Picnic at Hanging Rock* (Peter Weir, 1976, Australia), the entry in competition at the 1978 Cannes Film Festival of *The Chant of Jimmie Blacksmith* (Fred Schepisi, 1978, Australia), and the subsequent screening of some 20 other Australian films at Cannes (White, 1984), the Australian film industry gained international prominence. In the years following this, actors and directors from the Australian industry began to migrate to Hollywood. Some stayed permanently, while others worked for a while gaining experience before returning to Australia. For New Zealand, the migration came a little later following the flood of New Zealand films during the mid-1980s.

Actors

Two factors are at play in the migration of actors into the geographic Hollywood. The first is the desire for the increased opportunities that Hollywood offers (though for many the opportunities never materialize). The second is the invitations extended as a result of roles in domestic on non-Hollywood films that subsequently gain international exposure and acclaim. Although some actors make the direct move from New Zealand or Australia into Hollywood, for many their career path takes them through at least one other country first (such as the United Kingdom, or, for many New Zealanders, Australia). Actors from the two countries who have gained prominence in Hollywood include Nicole Kidman, Russell Crowe, Naomi Watts, Mel Gibson, Cate Blanchett, Heath Ledger, Geoffrey Rush, Anna Paquin, and Karl Urban. Although identified as a New Zealander, Paquin was born in Canada. This fluidity in national identity is quite common with Australians and New Zealanders. Nicole Kidman was born in the US, Roger Donaldson and Keisha

FIGURE 21.2   Baz Luhrmann directing Nicole Kidman during filming for *Moulin Rouge*
(2001), which was shot at the Fox studios in Sydney, New South Wales. Courtesy of
Bazmark Films/Ronald Grant Archive

Castle-Hughes were born in Australia, while Sam Neill was born in Northern
Ireland. It is common to find New Zealand actors, directors, and crews working
(and living) in Australia and vice versa.

The casting of actors with Hollywood credits (rarely A-grade stars) in domestically produced films is also a tool used to increase the marketability of those films
in the international marketplace. Examples of this include: Kirk Douglas in *The Man
from Snowy River* (George Miller, 1982, Australia), John Carradine in *The Scarecrow*
(Sam Pillsbury, 1982, NZ), Holly Hunter, Sam Neill, and Harvey Keitel in *The Piano*,
and Anthony Hopkins in *The World's Fastest Indian* (Roger Donaldson, 2005, NZ).
Although this strategy may help a producer secure investors, it does not always translate into box-office success.

FIGURE 21.3   Russell Crowe (right) working with director Peter Weir on the set of *Master and Commander: The Far Side of the World* (2004), a co-production between 20th Century Fox, Miramax, and Universal. Courtesy of 20th Century Fox/Ronald Grant Archive

Directors

A similar process has been at work with directors who have been able to use locally produced movies with international acclaim as calling cards to move into directing Hollywood movies. The early 1980s saw a number of Australian directors such as George Miller, Fred Schepisi, Bruce Beresford, Gillian Armstrong, and Peter Weir make their move into directing Hollywood movies. New Zealand directors followed shortly after as their films began to gain international exposure.

For New Zealand directors, the motivation to move to Hollywood has been varied. Aside from career opportunities, for the 1980s wave of directors, the closure of the tax loopholes and subsequent investigation into the industry by the New Zealand Treasury forced a number to seek offshore opportunities as local prospects dried up. Along with directors who originally established their careers in New Zealand (Geoff Murphy, Roger Donaldson, Lee Tamahori, Sam Pillsbury, and Vincent Ward for instance) were New Zealanders who moved into directing in other countries (Martin Campbell, Jane Campion, Andrew Niccol, and Andrew Adamson). Hollywood opportunities frequently followed experience in either Australia or London. The trend has continued, with directors such as Baz Luhrmann (Australia) and Niki Caro (New Zealand) taking on Hollywood assignments.

Many of the directors who headed to Hollywood have returned to their home country at some point to direct more personal or nationally distinctive works. Their return has added depth and experience to the industry, along with upward pressure on budgets. Roger Donaldson returned to New Zealand in 2004 to film *The World's Fastest Indian* with a budget of approximately $14 million (NZ$20.5 m.), while Vincent Ward returned about the same time to film the UK/NZ co-production of *River Queen* (2005) with an estimated budget of $19 million (NZ$28 m.). Both films had substantial international investment in addition to funding from New Zealand film agencies. On the Australian side of the Tasman, Phillip Noyce regularly returns to direct local films (such as *Rabbit Proof Fence*, 2002).

Hollywood Production in Australia and New Zealand

The exotic scenery seen in Australian and New Zealand films initially brought the localities to the attention of Hollywood filmmakers. But, interestingly, there has been a divergence in how Hollywood productions have used the localities. In Australia, Hollywood production has focused on studio facilities, utilizing the lower cost structures and more flexible labor environment. This has resulted in such films as *Scooby Doo* (Raja Gosnell, 2002, US), *Superman Returns* (Bryan Singer, 2006, US/Australia), *Star Wars: Episode II – Attack of the Clones* (George Lucas, 2002, US), and *The Matrix* (Andy and Larry Wachowski, 1999, US) being produced in either the Warner Roadshow Studios in Queensland or Fox Studios in Sydney.

The scenery and landscape of New Zealand, on the other hand, have served as the location and backdrop for many of the Hollywood movies shooting in the country. Mount Cook stood in as the Pakistani peak K2 in *Vertical Limit* (Martin Campbell, 2000, US/Germany), while Mount Taranaki became Mount Fuji in *The Last Samurai* (Edward Zwick, 2003, US) and portions of New Zealand represented Oregon State in *Without a Paddle* (Steven Brill, 2004, US). The only significant Hollywood movies produced in New Zealand primarily within a studio environment are *King Kong*, made in Jackson's Stone Street Studio, and *The Chronicles of Narnia: The Lion, the Witch and the Wardrobe*, based in the Henderson Valley Studios in Auckland.

The role of studio facilities in attracting Hollywood productions has been thoroughly covered by Goldsmith and O'Regan (2005). Australia is host to two major studio complexes, the Warner Roadshow Studios and Fox Studios Australia. These satellite production venues owned by Hollywood majors have attracted a number of big-budget Hollywood movies to Australia. A third studio complex is operating in Melbourne, though without the advantage of an ownership stake by a Hollywood major. In New Zealand there are two principal studio complexes, Henderson Valley Studios in Auckland and Peter Jackson's facilities in Wellington. Both have hosted big-budget Hollywood productions, although, as previously noted, many of the productions filming in New Zealand are primarily doing so for the scenery rather than the studio facilities.

Visual Effects/Post-Production

Typically, for Hollywood "runaway productions," the post-production and visual effects work has flowed back to the geographic Hollywood center. The expertise in facilities and visual effects (including physical effects) developed for the *Lord of the Rings* trilogy, however, has resulted in some work flowing instead to New Zealand rather than back to Hollywood. Among the films using New Zealand facilities and expertise have been *Van Helsing* (Stephen Sommers, 2004, US/Czechoslovakia), *Master and Commander: The Far Side of the World* (Peter Weir, 2003, US), *Peter Pan* (P. J. Hogan, 2003, US/UK), *I, Robot* (Alex Proyas, 2004, US), and *The Legend of Zorro* (Martin Campbell, 2005, US) (Weta Digital, 2006; Weta Workshop, 2006).

Peter Jackson

Although Hollywood had used New Zealand as a location prior to the *Lord of the Rings* trilogy – for instance *Willow* (Ron Howard, 1988, US) – and television series such as *Xena: Warrior Princess* (1995–2001, NZ/US) and *Hercules* (1995–9) had been based in New Zealand at Henderson Valley Studios in Auckland for a number of years, it was the *Lord of the Rings* which really established the country as a viable production location for big-budget Hollywood productions. The facilities built by Peter Jackson for the trilogy, and subsequently for *King Kong*, were equal to anything available internationally. Peter Jackson had begun working for Hollywood some years earlier when he produced *The Frighteners* (1996, NZ/US) for Universal.

FIGURE 21.4   Peter Jackson and actor Naomi Watts while filming *King Kong* (2005). Courtesy of Universal Pictures/Ronald Grant Archive

Following this, Universal invited Jackson to begin work on a remake of *King Kong*, subsequently canned after six months of pre-production work due to the poor performance of other creature movies at that time.

Peter Jackson has been able to build up a unique position in Hollywood. From his base in Miramar, he is able to produce big-budget Hollywood movies and undertake visual effects and post-production work. As part of his operation, he is a partner in one of the world's leading digital effects houses (Weta Digital) along with a massive scenic and physical effects workshop and facility (Weta Workshop). This integrated operation has enabled Jackson to complete the majority of work on each of his films in New Zealand (some aspects, such as orchestral recording, have still taken place overseas). Weta has also provided world-class facilities for other New Zealand directors (e.g. Jonathan King's 2006 horror film, *Black Sheep*, NZ/Korea), while other Hollywood films have been attracted to New Zealand for work particularly in the modeling and visual/physical effects area. Jackson's films are an example of the final step in the model: Hollywood productions produced outside of the Hollywood center, with creative and (some) financial capital outside of Hollywood, made for the Hollywood home market. Although other directors have accomplished this, Peter Jackson has been able to maintain a level of control and a share of the intellectual property, which places him in a powerful position with the Hollywood majors.

Government Support

Governments in both Australia and New Zealand have played a role in creating the environment and infrastructure for the domestic screen production industry to develop. Investment over many years by the Film Commissions in both countries has provided a base that Hollywood filmmakers have been able to exploit and develop further. Although initial government support was focused towards building domestic film industries, as Hollywood began to be interested in filming in each of the countries the governments moved to introduce economic incentives to attract internationally mobile productions. As of the middle of 2006, a refundable tax credit or grant of 12.5 percent was the primary incentive in both countries (with some differences in application). As of the middle of 2006, a refundable tax credit or grant of 12.5 percent was the primary incentive in both countries (with some differences in application). This changed with the Australian budget announcement in May 2007 when the government announced an increase to 15 percent along with a broadening of the program to include post-production expenditure as part of a comprehensive overhaul of government support to the Australian film industry. In New Zealand, it was the massive upfront tax deduction that Jackson and New Line Cinema were able to secure that resulted in work on the *Lord of the Rings* trilogy proceeding (Grant and Wood, 2004: 307). Subsequently, the tax loophole was closed and the Large Budget Screen Production Grant for certain productions introduced.

Local support for the development of studio complexes has been important. When the Warner Roadshow Studio was established on the Gold Coast, it was with considerable support in the form of soft loans and a long-term lease at a favorable rate (Goldsmith and O'Regan, 2005: 28). The Docklands studio development in Melbourne is projected to receive at least A$40 million over a 20-year period from the Victoria State Government (Goldsmith and O'Regan, 2005: 50). And when Peter Jackson decided to build a new sound stage in Wellington for *King Kong*, the local government injected $1.4 million (NZ$2 m.) of the $7 million (NZ$10 m.) cost (Positively Wellington Business, 2006). The construction of a new $4.2 million (NZ$7 m.) sound stage at the Henderson Valley Studios is a joint venture between the Waitakere City Council and a Malaysian investor with the support of a $650,000 (NZ$1 m.) grant from New Zealand Trade and Industry (Waitakere City Council, 2006). As Goldsmith and O'Regan (2005) demonstrate, local governments become heavily involved in the provision of suitable infrastructure due to the "loco-motive" value to the local economy (not to mention the prestige and PR value) that big-budget, Hollywood productions represent. Although not studio-based, *The Last Samurai* was estimated to have injected a total of $23 million (NZ$50 m.) into the Taranaki economy during 2002–3 and created the equivalent of 616 full-time positions in the region during production (Business and Economic Research Ltd, 2004: 4).

Conclusion

From the early days of cinema there have been flows between Hollywood and Aus-tralia and New Zealand. Movies have flowed from Hollywood to Australia and New Zealand, and people have migrated to Hollywood. In recent years, though, Austra-lians and New Zealanders have become more prominent. The Australian-born Rupert Murdoch acquired the 20th Century Fox Film Corporation and subsequently took US citizenship enabling him to add US television stations to his growing empire, though this didn't mean that he abandoned his business interests in Australia. In 1994, Murdoch announced the establishment of the Fox Studios Australia on the old Royal Agricultural Showgrounds in Sydney (Goldsmith and O'Regan, 2005: 67), which has subsequently provided the production base for a number of major blockbusters including *The Matrix* trilogy (Andy and Larry Wachowski, 1999–2003, US) and two of the *Star Wars* movies.

The emergence of Jackson in New Zealand as a major Hollywood director with his own production and post-production facilities (upgraded to world-class standards as a result of the *Lord of the Rings* trilogy) moved the country into the major league as a film production center. This was reinforced by the international success of *Whale Rider* (Niki Caro, 2002, NZ/Germany) around the same time. Instead of the periphery only receiving films from the Hollywood center, the periphery began providing films to the Hollywood market. No longer are New Zealanders and Australians simply on the receiving end of Hollywood-produced films or expatri-ates in geographic Hollywood. Both countries are now very much a part of the contemporary Hollywood, producing films for audiences internationally.

REFERENCES

Academy of Motion Picture Arts and Sciences (2006) "The Academy Awards," online at <http://www.oscars.org/aboutacademyawards/index.html> (accessed June 17, 2006).

Australian Minister for the Arts and Sport (2006) "Review of Film Support Measures," May 8, online at <http://www.minister.dcita.gov.au/kemp/media/media_releases/review_of_film_support_measures> (accessed May 14, 2006).

Business and Economic Research Ltd (2004) *Economic Impact Assessment for the filming of* The Last Samurai *in Taranaki*. New Plymouth: Venture Taranaki Trust.

Cinema.com (2004) "Lloyd Phillips," online at <http://www.cinema.com/people/004/210/lloyd-phillips/index.phtml> (accessed August 23, 2006).

Goldsmith, B., and T. O'Regan (2005) *The Film Studio: Film Production in the Global Economy*. Lanham, MD: Rowman & Littlefield.

Grant, P., and Wood, C. (2004) *Blockbusters and Trade Wars: Popular Culture in a Globalized World*. Vancouver: Douglas & McIntyre.

Innis, H. (1962) *The Fur Trade in Canada: An Introduction to Canadian Economic History*, revised edn. Toronto: University of Toronto Press.

Internet Movie Database (2006a) "All-Time USA Boxoffice," online at <http://www.imdb.com/boxoffice/alltimegross> (accessed July 2, 2006).

Internet Movie Database (2006b) "All-Time Worldwide Boxoffice," online at <http://www.imdb.com/boxoffice/alltimegross?region=world-wide> (accessed July 2, 2006).

Licuria, R. (2006) "Ozcars: Australians at the Academy Awards," online at <http://www.geocities.com/licuria/ausoscar.html> (accessed June 17, 2006).

Miller, T., N. Govil, J. McMurria, R. Maxwell, and T. Wang (2005) *Global Hollywood 2*. London: British Film Institute.

New Zealand Government (2006) "New Zealand's Star Continues to Shine at Oscars," March 4, online at <http://www.beehive.govt.nz/ViewDocument.aspx?DocumentID=25089> (accessed June 28, 2006).

Palmer, S. (1988) *A Who's Who of Australian and New Zealand Film Actors: The Sound Era*. Metuchen, NJ, and London: Scarecrow Press.

Positively Wellington Business (2006) "*Kong* Stage Benefits Are Clear," press release May 13, online at <http://www.positivelywellingtonbusiness.co.nz/mainsite/kong-stage-one-year-old.html> (accessed June 2, 2006).

Waitakere City Council (2006) "Lights, Camera . . . Action for $7 Million Studio Space," press release June 29, online at <http://www.waitakere.govt.nz/WhaHap/nm/mr/june06.asp#studiospace> (accessed July 10, 2006).

Wallerstein, I. (1974) *The Modern World System: Capitalist Agriculture and the Origins of the European World Economy in the Sixteenth Century*. New York: Academic Press.

Way, E. (1929) *Motion Pictures in Australia and New Zealand (Trade Information Bulletin No. 608)*. Washington, DC: Department of Commerce, Bureau of Foreign and Domestic Commerce.

Weta Digital (2006) "Filmography," online at <http://www.wetadigital.com/digital/company/filmography/> (accessed June 4, 2006).

Weta Workshop (2006) "Projects – Past Work," online at <http://www.wetaworkshop.co.nz/projects/filmography/film/> (accessed June 4, 2006).

White, D. (1984) *Australian Movies to the World*. Sydney/Melbourne: Fontana/Cinema Papers.

INDEX

Page numbers in **bold** indicate tables or figures; those in *italics* denote images.

A&E 110
Aardman **49**
ABC, *see* American Broadcasting Company
ABC exhibition chain 228
About Schmidt 32
Above the Rim 149
Abraham, F. Murray 245–6
Academy Awards 75, 246, 247, 295–6
Academy of Motion Picture Arts and
    Sciences 200, 203
accounting 55, 78–80
Ace Ventura: Pet Detective 178
actors 298–9
    background actors 161
Adamson, Andrew 295, 300
adaptations 44
Admira 269
Affleck, Ben **169**, 176, **179**
Africa 209, 287
African Queen, The 287
AFTRA, *see* American Federation of
    Television and Radio Artists
agencies 13, 14, 16, 25, 45, 50, 168, **179**,
    180
Agent Cody Banks 2: Destination London
    226
agents 168–71, 178
Ain't it Cool News 73
Air Force One 247
Akom 281
Aksoy, Asu 56, 75
Alexander 215, *216*, 246, 248

Alianza Films 30
Alien 71
All Over Me 149
Allen, Tim **49**
Allen, Woody 23
Almodóvar, Pedro 32
Alphaville Films 4, **49**
Altavista Films 266, 267
*Alvin and the Chipmunks Meet
    Frankenstein* 3
Amazon.com 85
Amblin Entertainment 21, 33
AMC, *see* American Multi-Cinemas
America Online 5, **26**, 27, 38, 85, 114
American Broadcasting Company 3, 13,
    22, **26**, 27, 107, 110, 190, 191
American Federation of Television and
    Radio Artists 140, 160, 162
American Graffiti 19, 146
American Multi-Cinemas 89, 92, **93**, 95,
    100, 228
    National Cinema Network 99, 100
American-Oriental Picture Co. 277
American Pie 244
American Playhouse 53
Amores Perros 267, *267*
Ampex 120
Anderson, Wes 151
Andreano, Simona 260
Andrews, Julie 169
Anhelo 266, 267
animation 281

AOL, *see* America Online
AOL Time Warner 229
Apoorva Sahodarargai 291
Apple iTunes 78, 85, 203
ARCO Corporation 53
ARD 241
Argentina 264, 265, 266, 272–3, **272**, 274
Argentina Sono Film 265
Argos Communications 269
Armageddon **215**, 289
Armstrong, Gillian 300
Arnez, Desi 16
Art Buchwald vs. Paramount 80
art films 17, 31, 67, 75, 100, 102
Arte 236
Artificial Intelligence: AI 139
As Good As It Gets **215**
Asia 97, 199, 200, 265, 277–83, 287, 289
   see also individual countries
Association of Film Commissioners 55
AT&T 38, 107
Atkinson, George 121, 123
attorneys 46, 168, 176–8, **179**
Aubrey, James 19
audiences 2, 6, 241–2
Australia **92**, 229, 245, 295, 298–301,
   303–4

Babelsberg 245
Babes in Toyland 149
Badlands 18
Baker Winokur Ryder 176, **179**
Bakshy, Alexander 209
Ball, Lucille 16
Bambi 288
Bangladesh 212
Bank of America 52
Banyan Tree **49**
Barnes, Morris, Klein, Mark, Yorn, Barnes
   and Levine 177, 178, **179**
Barrymore, Drew **169**
Basic 173
Basic Instinct 244
Batman 28, *28*, 115
Batman: The Animated Series 115
Batman Begins 35, 109, **216**, 226, *227*
Batman and Robin 34, 73, 149
Battlefield Earth: A Saga of the Year 3000
   173
Bauer-Benedek 168
Bean 224
Beautiful Creatures 222

Beautiful Joe 172
Belgium 212
Belton, John 97, 178
Benderspink **49**
Ben-Hur 288
Benjamin, Walter 86
Benny and Joon 146
Beresford, Bruce 300
Berliner Zeitang am Mittag 209
Berlusconi, Silvio 260
Betts, Ernest 230
Beverly Hills Cop 69
Biden, Joseph 191
Bielby, Denise D. and William T. 159
Big Chill, The **150**
Bikini Kill 149
Bill and Ted's Bogus Journey 173
Billboard 147, 149, 150
Binder, Chuck 172
Bing, Jonathan 88
Biograph 74
Birds of Prey 115
Biskind, Peter 89
Black Entertainment Television 112
Black, Jack **169**, **179**
Black, Shane 47
Black Sheep 303
Blade: Trinity 222
Blair Witch Project, The 73
Blanchett, Cate 298
Blay, Andre 122, 123
Blechtrommel, Die (The Tin Drum) 246
Blockbuster Video 25, **26**, 27, 95, 125, 127
blockbusters 19–20, 21, 28, 31, 37, 75,
   102, 125, 159
Bloom, Hergott, Diemer **179**
Bloom, Noel 123
Bludhorn, Charles 22
Blum, Léon 233
Bluth, Don 242
B-movies 15
Bodyguard, The 143, **150**
Bogart, Humphrey 215
Bollywood 212, 285
Bombay 288
Bonnie and Clyde 18
Bono, Sonny *202*
books 14, 44, 50, 195
Boot, Das (The Boat) 247
Borman, Moritz 246, 248
Bourdieu, Pierre 102
Bourne Supremacy, The 245, *246*

box office 221, 247
  admissions 88, 234, 241, 242, 252, **253**, 258, **258**
  data-gathering 90
  domestic 2, 6, 29, 48, 88, **91**
  Germany 242, 244
  gross **68**, 76, **77**
  international 2, 6, 28, **91**
  market share in Italy **254**, **257**
  receipts in the US **132**, **135**
  reporting in India 286
  revenues in the UK **221**
  theatrical 64
  world **215**, **216**
Boxing Cat **49**
Bragman, Nyman and Cafarelli 174, 175, **179**
Brazil 92, **92**, 100, 266, 270
Breakfast at Tiffany's 145
Bresler Kelly and Associates 172
Bridget Jones's Diary 224
Brillstein, Bernie 171
Brillstein-Grey Entertainment 172, **179**
British Board of Film Classification 226
British Satellite Broadcasting 229
Brittenham, Harry M. 176
Broderick, Matthew **179**
Brosnan, Pierce **49**
Bruce Almighty **68**
Bruckheimer, Jerry **49**, 69
Brunswick Records 144
Brussels 186
Bubble 204
Buchwald, Art 80
Bulgaria 212
Bullitt 18
Bullock, Sandra **169**, 177
Burger King **77**
Burke, Jason 212
Burr, Ty 213
Burton, Tim 34
Byrnes, James F. 233

CAA, *see* Creative Artists Agency
Cable Guy **177**, 178
Cage, Nicolas **169**, **179**
Caine, Michael **169**
Calcutta 287
California Labor Code 168
Calley, John 18
camcorder jamming 201
Cameron, James **49**, **98**, 270

Campbell, Martin 300
Campion, Jane 300
Canada 2, 58, **91**, 92, **92**, 93, 98, 100, 155, 163, 164, 188, 189, 210, 242, 245, 265, 270, 271
  Hollywood-North 164
Canal Plus 235
Canal Satellite 235
CanalPlay 238
Cannon 23, 124
Capcom **135**
Capital Cities 13, **26**, 27
Capitol 150
Capra, Frank 285
Carmike 92, **93**
Caro, Niki 300
Carolco 23, 124, 244
Carradine, John 299
Carrey, Jim **169**, 177, *177*, 178
Cars 70
Carsey-Werner Lakeshore **49**
Casablanca 215
Castle-Hughes, Keisha 298–9
Castle Rock Entertainment **26**, 29, 30, 115
Cattrall, Kim 177
CBS, *see* Columbia Broadcasting System
CBS Records 115, 125
CD, *see* compact disc
Cease Fire! 287
censorship 287
center–periphery model 296–7, **297**
Central Board of Censors 287
Centre National de la Cinématographie 237
Century Theaters **93**
Chain Reaction 173
Chan, Jackie 283
Chant of Jimmie Blacksmith, The 298
Chaplin, Charles 244
Charlie and the Chocolate Factory **216**, 226
Chase National 52
Chemical Bank 52
Cher 170
Cheyenne 108
Chick Flicks **49**
Chicken Little **216**
China 81, **92**, 189, 190, 193, 199, 200, 204, 211, 217, 277, 279, 280, 281, 282, 283, 284, 289, 297
China Film Corporation 280
Chouchou 238

Chronicles of Narnia, The: The Lion, the Witch and the Wardrobe **216**, 295, 301
Chronicles of Riddick, The 226
Cidade de Deus (City of God) 222
Cinderella Man 89
Cinecittà 259, 260
Cinema International Corporation 187, 228
CinemaNet 101
CinemaNow 85, 203
Cinemark 92, **93**, 100
Cinemax 21, 115
  ActionMAX 115
  MoreMAX 115
  ThrillerMAX 115
Cineplex Galaxy 92, 93, **93**
Cineplex Odeon 92, **93**
Cinesite 226
Citizen Ruth 32
City of Angels **215**
City Lights 236
City National 52
Clayton Act 185
Cleopatra 17, *17*
Clinton, Bill *184*, 188, 190
Clockwork Orange, A 18
Clooney, George 33, 34, **49**, **169**
Close, Glenn 246
Close Encounters of the Third Kind 20, 288, *288*
Closer 226
CNBC 110
Coca-Cola 22, 23
Cohen vs. Rosi 273
Colbert, Claudette 174
Cold Mountain 226
Collins, Lewis 295
Columbia 1, 14, 15, 18, 22, 23, 54, 65, 85, 115, 123, 125, 146, 171, 242, 273, 288, 292
  Columbia-TriStar 25, **26**, 33, 37, 115, 116, 220, 222, 237, 269
  Screen Gems 16, 30, 115, 116
Columbia Broadcasting System 22, 23, **26**, 27, 38, 95, 107, 110, 112, 190, 191
Columbia-EMI-Warners Distributors Ltd 228
Columbus, Chris 34, 35
Comcast Communications 38, 110, 115, 116, 117
Comedy Central 112

comic books 44, 109
Coming to America 80
Commando 78
Communication Workers of America *158*
Communications Act 1934 190
Communications Act 1996 190
Comodines (Cops) 272
compact disc 109, 121
conglomeration 5, **26**, 27, 229
Connery, Sean **169**, 170, 245
Constantin 244
Constantine 173, **216**
contracts 46
Contrafilm **49**
Conundrum **49**
Convention on the Protection and Promotion of the Diversity of Cultural Expression 210
Coppola, Sophia 32
copyright 44, 45, 122
  1909 Copyright Act 198
  Copyright Act of 1976 198
  Copyright Term Extension Act 201
  Digital Millennium Copyright Act 200, 201, 202
  Family Entertainment and Copyright Act 201
  first sale doctrine 123
  history 195–7
  No Electronic Theft Act 200, 201
Cornell University 156
Corporation for Public Broadcasting 53
Costner, Kevin 170
Cowan, Ruth Schwartz 121
Cox Communications 110, 115, 116
craft unions 163
craft workers 161
Craven/Maddalena **49**
Creative Artists Agency 13, 25, 168, 169, **169**, 170, **179**
Creative Coalition 158
Creature from the Black Lagoon 4
Crichton, Michael 50
crimen del Padre Amaro, El (The Crime of Father Amaro) 269
Criminal 273
Crow, The 150
Crowe, Russell **169**, 175, 176, **179**, 295, 298, *300*
Cruise, Tom **169**, 172, 175, 176, **179**
Cruz, Penelope **169**
Cuarón, Alfonso 35, 267, 268, 274

Cuban, Mark 204
cultural imperialism 254
current cinema 87
CW 112, 114, 115, 117

Da Vinci Code, The 94, 226
Dafoe, Willem 139
Dai Won 281
Dallas 218
Damon, Matt **169**, 176, **179**, 246
Dances With Wolves 244
Daniel, Sean 4
Daniels, Bill 50
Dark Water 283
Dart, Leslee 175
Davis, Geena 170
Day After Tomorrow, The **68**, 247
DC Comics 5
De Grazia, Victoria 211
De la Fuente, Anna Marie 270
De Lane Lea 226, 227
De Niro, Robert **49**, **179**
de Sica, Vittorio 252
De Vany, Arthur 64
deals 35
Decca 1, 3, 18, 145
Deep Impact **215**
Deewangee 291, 291
DeGeneres, Ellen 177
del Río, Dolores 265
del Toro, Guillermo 267, 274
DeLaurentiis Entertainment Group 23, 124
Deliverance 18
Denmark 212
Departed, The 283
Department of Commerce 58
Depp, Johnny 146, **169**, 176, **179**
deregulation 14, 23, 27, 108, 117, 126–7
Desilu 16, 108
Devil's Advocate, The 173
Devil's Pit, The 295
DGA, see Directors Guild of America
Dhallywood 212
Dhund 291
Diaz, Cameron **169**, 175, **179**
DiCaprio, Leonardo 176
Dicen que soy communista (They Say I'm a Communist) 265
Diesel, Vin **169**, **179**
digital cinema 97–101
  d-cinema 97, 98, 99, 100, 101, 102
  e-cinema 97, 98, 100, 101, 102

Digital Cinema Initiatives 97
digital video disc 3, 4, 26, 36, 85, 95, 96, 102, 106, 109, 127–8, 200, 202, 204, 258, **258**
  Blu-ray 128
  HD-DVD 128
  high-definition 38, 128
  video/DVD revenues 37, **77**, 86
Diller, Barry 22, 25
Dillon, Matt **49**
directors 247, 252, 267, 274, 283, 295, 300–1
Directors Guild of America 58, 159, 161, 162, 164, 264
direct-to-video movies 110
Dirty Dancing **150**
Dirty Harry 18
Disney 13, 14, 21, 22, 23, 24, **26**, 27, 29, 39, **49**, 65, 70, 95, 97, 106, 108, 109–10, 115, 116, 122, 123, 124, 125, 128, 129, 134, **135**, 164, 170, 187, **192**, 198, 199, 201, 213, 217, 222, 230, 243, 269, 274, 283
  ABC Family 110
  Buena Vista 65, 109, 220, 222, 235, 237, 242, 272, 273
  Buena Vista Television International 289
  Caravan Pictures 109, 110
  classics 109
  Disney Channel 23, 109
  Disney Corners 282
  Disneyland 16
  Hollywood Pictures 109, 110
  Toon Disney 110
  Touchstone Pictures 23, 31, 65, 109, 110, 226
Disney, Roy 109
Disney, Walt 109
Disneyland 108
distribution **24**, 63–81, 220–2, 225, 233–5
  deal 76
  domestic market 65
  international day-and-date releasing 94
  platform releasing 67, 94
  theatrical rentals 86
  wide releasing 67, 94
Doctor Dolittle (1967) 17
Doctor Dolittle (1998) **215**
DocuZone 101
Dollar Bottom, The 296

Donaldson, Roger 298, 300
Doordarshan 289
Dot Records 145
Double Negative 226
Douglas, Kirk 299
Douglas, Michael **169**, **179**
Dow Jones 110
Down and Out in Beverly Hills 23
Dracula 4
DreamWorks SKG 26, 27, 33, **49**, 65, **68**,
    110, 112, 124, 134, 177, 230
  DreamWorks Animation 139
Duel in the Sun 144
Dulles, Allen Welsh 210
Dulles, John Foster 210
Dumb & Dumber 29, 178
Dunst, Kirsten **179**
DVD, *see* digital video disc
DVD Forum 127

E! 110
Earthquake 19
Eastman Kodak Company 196
Eastwood, Clint 18, 33, **49**, **169**, **179**
Easy Rider 18, 146
Edison, Thomas 196
editors 161
Egypt 4
Eichinger, Bernd 245, 248
Eidos **135**
Eisner, Michael 13, 14, 22, 23, 25, 124
Election 32
Electronic Arts 135
Elsa and Fred 272
EMI 150
EMI-Capitol Music 148
Emmerich, Roland 247, 248
Empire Strikes Back, The 20
EM.TV 243
encryption 201
Endeavor Talent Agency 168, **169**, 178,
    179
Enemy at the Gates 245
English Patient, The 32
Ennis, Philip 101
Entertainment Data Incorporated 90
Entertainment Economy Institute 156,
    157
Entertainment Film Distributors 222
Entertainment Services and Technology
    Association 59
Entertainment Weekly 89

epinazo del Diablo, El (*The Devil's*
    Backbone) 267
Epstein, Edward Jay 36
ER 34
Erin Brockovich 33
ESPN 110
Estevez, Emilio 170
E.T. The Extra-Terrestrial 21, 54, *54*, 129,
    133
Eternal Sunshine of the Spotless Mind 31
Europe 100, 126, 135, 136, 199, 215, 229,
    230, **236**, 265, 266, 282, 298
  see also individual countries
European Audiovisual Observatory 214
Evergreen 100
Evolution Entertainment 30
exhibition 64, 83–102, 228–9
  opening weekend 64, **68**, 94, 95
  ownership 91–3
  screens 92, **92**
  ticket prices 88, 253
  windows 126
exhibition studies 87–8
Exodus 145
Exorcist, The 18, 19
exploitation films 17

Face/Off 173
Fadiman, William 167
Fahrenheit 9/11 90
Family Guy 130
Famous Players 92, **93**
Fantastic Four 37, **216**
Far and Away 175
Far from Heaven 33
Farrell, Joe 73
Fatal Attraction 73
FCC, *see* Federal Communications
    Commission
Federal Communications Commission 22,
    23, 27, 107, 108, 116, 117, 159, 161,
    198
Federal Trade Commission 186
Federation Against Copyright Theft 226
Feeling Minnesota 173
Fellini, Federico 252
Fernández, Emilio 268
Ferrell, Will 177, **179**
Fields, Bert 214
Fil-Cartoons 281
Film Bureau 282
Film Distributors' Association 226

film festivals 101
  Cannes 75, 298
  Guadalajara Iberoamerican Film Festival
    96
  Image + Nation International Film
    Festival 101
  Vues d'Afriques 101
Final Cut, The 100
Final Destination 2 222
Final Fantasy: The Spirits Within **135**, 138,
  139
financing 52–3, 259
  completion guarantees 53
  grants 259
  guarantee funds 259
  sources 52–3; hedge funds 52;
    investment capital 52; presales 52
  subsidized loans 259, 260
  see also merchandizing; product
    placement
Financing and Syndication Rules 23, 27,
  126, 127, 190
Finding Nemo 70, **138**, 139
Fiorentino, Linda 170
The Firm **179**
Five Easy Pieces 18
Flashdance 69, 147, 148, *148*, **150**
flexible specialization 56, 57
Flightplan **216**
Florida 164
Folkets Hus 100
Fondo Unico per lo Spettacolo 259,
  260
Football Factory, The 96
Footloose **150**
Forbes, Lou 144
Ford, Harrison **169**, 172, **179**
Ford Foundation 53
Forrest Gump 79, *79*, **150**
Fortnightly v. United Artists 198
Fortune 37
Foster, Jodie **169**, 175, **179**
Four Weddings and a Funeral 224
Fowler, Mark 23
Fox Film Corporation 1
Foxx, Jamie **169**
Framestore CFC 226
France **91**, **92**, 210, 211, 212, 215, 230,
  232–9, **236**, 242, 252
France 2 236
France 3 236, 241
Francefilm 187

franchises
  Back to the Future 28
  Batman 35, 70, 115
  Beverly Hills Cop 21
  Ghostbusters 28
  Halo 139
  Harry Potter 29, 34, 133, 224
  Indiana Jones 2, 28
  James Bond 18, 133, 224
  Lethal Weapon 28
  Lord of the Rings 29, 35, 133, 137, 222,
    296, 302, 304
  Matrix 35, 70, 137, 304
  Spider-Man 70, 76, **77**, 137
  Star Wars 29
  X-Men 35
Frankenstein 4
Free Trade of the Americas 269
Freeman, Morgan **49**
French Connection, The 19
Freston, Thomas E. 111
Friedman, Robert 67, 70, 74
Frighteners, The 302
Front Row 230
Full Frontal 33
FX Networks **77**

Gabler, Neal 13, 14, 39
Garcia, Andy **169**, **179**
Garr, Teri 170
Gaumont 235, 237
Gaumont Buena Vista International 235
Gaumont Columbia TriStar Home Video
  237
Gavaldón, Roberto 268
GE, *see* General Electric
Geffen, David **26**, 27
General Agreement on Tariffs and Trade
  210
General Cinema 93
General Electric **26**, 27, 106, 107, 109,
  110–11, 115, 116, 165, 189, **192**,
  224
  Bravo 110
  MUN2 110
  Telemundo Internacional 110, 111
  Universal HD 110
General's Daughter, The 173
Georgia Theater Company 98
Gere, Richard **169**, 175
German Internationale Medien und Film
  GmbH 246

Germany 3, **91**, **92**, 212, 215, 230, 233,
  240–8
 West Germany 122, 241, 242
Ghost 28
Ghostbusters 170
Giamatti, Paul **169**
Gibson, Mel 65, **169**, 172, **179**, 295, 298
Gilbert-Rolfe, James 72
Gingrich, Newt *202*
Gladiator 295
Glickman, Dan 97, 184, 193
globalization 225, 229
Godfather, The 18, 19
Godzilla **215**, 247
Gold Circle Films 30
Goldberg, Whoopi 175
Golden Globe 75
Goldfinger 145
Goldman, William 61
Goldman Sachs 126
Goldsmith, Ben 270, 301, 304
Goldwyn, Sam 15
González Iñárritu, Alejandro 267, 274
Goo Goo Dolls 149
Good Night, and Good Luck 33, 34, *34*
Good Will Hunting 32, **215**
Google 38, 39
Gotthelt, Michelle 176
Graduate, The 18, 146
Grant, Hugh **169**, 223, *223*, 224
Grease 20, **150**
Greenberg, Joshua 121
Greenburg Glusker **179**
Grokster 122, 202, 203
Groves, Don 94
Grudge, The 283
Grupo Financiero Inbursa 266
Guangzhou Jinyi Film and Television
  Investment Co. 282
Guback, Thomas H. 252
Guber, Peter 70
Guber-Peters Entertainment 115
Gulf + Western 19, 22
Gunga Din 287

Haber, Bill 168
Hackman, Gene **169**
Hall, Jason 139
Hall, Winter 295
Halo 2 133
Hanks, Tom 79, **169**, 170, 175, 177, **179**
Hard Day's Night, A 18, 145

Harris, Ed **169**
Harris, Richard 169
Harry Potter and the Chamber of Secrets
  68, **138**
Harry Potter and the Goblet of Fire **68**, 96,
  216
Harry Potter and the Prisoner of Azkaban
  68, 221
Harry Potter and the Sorcerer's Stone 67,
  138, 237
Hasbro 70
Hayes, Dade 88, 89
Hayes, Will H. 183, 213
Hayworth, Rita 174
HBO, *see* Home Box Office
Heaven's Gate 23, 125
Hello, Dolly! 17
Help! 18
Helú, Carlos Slim 266
Henderson Valley Studios 301, 302
Hengdian Group 282
Hercules 302
Hershey Foods 3
Heston, Charlton *163*
Hetzel, Ralph 183
high concept 19, 48, 67, 69
High Heels and Low Lifes 222
Highlight 244
hijo de la novia, El (*Son of the Bride*) 273
Hirsch, Wallerstein, Hayum, Matlof and
  Fisherman **179**
History Channel 110
Hitachi 127
Hitch **216**
Hoffman, Dustin **169**, 170, **179**
Hollywood Reporter, The 63
Home Alone 28, 34
Home Box Office 5, 21, 23, 30, 53, 115,
  258, 292
 HBO2 115
 HBO Comedy 115
 HBO Films 30
 HBO Signature 115
home market economic model of film
  trade 255
Hong Kong 212, 217, 278, 279, 280, 282,
  283
Hoover, Herbert 183, 187, 193
Hopkins, Anthony 299
Horse Whisperer, The **215**
Hostel 30
House of Spirits, The 246

Hoyts Cinemas **93**
Huayi Brothers 282
Hudson, Kate 175, **179**
Hughes, Howard 16
Hulk 286
Humraaz 291
Hunter, Holly 299
Huntington, Samuel P. 217
Huvane Baun Halls 175
Hyde Park **49**

I Know What You Did Last Summer 291
I, Robot 222, 302
Iapadre, Lelio 260
ICM, *see* International Creative
    Management
Icon Pictures 65
ID Public Relations 176, **179**
IFC Films 267
Iger, Robert 213
iHQ 278
Illinois 164
Illuminados por el fuego (*Blessed by Fire*)
    272
ImageMovers **49**
Imagine **49**
IMCINE, *see* Instituto Mexicano de
    Cinematografía
IMF, *see* International Monetary Fund
In the Line of Fire 247
INCAA, *see* Instituto Nacional de Cine y
    Artes Audiovisuales
Incredibles, The **138**
iNDEMAND 110, 115, 116, 117
Independence Day 247, *247*
Independent Film Channel 30
    IFC Films 30
independent film movement 29–31
Independent Motion Picture Corporation
    74
independent producer-distributors 31
independent producers 16, 52, 75–6
India **91**, **92**, 100, 187, 189, 193, 211, 212,
    278, 281, 282, 285–93, 297
Indiana Jones and the Temple of Doom 289
indie blockbusters 32
Indiewood 32
Indonesia 212
Industrial Light and Magic 4
Informa Media 230
Initial Entertainment Group 244
Inkeles, Alex 217

Innis, Harold 86, 296
Insomnia 35
Instituto Mexicano de Cinematografía
    266, 274
Instituto Nacional de Cine y Artes
    Audiovisuales 272, 273
intellectual property 5–6, 81, 195–204
    patents 196, 197
    trademarks 196
    see also copyright
Interamerican Entertainment Corporation
    266
International Creative Management 25,
    168, **169**, 172, **179**
International Intellectual Property Alliance
    290
International Monetary Fund 189
internet 38, 238
    download-to-burn services 203
    video-on-demand 203, 204, 238
Interpreter, The 73
Interpublic 175, 176, 178
InterTalent 168, 170
Irish DreamTime **49**
Irons, Jeremy 246
Israel 210, 289
Italy 3, **91**, **92**, 195, 212, 233, 241, 242,
    251–62, **253**, **254**, **256**, **258**

Jackman, Hugh **169**
Jackoway, Tyerman, Wertheimer, Austen,
    Mandelbaum and Morris **179**
Jackson, Michael 170
Jackson, Peter 35, 295, 296, 301, 302–3,
    302, 304
Jackson, Samuel L. **169**, 177, **179**
Jakarta 187
JAKKS Pacific 3
Japan **91**, **92**, 121, 135, 136, 211, 212, 215,
    241, 242, 278, 279, 283, 286, 289
Jaws 19, 20, *20*, 66, 125
Jewel 149
Johansson, Scarlett **169**, 178
Johnny English 224
Johnson, Anne-Marie 161
Johnson, Randal 266
Johnston, Eric 183
Jolie, Angelina **169**
Jones, Tommy Lee **169**
Jordan 4
Jungle Book, The 144
Jurassic Park 2, 33, 289, *290*, 295

Justice Department 19, 22
JVC 115, 127
  Video Home System 120, 121

Kaante 291
Kaige, Chen 283
Kamchatka 273
Kantana 281
KanZaman s.a.m. 4
Karl, Stuart 123
Katzenberg, Jeffrey 23, **26**, 27, 124, 129
Kawin, Bruce 60
Keaton, Diane **169**
Keeble, David 226
Keightley, Keir 86
Keitel, Harvey 299
Kellerman, Annette 295
Kelly, R. 149
Kennedy/Marshall **49**
Kerasotes Showplace **93**
Kerkorian, Kirk 19, 23
Kidman, Nicole **169**, 175, **179**, 298, *299*
Kinetoscope 196, 204
King Arthur 226
King Kong (1933) 60
King Kong (2005) **216**, 295, 301, 302,
    304
Kingdom of Heaven **216**
Kingsley, Pat 174, 175
Kinney Corporation 19
Kinowelt 244
Kirch, Leo 241, 243
Kirch Group 244
Klein, Deborah 177
Klein, Howard 172
kleine Eisbär, Der (*The Little Polar Bear*)
    222
Klute 18
Knockin' on Heaven's Door 243
Kodak 226
Kokoda Front Line! 296
Kopelson, Anne and Arnold 244
Korea 278
  North Korea 211
  South Korea **91**, **92**, 199, 212, 215, 278,
    279, 280, 281, 286, 289, 297
Korean Film Council 278
Kornblau, Craig 3, 4
Knowles, Harry 73
Krane, Jonathan 173
Krauss, Alison 149
Krim, Arthur 23

KTH 278
Kunstler, James Howard 217

labor 58, 155–65
Ladies' Night 269
Laemmle, Carl 74
Landscape **49**
Lange, André 214
Lansing, Sherry 78
Lara Croft: Tomb Raider **135**, *134*
Large Budget Screen Production Grant 303
Last Boy Scout, The 47
Last Dance 172
Last Picture Show, The 18
Last Samurai, The 35, 301, 304
Latin America 200, 229, 264–74
  see also *individual countries*
Law, Jude **169**
Lawrence, Florence 74
Leading Artists Agency 168
League of Their Own, A 170
Ledger, Heath 298
Lee, Ang 31, 283
Lee, Roy 283
Lee, Spike 25
Legal Eagles 170
Legend of Zorro, The 302
Legendary Pictures 35
Leiner, Dylan 273
Lenin 182
Leone, Sergio 18
Lethal Weapon 47
Lethal Weapon 4 **215**
Li, Gong 283
Lieberfarb, Warren 128
life-cycle of films 94, 95, 96
Lifetime 110
Lifetime Movie Network 110
Lightstorm **49**
Lilo and Stitch 110
Lilo and Stitch: The Series 110
Lilo and Stitch 2: Stitch has a Glitch 110
line producer 51
Lion King, The **150**
Lion Rock **49**
Lionsgate (formerly Lions Gate) 30, 85,
    100, 128
Little Mermaid, The 23
Liu, Lucy **169**
LIVE 123, 124
lobbying 191–2, **191**, **192**
Loews 1, 92, **93**, 99, 100, 197

London 225–8, 231, 287
  Soho 226
Long Kiss Goodnight, The 47, 47
Long Time Dead 222
Look Who's Talking 173
Lopez, Jennifer **169**, **179**
Lord of the Rings: The Return of the King
  138, 295
Lord of the Rings: The Two Towers **138**,
  237, 295
Loren, Sophia 252
Los Angeles 157, 158, 160, 161, 164, 225
Los Angeles magazine 175
Los Hooligans **49**
Lost World: Jurassic Park, The 2
Love Story 18, 19
Lovely, Louise 295
Lowe, Jim 121
Lucas, George 20, 21, 125
Lucasfilm 21
Luhrmann, Baz *299*, 300
Lui, Francis 217
Lung fu fong wan (*City of Fire*) 291
Luxford, Nola 295

M6 235
McCabe and Mrs Miller 18
McCann-Erickson WorldGroup 175
McCombs, Maxwell 129
McDonald's 85
McGregor, Ewan 139
Machinima 138–9
Madagascar **216**
made-for-television movies 108
Madonna 170
Magnetic Video 122, 123
Maguire, Tobey 139
Malaysia 212, 280
Malkovich, John **49**
Malpaso Productions 33, **49**
Man in the Iron Mask, The **215**
Man from Snowy River, The 299
Management 360 172, **179**
managers 45, 168, 171–3, 178, **179**, 180
  producer-managers 172–3
Mandalay **49**
Manuelita 273
Marich, Robert 72, 73
MarketCast 73
marketing 66, 69–75
  advertising 71, **72**
  costs 37, 63, **63**

market research 72–3
  trailers 71
  websites 2
Marshall, Garry **49**
Marshall, Penny 170
Martin Baum Associates 168
Martin, Steve **169**
Marvel 77
Mask, The 29
Mask of Zorro, The **215**
Maslansky-Koenigsberg 174
Master and Commander: The Far Side of
  the World 270, 302
Mastroianni, Marcello 252
Matrix, The 173, 301
Matrix Reloaded, The **68**, **138**
Matrix Revolutions, The 203–4
Matsushita 1, 25, **26**, 27, 38, 115, 120, 121,
  125, 127, 128, 147, 228
Mauritius 212
MCA, *see* Music Corporation of America
Mean Streets 18
Medavoy, Brian 172
Media21 278
Meet the Fockers **216**
megaplexes 85, 86, *87*
Memento 35
Mephisto 247
merchandizing 14, 28, 53
Merrill Lynch 64
Metrodome 65
Metro-Goldwyn-Mayer 1, 15, 16, 18, 19,
  23, **49**, 66, 97, 116, 145, 197, 202, 203,
  226, 230, 241, 292
  MGM Home Entertainment 30
Metropolitan 237
Mexico 30, **92**, 189, 264, 265, 266–71, **266**,
  267, 273, 274
Mexico City 187
Meyer, Ron 168
MGM, *see* Metro-Goldwyn-Mayer
MGM v. Grokster 203
MGM Parade 108
MGM/UA 23, **26**, 27, 38, 65, 242
Microsoft 110, 133, 135, 177
Midnight Cowboy 146
Midway **135**
Middle East 199
  see also individual countries
Miller, George 300
Miller, Toby 296
Million Dollar Baby 33, **216**

Mirage 49
Miramax Films 26, 29, 32, 65, 109, 110,
     125, 226
   Dimension Pictures 30, 109, 110
Miravista 269
Mitchum, Robert 232
Mitsubishi 127
Modern Times 236, 244
Momentum 175
Monogram 15
Moonves, Leslie 111, 112
Moore, Demi 169, 179
Moore, Julianne 169
Moore, Michael 32
More, Erwin 172
More Medavoy Management 172
Moretti, Franco 217
Morgan Creek 49
Morita, Akio 121
Morocco 4, 215
Morris, Kevin 177
Mortal Kombat 135
Mortal Kombat: Annihilation 135
Motion Picture Association of America 2,
     23, 36, 48, 49, 51, 58, 63, 65, 96, 97,
     164, 182–8, 189, 190, 191, 192, 192,
     193, 199, 200, 201, 202, 203, 213, 226,
     251, 255, 260, 264, 279, 284, 286
   Motion Picture Association (MPA) 36,
     36, 185, 186, 192, 266, 268–9, 274,
     290
   Motion Picture Export Association
     (MPEA) 184–5, 192, 286, 288
Motion Picture Patents Company 196
Motion Picture Producers and Distributors
     of America 183, 213
Mount, Thom 149
Movie Channel, The 21
Moviefone 85
moviegoing 89
Movielink 85, 203
Moving Picture Company 226
Moving Picture World 74
MPA, see under Motion Picture
     Association of America
MPAA, see Motion Picture Association of
     America
MPEA, see under Motion Picture
     Association of America
Mr & Mrs Smith 216
Mr Mudd 49
Mrs. Doubtfire 34

MSNBC 110, 190
MTV 49, 112, 147
Mukta Adlabs 100
Mulan 215
Mullis Capital 278
Mulroney, Brian 188
multiplexes 85, 99, 228–9, 242, 280, 282,
     289
Mummy, The (1932) 1, 2, 4
Mummy, The (1999) 1, 2, 3, 4, 5
Mummy: The Animated Series, The 3
Mummy Returns, The 1, 2, 3
Murdoch, Rupert 27, 38, 112, 114, 189,
     190, 193, 304
Murphy, A. D. 21
Murphy, Brittany 169
Murphy, Eddie 21, 49, 80
Murphy, Geoff 170, 300
Murray, Bill 170, 171
Music Corporation of America 1, 13, 16,
     18, 19, 26, 121, 123, 145
   Revue 19
   see also Universal
music video 147
Mussolini, Benito 259
My Beautiful Launderette 224
My Big Fat Greek Wedding 30, 67, 68
My Left Foot 29
Myers, Mike 169, 179
MySpace 38, 190
Mystic River 33

NAB, see National Association of
     Broadcasters
Nachum, Lilach 226
Name of the Rose, The 245
Napoleon Dynamite 37
Napster 122
National Amusements 6, 93, 95, 106, 109,
     110, 111–12, 114, 115, 116, 117
   Showcase 228
National Association of Broadcast
     Employees and Technicians 158
National Association of Broadcasters 189,
     190, 191
National Association of Theatre Owners
     100
National Broadcasting Company 19, 22,
     27, 107, 110, 111, 159, 190, 191, 197,
     224, 229
National Geographic 110
National Research Group 73

National Science Foundation 53
Navarro, Ramón 265
NBC, *see* National Broadcasting Company
NBC Universal **26**, 27, 165
Neill, Sam 295, 299
Never on a Sunday 145
Neverending Story, The 245, 247
New American Cinema 18
New Delhi 186
New German Cinema 246–7
New Hollywood 19–21
New International Division of Cultural
    Labor 211
New Line Cinema 5, 23, **26**, 29, 30, 31, 35,
    49, 65, 115, 125, 128, **135**, 222, 303
  Fine Line Films 29, 30, 115
New Regency **49**
New Straits Times 212
New York 157, 160, 161, 162, 165
New Zealand 237, 270, 295–6, 298–304
New Zealand Trade and Industry 304
Newell, Mike 35
Newman, Paul 170
Newmarket 127
News Corporation 14, 22, **26**, 27, 37, 38,
    106, 109, 110, 112–14, 116, 117, 125,
    190, **192**, 229
  BSkyB 112, 229
  DirecTV 112, 177
  FOX Broadcasting Company 22, 77,
    113, 114, 190, 191
  Fox Kids 112
  FUEL 112
  FX 112
  My Network 114
  Sky Box Office 230
  Sky Cinema 230
  SPEED 112
Niccol, Andrew 300
Nicholson, Jack 172
Nickelodeon 112
Nickelodeon Revelations **49**
Nielsen Media Research 72, 73, 90, 91
Nigeria 129
Night of the Hunter, The 232
Night of the Iguana 270
Nintendo **135**, 135, 136
Nolan, Christopher 35
North America 135
  see also individual countries
North American Trade Agreement 271
North Carolina 164

Notting Hill 223, *223*, 224
novelization 109
NOW That's What I Call Music! 150
Noyce, Phillip 301
Nueve reinas (Nine Queens) 273
Nyman, Michael 174

O Brother, Where Art Thou? **150**
Ocean's Eleven 33, 34
Odeon 228
Ogilvy Public Relations Worldwide 176
O'Hare, Sharon L. 129
Omnilife 266
One Hour in Wonderland 108
Online Testing Exchange 73
Oranan, Erol 121
O'Regan, Tom 270, 301, 304
Orion 23, 124, 244
  Orion Classics 30
Ovitz, Michael 13, 14, 25, 168, 170
Oxford Economic Forecasting 226

Pacifier, The **216**
Pacino, Al 175
packaging 13, 16
Paltrow, Gwyneth **169**, 175, 176
Paquin, Anna 298
Paramount 1, 2, 6, 14, 15, 16, 18, 19, 21,
    22, **26**, 27, **49**, 65, 67, 79, 85, 95, 97,
    111, 112, 123, 125, 128, **135**, 145, 187,
    197, 203, 220, 228, 230, 233, 235, 242,
    278, 286, 292
  Paramount Classics 30, 112
  Paramount Home Entertainment 112
  UPN 27, 114, 117
Paramount Communications 22, 228
Paramount decree 16, 22, 66, 107, 108,
    126, 127, 145, 186, 190, 192
Parker, Trey 177
Parole Officer, The 22
pasi 281
Passion of the Christ, The 67, 90, 127
Patagonik 272
Pathé 223, 232, 286
Pathé Communications **26**, 27
Patoruzito 273
Patriot, The 247
Paxson Communications 110
  PAX 110
Payne, Alexander 32, 33
Pearl Harbor 270
peer-to-peer networks 200, 202, 203

Penn, Sean **169**
Pepsi 70
Perfect Murder, A 291
Perfect Storm, The 34, 247
Perkins, Rowland 168
Peter Pan 302
Petersen, Wolfgang 247, 248
Pfeiffer, Michelle **169**, 175, **179**
Phenomenon 173
Philippines 280, 281, 287
Philips 121, 128
Phillips, Lloyd 296
Piano, The 296, 299
Pickwick Public Relations 174
Picnic at Hanging Rock 298
Picturehouse 30
Pillsbury, Sam 300
Pinewood Shepperton 226
Pinewood Studios 4, 226
Pinocchio 124
Pioneer 127
piracy 95–6, 97, 102, 195, 196, 199, 200,
    259, 280, 290, 291
    internet 203, 238, 279
Pitfall 133
Pitt, Brad **169**, 176, **179**
Pixar 70, 109, 139, 177
Pleitgen, Fritz 210
PMK 174, 175
PMK/HBH 175, 176, **179**
Poitier, Sidney 169
Pokemon: The First Movie **135**
Pokemon: The Movie 2000 **135**
Pokemon 3: The Movie **135**
Poland 289
Polaroid 3
Pol-Ka 272
Pollack, Sydney 170
Pollock, Tom 25
PolyGram 224
Poulsen, Valdemar 120
Premiere 25
prestige pictures 15, 17
Pretty Woman 28
Prey 50
Price, Frank 25
Primal Fear 291
primary movie spending 256, **256**, 257
Prince 170
Priority **49**
Proclaimers, The 146
producer-directors 21

producers 46, 255
product placement 45, 53, 273
production 24, 43–60, 252, **253**, 301
    co-productions 17, 53, 252, 281, 282,
        288
    costs 2, 21, 51, **63**, **68**, **77**; above-the-
        line 51; below-the-line 51
    deals **49**; distribution deal 49; equity
        partnership 49; first look deal 49
    development **43**, 44–50
    film commissions 55–6
    German-American collaborations 244
    German investment 244
    locations 55–6, 281
    outsourcing 163, 281
    post-production **43**, 59–60
    pre-production 43, 54–8
    principle photography 58–9
    project organization 4, 43
    remakes 283, 290–1
    runway production 57–8
    services 59
    tax shelters 244
Production Code 18
profit participation 51, 76, 79
profits 79, 80
P2P networks, *see* peer-to-peer networks
publicists 168, 173–6, 178, **179**, 180
publicity 66, 74–5, 173–4
    press junkets 74
    reviews 75
Pullman, Bill *247*
Pulp Fiction 29
Puños Rosas 96
Purple Rain **150**

Qayamat 291
Quick and the Dead, The 172
quotas 233, 259, 265, 273, 274, 279, 280

Rabbit Proof Fence 301
radio 107, 116, 145
Radio Corporation of America 107, 110,
    120, 121, 197
Radio-Keith-Orpheum 1, 15, 16, 17, 197,
    265
Raiders of the Lost Ark 20, 133
Rain Networks 100
Ramis, Harold 170, *171*
Ramoji Film City 292
RCA, *see* Radio Corporation of America
RCA Victor 144

Reagan, Ronald 23, 188, 189
recorded music 143–51
    cross-promotion 146, 147
    licensing revenues 148
    soundtrack albums 145, 146, 148, 149,
        150, **150**
    synchronization fees 148
Recording Industry Association of America
    189, 202
Red Hot Chili Peppers 149
Redford, Robert 112, 170, 175
Redstone, Sumner 38, 111, 190, 193
Reed Elsevier 73
Reeves, Keanu **169**, 173, 177, **179**
Regal Entertainment Group 92, **93**
    Digital Content Network 98, 100
    National Cinemedia 100
Reitman, Ivan 170
R.E.M. 149
Rentrak 90, 91, 127
Republic 15
Reservoir Dogs 291
Resident Evil **135**, 245
Revenge of the Mummy: The Ride 3
Revolution **49**
Reyes Mejilla, Hugo Alonso 270
Richardson, Bonnie 164
Ring, The 283
Rio de Janeiro 187
Rising: Ballad of Mangal Pandey, The 292
risk 61, 65
River Queen 301
River Road **49**
RKO, *see* Radio-Keith-Orpheum
Robbins, Tim **169**
Roberts, Julia 33, **169**, 172, **179**, 223, *223*
Robins, Kevin 56, 75
Robots **216**
Rock, The 291
Rock, Chris 176, **179**
Rocky 20
Rocky IV 21
Rodriguez, Robert **49**
Rogers, Henry 174
Rogers & Cowan 174, 175, **179**
Rosemary's Baby 18
Rosenfeld, Mike 168
Ross, Diana 149
Ross, Steve 25
Rosza, Miklos 144
Rugrats 112, *113*
Rugrats Go Wild! 112

Rugrats Movie, The 112
Rugrats in Paris 112
Rush, Geoffrey 298
Rush Hour **215**
Russia **92**, 200
Ryan, Meg **169**, 176, **179**
Ryder, Winona 176, 246

S Club: Seeing Double 222
Sabu 144
SAG, *see* Screen Actors Guild
Sandler, Adam 176
Sarandon, Susan **169**
SARFT, *see* State Administration of Radio,
    Film, and Television
Sasson, Donald 211–13
Saturday Night Fever 20, 143, 144, 147,
    147, **150**
Saturday Night at the Movies 197
Saving Private Ryan **215**
Saw 30
SBC International Cinemas 229
Scandinavia 126
Scanner Darkly, A 33
Scarecrow, The 299
Schamus, James 31
Schepsi, Fred 300
Schindler's List 33
Schühly, Thomas 246
Schumacher, Joel 34
Schwarzenegger, Arnold 79, 172
Scooby Doo 301
Scorpion King: Rise of the Akkadian, The 3
Scorsese, Martin 25, 32
Scott, Allen J. 225
Scott Free **49**
Screen Actors Guild 58, 140, 161, 162,
    189, 264
Screen Digest 211
Screen International 63
Screening Room Digital Cinemas 101
Screenvision 99
Scripps, Charles 129
scripts 45, 46–8, 53, 60
Seagram 1, 13, 27, 128, 224, 228
Section Eight Ltd. 34, **49**
Securities and Exchange Commission 111
Seltzer, Nancy 175
Selznick, David O. 15, 144
Semel, Terry 28
Senator 243
Seoul Movie 281

SES Global 110
Set It Off 149
Seven Arts 19
sex, lies and videotape 29, 33
Sexo, Pudor y Lagrimas (*Sex, Shame and Tears*) 269
Shaft 146
Shakespeare in Love 32
Shall We Dance 283
Shandwick 175
Shattered Jade Fated To Be Reunited 277
Shawshank Redemption, The 29
Shepperton Studios 4, 224, 226
Sherman Antitrust Act 185
Shi mian mai fu (*House of Flying Daggers*) 283
Shin-EGV Theaters 101
ShopNBC 110
Shout 170
Shout Africa 101
Showtime 21, 110, 112
Shrek 138–9
Shrek 2 **68**, 222, 295
Shyamalan, M. Night 47
Side Street **49**
Sideways 31, 32, 37
Sidus FNH 278
Simpson, Don 69
Since You Went Away 144, 145
Singapore 187, 199, 212, 278
Singer, Bryan 35
Singles 149
Singleton, John 177
Sisterhood of the Traveling Pants, The 96
Six Days, Seven Nights **215**
Sixth Sense, The 48
Sky 229
Slater, Christian 246
Smashing Pumpkins 149
Smith, Lois 174, 175
Smith, Will **169**, **179**
Snipes, Wesley **169**
Snow White and the Seven Dwarfs 122, 144, 283
Soderbergh, Steven 32, 33, 34, **49**, **95**, 204
Sony 14, 25, **26**, 27, 38, **49**, 106, 109, 115–16, 117, 121, 122, 125, 128, **135**, 135, 136, 147, 150, 198, 203, 220, 226, 230, 292
  Betamax 21, 115, 120, 121, 198
  Blu-ray Disc 38

PlayStation 3
PlayStation Portable 85, 137
Sony Corporation of America 115
Sony Home Entertainment 30
Sony Pictures Classics 29, 115, 116, 273
Sony Pictures Entertainment 37, 65, **68**, 97, 115, 116, 164, **192**, 269
Sony Theaters 93
Sound of Music, The 17
SoundScan 90
soundtrack albums 3, 14
South Africa 101
South Park 177
Sovexport Film 187
Space Jam **150**
Spacey, Kevin **169**
Spaghetti Westerns 18
Spain 3, **91**, **92**, 212, 230, 266
special effects 59, 281, 292
Specialist, The 172
specialty films 30, 31, 33, 37
Speed 289
Spellbound 144
Spider-Man **68**, 77, *78*, **138**
Spider-Man 2 **68**, 77, **138**
Spielberg, Steven 19, 21, 25, **26**, 27, 33, 125, 129, 139, 288–9
Spike TV 112, 139
Spiritdance **49**
Splash 23
Spyglass **49**
Square **135**
Sri Lanka 212, 289
Stallone, Sylvester 21, 169, **179**
Stand and Deliver 53
Standard Chartered 278
Star! 17
star system 167–80, 281
  packaging 170–1, *171*
  post-studio system 167–8
Starbucks 85
Stargate 247
stars 21, 66, 74, 167, 168, 251, 283
  computer-generated 138
  salaries 178
Star Trek: The Movie 123
Star Trek II: The Wrath of Khan 123, *124*
STAR TV 189, 292
star vehicles 15, 31, 37
Star Wars 20, 66, 70, 125, 136
Star Wars: Episode II – Attack of the Clones 301

Star Wars: Episode III – Revenge of the Sith
    37, **68**, 89, **138**, **216**
State Administration of Radio, Film, and
    Television 280, 282, 284
State Street **49**
Stead, W. T. 217
Steiner, Max 144, 145
Stewart, Jon 165
Stiller, Ben **169**, **179**
Sting, The 19
Stoff, Erwin 173
Stone, Matt 177
Stone, Oliver 25, 215, 246
Stone, Sharon **169**, 172, 175, **179**
Stone Street Studio 301
Storper, Michael 56
Straw, Will 86
Streamcast 202
Streep, Meryl **169**, 246
Street Fighter **135**
Streisand, Barbra 170
Stripes 170
studio system
    classical 14–16, 66
    Conglomerate Hollywood 14, 25–9, 30,
        32, 33, 35, 37, 38, 39
    contract system 15
    vertical integration 14–15
Sundance Channel 30, 112
Sundance Film Festival 30, 112
Super Mario Bros. **135**
Superfly 146
Superman 20
Superman Returns 35, 301
Sutherland, Donald **169**
Sutherland, Kiefer 170
Swank, Hilary **169**, **179**
Sweden 100
synergy 19, 22, 109, 126, 147
Syriana 33

Tagliavini, Gabriela 269
Taiwan 199, 212, 278, 279, 280, 281, 282,
    286
Takayanagi, Kenjiro 121
Talent Agency Act 172
Tamahori, Lee 300
Tarantino, Quentin **49**, 151
Taylor, Richard 296
TBS, *see* Turner Broadcasting System
Teenage Mutant Ninja Turtles 29
Telecommunications Act of 1996 27

telefilm production 16, 19
Telefónica Media 272
Telepui 258
Televisa Mexico 269
television 5, 14, 16, 67, 106–17, 197,
    235–6, 241, 243, 252, 257, 258, **258**,
    261, 292
    cable 21, 22, 23, 30, 36, 52, 106, 109,
        117, 160, 197–8, 204, 291, 292
    films on **236**
    HDTV 97, 128
    network 106, 109
    pay-per-view 86, 106, 109, 110, 115,
        116, 230
    pay-television 229–30, 259, 261
    revenues 37, 77
    sale of films to 17
    satellite 22, 117
    syndication 17, 106, 109
    video-on-demand 230
Television Without Frontiers directive 235
Ten Commandments, The 288
Terminator 3: Rise of the Machines 248
Terra Firma 229
Texas 164
TF1 235, 236
Thailand 101, 212, 215, 278, 281, 282
Thatcher, Margaret 189
theme parks 14
There's Something About Mary **215**
Thomson 128, 226
Thornton, Billy Bob **169**
3 Arts Entertainment 172, 173, **179**
Three Kings 34
Thurman, Uma **169**
tie-ins 3, 28, **77**
Tiempo de valientes (On Probation) 272
Time Inc. 5, 23, 25, **26**, 228
Time Warner 5, 13, 14, **26**, 27, 30, 34, 38,
    39, 106, 109, 110, 112, 114–15, 116,
    117, 125, 128, 134, 147, **192**, 222
    Entertainment Weekly 114
    Time Warner Cable 5
    Warner Books 114
Titanic 79, 136, 143, 150, **150**, **215**, 270,
    271, *271*
TMC, *see* The Movie Channel
Tobias 244
Tom Jones 17–18
Tom Online 282
Tomorrow Never Dies 214, *214*, **215**
Tootsie 170

Top Gun 69, *69*, **150**
Tora! Tora! Tora! 17
Toronto 187
Toshiba 38, 128
Toy Island 3
Toy Story 70
TPS 235
Traffic 33
Transmerica 19, 23
Travolta, John 170, 173, **179**
Triad Artists 168
Tribecca **49**
TriStar 13, 23, 173, 292
Troy 35, 247
Truman Show, The **215**
Turner, Ted 23
Turner Broadcasting System 5, 13, 23, **26**, 27, 29, 53, 115
    Cartoon Network 115
Turner Classic Movies 115, 230
Turner Network Television **77**, 115
Turner International 292
Twain, Shania 149
20th Century Fox 14, 15, 16, 17, 19, 20, 22, **26**, 27, 30, 37, **49**, 50, 65, **68**, 70, 89, 90, 97, 112, 122, 123, 125, 127, 128, 134, 146, 170, 173, 197, 203, 220, 222, 223, 226, 229, 230, 235, 237, 242, 269, 271, 292, 304
    Fox Searchlight 30, 31, 32, 37, 112
    Fox Studios Australia 301, 304
    Fox Studios Baja 270, 271, *271*
    Fox 2000 112
    20th Century Fox Animation 112
    20th Century Fox Home Entertainment 112
20th Century Fox Hour, The 108
24 37
Twins 291
Twisted Pictures 30
Twister 149
200 Cigarettes 150
2929 Entertainment 95

UA, *see* United Artists
UATC 92, **93**
UCI, *see* United Cinemas International
UFD 235
UGC 235
UIP, *see* United International Pictures
UK Film Council 226
Under Siege 69

Unforgiven 33
Union of Cinema Production Workers 270
Union of Soviet Socialist Republics 211
United Artists 15, 16, 17, 18, 19, 23, **49**, 116, 125, 145, 146
    United Artists Records 145
    United Artists Theaters 289
United Artists v. Fortnightly 198
United Cinemas International 228, 229, 242
United International Pictures 65, 187, 220, 222, 224, 235, 242, 244, 289
United Kingdom 4, **91**, **92**, 195, 211, 212, 215, 220–31, **221**, 233, 241, 242, 245
United States 2, 4, 91, 92, **92**, 98, 100, 101, 120, 121, 123, 126–7, 128, 129, 136, 157, 158, 164, 188, 195, 210, 212, 217, **256**, 257, **258**, 282
United Talent Agency 168, **169**, **179**
Universal 1, 2, 3, 4, 13, 15, 18, 19, 21, **26**, 27, 33, **49**, 54, 65, **68**, 85, 97, 111, 122, 123, 128, **135**, 145, 146, 149, 159, 175, 187, 189, **192**, 198, 203, 220, 224, 228, 229, 230, 235, 242, 244, 269, 278, 287, 292, 303
    Focus Features 30, 31, 32, 33, **49**
    MCA-Universal 13, 19, 25, **26**, 27, 125
    Universal City 4
    Universal Studios Consumer Productions 3
    Universal Studios Home Video 3
    Universal Studios theme parks 3
Universal Music Group 1, 3
Urban, Greg 86
Urban, Karl 298
US Chamber of Commerce 183
US Copyright Office 196
US House of Representatives 188
US Justice Department 108, 186
US Senate 188
US State Department 209, 213
US Supreme Court 16, 21, 107, 122, 198, 202
US Trade Representative 187, 260, 279
US v. Southwestern 198
USA Network 53
    USA Films 33
Usual Suspects, The 35
UTA, *see* United Talent Agency

V 189
Valenti, Jack 23, 96, 183, 184, *184*, 185, 186, 188, 191, *202*

Value Vision Media 110
Van Halen 149
Van Helsing 302
Vancouver 164
Variety 63, 85, 186
vaudeville 196
Vaughn, Vince 177, **179**
Vélez, Lupe 265
Vergara, Carlos 266
Verizon 38
Vertical Limit 301
Vestron 23, 123, 124
VH1 112
Viacom 6, **26**, 27, 33, 38, 39, 92, 95, 110,
    111, 125, 190, **192**, 228
Victor Records 144
video 3, 4, 5, 6, 14, 21, 26, 52, 115,
    120–30, 198–9, 237–8, 258, **258**, 259,
    261
  distribution 222–3
  kidvid 124
  market 126
  rental 86, 123
  revenue sharing 127
  sell-through 123–4
  two-tier pricing 124
  VCR ownership 123
  see also digital video disc
video games 3, 44, 132–40
  audiences 136–7
  games based on movies **138**
  history of games and films 133–4
  labor 139
  sales **138**
  software sales in the US **132**, **135**
  unionization 139–40
videodisc 121
Videophile's Newsletter, The 121
Vietnam 280, 289
Village Roadshow **49**, 228, 289
Visconti, Luchino 252
Vitagraph 225
Vitaphone 144
Vitti, Monica 252
Vivendi 1, **26**, 111, 224, 228, 229
Vivendi Universal **26**, 27, 111, 229
VNU 73, 90
Vogel, Harold 78, 80

Wachowski, Andy and Larry 35
Wagner, Todd 204
Wahlberg, Mark **169**

Waitakere City Council 304
Waiting to Exhale 149, **150**
Walken, Christopher **169**
Wall Street Journal 213
Wallerstein, Immanuel 296
Wal-Mart 85, 127
Walt Disney Christmas Special, The 108
Walt Disney Latin America 269
Wanda Group 282
Wang Productions 281
War of the Worlds **216**
Ward, Vincent 300, 301
Warner Bros. 1, 5, 6, 14, 15, 16, 18, 19,
    30, 33, 34, 35, 37, **49**, 65, 66, 67, **68**,
    85, 96, 97, 108, 123, 128, **135**, 139,
    144, 146, 149, 164, 167, 173, 187, 203,
    215, 220, 221, 222, 226, 230, 237, 242,
    246, 269, 282, 292
  Kids' WB 3
  Warner Bros. Animation 115
  Warner Bros. Consumer Products 5
  Warner Bros. Entertainment 5
  Warner Bros. Home Entertainment
    Group 5
  Warner Bros. Independent Pictures 5,
    30, 34, 115, 273
  Warner Bros. International Television
    292
  Warner Bros. International Theaters 5,
    228, 229, 289
  Warner Bros. Pictures 5, 115
  Warner Bros. Pictures International 5
  Warner Bros. Studio Facilities 5
  Warner Bros. Television Group 5
  Warner Home Video 115, 128
  WB 27, 114, 115, 117
Warner Brothers Presents 108
Warner Communications 22, 25, **26**,
    228
Warner Roadshow Studios 301, 303
Warner Village 229
Washington, Denzell **169**, 175, **179**
Wasserman, Lew 13, 23, 25, 145, 189
watermarking 201
Watts, Naomi **169**, 298, 302
Wayans, Keenan Ivory 177
Weaver, Sigourney **169**
Weber Shandwick 175
Webb–Pomerene Export Trade Act 185,
    187
  Export Trading Company Act 1982
    186

Wedding Crashers 151, *151*, **216**
Weinstein, Harvey 53
Weinstein Company, The 53
Weintraub, Jerry **49**
Weir, Peter 300, *300*
Wells, Frank 23
Westdeutschen Rundfunks 210
Westinghouse 107
Weta Digital 296, 303
Weta Workshop 296, 303
Whale Rider 304
Whitaker, Forest **49**
Who Killed Roger Rabbit? 78
Wick, Ted 144
Wild Bunch, The 18
William Morris Agency 13, 16, 25, 168, 169, **169**, 170, **179**
Williams, Raymond 86, 129
Williams, Robin **169**, 170
Willis, Bruce **169**, 177, **179**
Willow 302
Wilson, Harold 213
Wilson, Owen **169**
Win a Date with Tad Hamilton! 89
Winger, Debra 170
Winslet, Kate **169**
WIPO, *see* World Intellectual Property Organization
Wish You Were Here 224
Witherspoon, Reese **179**
Without a Paddle 301
Wiz, The 149
WMA, *see* William Morris Agency
Wolf-Kasteler 176, **179**
Wolf Man, The 4
Wolff, Michael 170
Woo, John **49**, 283
Wood, William C. 129
Woodstock 16
Woodward, Joanne 169
Working Title **49**, 224
World Bank 189

World Intellectual Property Organization 201
World Trade Organization 193, 199, 201, 279, 280
World's Fastest Indian, The 299, 301
WPP 176
writers 45
Writers Guild of America 177
WTO, *see* World Trade Organization
Wu, Vivian 283
Wyatt, Justin 67, 69

Xena: Warrior Princess 302
X-Files, The 113
X-Files: The Movie 113, **215**
X2: X-men United 286

Y tu mama también 30, 267, 268, *268*
Yahoo 38, 39
Yash Raj Studios 292
Yeoh, Michelle 283
Yimou, Zhang 32, 283
Ying xiong (Hero) 283
Yorn, Kevin 178
Young Guns II 170
YouTube 38, 39, 190

Zabriskie Point 146
Zanuck **49**
Zee Television 292
   Zee Movies 292
Zellweger, Renée **169**, 176, **179**
Zelnick, Strauss 75
Zemeckis, Robert **49**, 79
Zeta-Jones, Catherine **169**, 177, **179**
Ziffren, Brittenham, Branca, Fischer, Gilbert-Lurie, Stiffelman and Cook 176, 177, **179**
Ziffren, Ken 176, 177
Zimmer, Hans 247
Ziv 108
Ziyi, Zhang 283